MARILYN MONROE AND THE CAMERA
Foreword by Jane Russell
Interview by Georges Belmont

Many different, often contradictory, things have been written about Marilyn Monroe, but one truth remains constant—the camera loved her. Whether posing kittenishly in a pinup shot or dramatically for a classic portrait, this shy, vulnerable, enormously insecure woman was transformed by the lens.

Marilyn posed for nearly every major photographer of her day, and this pictoral chronicle of her affair with the camera, featuring shots from Richard Avedon, Cecil Beaton, Henri Càrtier-Bresson, Alfred Eisenstaedt, Elliott Erwitt, Philippe Halsman, Weegee, and thirty other artists, brings together the most beautiful and unusual images available. From her early days as a "fashion model" for ads and pinup calendars, through the film stills that follow her career as a minor actress and then major starlit, to the now-famous portraits by Richard Avedon, and Cecil Beaton, as well as the paparazzi shots from the hordes of photographers who trailed her every move—Marilyn emerges in all her many moods: girlish and gay, sexy and serious, glamorous and girl-next-door. And, in a fascinating and revealing interview with French writer George Belmont, Marilyn sets the record straight about much of her early life, and about her ambitions, fears, and dreams.

Jane Russell, Marilyn's friend and costar in *Gentlemen Prefer Blondes*, enhances this portrait with an affectionate foreword that describes what it was like to work with the young actress. Although we will never know the "real" Marilyn, this sumptuous volume goes a long way toward preserving the memory of an utterly unforgettable woman.

Georges Belmont, born in Belley, France, in 1909, is a writer, journalist, and the renowned translator of such authors as Henry Miller, Evelyn Waugh, Graham Greene, Henry James, and Erica Jong. He lives in Aix-en-Provence.

Jane Russell has starred in numerous motion pictures, including *The Outlaw, Son of Paleface, Gentlemen Prefer Blondes,* and *The Tall Men.* She lives in Southern California.

248 pages, 104 duotone and 48 color plates
ISBN 3-8238-5467-4

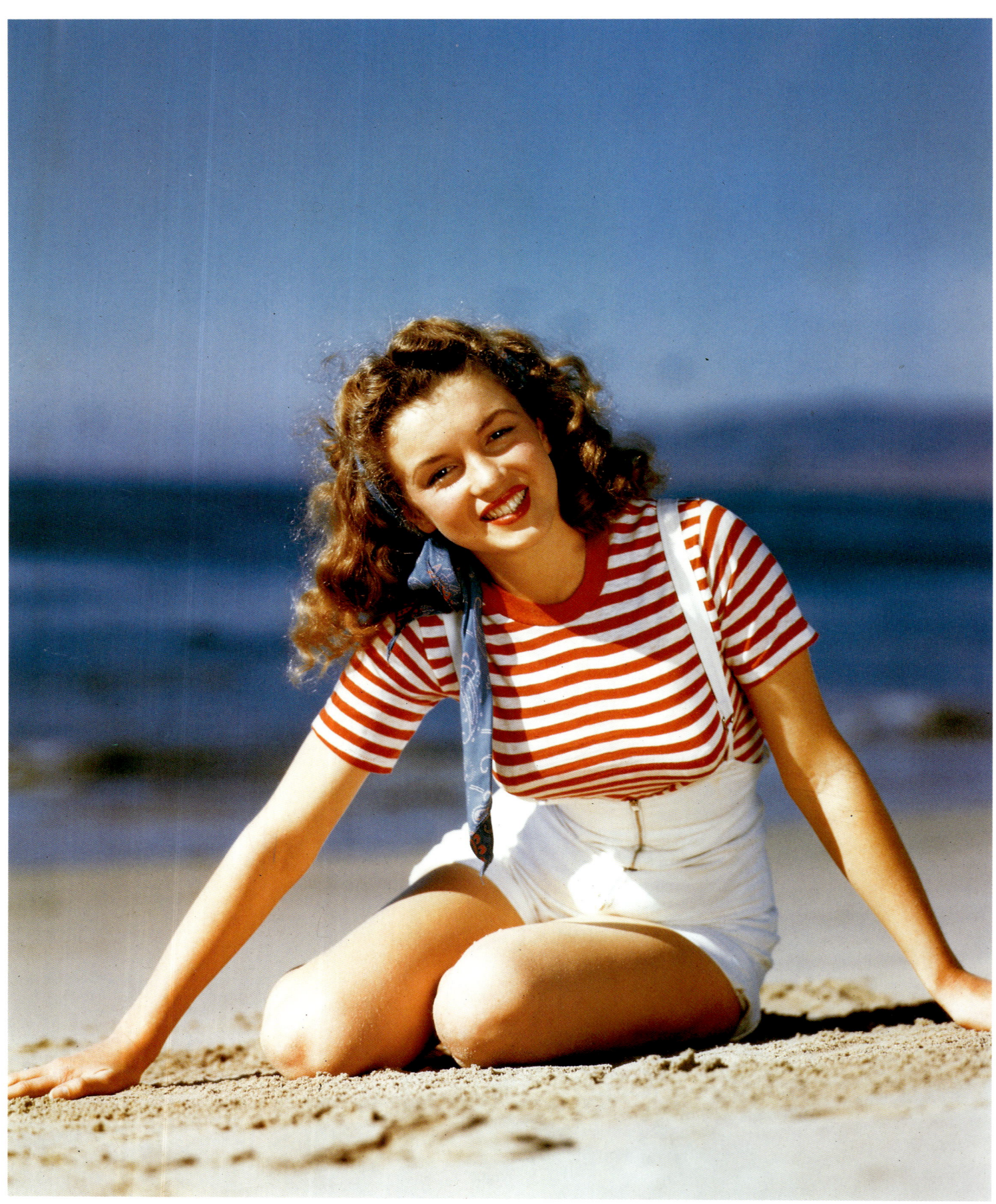

Marilyn Monroe at Malibu Beach photographed by André de Dienes, 1945.

Marilyn Monroe

and the Camera

With a Foreword by Jane Russell
and an Interview by Georges Belmont

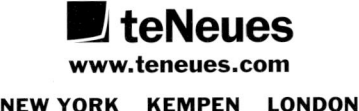
teNeues
www.teneues.com
NEW YORK   KEMPEN   LONDON

Published in the U.S.A. and Canada
by te Neues Publishing Company, New York

Conception by Lothar Schirmer
Translation by Paul Kremmel

The Georges Belmont interview was originally published
in French in the magazine *Marie Claire*, 1960

Printed in Italy by EBS, Verona

ISBN 3-8238-5467-4
A Schirmer/Mosel Production

Acknowledgments

This book is dedicated to the memory of Marilyn
Monroe.

Many people and friends have contributed to making
this project possible. I especially wish to thank Maria
Höhnigschmied, Carol Judy Leslie, Susanne Porsche,
Hanna Schygulla, Cindy Sherman, and Bert Stern,
who have all helped in their own ways to bring the
idea behind this book to fulfillment.
For help in the acquisition of the pictures as well as
for contributions, hints and helpful support, I wish to
thank Sid Avery, Susann Babst, Katherine Bang,
Georges Belmont, Susan Bernard, Christiane Bötzl,
Dieter Boldt, Jean-Pierre Boscq, Leo Caloia, Debra
Cohen, Simon Crocker, Lydia Cullen, Nancy
D'Antonio, Henri Dauman, Nancy M. Davis, Shirley
de Dienes, Nora and Alex Ester, Jackie Fixot, John
Florea, Alexander Haas, Yvonne Halsman, François
Hébel, Elisabeth Heidt, Stevie Holland, Ken
Johnston, Tom Kelley, Jr., David Kent, Margot
Klingsporn, John Kobal, Hilaneh von Kories, Ned
Leavitt, Renate Lust, Anne de Margerie, Michael Ochs,
Onur Olgun, Randall Riese, Nicole Rudschinat, Uschi
Sandvoss, Peter Schnug, Ina Seibold, David Seidner,
Marcia Terrones, Johanna Thorman, Peter Tomlinson,
Annemarie Weber, Ray Whelam, Bob Willoughby, Sue
Wookey.
Finally I should like to warmly thank all the contri-
buting photographers and Miss Jane Russell for
generously contributing a lively foreword to the
book.

Munich, Autumn 1989   *Lothar Schirmer*

Foreword

The first time I met Marilyn she was dancing with her first husband, Jim Dougherty, a past schoolmate of mine. He was in uniform and called out to me, "Hey, outlaw! I want you to see my wife, Norma Jeane." I looked up from the table and saw a little thing with ash-brown hair and a very sweet smile. We waved hi. She was curled literally over his arm. A year or so later I was riding with the director Nick Ray on the RKO lot when we passed a girl wearing very "stressed" blue jeans and a man's shirt tied under her bosom and showing quite a lot of midriff. Nick stopped the car and said, "I'd like you to meet this kid. . . . She's having a tough time on her picture with the lady star, who is being very sarcastic to her." As she walked alongside, he called, "Marilyn, I want you two to meet. Jane, this is Marilyn Monroe." Her hair was blonder now – tousled, but definitely blonder. Nick was very concerned, caring, protective.

I believe that the outstanding quality that made Marilyn different from other so-called sex symbols was her . . . vulnerability. Everyone wanted to take care of her, to help. She brought out protectiveness in all but the insensitive, or those who, of course, simply wanted a more sophisticated adult world where everyone was responsible to himself, a world of caustic humor, a take-as-much-as-you-give world. I was accustomed to that world, but Marilyn could get terribly hurt. She simply could not understand people being mean. She was super sensitive – and with good reason, considering her rudderless past and unsure future.

Marilyn had a never-ending thirst for knowledge and self-improvement. She loved poetry and music and was instinctively drawn to culture, to all the arts, but money and power were not to be gained by coercion; especially not when applied to Marilyn. She would flit off like a butterfly. I remember her saying, "If they aren't going to be fair and nice, I can always leave. I can get by on very little. After all, I've done it before."

When we started making *Gentlemen Prefer Blondes* she was in her very first "star" dressing room, even though she had already starred in a picture. She was determined that her bosses at Fox were going to take her seriously. She worked night and day rehearsing the dance numbers, or she'd shoot the film all day and then go over the script with her coach at night. I'd go home exhausted and ready to relax, but Marilyn worked on into the night. The next day she would arrive a good hour before I did. She was always ready but could not make herself get out on the set. She puttered, seemingly frozen there. It got a little tense on the set for a couple of days – you just didn't keep Howard Hawks waiting without getting the steely blue eye! Whitey, her makeup man, confided to us in my dressing room that he felt that she was afraid to go out on the set – to face the "tiger," as it were. So, from then on, I would stop by her dressing room and say, "Come on, Blondel, it's five of. Let's go get 'em!" Marilyn would look up and in her little-girl whisper say, "Oh . . . O.K.," and we'd trot out together.

We all found her very cooperative, sweet, and humorous, and when the camera rolled she *glowed*. Physically, she seemed to have no bones . . . she curved every which way . . . undulating flesh . . . and yet, the innocence of a child was ever present. If you raised your voice at her or were too harsh, she'd cry – you knew that.

Still photographers are the gentlest of creatures. They coax the very best out of their subjects. They have to, or they'd lose you . . . and our girl Marilyn responded to them like a flower opening to the sun – as you can see in the following pages.

– Jane Russell

The Photographers

Eve Arnold
Richard Avedon
Baron
Cecil Beaton
Bruno Bernard
Leo Caloia
Carone
William Carroll
Henri Cartier-Bresson
Ed Clark
Henri Dauman
André de Dienes
Alfred Eisenstaedt
John Engstead
Elliott Erwitt
Jack Esten
J. R. Eyerman
Ed Feingersh
John Florea
Milton H. Greene
Ernst Haas
Philippe Halsman
Bob Henriques
Tom Kelley
Gene Kornman
Madison Lacy
Frank Maestro
Leonard McCombe
Richard C. Miller
Earl Moran
Frank Powolny
Bert Reisfeld
Willy Rizzo
Slade
Steinberg
Bert Stern
Weegee
Bob Willoughby

Contents

Marilyn's Interview

with Georges Belmont

Rupert Allan, who took care of Marilyn Monroe's publicity, arranged the famous 1960 interview Marilyn gave Georges Belmont, who was then the editor of the French magazine Marie Claire. *The interview took place while* Let's Make Love *was being shot, a film which of course received everybody's attention in France because of costar Yves Montand. Georges Belmont soon managed to gain Marilyn's confidence by promising to give her a transcript of the interview and to keep strictly to her actual words when using the text. All those who heard the interview later realized to their surprise that they had never heard Marilyn talk about herself so naturally. Georges Belmont describes the atmosphere: "I just let her go ahead and speak. The only pressure I exerted was silence. When she was silent, I didn't say anything either, and when she couldn't stand it any longer and then continued talking, she usually said something very important, something very moving." In view of the photographs in this book, which record Marilyn's career in all its glamour and glory virtually from the very first to the very last photo, we think it necessary and right that Marilyn herself has a chance to speak in this book.*

MM: I'd much rather answer questions. I simply can't tell the whole story, that's terrible.... Where to begin? How? There are so many twists and turns.

GB: *Still, it began somewhere. Your childhood?*

MM: Well, that ... no one knew anything about it, except through pure coincidence. For a long time my past, my life, remained completely unknown. I never spoke about it. No particular reason, but simply because I felt it was my affair and not something for other people. Then one day a Mr. Lester Cowan wanted to put me in a film with Groucho Marx, called *Love Happy*. At that time I was under contract to Fox and Columbia, although they wanted to drop me.... He offered me a small part, this Mr. Cowan;

but he was interested in putting me under contract. So he called. I was still very young, and he said he wanted to speak to my father and mother. I told him, "Impossible." "Why?" he insisted. So I briefly explained the situation: "I never lived with them." That was the truth, and I still don't see what was so unusual about it. But then he called Louella Parsons and told her the whole story, and it all appeared in Louella's column. That's the way it all began. Since then so many lies have been spread around.... My goodness, why shouldn't I simply tell the truth now?

GB: *What are your earliest childhood memories?*

MM: [long silence] My earliest memories? ... It's the memory of a struggle for survival. I was still very small – a baby in a little bed, yes, and I was struggling for life. But I'd rather not talk about it, if it's all the same to you. It's a cruel story, and it's no one's business but my own, as I said.

Anyway, as far back as I can remember, I can see myself in a baby carriage, in a long white dress, on the sidewalk of a house where I lived with a family that wasn't my own.

It's true that I was illegitimate. But everything that's been said about my father – or my fathers – is wrong. My mother's first husband was named Baker. Her second was Mortensen. But she'd been divorced from both of them by the time I was born. Some people say my father was Norwegian, probably because of the name Mortensen, and that he was killed in a motorcycle accident right after my birth. I don't know if that's true, because he wasn't related to me. As far as my real father is concerned, I wish you wouldn't ask ... but there are a couple of things that could clear up some of the confusion. When I was very young, I was always told that my father was killed in a car crash in New York before I was born. Strangely enough, on my birth certificate under father's profession there's the word "baker," which was the name of my mother's first husband. When I was born – illegitimate, as I said – my mother had to give me a name. She was just trying to think quickly, I guess, and said "Baker." Pure coincidence, and then the official's confusion.... At least, I think that's the way it was.

Anyway, my name was Norma Jeane Baker. It was in all my school records. Everything else that's been said is crazy.

GB: Your mother ... I read somewhere that to you she was just "the woman with the red hair"?

MM: I never lived with my mother. That's the truth, no matter what some people have said. As far back as I can remember I always lived with other people.

My mother was mentally ill. She's dead now. And both of her parents died in mental institutions. My mother was also committed. Sometimes she got out, but she always had to go back.

Well, you know how it is.... When I was real little, I'd say to every woman I'd see, "Oh, there's a mommy!" And if I saw a man, I'd say, "Oh, there's a daddy." But one morning – I was only about three – I was taking a bath and I said, "Mommy" to the woman who was taking care of me. And she said, "I'm not your mommy. Call me 'Aunt.'" "But he's my daddy!" I said and I pointed to her husband. "No," she said, "we're not your parents. The one who comes here with the red hair, she's your mother." It was quite a shock to hear that. But since she didn't come very much, it's true that to me she was always "the woman with the red hair."

Anyway, I knew that she existed. Then later on, when I was in an orphanage, I had another shock. I could read then, and when I saw the word "orphanage" in gold letters on a black background, they had to drag me in. I screamed, "I'm not an orphan! I have a mother!" But then I thought, "I'd better believe she's dead." And later people said, "It is better that you forget about your mother." "But where is she?" I asked. "Don't think about it," they said. "She's dead."

And then a little bit later I suddenly heard from her.... And that's the way it went for years. I thought she was dead, and I said so, too. But she was alive. So some people accused me of making it up that she was dead because I didn't want to admit where she was. It's crazy.

Anyway, I had – let's see – ten, no, eleven families.

The first one lived in a small town near Los Angeles – I was born in Los Angeles. Along with me they had a little boy they later adopted. I stayed with them until I was around seven. They were terribly strict. They didn't mean any harm – it was their religion. They brought me up harshly, and corrected

me in a way I think they never should have – with a leather strap. That finally came out, and so I was taken away and given to an English couple in Hollywood. They were actors, or I guess I should say extras, with a twenty-year-old daughter who was the spitting image of Madeleine Carroll. Life with them was pretty casual and tumultuous. That was quite a change from the first family, where we weren't allowed to talk about movies and actors or dance or sing, except maybe for psalms.

My new "parents" worked hard, when they worked, and they enjoyed life the rest of the time. They liked to dance and sing, they drank and played cards, and they had a lot of friends. Because of that religious upbringing I'd had, I was kind of shocked – I thought they were all going to hell. I spent hours praying for them.

I remember something ... after a few months my mother bought a small house where we were supposed to live. Not for very long – maybe three months. Then my mother had to be committed again. And that was a big change. After she left, we moved back to Hollywood.

The English family kept me as long as there was money – my mother's money from her savings and from an insurance policy she had.

Through them I learned a lot about the movies. I wasn't even eight. They used to take me to one of the big movie theaters in Hollywood, the Egyptian or Grauman's Chinese. I used to watch the monkeys in the cages outside the Egyptian, all alone, and I tried to fit my feet into the footprints in front of Grauman's, and I could never get my feet in because my shoes were too big.... It's funny to think that *my* footprints are there now, and that other little girls are trying to do the same thing I did.

They took me there every Saturday and Sunday. That was a break for them, I think; they worked very hard and they didn't want to be bothered with this child around the house all the time. It was probably better for me, too.

I'd wait till the movie opened and then for ten cents I'd get in and sit in the front row. I watched all kinds of movies there – like *Cleopatra* with Claudette Colbert; I remember that so well.

I'd sit there and watch the movie over and over. I had to be home before it got dark, but how was I supposed to know when it was dark? The folks were good to me: even if I didn't get anything to eat when I was hungry I knew they'd save something for me at home. So I stayed at the movies.

I had favorite stars. Jean Harlow! I had platinum blonde hair and people used to call me "tow-head." I hated that and I dreamed of having golden hair ... until I saw her, so beautiful and with platinum blonde hair like mine.

And Clark Gable. I'm sure he wouldn't mind if I say it, because in a Freudian sense it's supposed to be very good . . . I used to think of him as my father. I'd pretend he was my father – I never pretended anyone was my mother, I don't know why – but I always pretended he was my father. . . . Where was I?

GB: *The English couple. And when the money ran out . . .*

MM: Oh, yes. They put me in an orphanage. No, wait a minute. When the English couple couldn't keep me anymore, I went to stay with some people in North Hollywood, people from New Orleans. I remember that because they always called it "New Orleeens." I didn't stay there long, two or three months. I only remember that he was a cameraman and that one day he suddenly took me to the orphanage.

I know a lot of people say that the orphanage wasn't so bad. But I do know that it's changed in the meantime. Perhaps it's not as gloomy. . . . But of course even the most modern orphanage is still an orphanage – if you know what I mean.

At night, when the others were sleeping, I'd sit up in the window and cry because I'd look over and see the RKO studio sign above the roofs in the distance, where my mother had worked as a cutter. When I went there to work, years later, in 1951, doing *Clash by Night,* I went up to see if I could see the orphanage. But there were too many tall buildings in the way.

I once read, I don't know where, that there were only three or four of us in a room in the orphanage. That's not true. I slept in a room with twenty-seven beds, where you could work your way to the "honor" bed, if you behaved. And then you could work yourself into the other dormitory, which had only a few beds. I got to the honor bed once. But one morning I was late and was putting on my shoes when the matron said, "Come downstairs!" I tried to tell her I was tying my shoes, but she said, "Back to the twenty-seventh bed."

We'd get up at six in the morning, and we did our work before we went to the public school. We each had a bed, a chair, and a locker. Everything had to be very clean, perfect, because of inspection. For a while I cleaned the dormitory where I slept. Every day you moved the beds and you swept and then you dusted. The bathrooms were easier; there was less dust because of the cement floors. And I worked in the kitchen, washing dishes. There were a hundred of us, so I washed a hundred plates and all those spoons and forks. . . . We didn't have knives or glasses and we drank out of mugs. But in the kitchen you could earn money. We made five cents a month. They took a

penny out for Sunday school, so that you had one penny left at the end of the month if there were four Sundays. We'd save that to buy a friend a little thing for Christmas.

I can't say I was very happy there. I didn't get along very well with the matrons. But the superintendent was very nice. I remember one day she called me into her office and said, "You have very fine skin, but it's always so shiny. Let me put a little powder on to see if it helps." I felt honored. She had a little dog, a Pekinese, who wasn't allowed to be around the children because he would bite them. But the dog was very friendly to me and I really loved dogs. . . . I was really very honored; I mean, I was walking on air.

Later, I tried to run away with some of the other girls. But where to? We couldn't decide, we hadn't the slightest idea. We only got as far as the bump in the front lawn when we were caught. The only thing I said was, "Please don't tell the superintendent!" – because she'd made me smile and put powder on my nose and let me pet her dog.

In the orphanage I began to stutter. The day they brought me there, after they pulled me in, crying and screaming, suddenly there I was in the large dining room with a hundred kids sitting there eating, at five o'clock, and they were all staring at me. So I stopped crying right away. Maybe that's a reason along with the rest: my mother and the idea of being an orphan. Anyway, I stuttered. That was the first time. Later on, in my teens, when I was at Van Knight High School, they elected me secretary of the English class, and every time I had to read the minutes I'd say, "Minutes of the last m-m-m-meeting." It was terrible. That went on for two years, I guess, until I was fifteen.

Sometimes it even happens to me today if I'm very nervous or excited. Once when I had a small part in a movie, in a scene where I was supposed to go up the stairs, I forgot what was happening and the assistant director came and yelled at me, and I was so confused that when I got into the scene I stuttered. Then the director himself came up to me and said, "You don't stutter." And I said, "That's what you think." It was painful. And it still is if I speak very fast or have to make a speech. Terrible . . . [silence].

I stayed about a year and a half in the orphanage. We went to the public school. It's very bad to have children from an institution like that go to a public school because the other kids point their fingers: "Oh, they're from the home, they're from the home." We were all ashamed to be from the orphans' home.

In school I liked singing and English. I hated arithmetic. I never had my mind on it, you know? I was always dreaming in a window. But I was good at sports.

I was pretty tall. At the orphanage, the first day,

they didn't believe me when I said I was nine years old. They thought I was fourteen. I was almost as tall as I am now – five feet six inches. But I was very, very thin until I was eleven. Then things changed.

Suddenly, I wasn't in the orphanage anymore. I complained so bitterly to my guardian that she got me out. My guardian – Grace McKee. She'd been my mother's best friend. She died eleven years ago. While she was my legal guardian she worked as a film editor at Columbia. But she was fired, and she married a man ten years younger than herself and he had three children. They were very poor, so they couldn't care for me. And I think she felt that her responsibility was to her husband, naturally, and to his kids.

But she was always wonderful to me. Without her, who knows where I would have landed! I could have been put in a state orphanage and kept there till I was eighteen. My orphanage was private, and Grace used to visit me and take me out. Not as often as they say, but she used to come and take me out sometimes and I could put on her lipstick. I was only nine then. She'd take me someplace to get my hair curled, which was unheard of because it wasn't allowed and because I had straight hair. Things like that meant a great deal to me.

Besides, she was the one who got me out of that orphanage after I complained so much, as I said. Of course that meant a new "family." I remember one where I stayed for just three or four weeks. I remember them because the woman delivered things her husband made. She'd take me along and I'd get so carsick! I don't know if they were paid for taking me in. I only know that after them I kept changing families. Some took me at the end of the school year and then they had enough after the vacation. But maybe that's what had been arranged.

Then Los Angeles County took over my support. It was awful. I hated it. Even in the orphanage when I went to school, I tried not to look like an orphan. But now this woman would come around and say, "Now let's see, I think you need some shoes." And she would write it down: one pair of shoes. Then, "And does she have a sweater?" Or, "I think the poor girl needs two dresses, one for school and one for Sunday."

Well, the sweaters were ugly, they were made of cotton, and the clothes all looked like they were made of flour sacks . . . terrible. And the shoes! I'd say, "I don't want them." I always tried to get clothes from grown-ups that would be altered for me. And I wore tennis shoes a lot. You could get them for ninety-eight cents.

I must have looked pretty funny then – I was so tall, as I said, and I ate everything. I know because the families I lived with said they'd never seen a child who ate everything. I'd eat anything.

I also know that I was very quiet, at least in front of adults. They used to call me "the mouse." I didn't say very much except to other children, and I had a lot of imagination. The other kids liked to play with me because I could think of things. I'd say, "Now we're going to play murder . . . or divorce." And they'd say, "How do you think of things like that?"

I was probably a lot different than the others. Kids usually refuse to go to bed, but I never did. Instead, I'd say, "I think I'll go to bed now." I loved the privacy of my room, my bed. I especially loved to act out every part of the last movie I'd seen. You know, standing on my bed, being even taller, I'd act out all the parts, the men as well as the women, and I'd work out what happened before or after. It was wonderful. . . . So was acting in school plays. Once I played the part of a king and once the part of a prince – that's because I was so tall.

I had a real happy time while I was growing up when I went to live with a woman I called "Aunt Anna." She was Grace McKee's mother. She was a lot older, she was sixty, I guess, or somewhere around there, but she always talked about when she was a girl of twenty. There was real contact between us because she understood me somehow. She knew what it was like to be young. And I loved her dearly. I used to do the dishes in the evening and I'd always be singing and whistling, and she'd say, "I never heard a child sing so much." So I did it during that time. Aunt Anna . . . I adored her.

When I was fifteen, turning sixteen, Grace McKee arranged a marriage for me. There's not much to say about it. She and her husband wanted to move to West Virginia. In Los Angeles the county paid them twenty dollars a month for me. If I'd gone with them to West Virginia, they wouldn't have gotten that money, and since they couldn't support me they had to work out something. In the state of California a girl can marry at sixteen. So I had the choice: go to a home till I was eighteen or get married. And so I got married.

His name was Dougherty. He was twenty-one at that time and worked in a factory. Then the war came and he was going to be drafted, but he went into the Merchant Marine, and I stayed with him for a while at Catalina, where he was a physical training instructor. Around the end of the war I went to Las Vegas to divorce him. I was twenty. He's a policeman now.

During the war I worked in a factory. I was in what they called the "dope room" – I had to paint "dope" on the fabric used in making target planes. The work was very boring and life was pretty awful there. The other girls would talk about what they'd done the night before and what they were going to do the next weekend. I worked near where the paint sprayers were – nothing but men. They used to stop their work to write me notes.

The work was so boring I worked very fast just to get it over with. They thought I was doing something wonderful. There was an assembly for the whole plant and the president of the plant called my name and gave me a gold medal and a twenty-five-dollar war bond for "exemplary willingness," as he put it. The other girls were furious when I got it and they'd bump into me and make me spill my can of dope when I'd go for a refill. Oh my goodness, they made life miserable.

And then one day the Air Force wanted to take pictures of our factory. I'd just come back from my vacation when the office called me in. "Where have you been?" I nearly died and I said, "But I had permission for a vacation!" – which was true. They said, "It's not that. Do you want to pose for some pictures?"

Well, the photographers came and took the pictures. They wanted to take more, outside the factory, but I didn't want to get in trouble – because I would have missed work – so I said, "You'll have to get permission." Which they got, so I worked as a model here and there for several days, holding things in my hand, pushing things around, pulling them …

The pictures were developed at Eastman Kodak and the people there asked who the model was and one of the photographers – David Conover – came back and said to me, "You should become a model. You'd easily earn five dollars an hour." Five dollars an hour! I was earning twenty dollars a week for ten hours a day and I had to stand all day on a concrete floor. Reason enough to give it a try.

I started off slowly. The war was over, so I left the factory and went to an agency. They took me on, for ads and calenders – not the one that caused so much trouble; we'll come to that – but others, where I was a brunette, then a redhead, then a blonde. And I really did earn five dollars an hour!

And I was able to pursue one of my dreams. From time to time I took drama lessons, when I had enough money. They were expensive; I paid ten dollars an hour.

I got to know a lot of people, people different from those I'd known, both good and bad. Sometimes when I was waiting for a bus a car would stop and the man at the wheel would roll down the window and say, "What are you doing here? You should be in pictures." Then he'd ask me to drive home with him. I'd always say, "No, thank you. I'd rather take the bus." But all the same, the idea of the movies kept going through my mind.

Once, I remember, I did accept an offer from a man I met like that – an offer to audition in a movie studio. He must have been pretty persuasive. Anyhow, I went. It was on a Saturday and the place was deserted. I should have been suspicious, but I was still awfully naive. Well, the man led me into an office. We were alone. He held up a script and said there was a part in it, but he'd have to see. Then he told me to read the part and to pull up my dress. It was summer and I was wearing a bathing suit under my dress. But when he said, "Higher," I got scared and turned red and blurted out, "Only if I can keep my hat on!" That was stupid, of course, but I was really scared and desperate. I must have looked ridiculous, standing there holding on to my hat. Finally he got very mad. I was terribly frightened and ran away. I told the agency about this and they called the studio and other places to try to find this guy, but they didn't. He must have had a friend or somebody who let him use his office.

This incident frightened me so much that for a long time I was determined never to become an actress, after all. It was a difficult time in my life. I was living in rooms here and there – not in hotels, because they cost too much.

And then, as luck would have it, I was on the covers of five magazines in one month, and Fox called me up. And so I was waiting on those hard benches with lots of other people, all ages and sizes and everything. There was a long wait until Ben Lyon, the head of casting, came out of his office. He was hardly out when he pointed at me and said, "Who's this girl?" I was wearing a white cotton dress that Aunt Anna – I was living with her then for a little while – had washed and ironed for me. Everything had come up so suddenly that I couldn't do both – iron the dress and get myself ready – so she said, "I'll do the dress, you just put on your makeup." After that long wait, I felt beat, but Lyon was so nice. He said I looked so fresh and young and I don't know what all. He even said, "I've only discovered one other person – and that was Jean Harlow." Imagine that, my favorite actress!

They made a Technicolor test the next day, which was unusual because they should have had the director's permission. And then Fox put me under contract – a stock contract for a year.

But nothing came of it, and I never understood why. They hired a lot of girls and some boys, but they dropped them without ever giving them any chances. After they dropped me, I tried to see Mr. Zanuck, but that was impossible. They always told me he was in Sun Valley. I'd come back a week later and they'd say, "He's in Sun Valley, we're very sorry, he's very busy." After a while you just give up. And then, when I was hired back, after *Asphalt Jungle,* he said to me, "I understand you used to be here?" I said, "That's right." Well, things are a lot different now. And he said I had a three-dimensional quality, reminiscent of Harlow, which was interesting since Ben Lyon had been saying that.

I owe a lot to Ben Lyon. He was the first to believe in me. He even gave me my name. One day we were looking for a stage name for me. I couldn't very well take my father's name, but I wanted at least something that was related, so I said, "I want the name 'Monroe,'" which was my mother's maiden name. And so, since he always said I reminded him of Jean Harlow and Marilyn Miller, the great Broadway musical star, he said, "Well, Marilyn goes better with Monroe, so – Marilyn Monroe." And now I end up being Marilyn Monroe even on my marriage license!

But to get back to where I was . . . I was pretty desperate. Fox dropped me and the same thing happened later at Columbia, even though it was a little different. They at least put me in a movie called *Ladies of the Chorus*. It was really dreadful. I was supposed to be the daughter of a burlesque dancer some guy from Boston falls in love with. It was a terrible story and terribly badly photographed – everything was awful about it. So they dropped me. But you learn from everything.

I saw no way out. It was the worst time for me. I lived in the Hollywood Studio Club and I couldn't stand it there. It reminded me of the orphanage.

I was broke and behind in the rent. In the Studio Club they'd let you get about a week behind in the rent and then they'd write you, "You're the only one who doesn't support this wonderful institution." When you lived there, you'd get two meals a day – breakfast and dinner – and you had a roof over your head. Where else could I have gone? I had no family and I was really hungry.

Of course, a lot of people said, "Why don't you go and get a job in a dimestore?" But I don't know; once I tried to get a job at Thrifty's and because I didn't have a high school education they wouldn't hire me. And it was different, really – being a model, trying to become an actress, and I should go into a dimestore?

There are a lot of stories told about those calendar pictures. When the story came out, I'd already done *Asphalt Jungle* and was rehired at Fox with a seven-year contract. I still remember the publicity department calling me on the set and asking, "Did you pose for a calendar?" And I said, "Yes, anything wrong?" Well, they were real anxious and they said, "Don't say you did, say you didn't." I said, "But I did, and I signed the release, so I feel I should say so." They were very unhappy about that. And then the cameraman who was working on the film then got hold of one of the calendars and asked me if I'd sign it, and so I said yes, I would. I signed it and wrote " To . . ."

and then his name, and I said, "This isn't my best angle, you know." And of course the studio got even madder.

Anyone who knows me knows that I can't lie. Sometimes I leave things out or I don't elaborate, to protect myself or other people – who probably don't even want to be protected – but I can never tell a lie.

I was very hungry, four weeks behind in my rent, and needed money desperately. I remembered that I'd done some beer ads for Tom Kelley and his wife, Natalie, and that they had asked me to pose nude. They told me there was nothing to it and that I would earn a lot – fifty dollars, the amount I needed. Because they were both very nice to me I called them up and asked Tom, "Are you sure they won't recognize me?" He said, "I promise." Then I said, "Well, if it's at night and you don't have any helpers . . . you know how to put up the lights . . . I don't want to expose myself to all the people you have." He said, "All right, just Natalie and me." So we did it. I felt shy about it, but they were real delicate, you know, about the whole situation. They just spread out some red velvet and had me lie down on it. And it was all very simple – and drafty! – and I was able to pay the rent and buy myself something to eat.

People are funny. They ask you a question and when you're honest, they're shocked. Someone once asked me, "What do you wear in bed? Pajama tops? Bottoms? Or a nightgown?" So I said, "Chanel Number Five." Because it's the truth. You know, I don't want to say "nude," but . . . it's the truth.

There came the time when I began to – let's say, be known, and nobody could imagine what I did when I wasn't shooting, because they didn't see me at previews or premieres or parties. It's simple. I was going to school. I'd never finished high school, so I started going to UCLA at night, because during the day I had small parts in pictures. I took courses in the history of literature and the history of this country, and I started to read a lot, stories by wonderful writers.

It was hard to get to the classes on time because I worked in the studio till six-thirty. And since I had to get up early to be ready for shooting at nine o'clock, I was tired in the evening and sometimes I would fall asleep in the classroom. But I forced myself to sit up and listen. And I was really lucky to sit next to a Negro boy who was absolutely brilliant. He worked for the post office – now he's head of the Los Angeles Post Office.

The professor, Mrs. Seay, didn't know who I was and found it odd that the boys from other classes often looked through the window during our class and whispered to one another. One day she asked about me and they said, "She's a movie actress." And she said, "Well, I'm very surprised. I thought she was a young girl just out of a convent." That was one of the nicest compliments I ever got.

But the people I just talked about – you know, they liked to see me as a starlet: sexy, frivolous, and dumb.

I have a reputation of always being late. Well, I don't think I'm late all the time. People just remember the times I come too late. Besides, I really don't think I can go as fast as other people. They get in their cars, they run into each other, they never stop. I don't think mankind was intended to be like machines. Besides, it's a great waste of time – you get more done doing it more sensibly, more leisurely. If I have to get to the studio to rush through the hairdo and the makeup and the clothes, I'm all worn out by the time I have to do a scene. When we did *Let's Make Love,* George Cukor thought it would be better to let me come in an hour late, so I'd be fresher at the end of the day. I think actors in movies work too long hours anyway.

I like to have time for the things I do. I think that we're rushing too much nowadays. That's why people are nervous and unhappy – with their lives and with themselves. How can you do anything perfect under such conditions? Perfection takes time.

I'd like very much to be a fine actress, a true actress. And I'd like to be happy, but who's happy? I think trying to be happy is almost as difficult as trying to be a good actress. You have to work at both of them.

GB: I suppose the portrait of Eleonora Duse on the wall is there for some reason.

MM: Yes. I feel a lot for her because of her life and also because of her work. How shall I put it? She never settled for less, in either.

Personally, if I can realize certain things in my work, I come the closest to being happy. But it only happens in moments. I'm not just generally happy. If I'm generally anything, I guess I'm generally miserable. I don't separate my personal life from my professional one. I find that in working, the more personally I work the better I am professionally.

My problem is that I drive myself, but I do want to be wonderful, you know? I know some people may laugh about that, but it's true.

Once in New York my lawyer was telling me about my tax deductions and stuff and having the patience of an angel with me. I said to him, "I don't want to know about all this. I only want to be wonderful." But if you say that sort of thing to a lawyer, he thinks you're crazy.

There's a book by Rainer Maria Rilke that's helped me a lot: *Letters to a Young Poet.* Without it I'd probably think I *was* crazy sometimes. I think that when an artist – forgive me, but I do think I'm becoming an artist, even though some people will laugh; that's why I apologize – when an artist tries to be true, you sometimes feel you're on the verge of some kind of craziness. But it isn't really craziness. You're just trying to get the truest part of yourself out, and it's very hard, you know. There are times when you think, "All I have to be is true." But sometimes it doesn't come so easily. And sometimes it's very easy.

I always have this secret feeling that I'm really a fake or something, a phony. Everyone feels that way now and then, I guess. My teacher, Lee Strasberg, at the Actors Studio, often asks me, "Why do you feel that way about yourself? You're a human being." I answer, "Yes, I am, but I feel like I have to be more." "No," he says, "you have to start with yourself. What are you doing?" I said, "Well, I have to get into the part." He says, "No, you're a human being so you start with yourself." "With *me?*" I shouted the first time he said that. "Yes, with you!"

I think Lee probably changed my life more than any other human being. That's why I love to go to the Actors Studio whenever I'm in New York.

My one desire is to do my best, the best that I can from the moment the camera starts until it stops. That moment I want to be perfect, as perfect as I can make it.

When I worked at the factory, I used to go to the movies on Saturday nights. That was the only time I could really enjoy myself, really relax, laugh, be myself. If the movie was bad, what a disappointment! The whole week I waited to go to the movies and I worked hard for the money it cost. If I thought that the people in the movie didn't do their best or were sloppy, I was really angry when I left because I didn't have much money to go on for the next week. So I always feel that I work for those people who work hard, who go to the box office and put down their money and want to be entertained. I always feel I do it for them. I don't care so much about what the director thinks. I used to try to explain this to Mr. Zanuck....

Love and work are the only things that really happen to us. Everything else doesn't really matter. I think that one without the other isn't so good – you need both. In the factory, though I worked so fast because it was boring, I used to take pride in doing my work really perfectly, as perfectly as I could.

And when I dreamed of love, then that was also something that had to be as perfect as possible.

When I married Joe DiMaggio in 1954, he had already retired from baseball, but he was a wonderful athlete and had a very sensitive nature in many respects. His family were immigrants and he'd had a very difficult time when he was young. So he understood something about me, and I understood something about him, and we based our marriage on this.

But just "something" isn't enough. Our marriage wasn't very happy, and it ended in nine months.

My feelings are as important to me as my work. Probably that's why I'm so impetuous and exclusive. I like people, but when it comes to friends, I only like a few. And when I love, I'm so exclusive that I really have only one idea in my mind.

Above all, I want to be treated as a human being.

When I met Arthur Miller the first time, it was on a set, and I was crying. I was playing in a picture called *As Young As You Feel,* and he and Elia Kazan came over to me. I was crying because a friend of mine had died. I was introduced to Arthur.

That was in 1951. Everything was pretty bleary for me at that time. Then I didn't see him for about four years. We would correspond, and he sent me a list of books to read. I used to think that maybe he might see me in a movie – there often used to be two pictures playing at a time, and I thought I might be in the other movie and he'd see me. So I wanted to do my best.

I don't know how to say it, but I was in love with him from the first moment.

I'll never forget that one day he said I should act on the stage and how the people standing around laughed. But he said, "No, I'm very serious." And the way he said that, I could see he was a sensitive human being and treated me as a sensitive person, too. It's difficult to describe, but it's the most important thing.

Since we've been married we lead – when I'm not in Hollywood – a quiet and happy life in New York, and even more so on the weekends in our country house in Connecticut. My husband likes to start work very early in the morning. Usually he gets up at six o'clock. Then he stops and takes a nap later on in the day. Our apartment isn't very large, so I had his study soundproofed. He has to have complete quiet when he works.

I get up about eight-thirty or so, and sometimes when I'm waiting for our breakfast to be ready – we have an excellent cook – I take my dog, Hugo, for a walk. But when the cook is out, I get up early and fix Arthur's breakfast because I think a man should never have to fix his own meals. I'm very old-fashioned that way. I also don't think a man should carry a woman's belongings, like her high-heeled shoes or her purse or whatever. I might hide something in his pocket, like a comb, but I don't think anything should be visible.

After breakfast, I'll take a bath, to make my days off different from my working days, when I get up at five or six in the morning and take a cold shower to wake me up. In New York I like to soak in the tub, read the *New York Times,* and listen to music. Then I'll get dressed in a skirt and a shirt and flat shoes and a

polo coat and go to the Actors Studio – on Tuesdays and Fridays at eleven o'clock. On other days I go to Lee Strasberg's private classes.

Sometimes I come home for lunch, and I'm always free just before and during dinner for my husband. There's always music during dinner. We both like classical music. Or jazz, if it's good, but mostly we put it on when we have a party in the evening, and we dance.

Arthur often goes back to work after his nap, and I always find things to do. He has two children from his first marriage, and I try to be a good stepmother. And there's a lot to do in the apartment. I like to cook – not in the city, where it's too busy, but in the country. I can make bread and noodles – you know, roll them up and dry them, and prepare a sauce. Those are my specialties. Sometimes I invent recipes. I love lots of seasonings. I love garlic, but sometimes it's too much for other people.

Now and then the actors from the studio will come over and I'll give them breakfast or tea, and we'll study while we eat. So my days are pretty full. But the evenings are always free for my husband.

After dinner we often go to the theater or to a movie, or we have friends in, or we visit friends. Often we just stay home, listen to music, talk, read. Or we go for a walk after dinner in Central Park, sometimes; we love to walk. We don't have a set way of doing things. There are times when I would like to be more organized than I am, to do certain things at certain times. But my husband says at least it never gets dull. So it's all right. I'm not bored by things; I'm just bored by people who are bored.

I like people, but sometimes I wonder how sociable I am. I can easily be alone and it doesn't bother me. I don't mind it – it's like a rest, it kind of refreshes myself. I think there are two things about human beings – at least, I think there are about me: they want to be alone and they also want to be together. I have a gay side to me and also a sad side. That's a real problem. I'm very sensitive to that. That's why I love my work. When I'm happy with it, I feel more sociable. If not, I like to be alone. And in my private life, it's the same way.

GB: If I asked you what does it feel like being Marilyn Monroe, at this stage in your life, what would you answer?

MM: Well, how does it feel being yourself?

GB: Sometimes I'm content with myself, at other times I'm dissatisfied.

MM: That's exactly how I feel. And are you happy?

GB: *I think so.*

MM: Well, I am too, and since I'm only thirty-four and have a few years to go yet, I hope to have time to become better and happier, professionally and in my personal life. That's my one ambition. Maybe I'll need a long time, because I'm slow. I don't want to say that it's the best method, but it's the only one I know and it gives me the feeling that in spite of everything life is not without hope.

Marilyn Monroe made her media debut as Norma Jeane Mortensen, chosen and discovered by
David Conover, photographer for the U.S. Army's First Film Unit. Conover was assigned
by his commanding officer, Ronald Reagan (later president of the United States), to photograph beautiful
young women working at jobs vital to the war effort for publicity purposes. On June 26, 1945, in the
Radio Plane Corporation, a company owned by Reagan's friend Reginald Denny that produced
radio-controlled target planes, Conover met Norma Jeane, who was working there for twenty
dollars a week. He recognized her talent, photographed her, and recommended that she become a professional model. In addition, he introduced her to his photographer friend William Carroll, who took
this picture of Norma Jeane in a red sweater and white shorts with suspenders against the
background of the blue sky and the Pacific Ocean. Carroll took the photo for an advertising brochure
that was meant to demonstrate the quality of a color-processing photo lab.

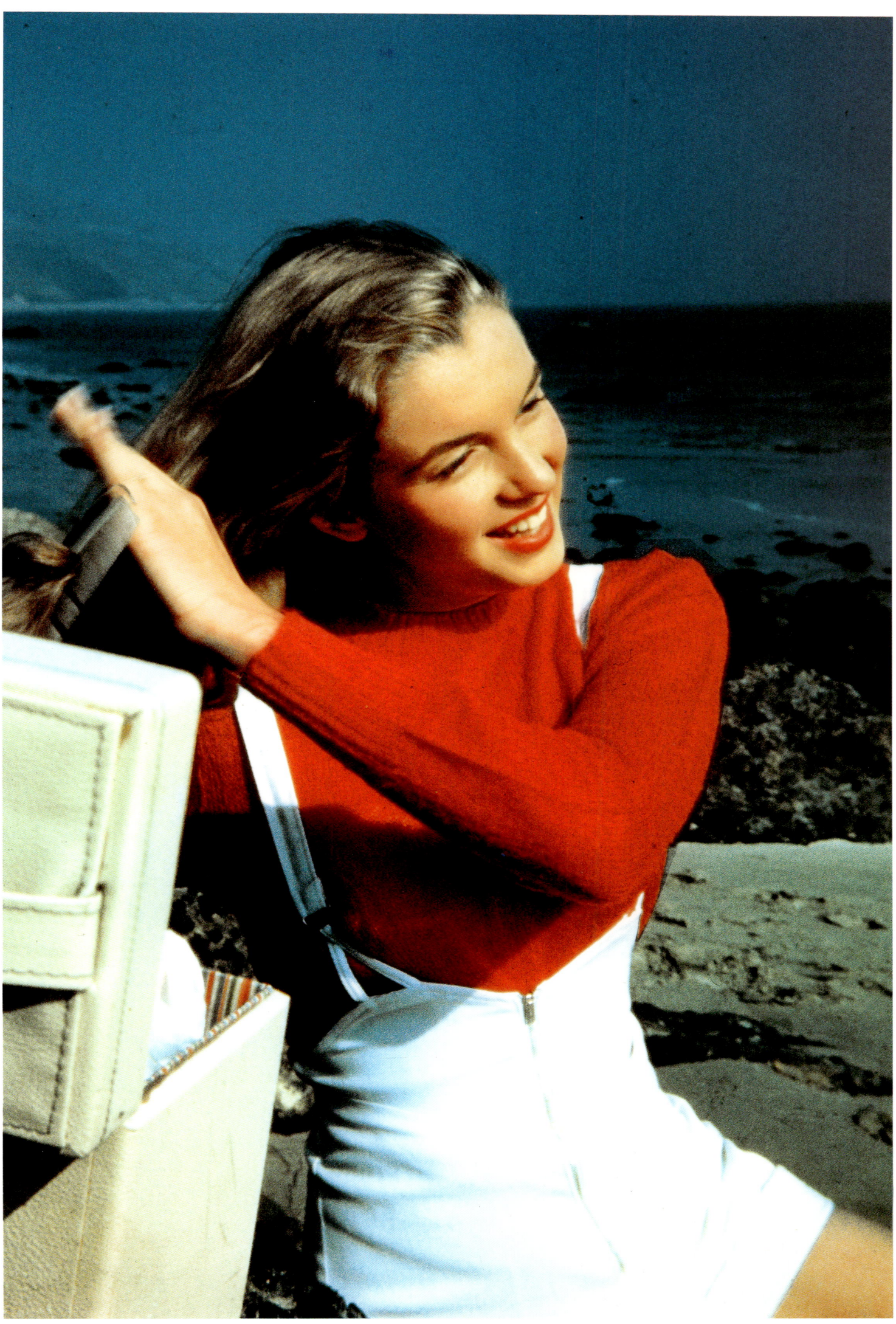

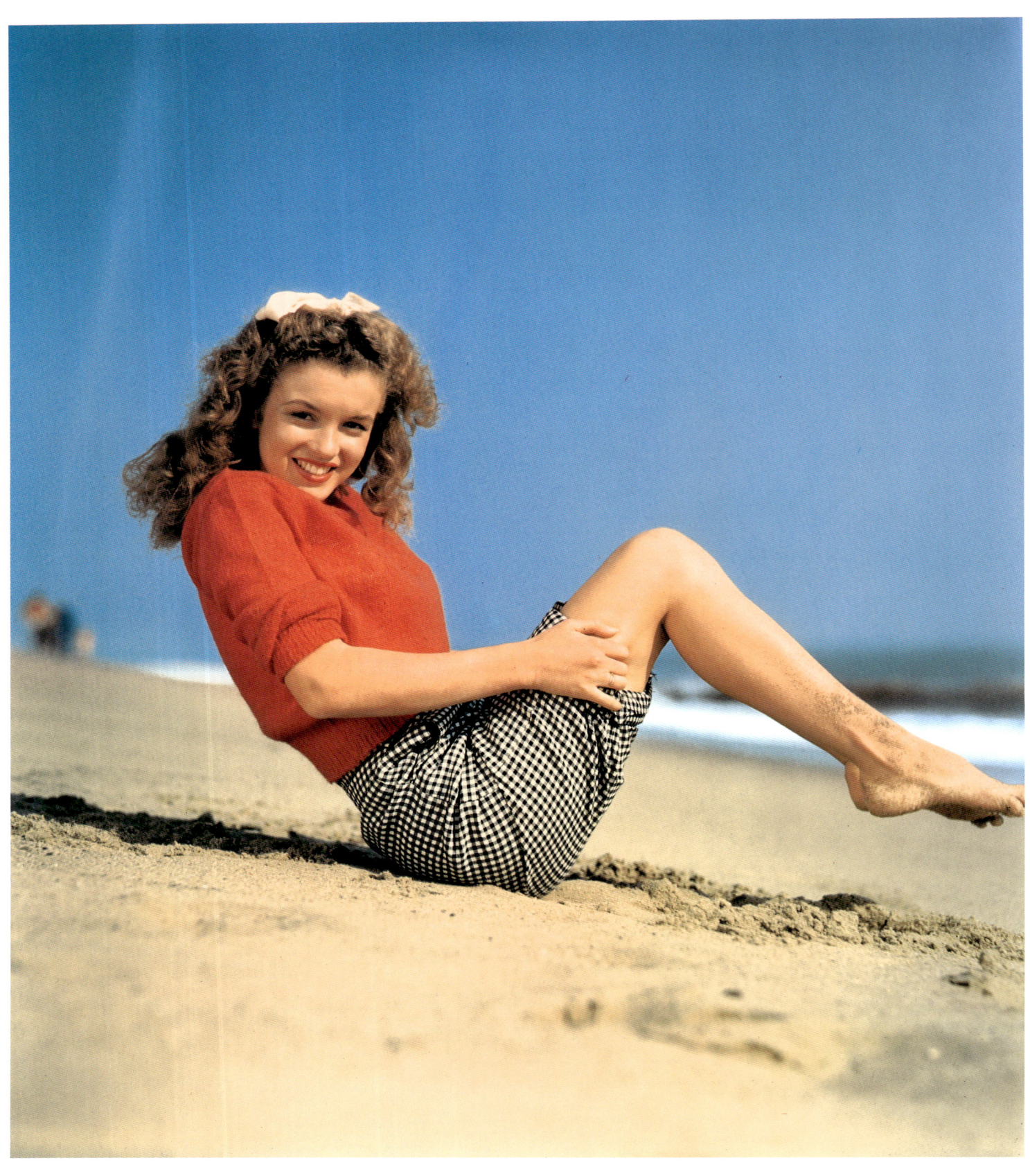

The man who discovered Norma Jeane's artistic talent was the
Hungarian-born photographer André de Dienes. He was looking for a model who would
also be willing to pose nude for him. The girl sent to him by the
Blue Book Modelling Agency was Norma Jeane. De Dienes was immediately taken by her
charm and hired her for $100 a week, plus expenses and props. The first pictures by André
de Dienes show Norma Jeane as a little devil in a schoolgirl skirt on the beach, 1945.

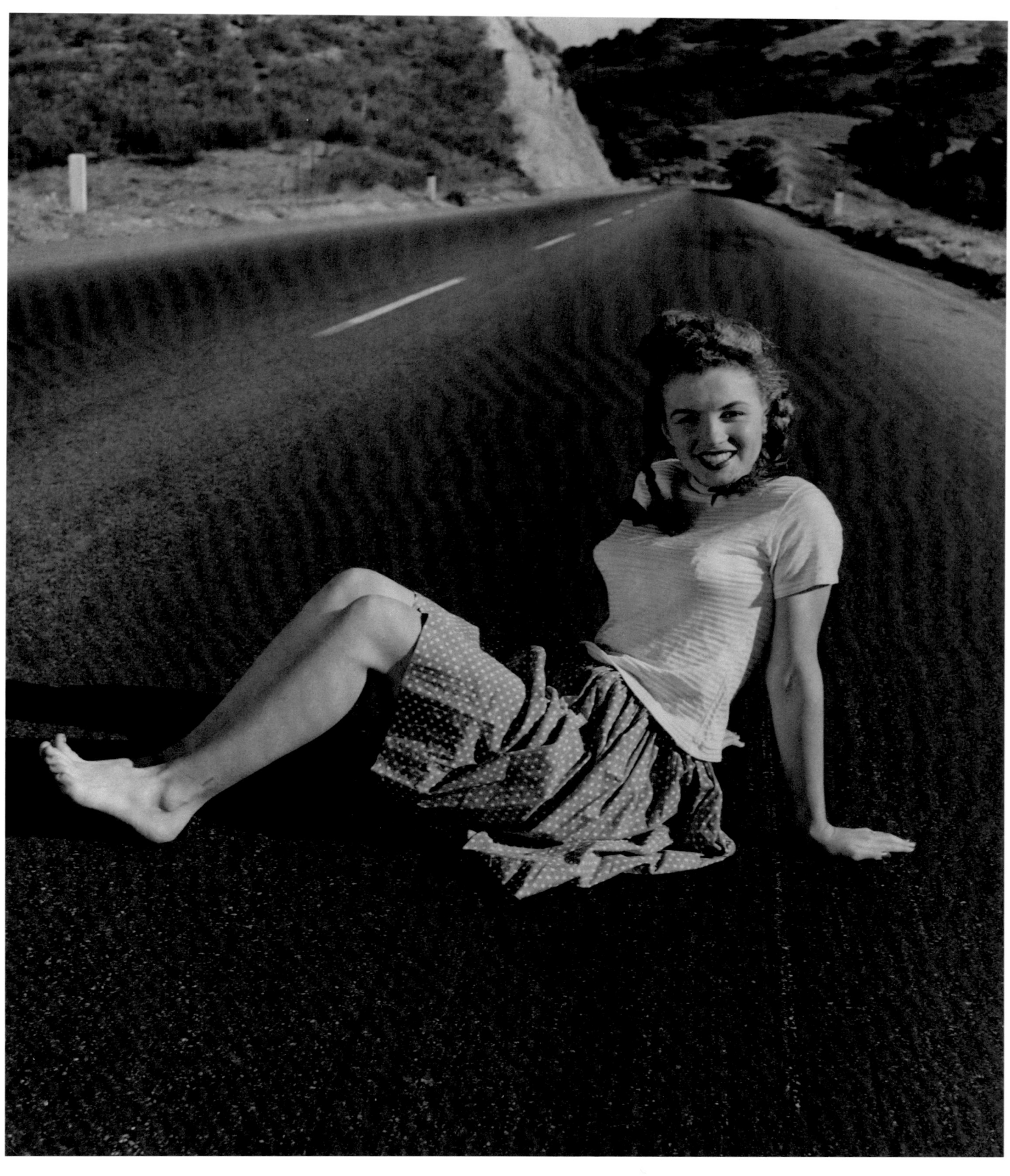

A picture full of symbolism, also by André de Dienes, on his first extended
photo expedition with Norma Jeane in the summer of 1945. With the words:
"Sit on the highway, it represents life. You have a long way to go,"
André de Dienes inspired this pose by Norma Jeane.

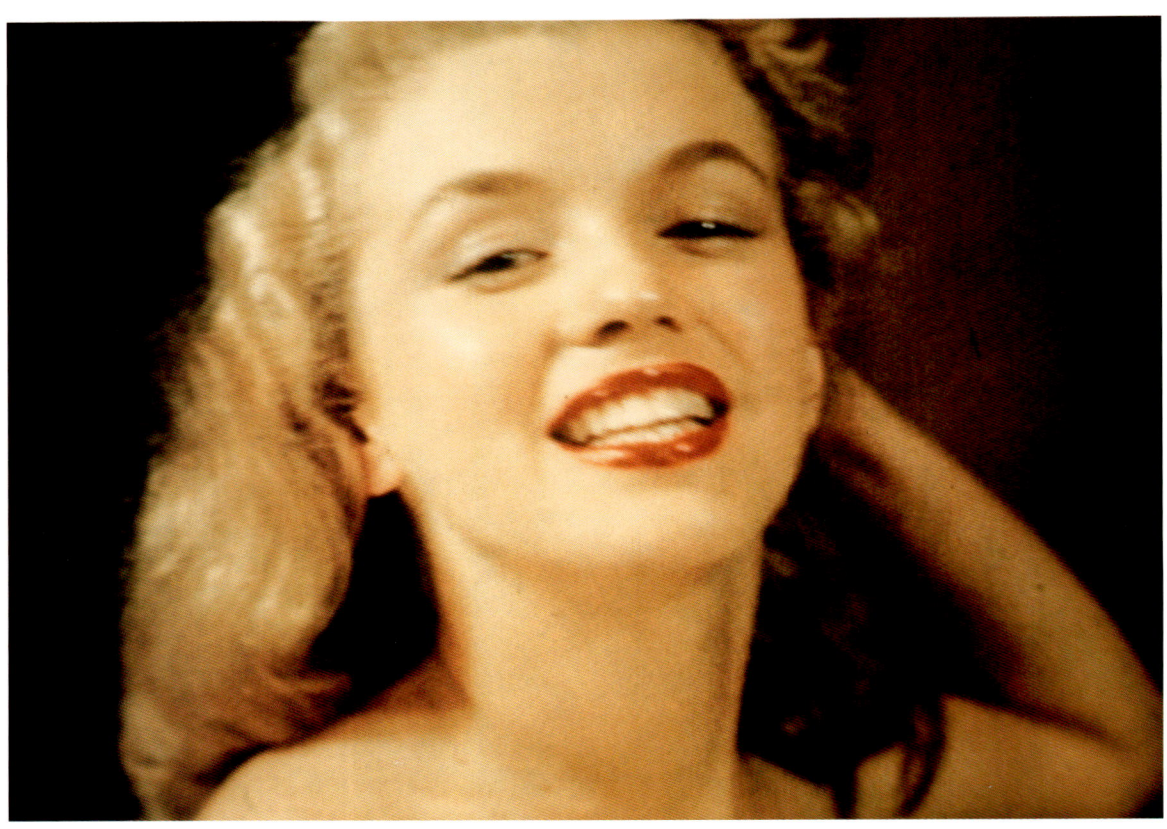

The photographer Leo Caloia made this movie still in 1946
at the Ambassador Hotel in Hollywood. Radio KFI in Los Angeles was hosting a talk show
on photo-artistic techniques. On the stage were seven models, including
Norma Jeane. In the picture, Norma Jeane's extraordinarily photogenic qualities can be
detected. It is evident how effectively light enhances the features of her face.

André de Dienes's portrait of Norma Jeane with her hair up and wearing
a mohair jacket recalls the style of family photos in the forties,
and also gives a hint of the feelings the photographer was soon to feel for his model.

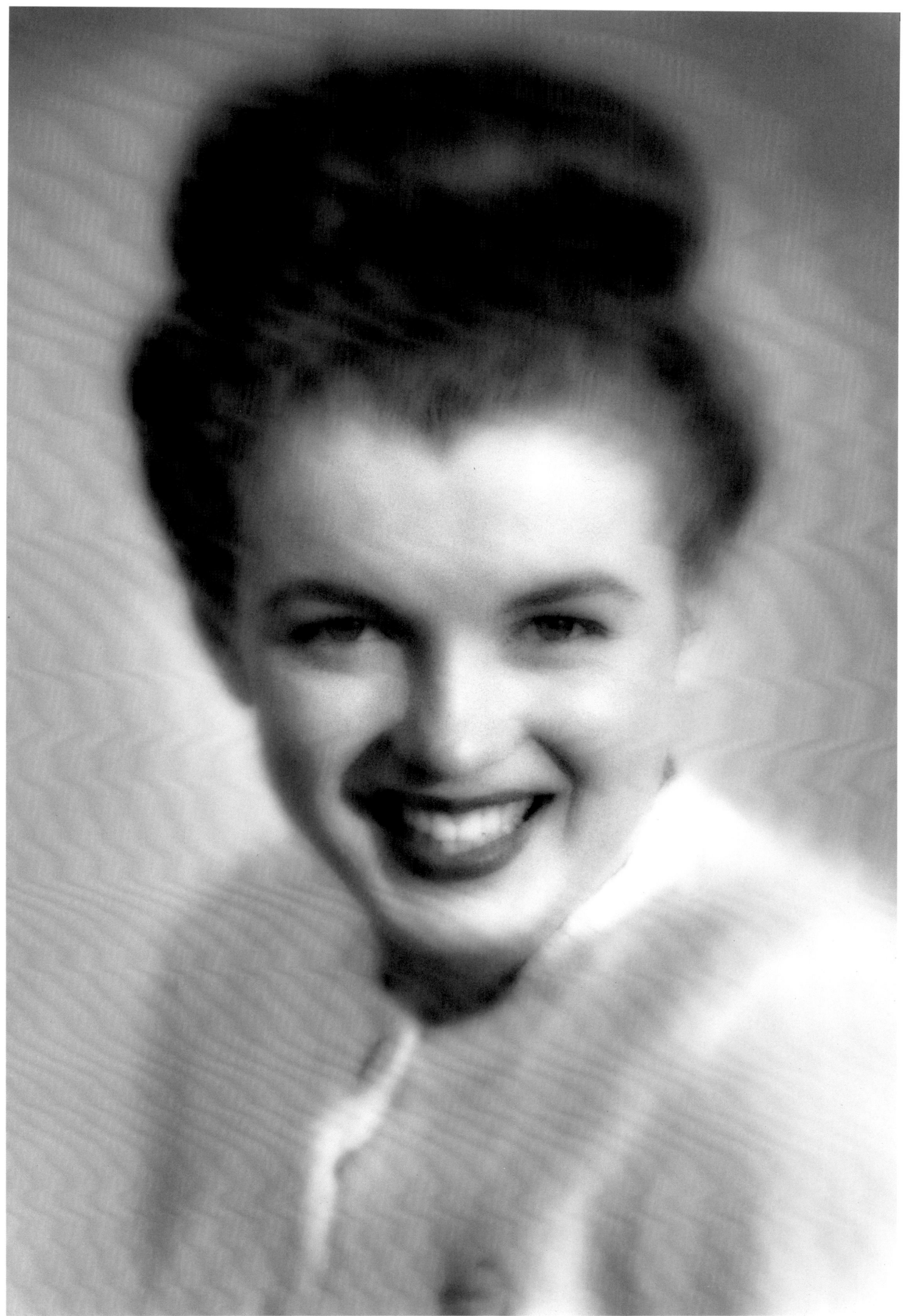

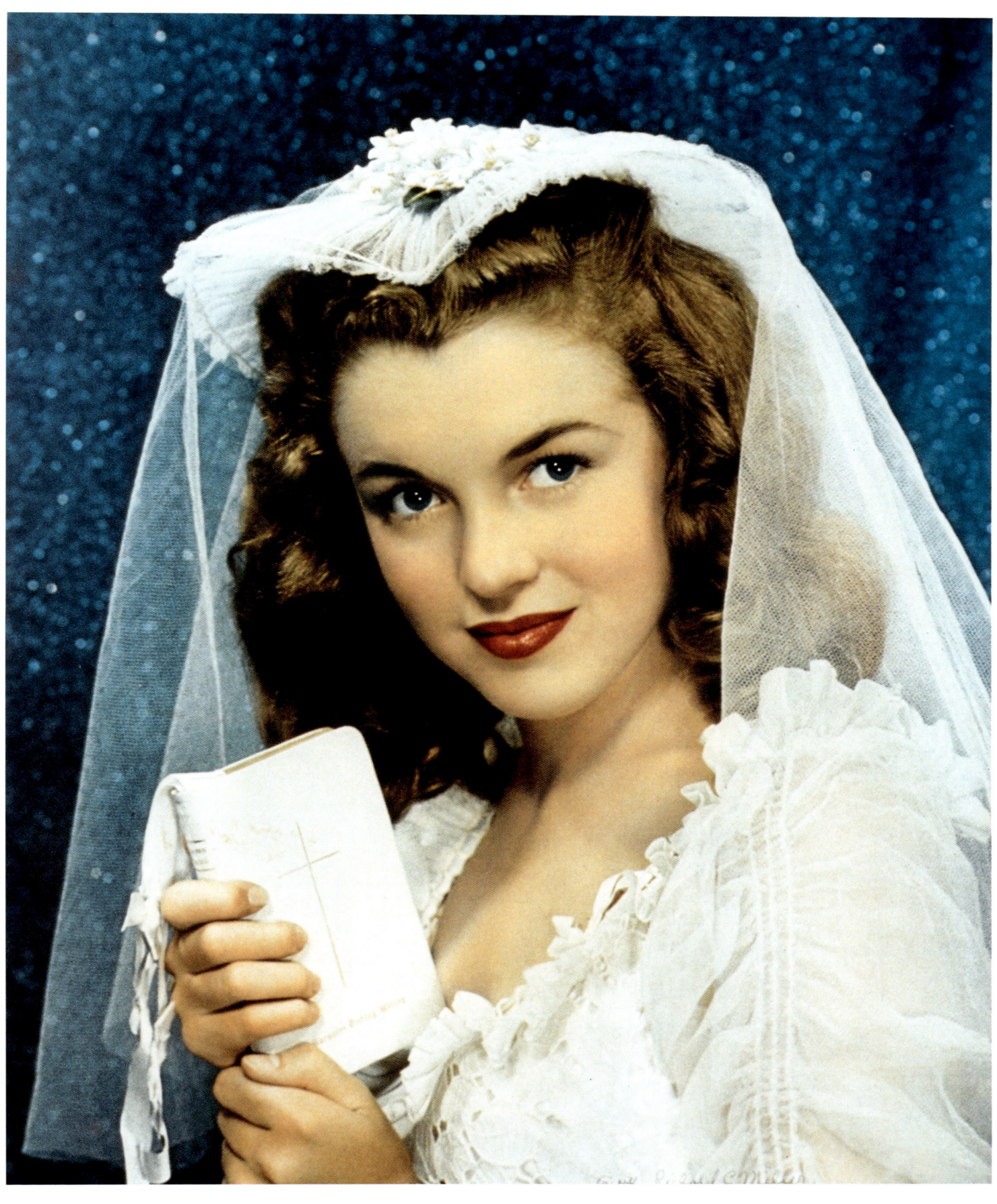

For this advertisement photographed by Richard C. Miller in 1946,
Norma Jeane posed in her own wedding dress from her first marriage to Jim Dougherty
and with the prayer book of the photographer's wife.

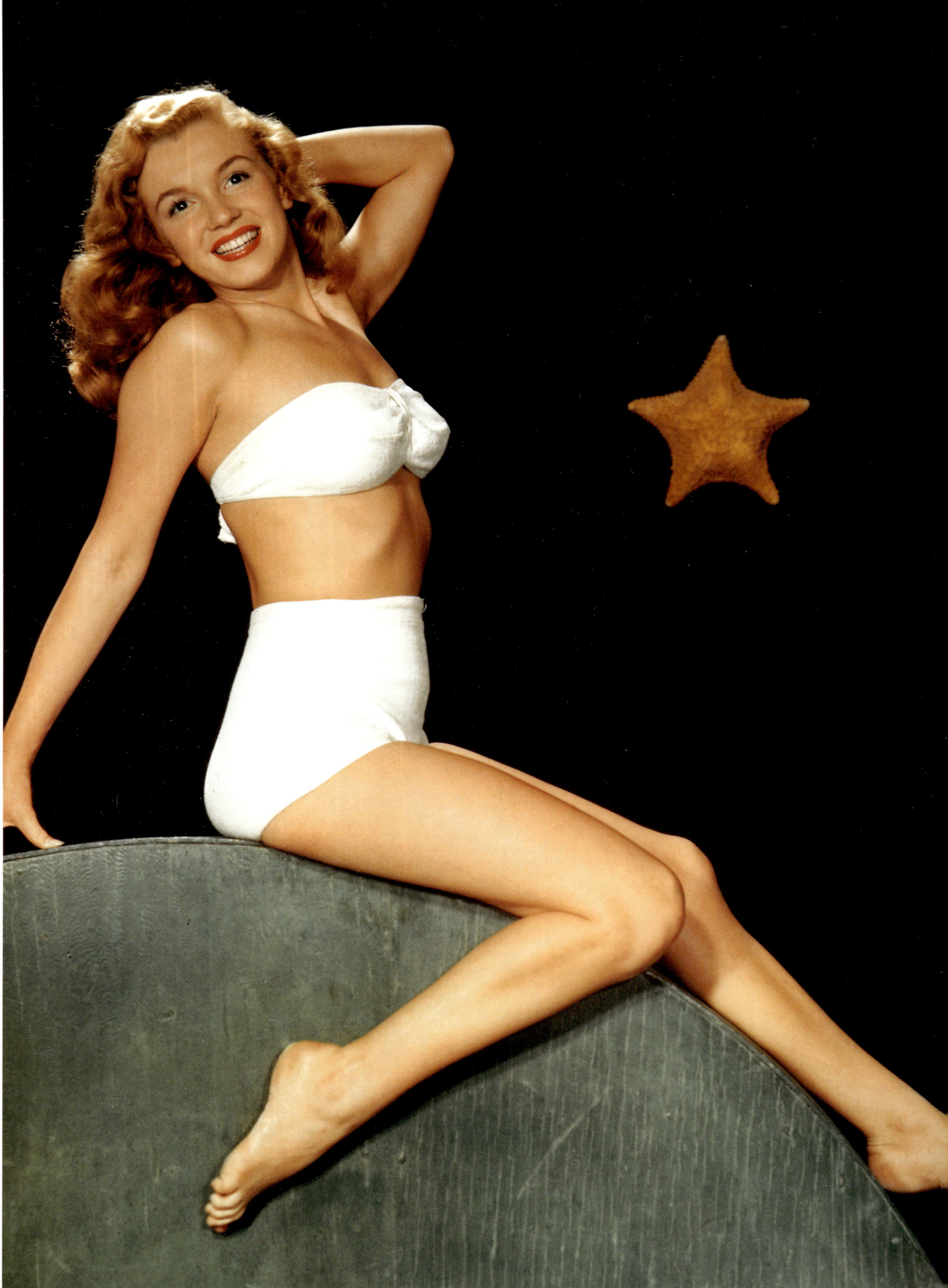

Another photographer who could lay claim to having discovered
Norma Jeane was the German-born Hollywood photographer Bruno Bernard, who was
famous in the forties and fifties as "Bernard of Hollywood." He met
Norma Jeane one late September day in 1945 on the street and arranged a sitting with her.
This picture from 1946 already shows all the qualities of a classic pinup.
One photo from the series soon appeared on the cover of the magazine *Laff* and helped
Norma Jeane to get her first screen test
at 20th Century-Fox, where she was given her first film contract.

A sitting with Bruno Bernard in 1949 at the Racquet Club
in Palm Springs had far-reaching consequences for Norma Jeane, who now called herself
Marilyn and who already had a limited 20th Century-Fox film contract.
On this occasion she met Johnny Hyde, who ran the office of the famous William Morris
Agency on the West Coast, and who was to become her friend and mentor.
The picture shows Marilyn in a two-piece bathing suit and sandals with high cork heels,
so typical for the time, on the diving board at the club.

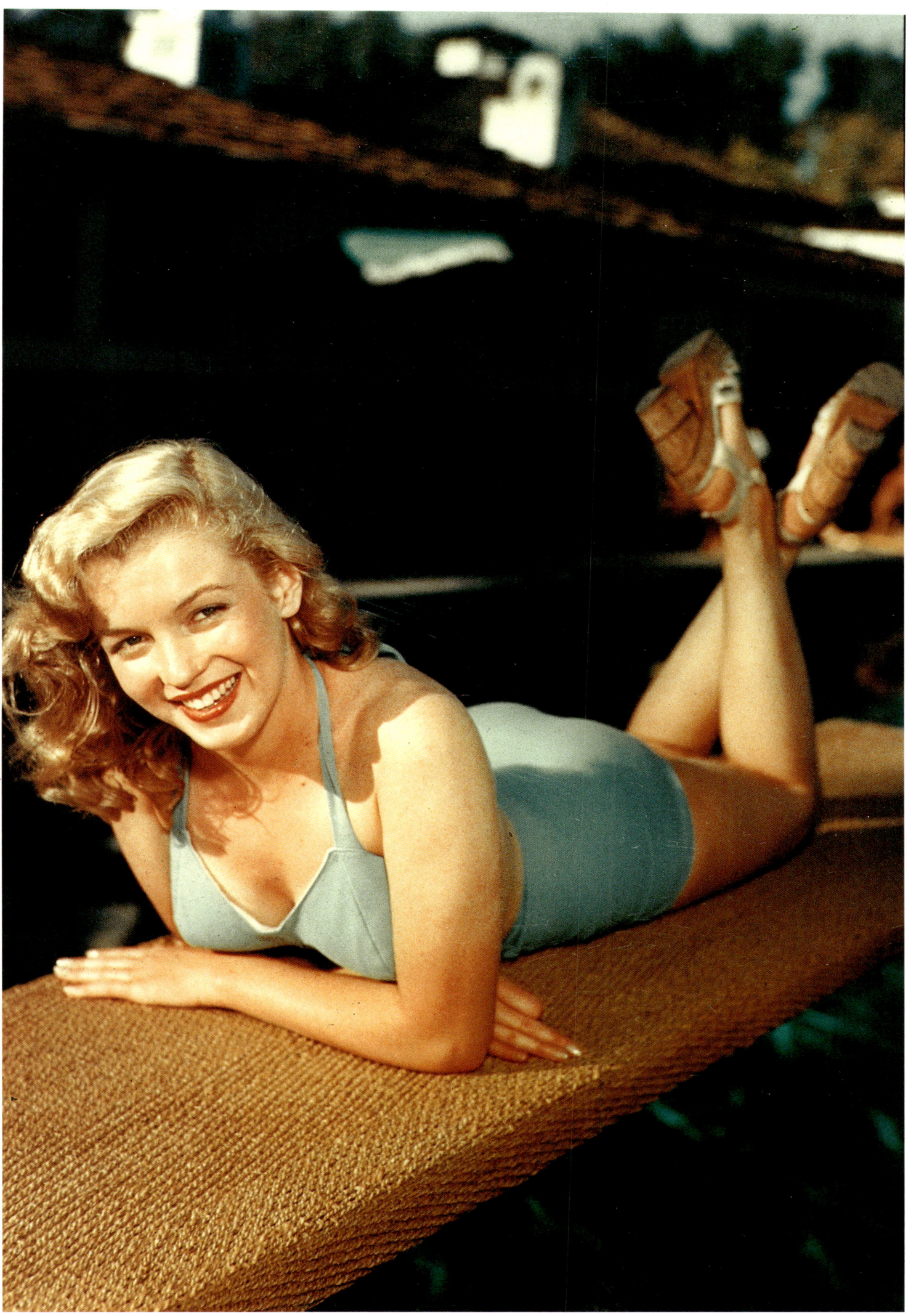

Fashion photograph by John Engstead, about 1947.

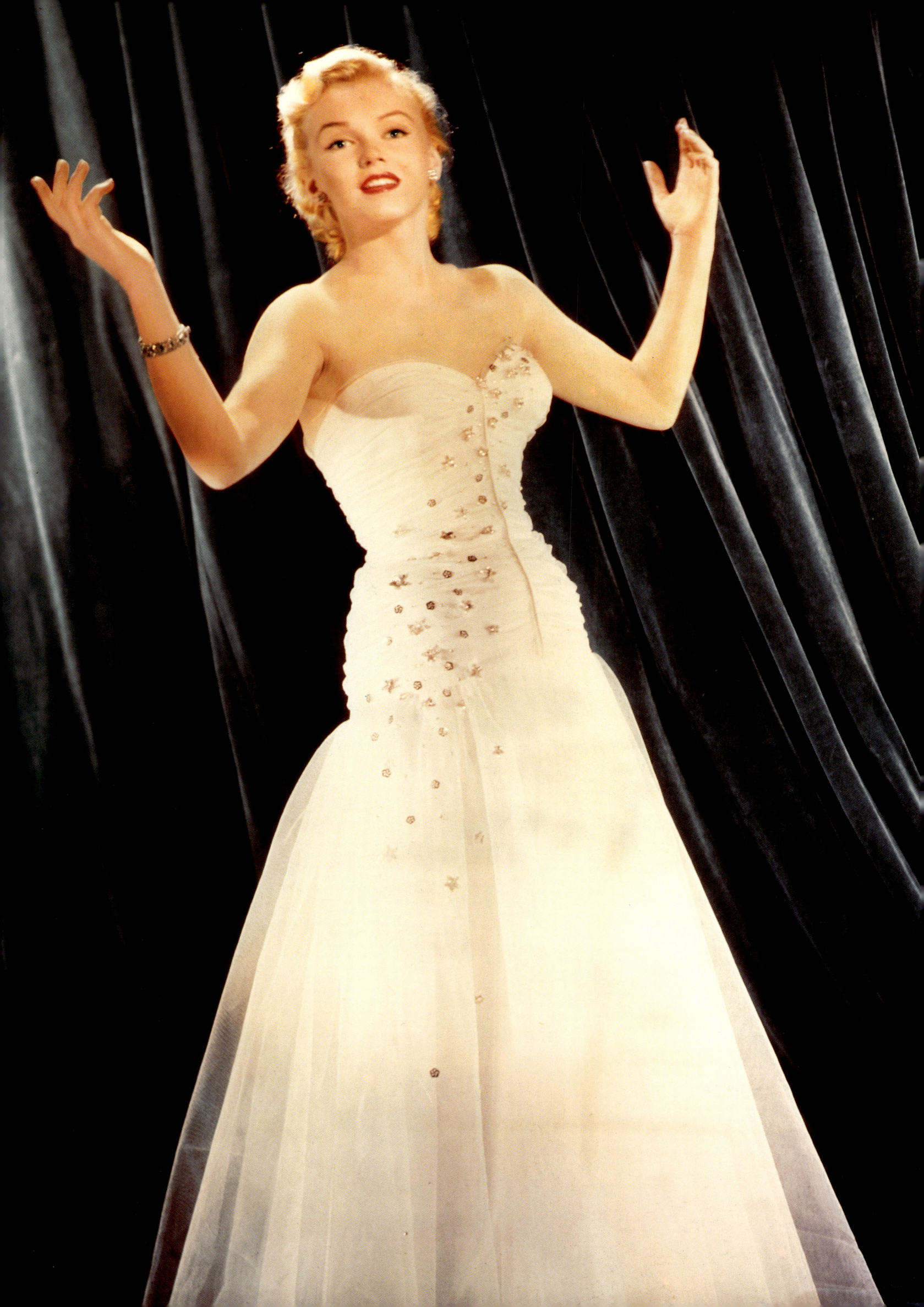

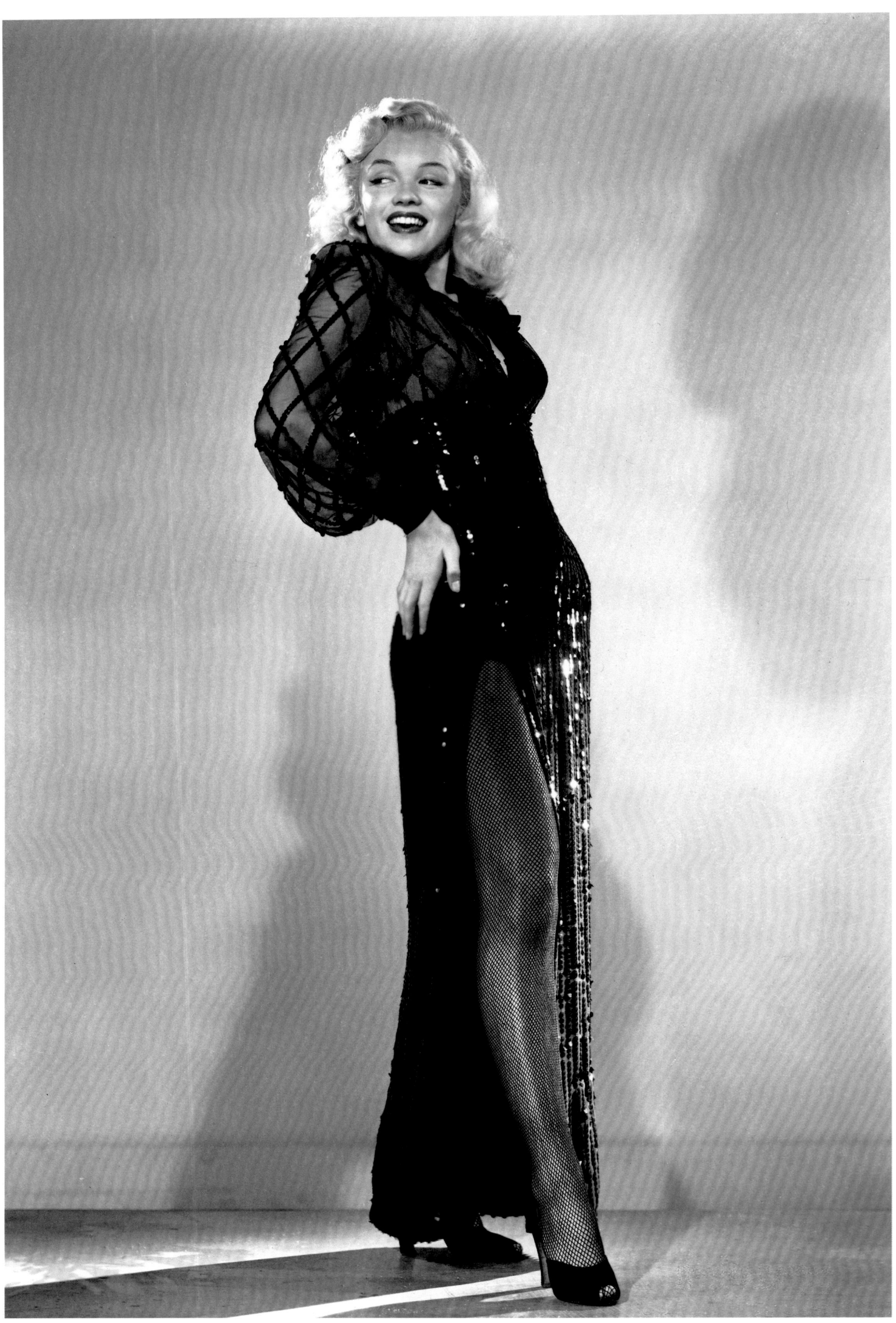

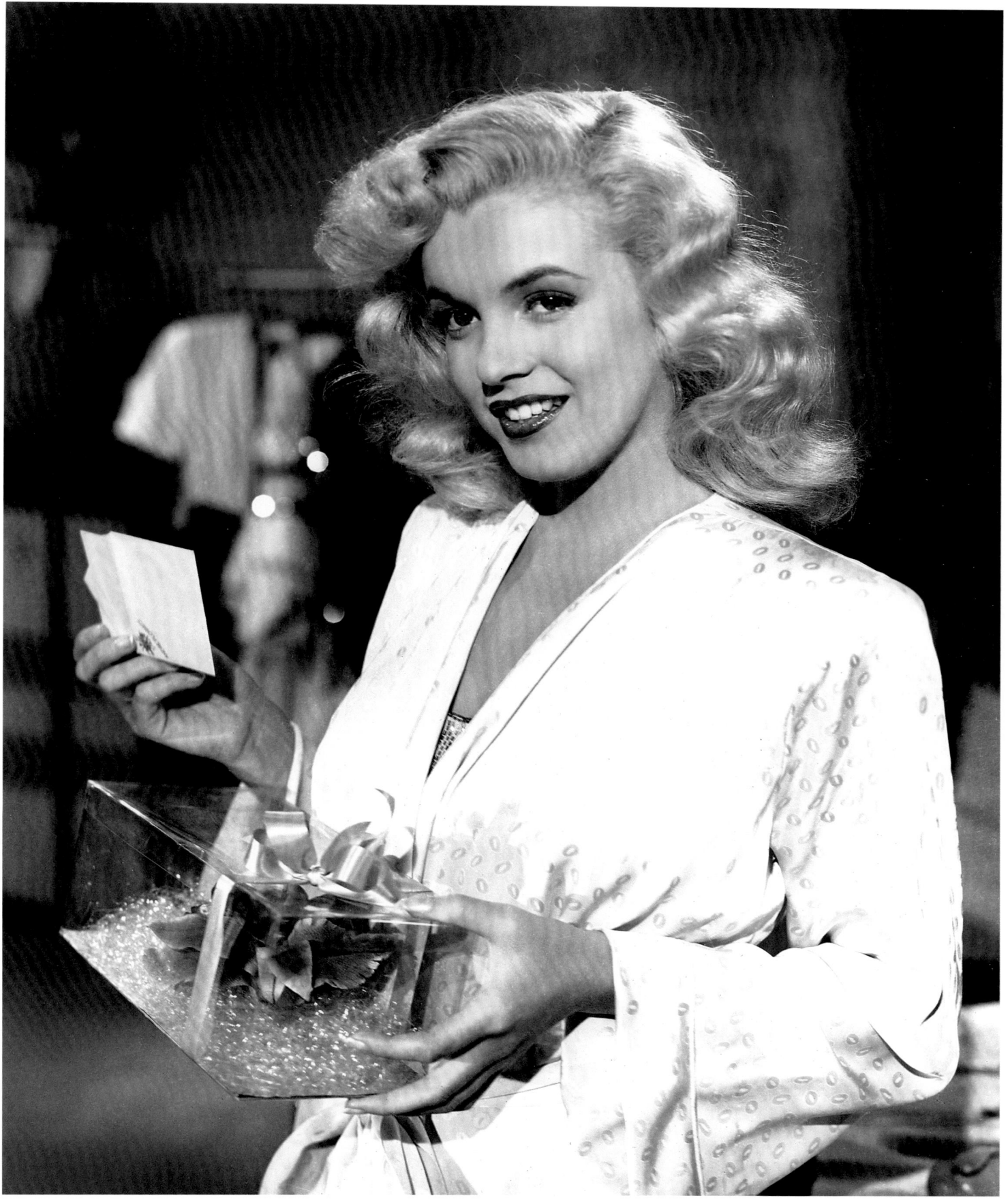

Ladies of the Chorus (1948) was the first film in which Marilyn was allowed to talk,
sing, and dance. On this occasion she met Natasha Lytess, who would personally manage her
until the completion of *The Seven Year Itch* in 1955. These two publicity shots from
the film show Marilyn as the chorus girl Peggy Martin. Her appearance already hints
at her star quality, and she sang two songs in the film about which Tibor Krekes
commented in *Motion Picture Herald:* "One of the bright spots is Miss Monroe's singing.
She is pretty and, with her pleasing voice and style, she shows promise."

Publicity shot in 1948 for United Artists, which signed her up for the film *Love Happy*.

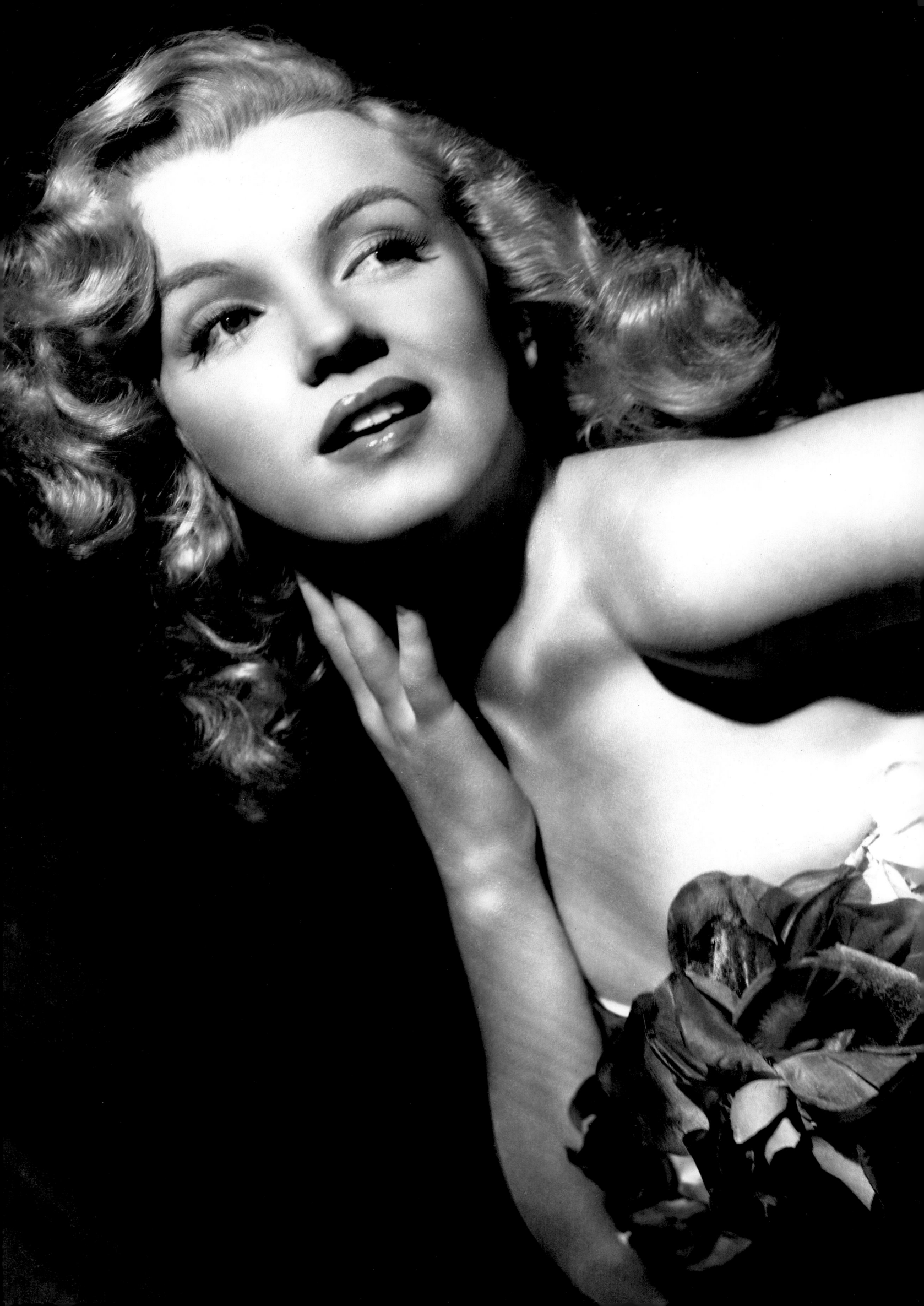

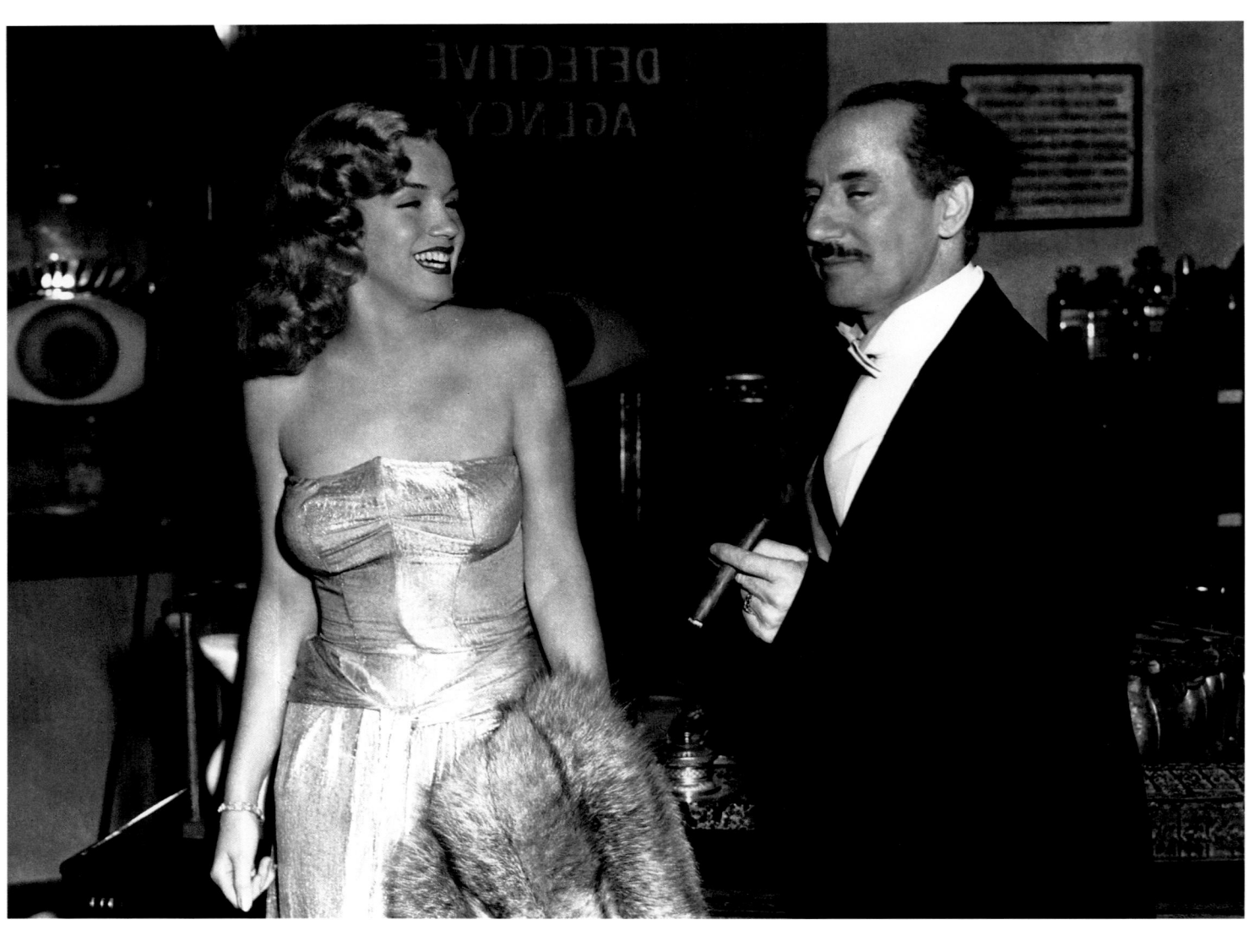

Still photo from *Love Happy* with Groucho Marx,
the first famous film personality with whom Marilyn appeared on the screen. He was looking
for a "young lady who can walk by me in such a manner as to arouse
my elderly libido and cause smoke to issue from my ears." Marilyn got the role.

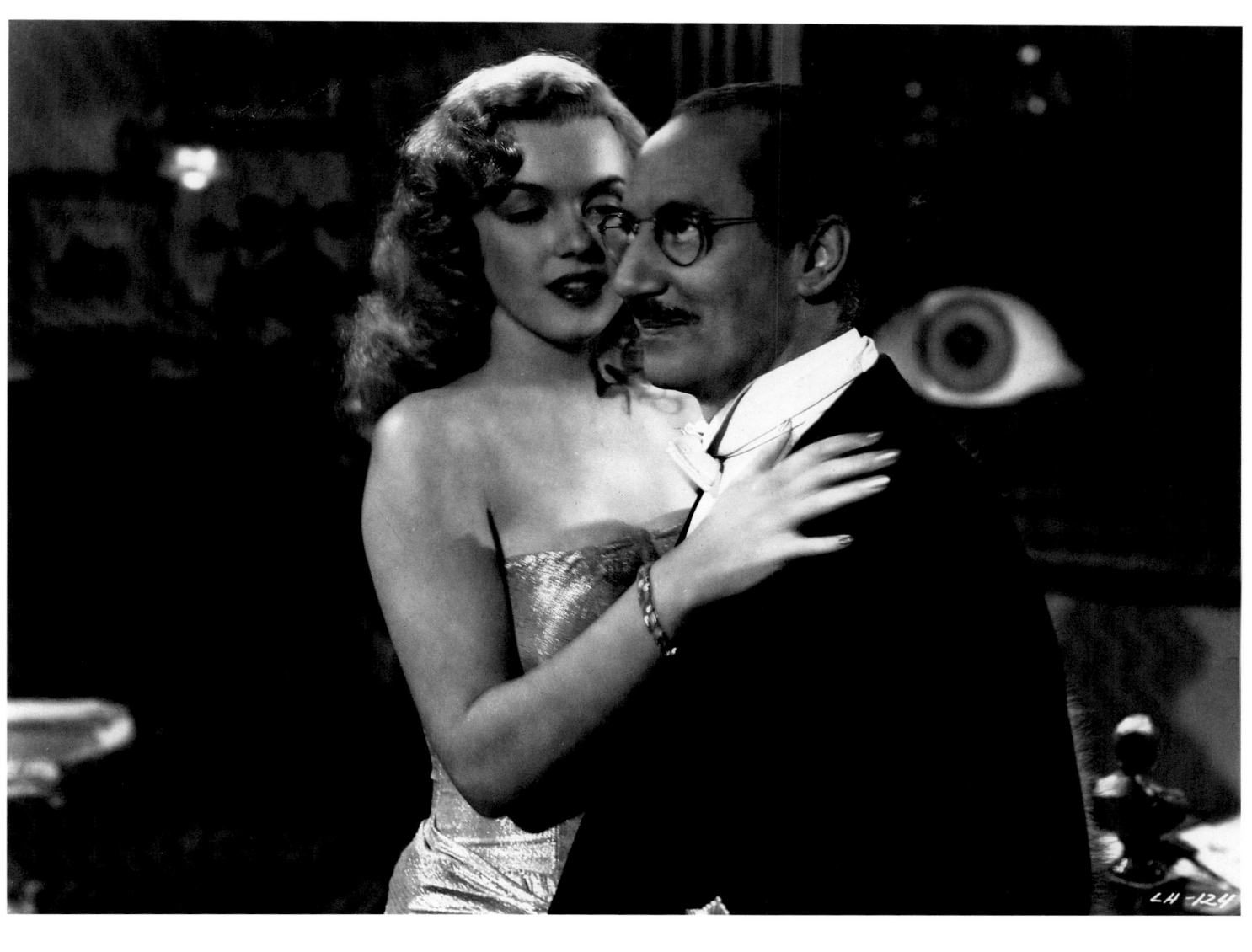

Still photo from *Love Happy*.
While the detective Grunion (Groucho Marx) is trying to track down
some missing diamonds, he is asked for help by a
voluptuous blonde (Marilyn Monroe) because men keep following her. To which
Groucho replies: "Really? I can't understand why."

Marilyn posing for *Life* in a costume from *Love Happy*.
Photograph by J. R. Eyerman, 1948.

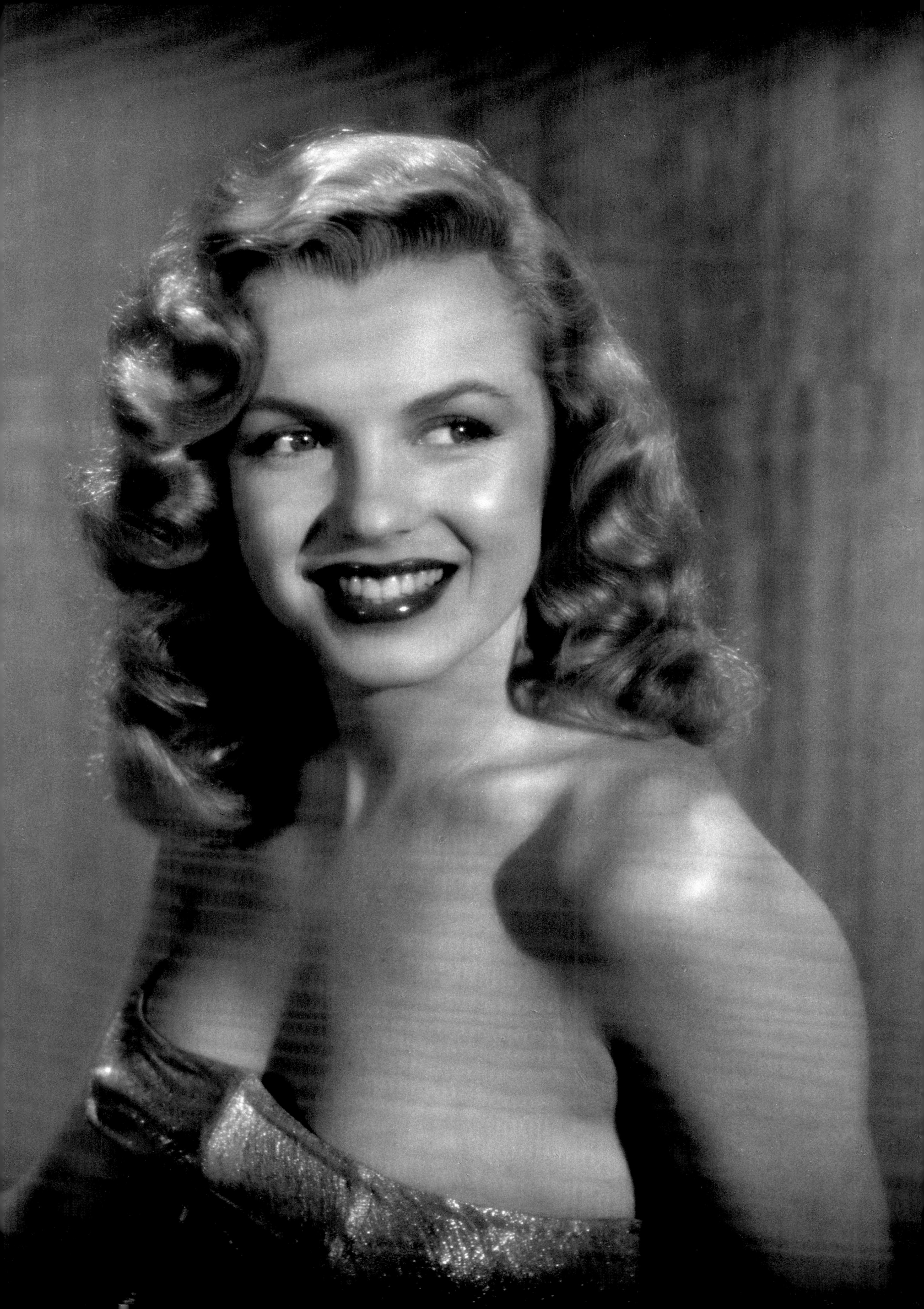

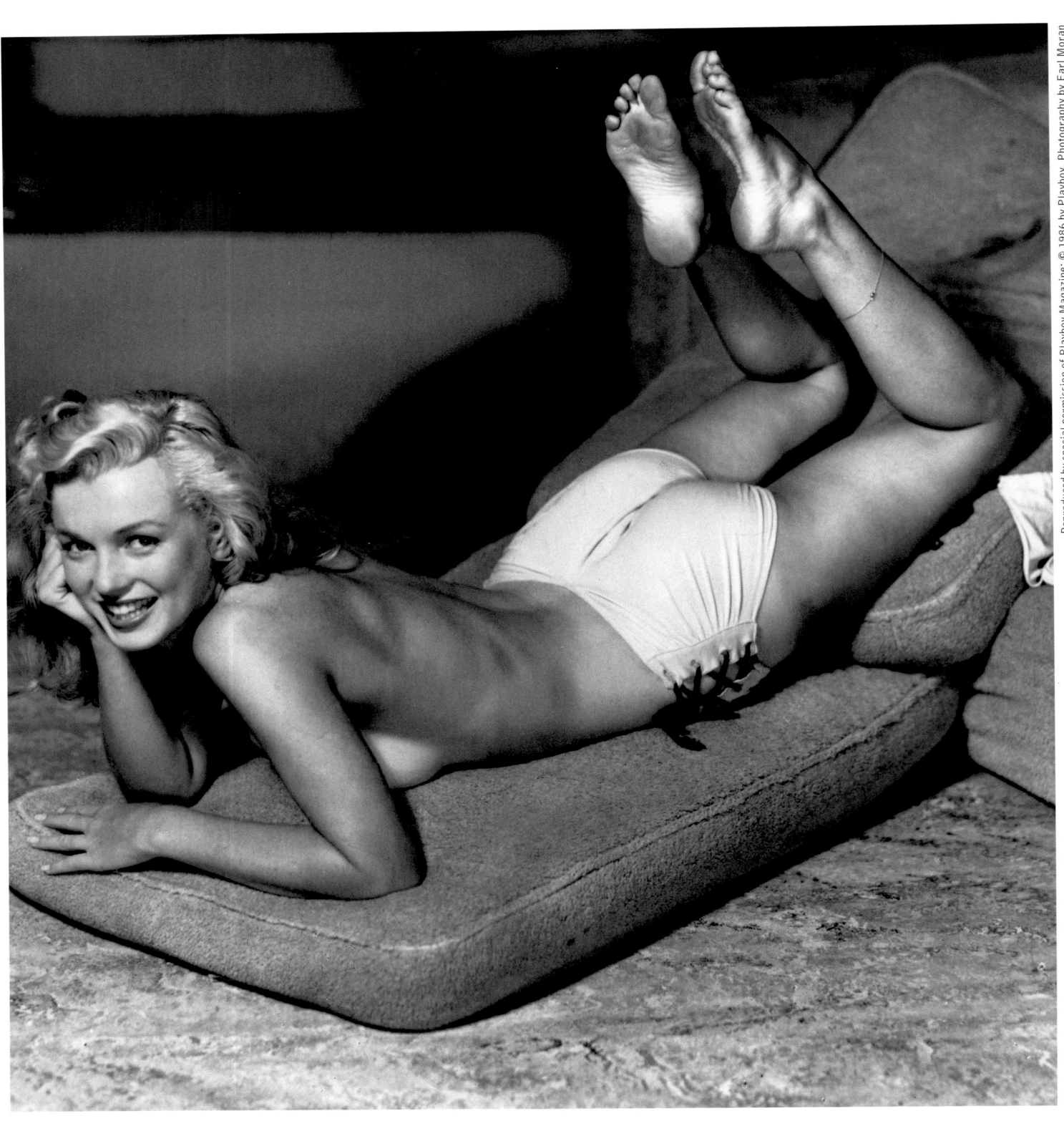

During the time of the shooting for *Love Happy,*
these pictures were taken by the artist and illustrator Earl Moran. Marilyn posed regularly
for him for several years, starting in 1946.
The photos served as the basis for his pinup drawings.

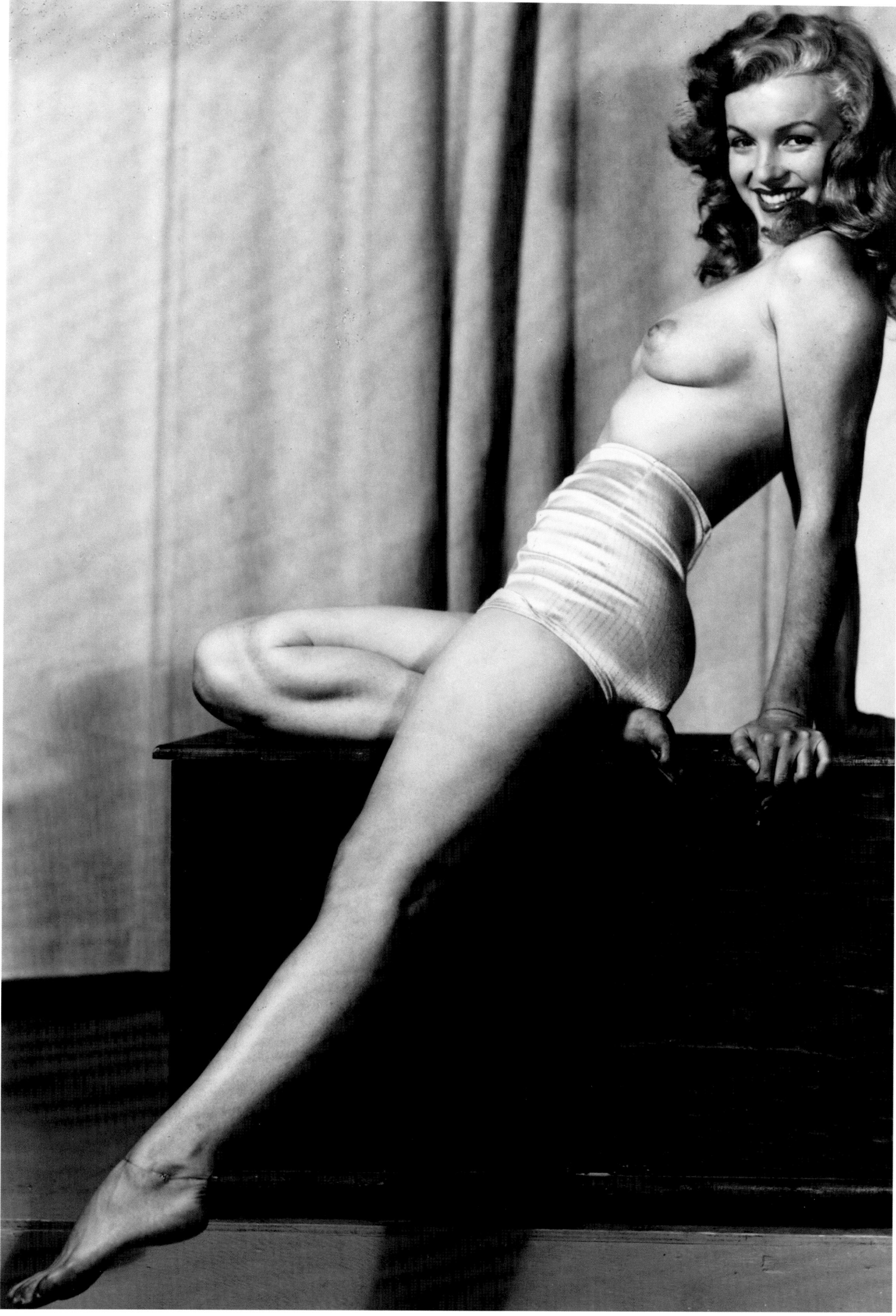

In May 1949 this famous photograph was taken by the Hollywood photographer
Tom Kelley in his studio. It was to cause a scandal when it was revealed almost three years
later in March 1952, that Marilyn Monroe, the young star of the future, had posed in the nude
for this photograph, which had since been published in a pinup calender. The scandal
reached Marilyn while *Don't Bother to Knock* was being shot. When Marilyn stood uo to the
situation and admitted to the photograph, the public was immediately on her side.
On April 7, 1952, probably as a direct effect of the calendar scandal, she appeared for the first
time on the front cover of *Life* magazine.

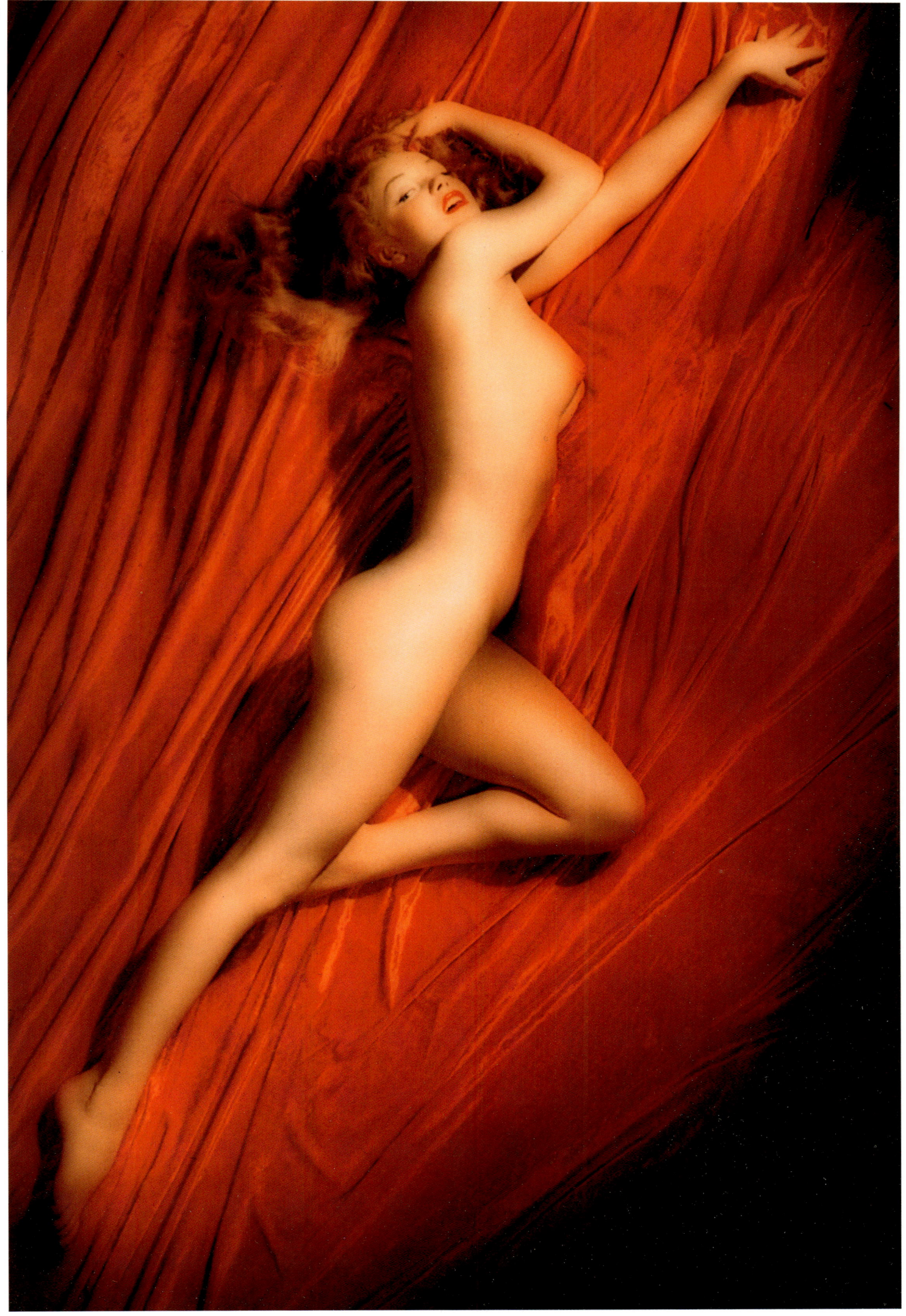

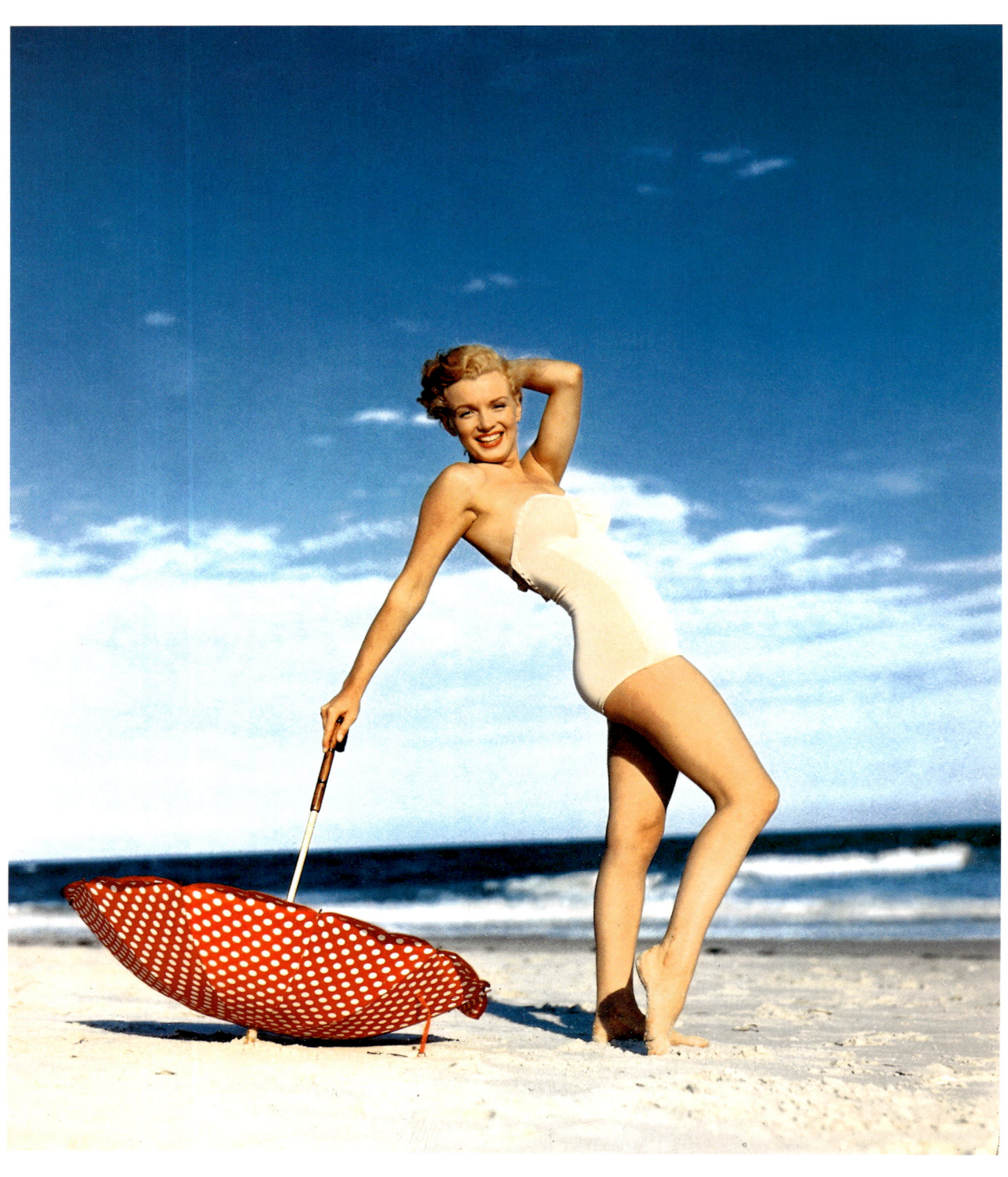

In 1949 Marilyn was asked to take part in a promotion tour for *Love Happy*.
The tour took her through several cities, including New York, where she stayed at the Sherry
Netherlands Hotel. There she arranged a sitting with André de Dienes, who was also staying on the
East Coast. That resulted in some of the most beautiful pictures ever taken of Marilyn. These and
the following picture were shot at Tobey Beach, Long Island. The pink and the white swimsuits, as
well as the dotted and colored umbrellas, were purchased for Marilyn by André de Dienes.

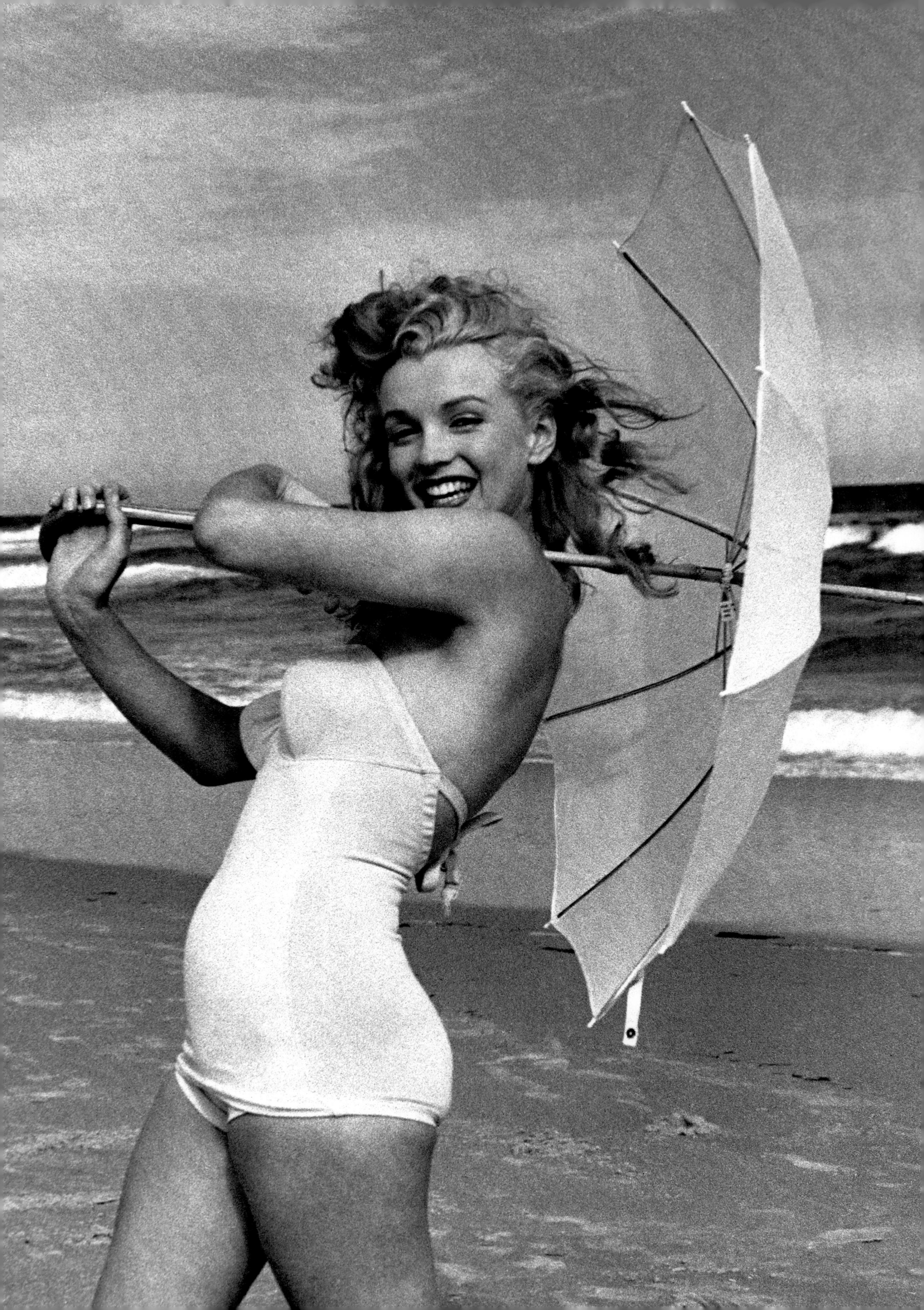

A beaming Marilyn, sitting cross-legged on Tobey Beach.

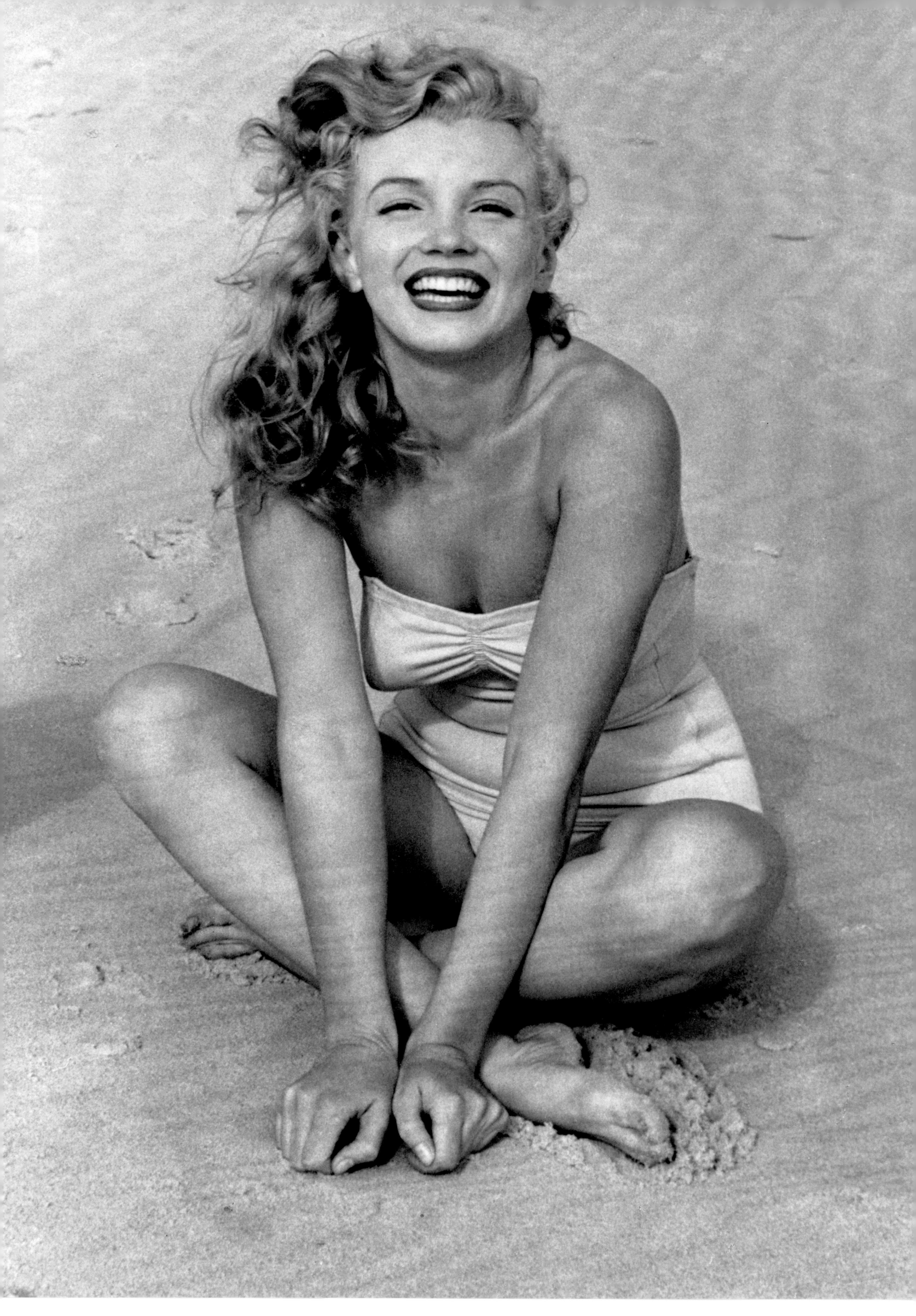

Publicity still for *The Asphalt Jungle,* 1950,
probably photographed by Frank Powolny. *The Asphalt Jungle,* directed by John Huston,
piqued the curiosity of a broad public about Marilyn Monroe.
Her role as the young lover of an aging gangster gave rise to a question that spread like
wildfire: "Who's the blonde?"

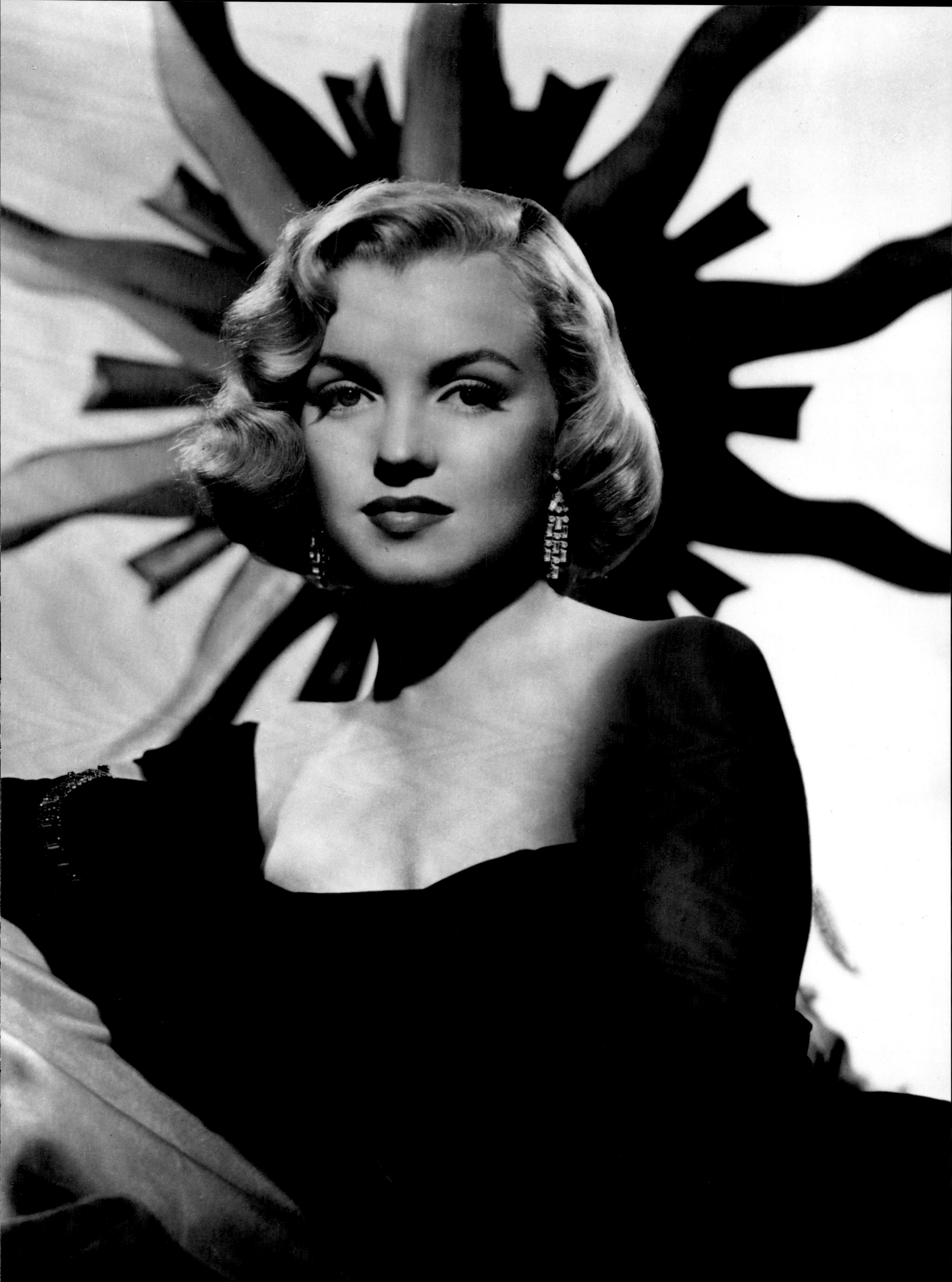

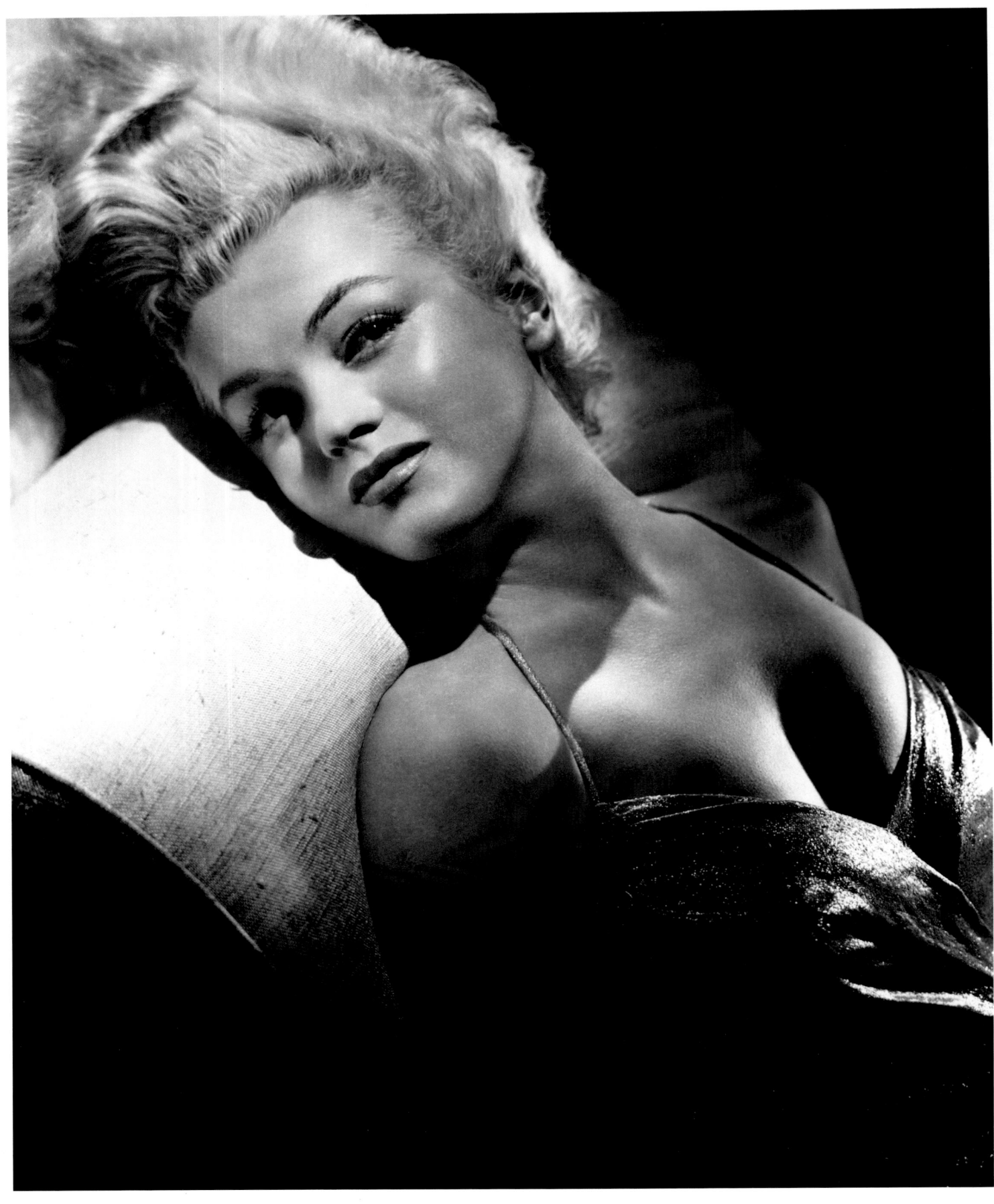

Publicity shot by Frank Powolny, 1950, in a dress for *All About Eve*. In this Oscar-winning film, starring Bette Davis, Anne Baxter, and George Sanders, Johnny Hyde had managed to get Marilyn a small role. The critics were very impressed with her performance. Darryl Zanuck, head of 20th Century-Fox, and certainly no great fan of Marilyn's, gave her another contract as a result.

Photograph by Ed Clark for *Life*. After her small roles in *The Asphalt Jungle* and *All About Eve,* the press begins to celebrate Marilyn's erotic aura.

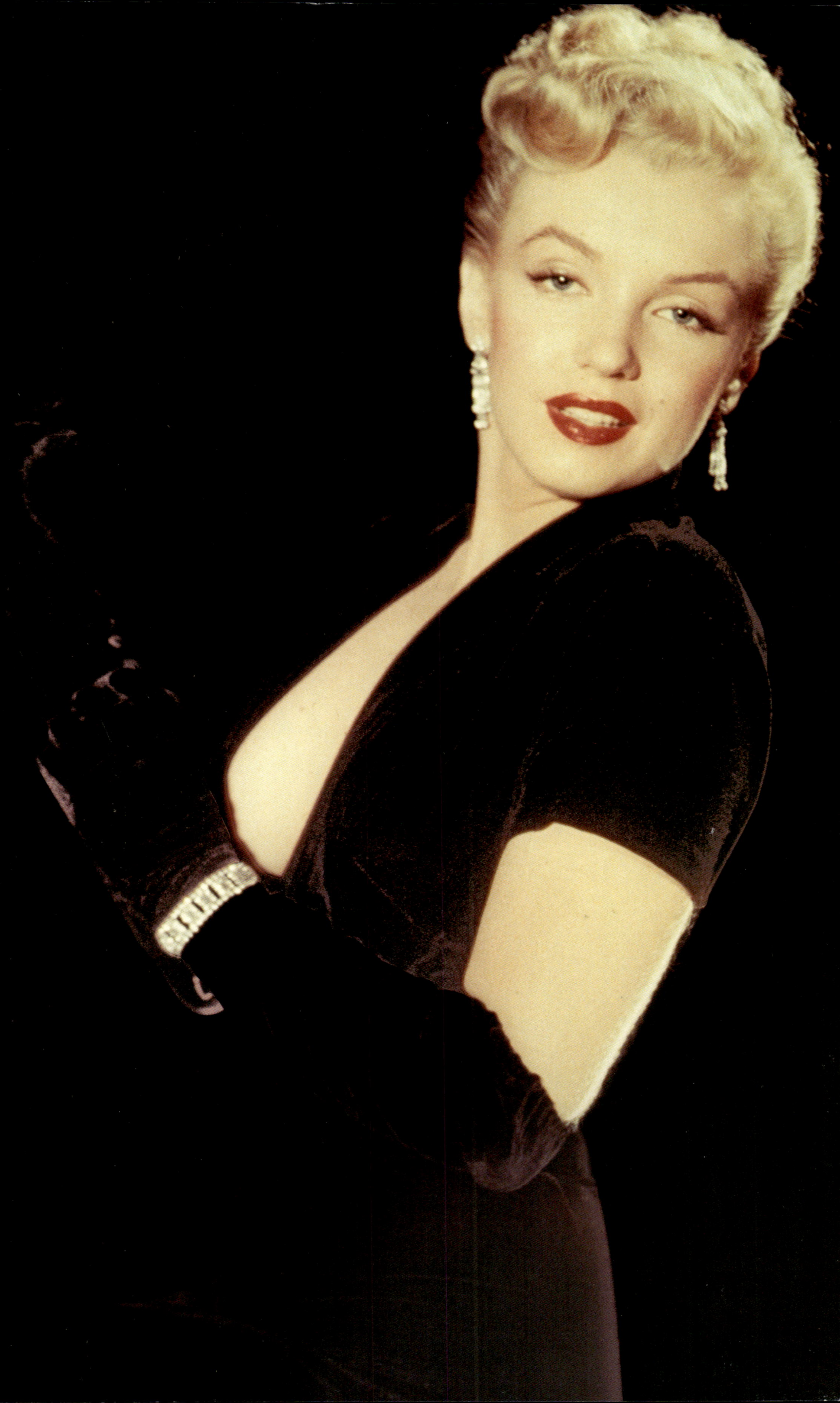

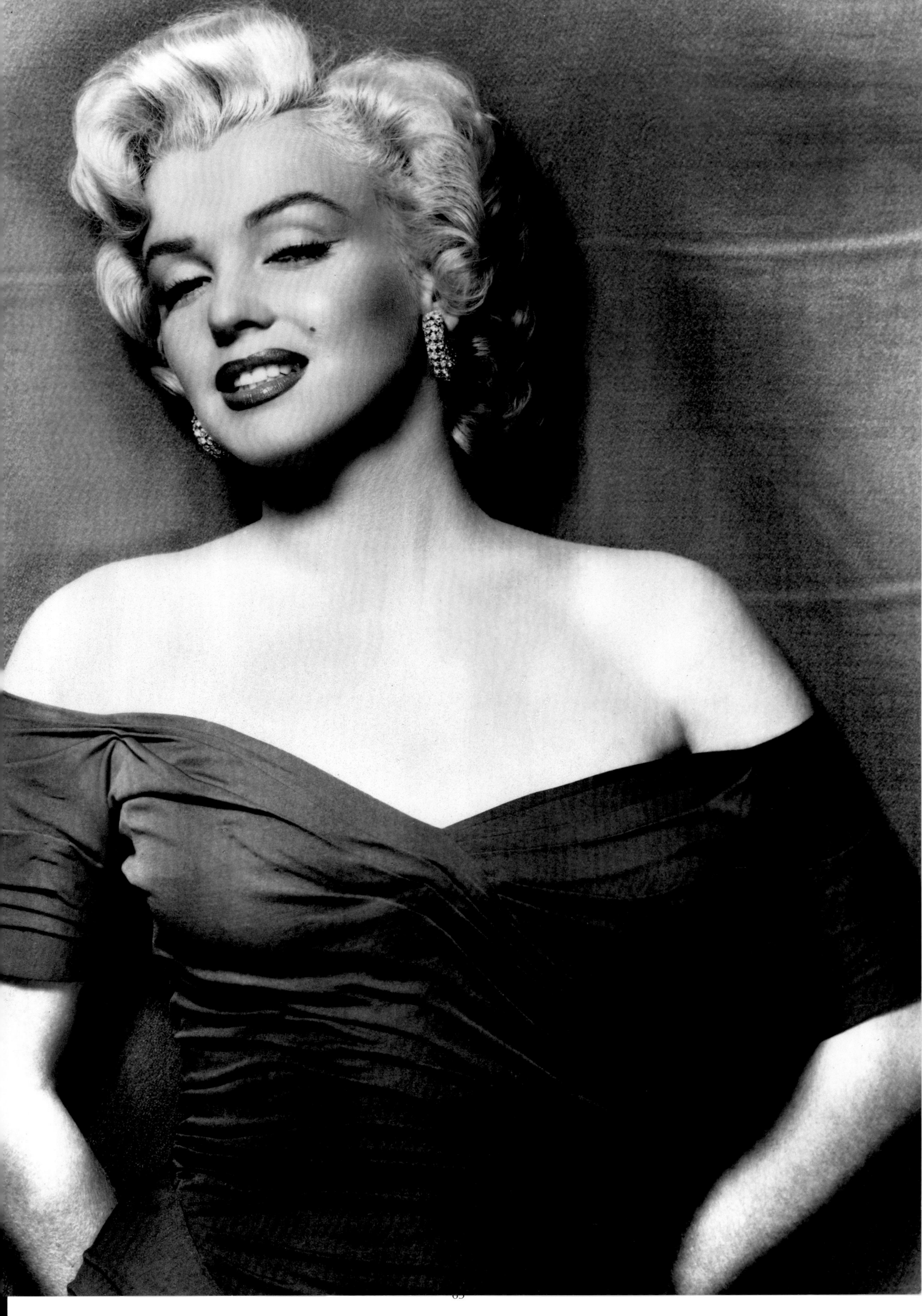

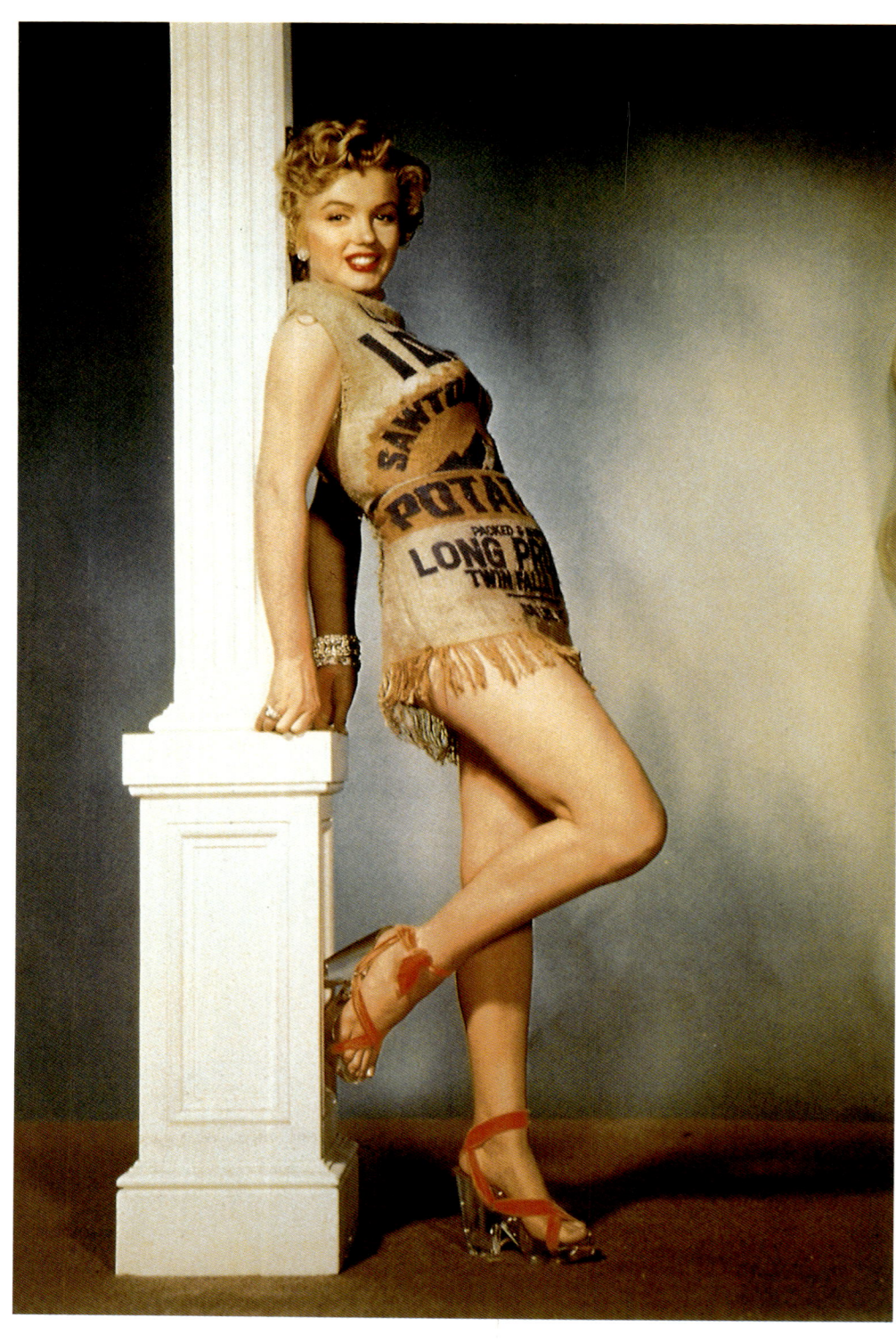

Besides her films, an almost endless number of pinup photographs
for publicity purposes were taken of Marilyn. They built on her image as a glamour girl.
The accessories were always the same: high-heeled shoes, T-shirts or bathing
suits, and, in this case, even a potato sack. These are two publicity stills from about 1952.

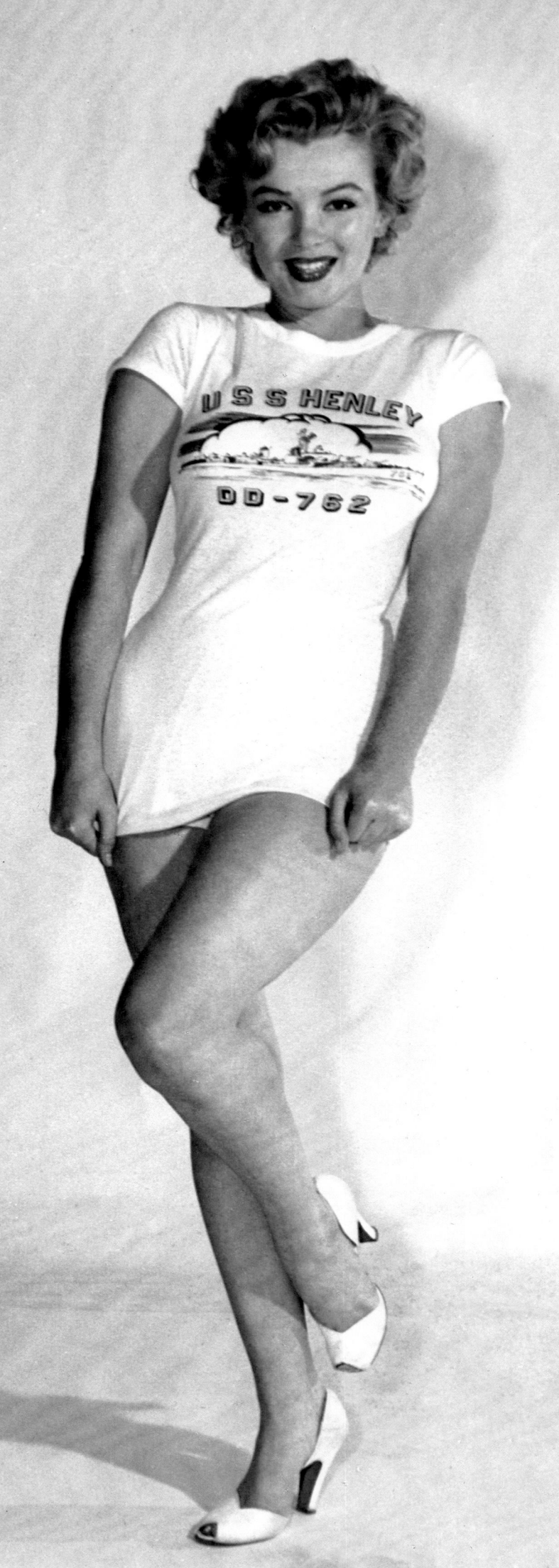

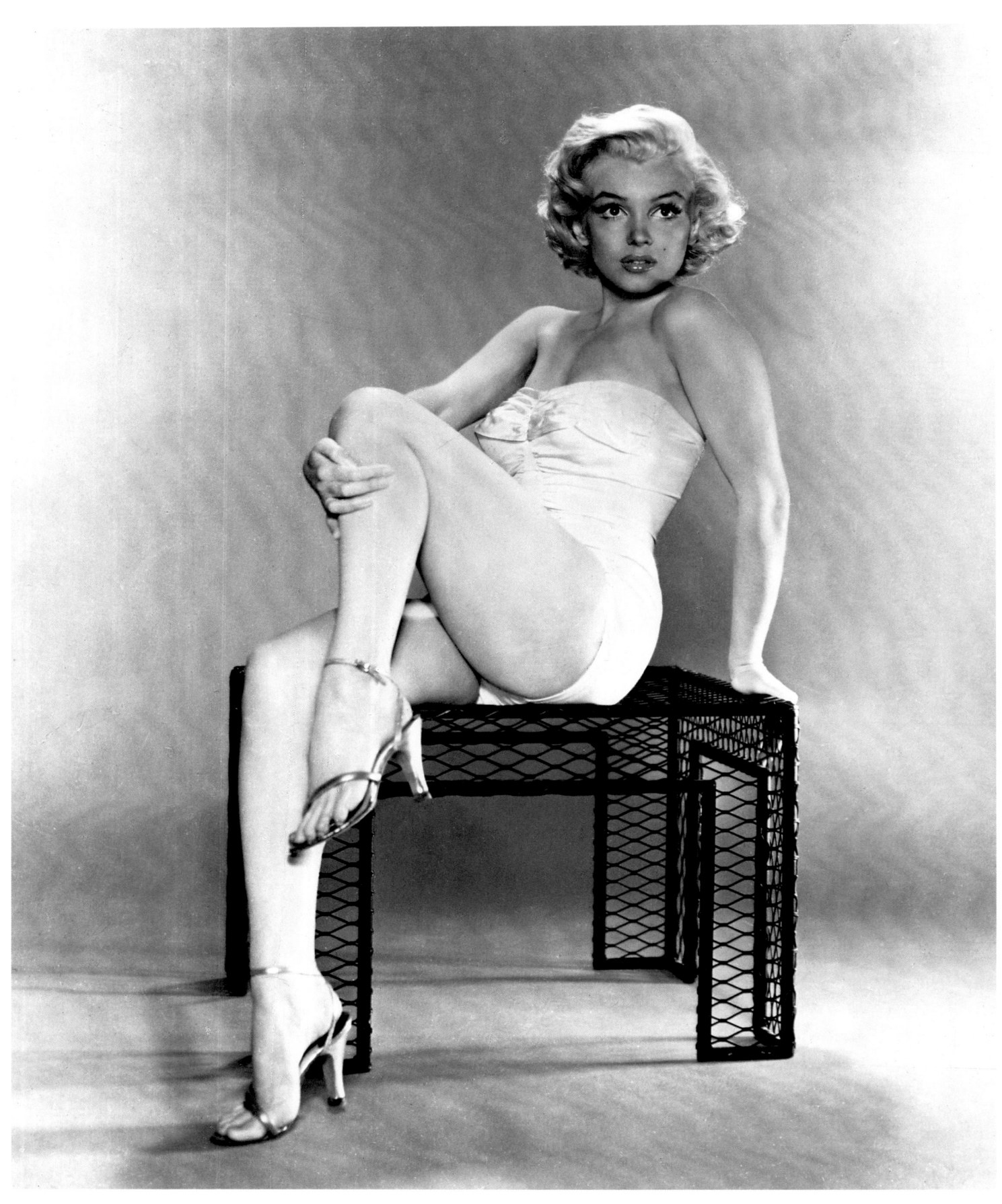

Marilyn's hairstyle in 1952 is youthful and modern.
She plays with Barbara Stanwyck in Fritz Lang's *Clash by Night*. Irene Thirer writes in the
New York Post: "That gorgeous example of bathing beauty art,
Marilyn Monroe, is a real acting threat to the season's screen blondes."

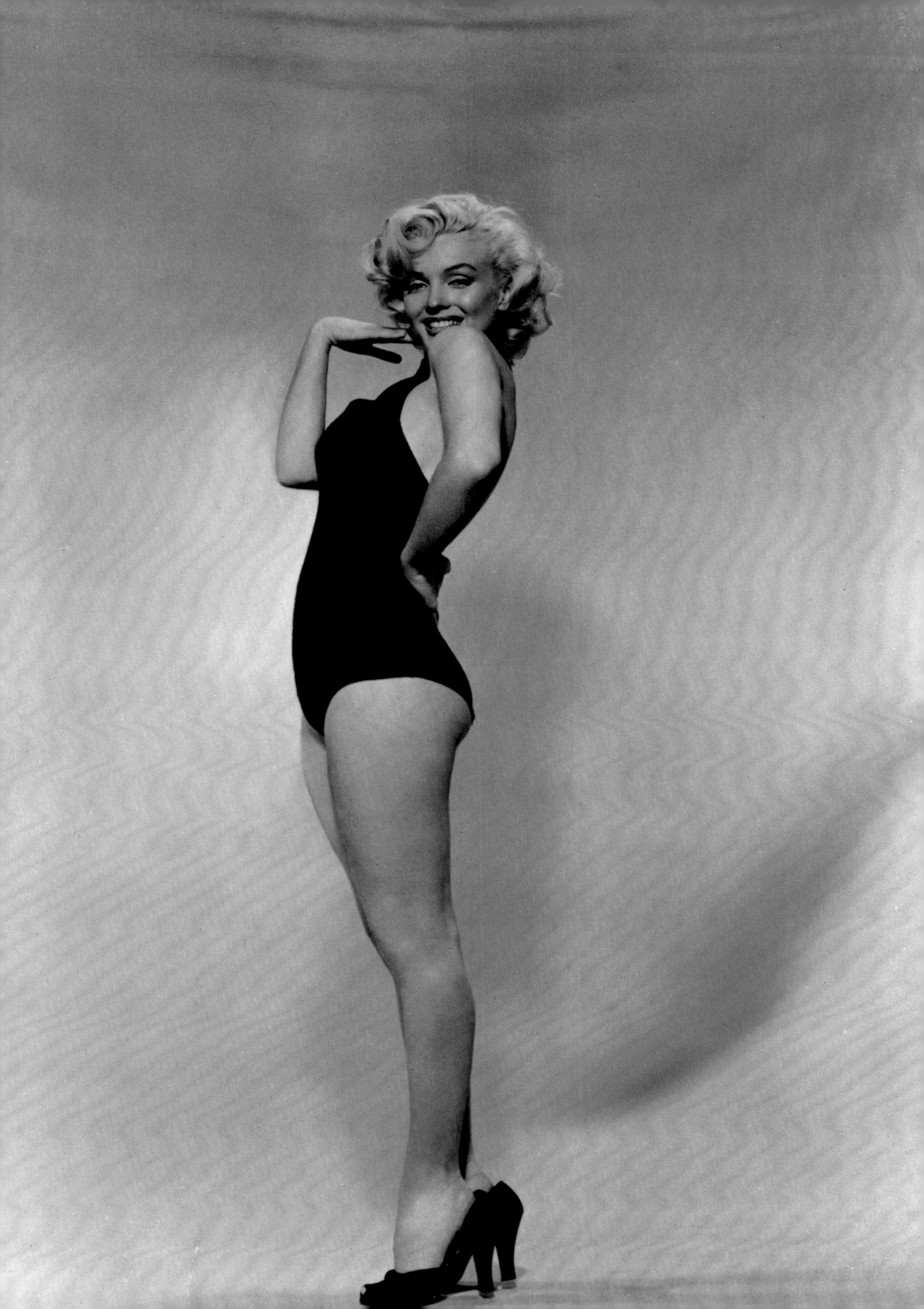

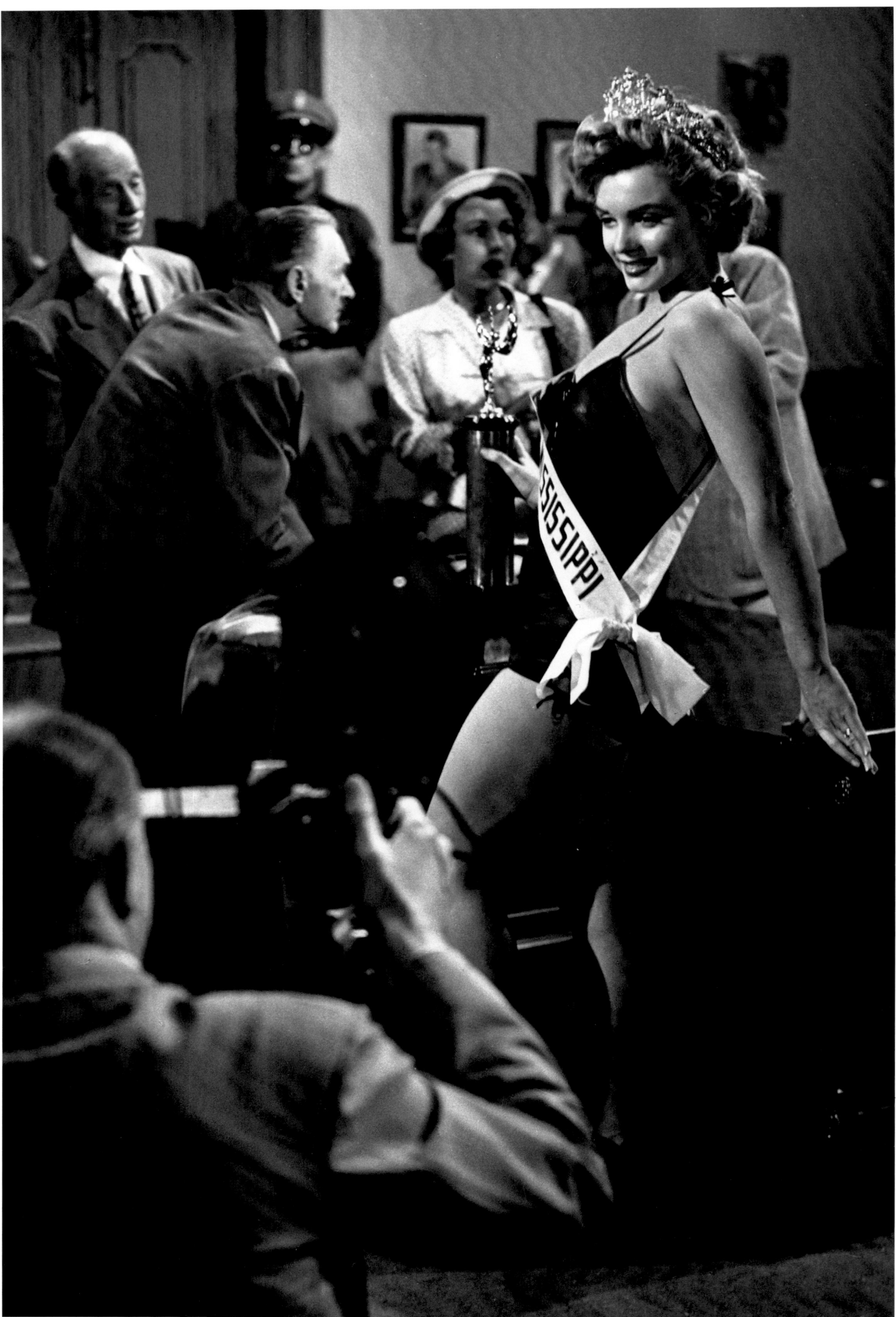

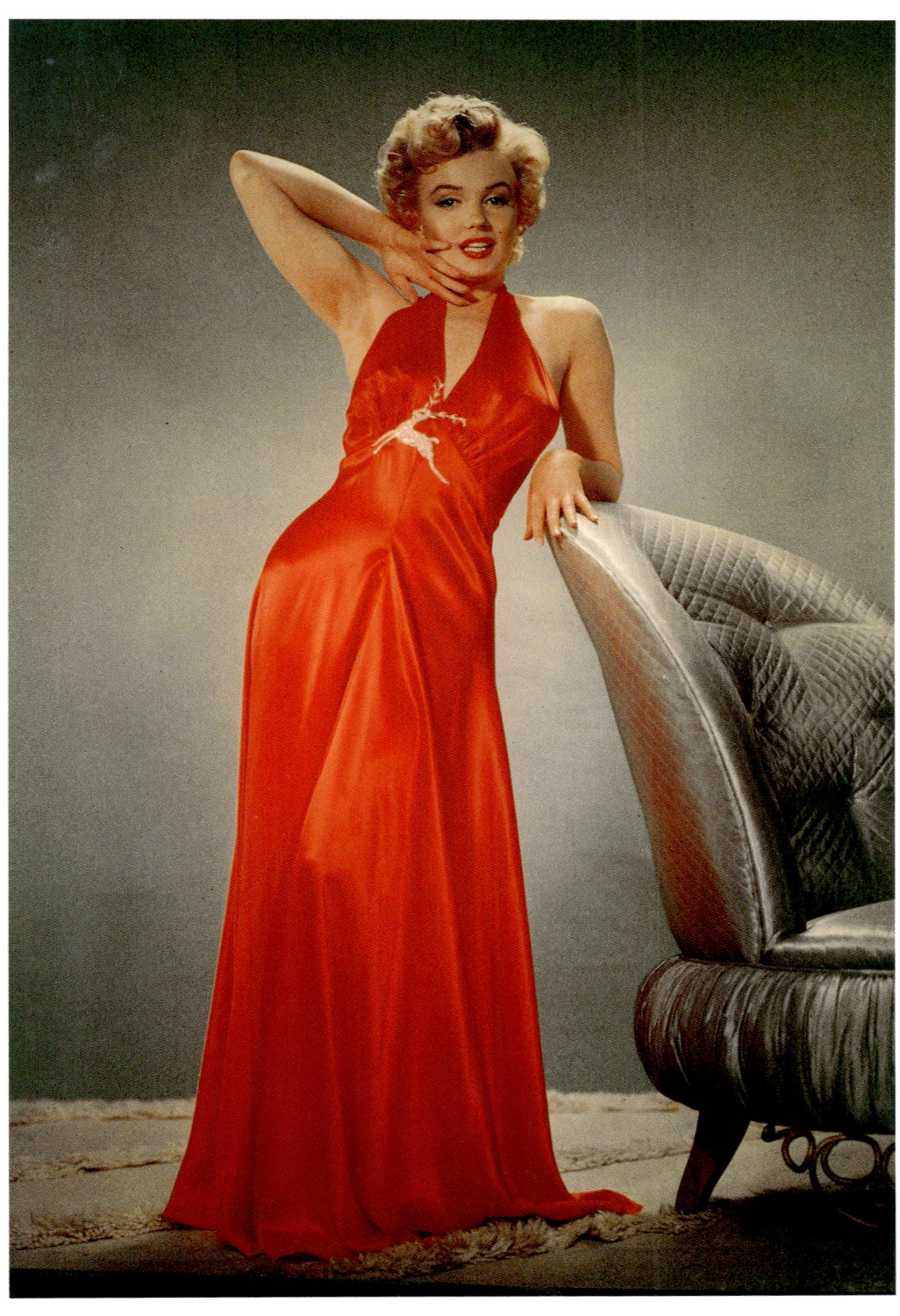

In the film *We're Not Married* Marilyn appears as Annabel Norris,
the winner of a beauty contest for Mrs. Mississippi. When the truth comes out that she is not
legally married to her husband, Jeff (David Wayne),
she then takes part in the Miss Mississippi contest and wins it. The comedy concludes
with a second, this time legal, marriage.

Publicity still from 1952. This shows Marilyn
at the provisional end of the bikini era in a luxurious nightgown.

Publicity still for *Don't Bother to Knock,* Marilyn's sixteenth film.
In this film she had her first dramatic leading role, that of a psychotic baby-sitter, costarring
with Richard Widmark. The role was particularly difficult for her,
having up to that time played only sexy blondes. The reaction of the critics was mixed.

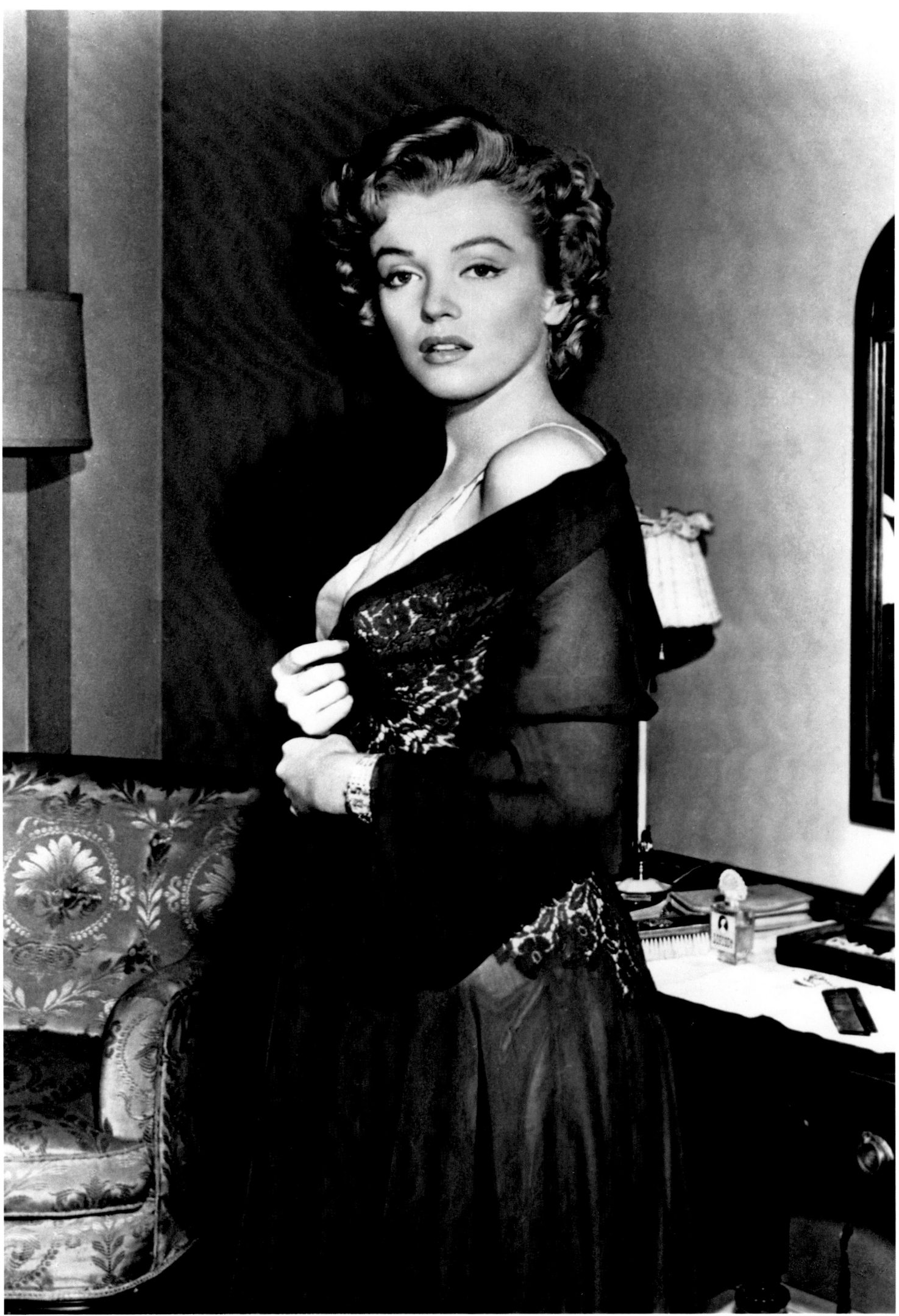

Marilyn as a vamp. Publicity still by Frank Powolny, 1953.

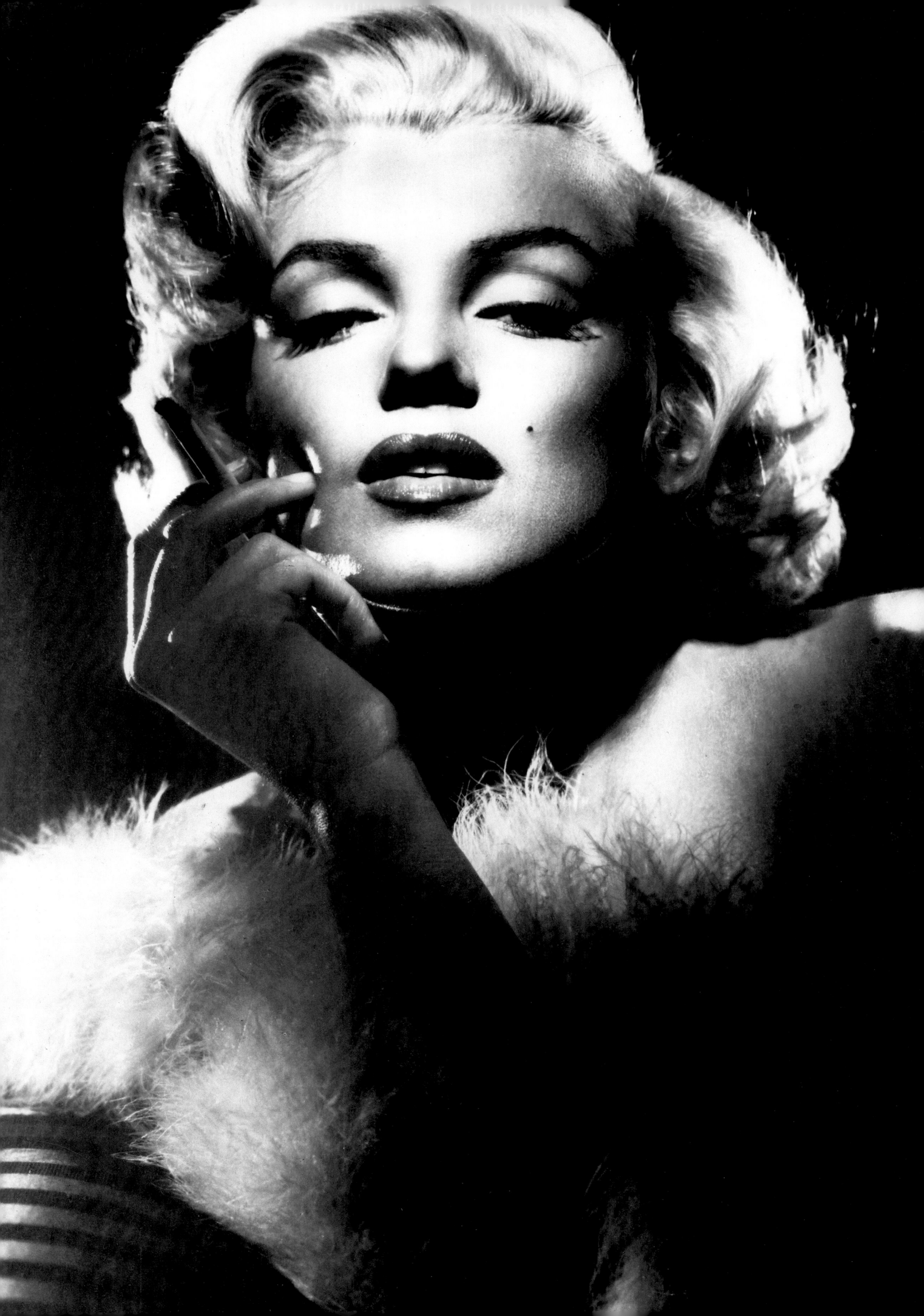

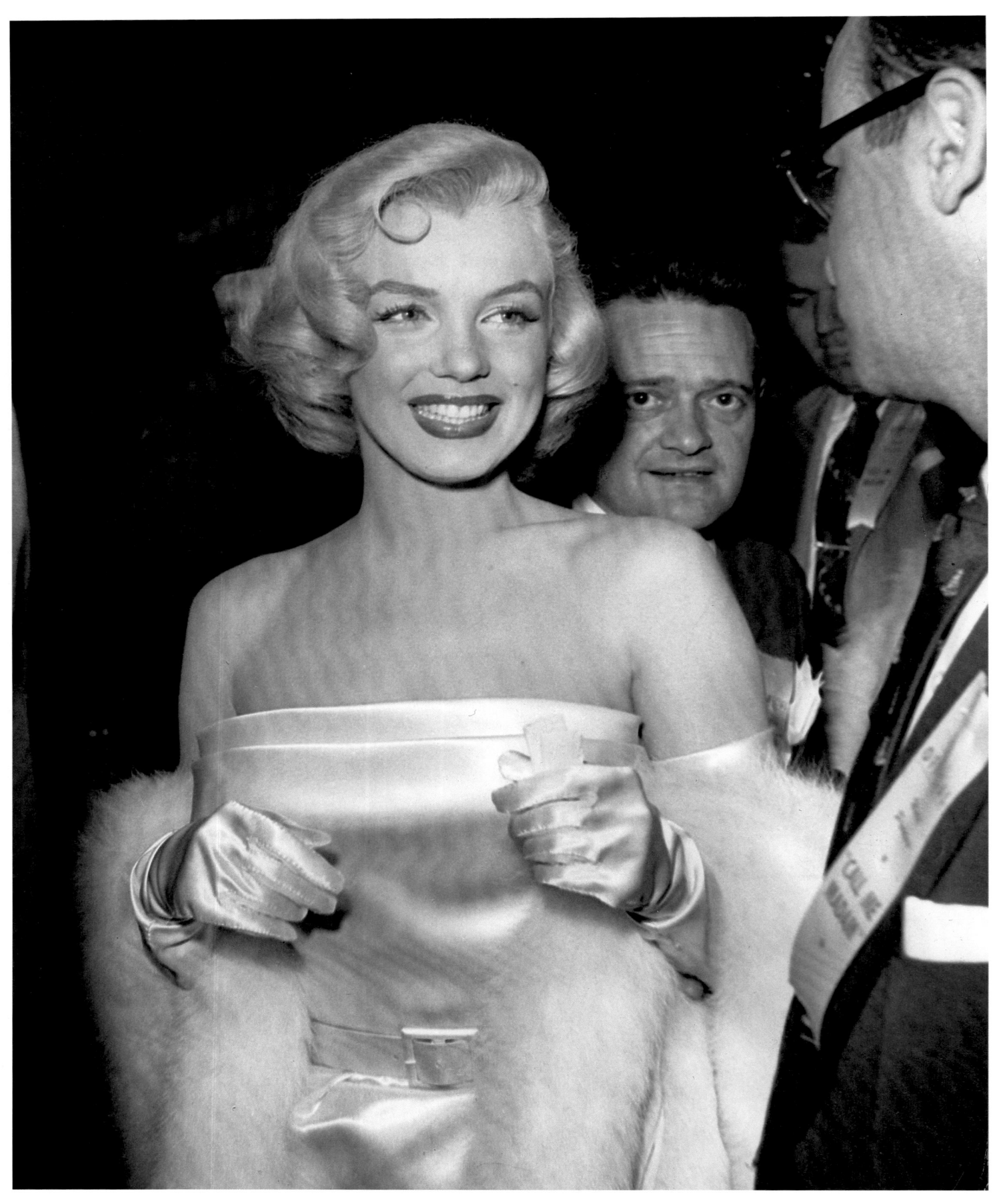

Marilyn arriving at a film premiere in Hollywood.
Unknown photographer, about 1952.

Color portrait as a vamp in a fluffy fur stole, about 1952.

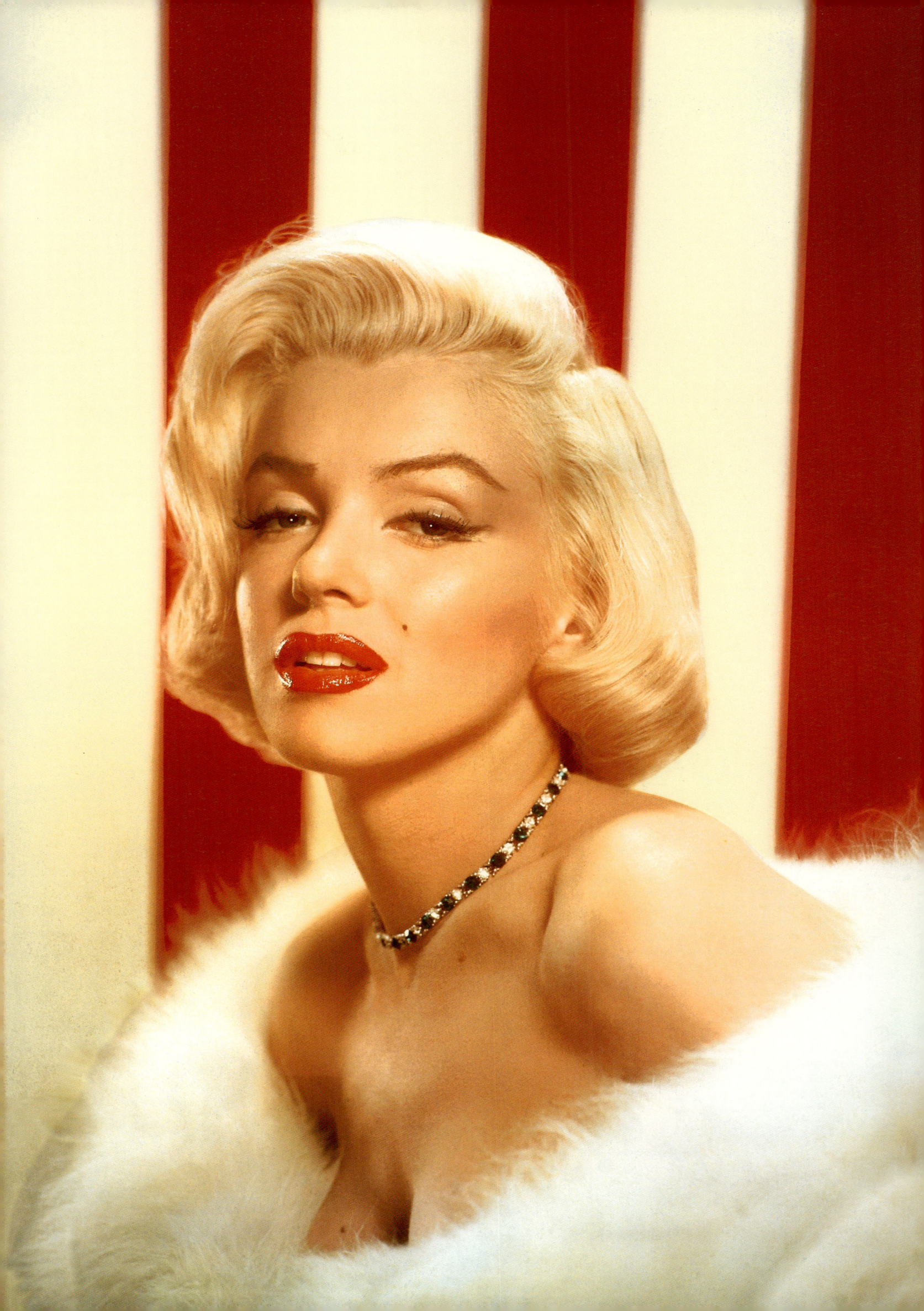

Publicity shot by Frank Powolny, 1952.

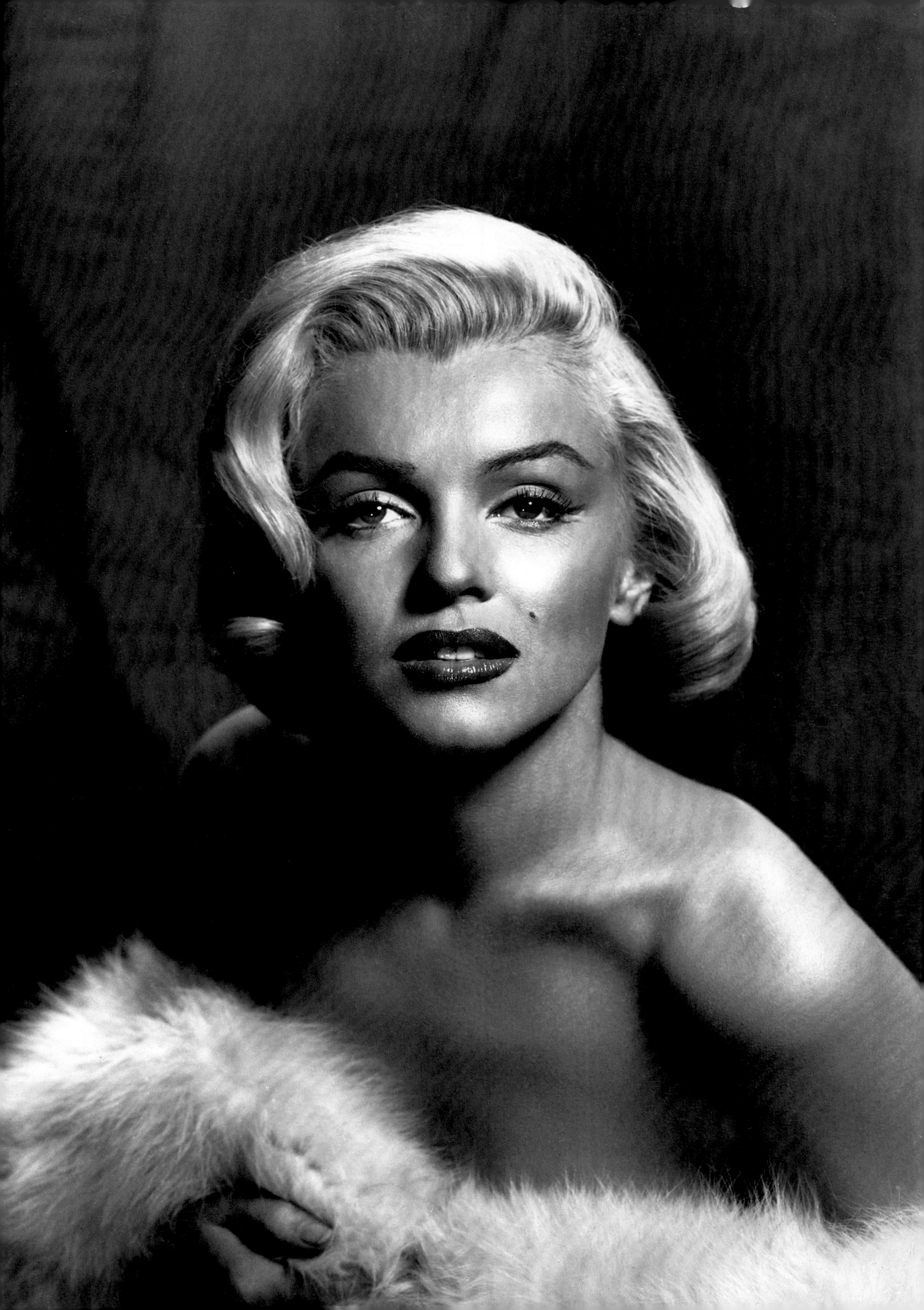

Of all the Marilyn photographs, it was this portrait by Frank Powolny
that immortalized her. Andy Warhol chose this picture as the basis for his famous silk-screen
series. One version of this print on a red background
(in a relatively small format, 101 x 101 cm, on canvas) was recently sold at a New York auction
for the astronomical sum of $3.8 million.

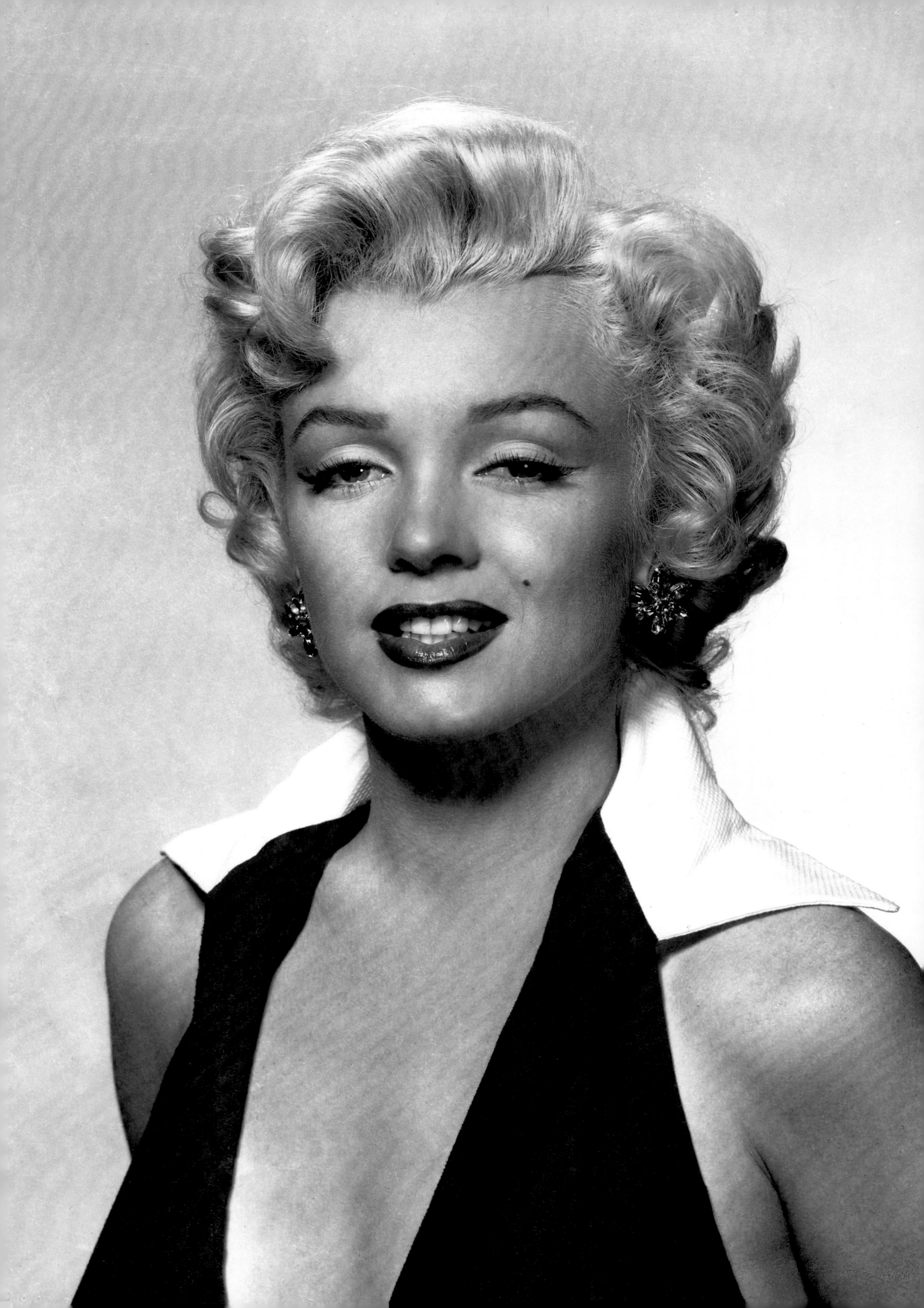

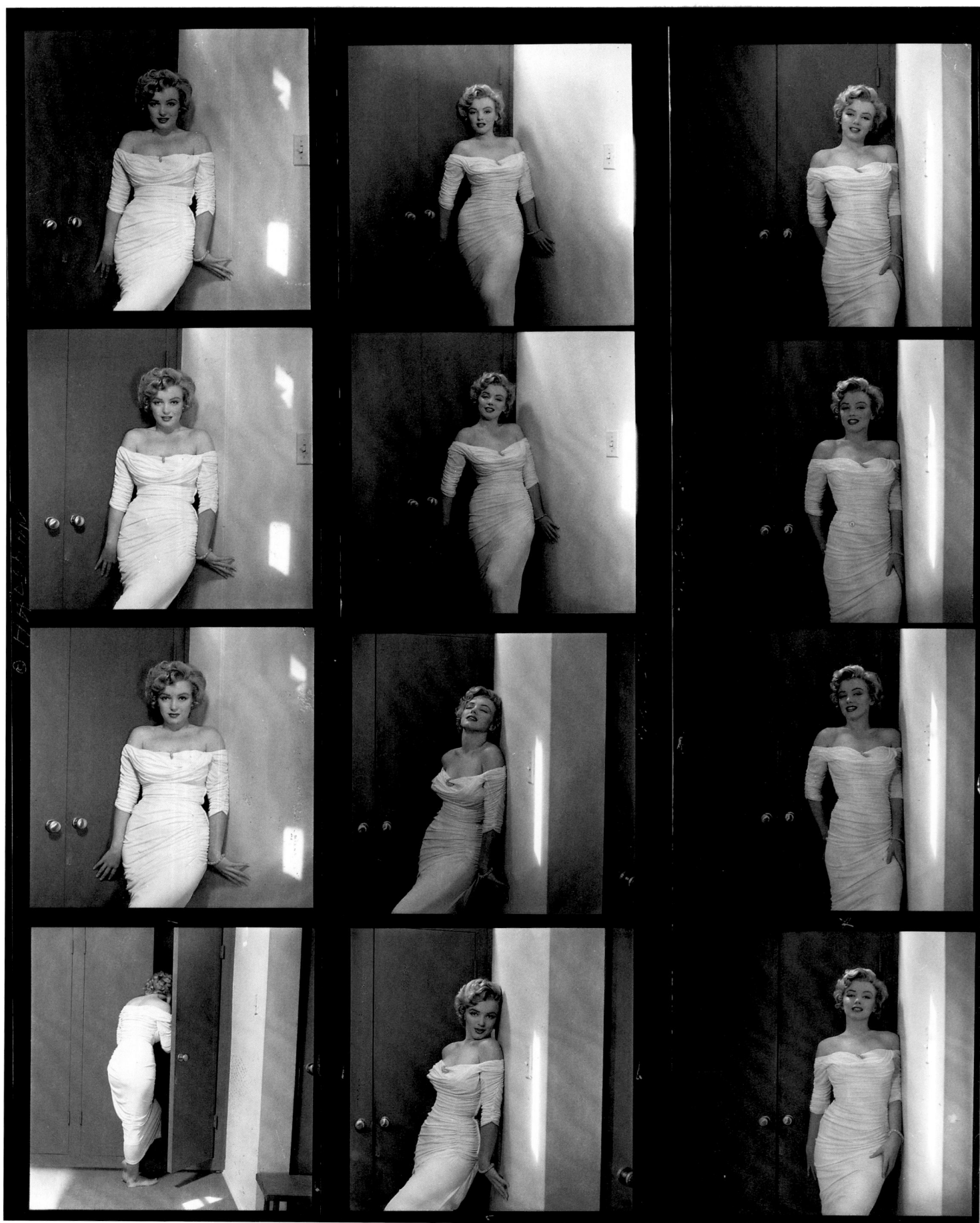

Through Philippe Halsman's famous series of 1952, Marilyn Monroe made it to the
cover of *Life* for the first time. Photographing the twenty-six-year-old Marilyn with half-closed eyes
and slightly parted lips, Halsman made her into a sex goddess. He described the situation:
"Finally I asked her to stand in the corner of the room. I was facing her with my camera, the *Life*
reporter and assistant at my side. Marilyn was cornered and she flirted with all three of us,
and the photograph eventually made the cover of *Life*. The cover gave her the status of a star...."
The pictures on the left are contact prints of the series.

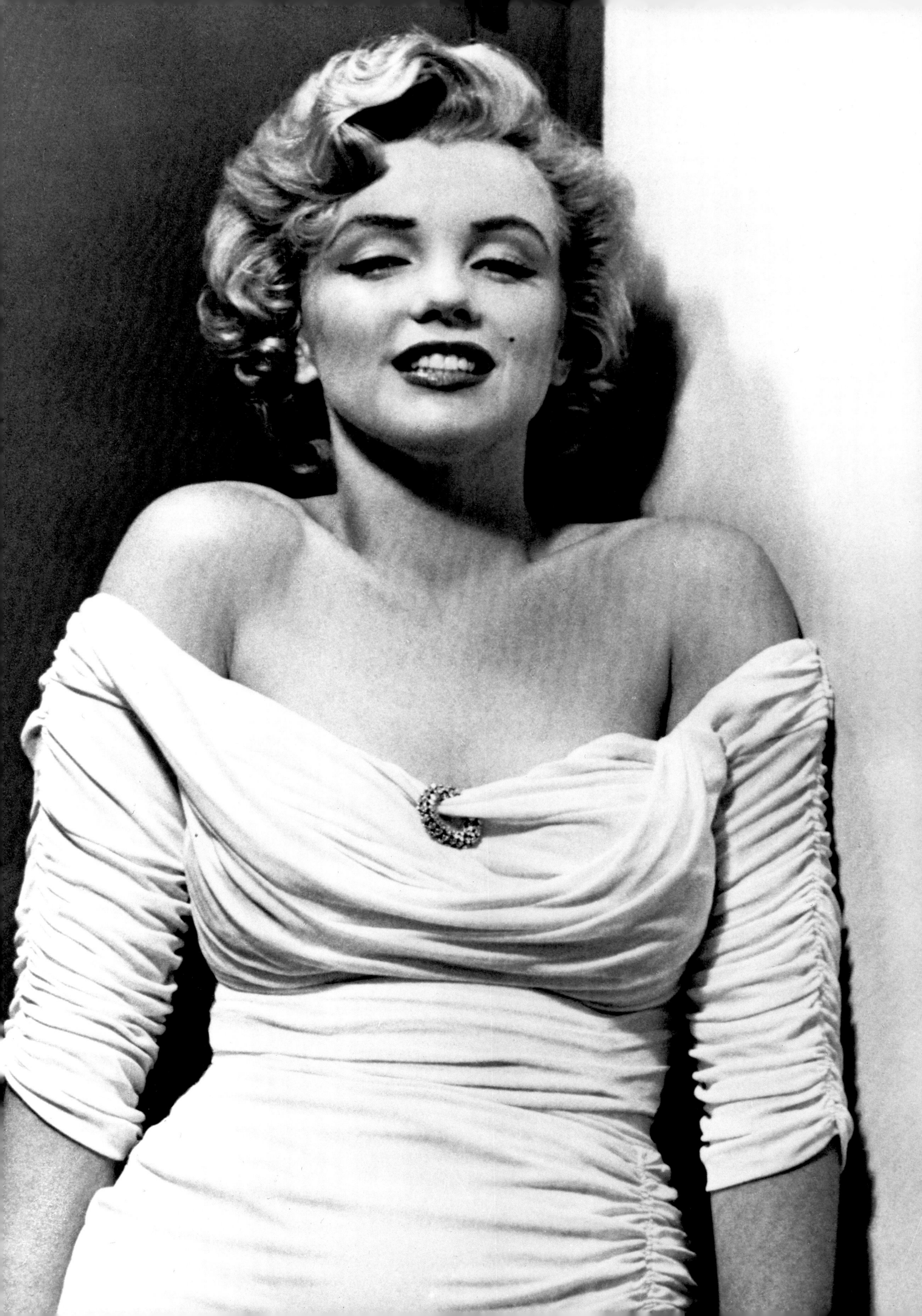

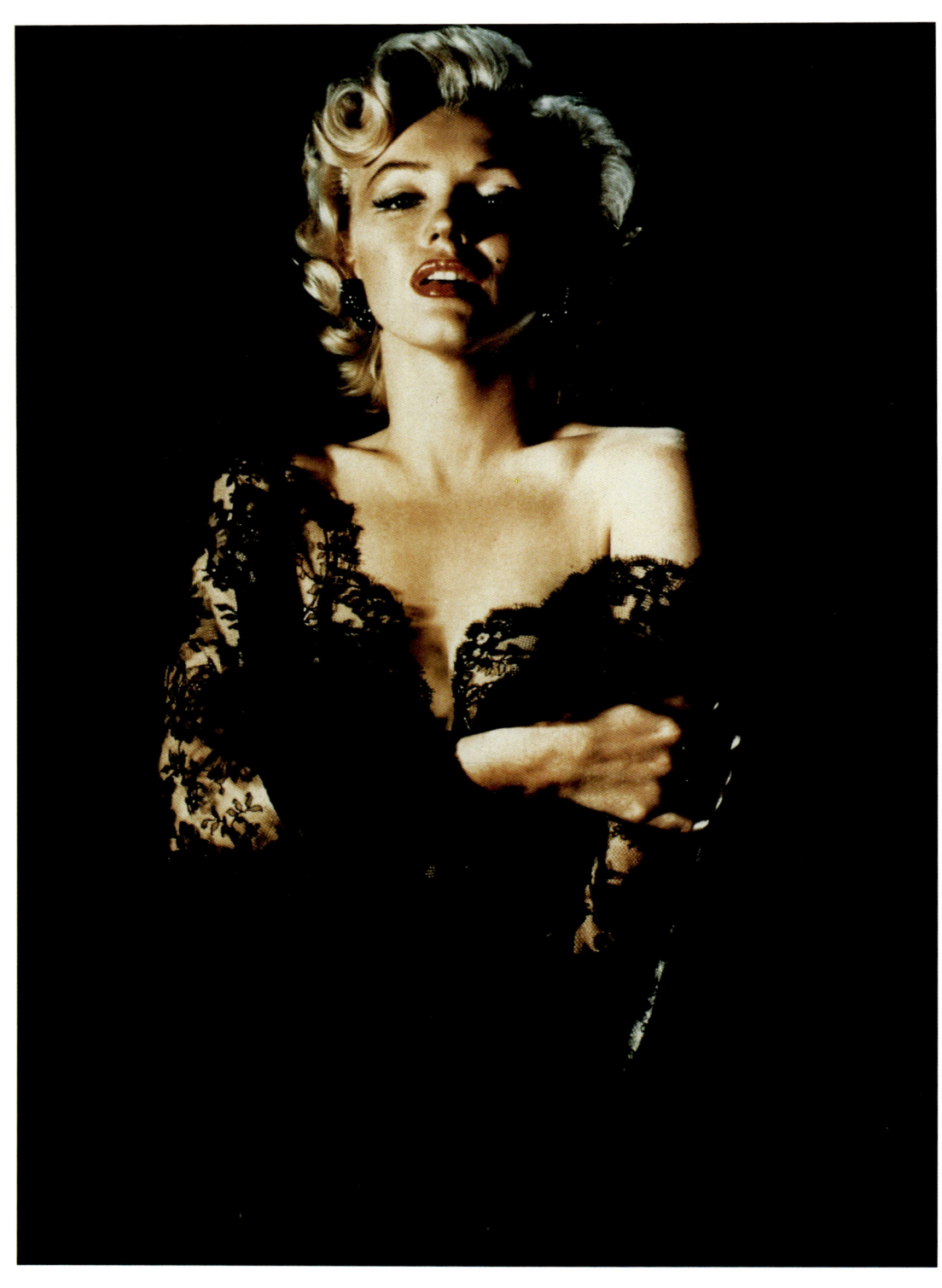

Glamour photo in a lace negligee by Bernard of Hollywood, 1952.

Marilyn in a negligee, eyes closed, in her apartment in a suburb of Los Angeles, 1952. Philippe Halsman, traveling for *Life* at the time, remarked on the furnishings: "What impressed me in its shabby living room was the obvious striving for self-improvement of the alleged dumb blonde. I saw a photograph of Eleonora Duse and a multitude of books which I did not expect there either, such as the works of Dostoyevski, Freud, *The History of Fabian Socialism,* etc."

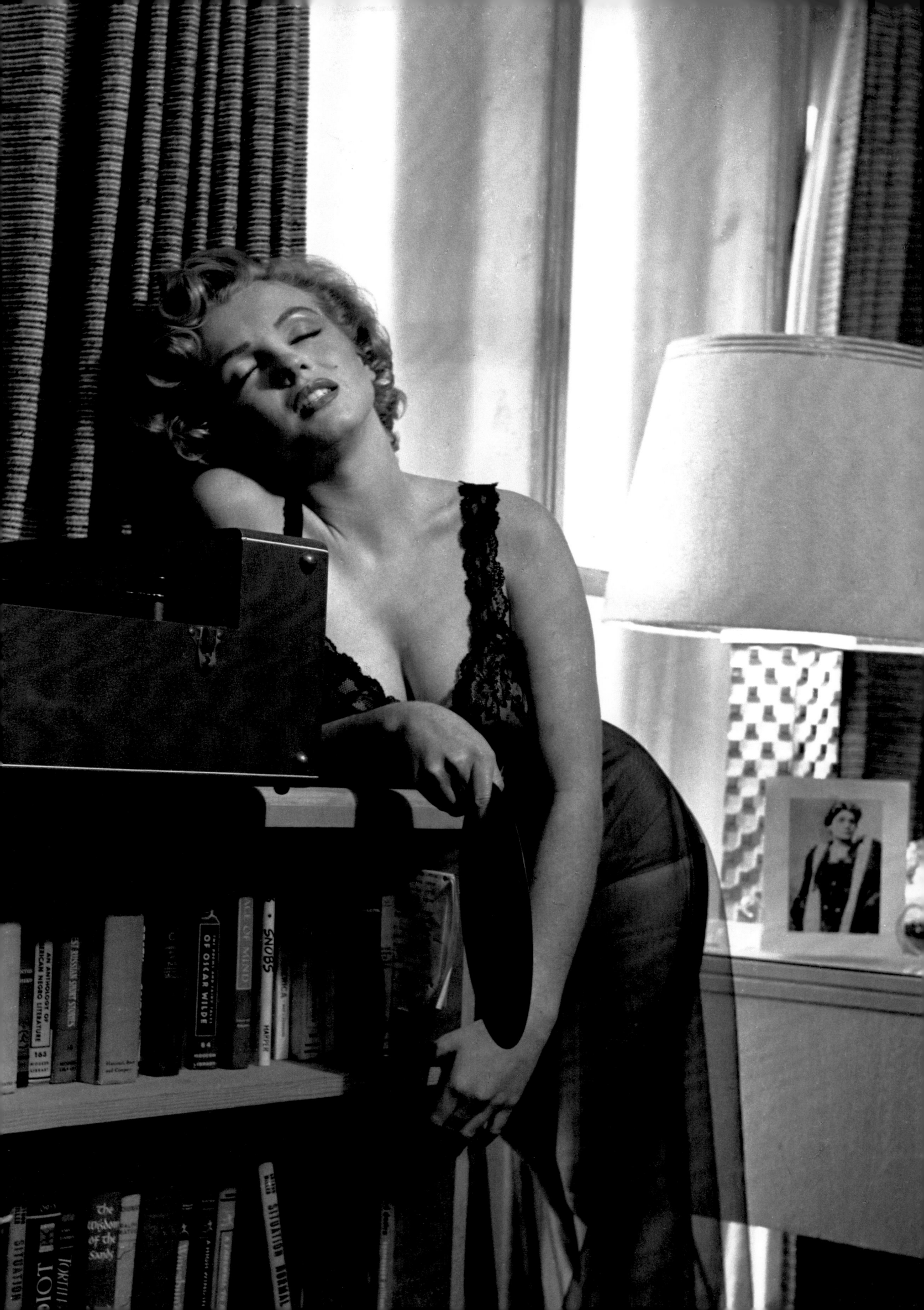

Philippe Halsman continued: "On the floor were two barbells. 'Are you using them?' I asked. 'Yes,' she replied. 'I'm fighting gravity.'" Photograph by Philippe Halsman, 1952.

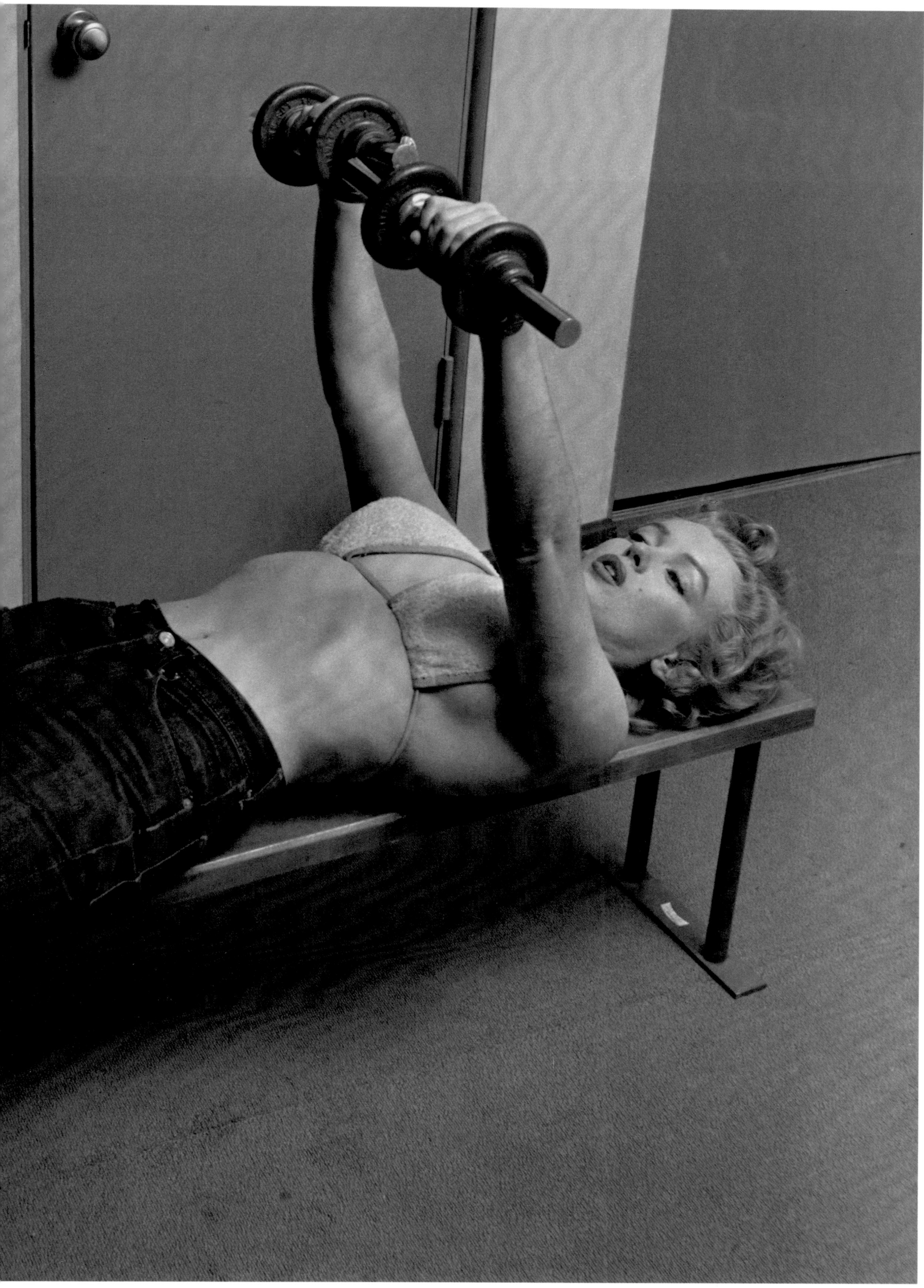

Marilyn reading James Joyce's *Ulysses*. Photograph by Eve Arnold, about 1952.

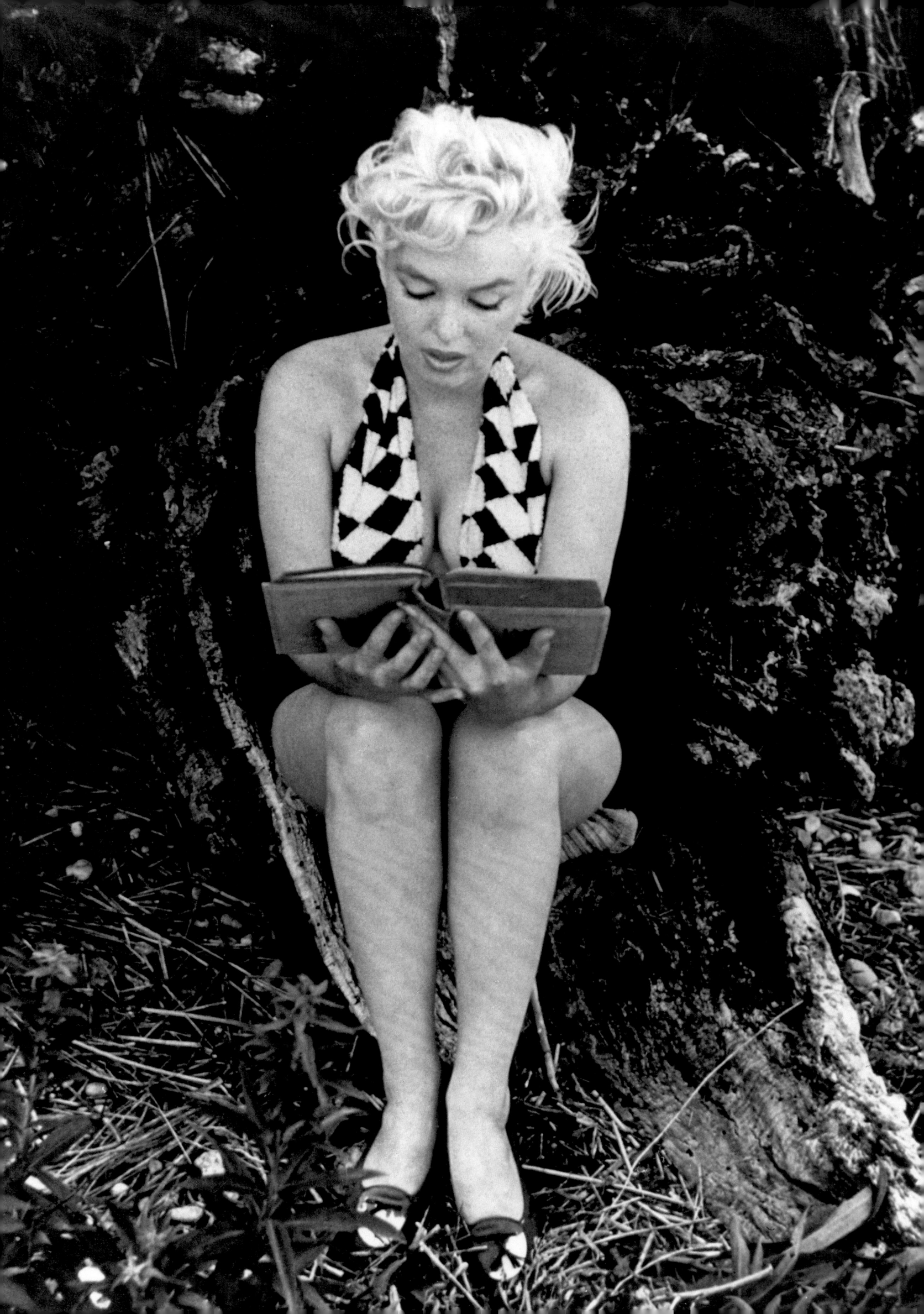

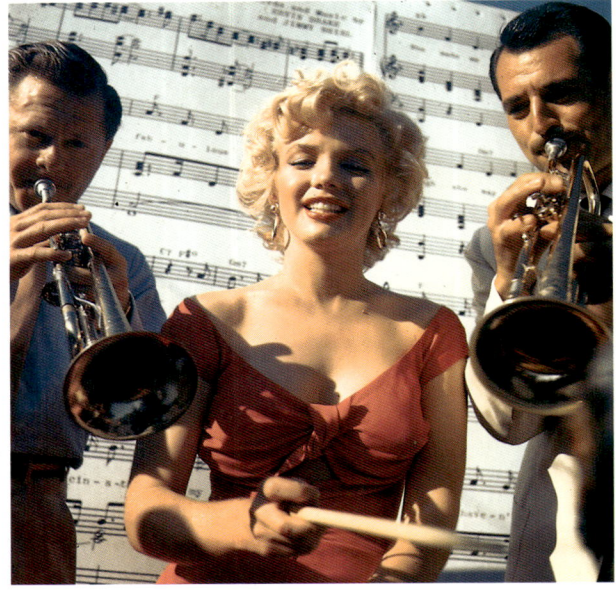
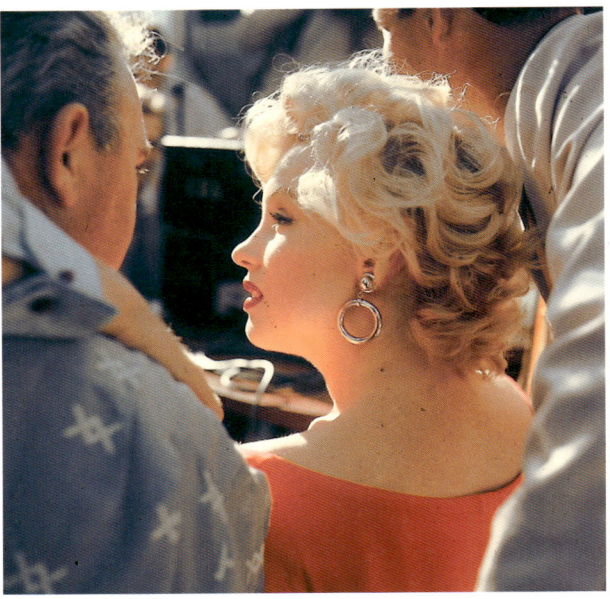
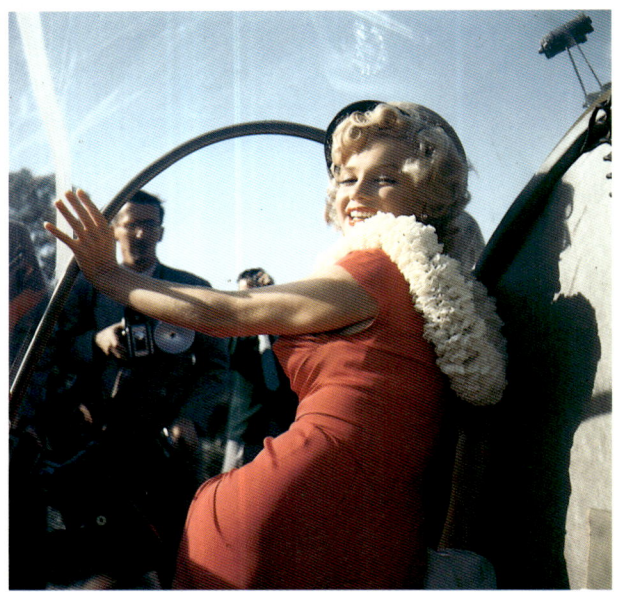
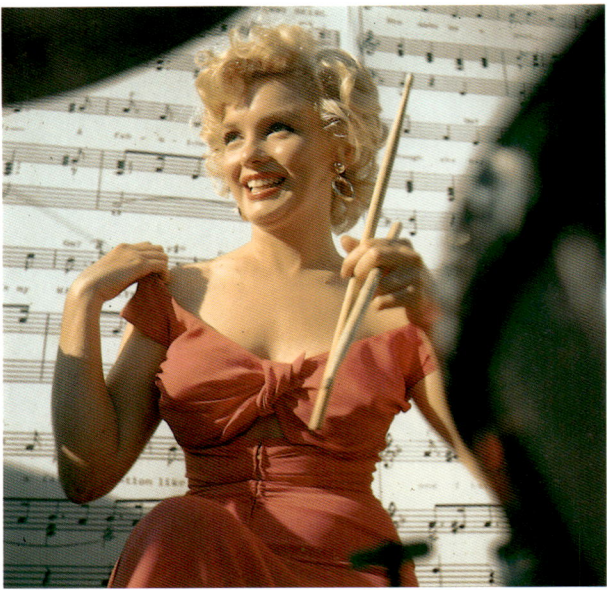

In 1952 bandleader Ray Anthony composed and arranged a song entitled "Marilyn."
For the presentation of the song at a press conference
in Hollywood, Marilyn was flown in by helicopter. Photographs by Bob Willoughby.

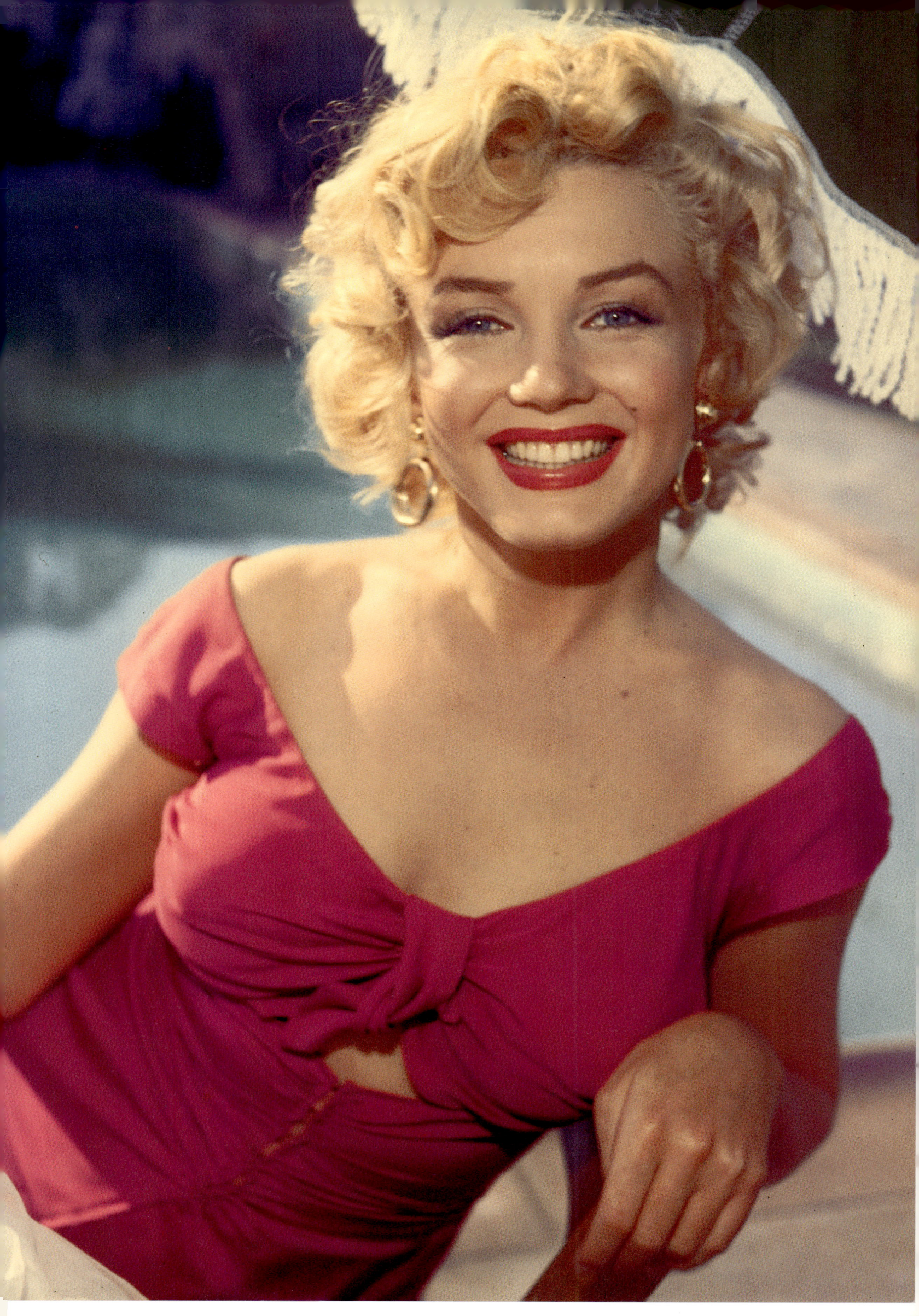

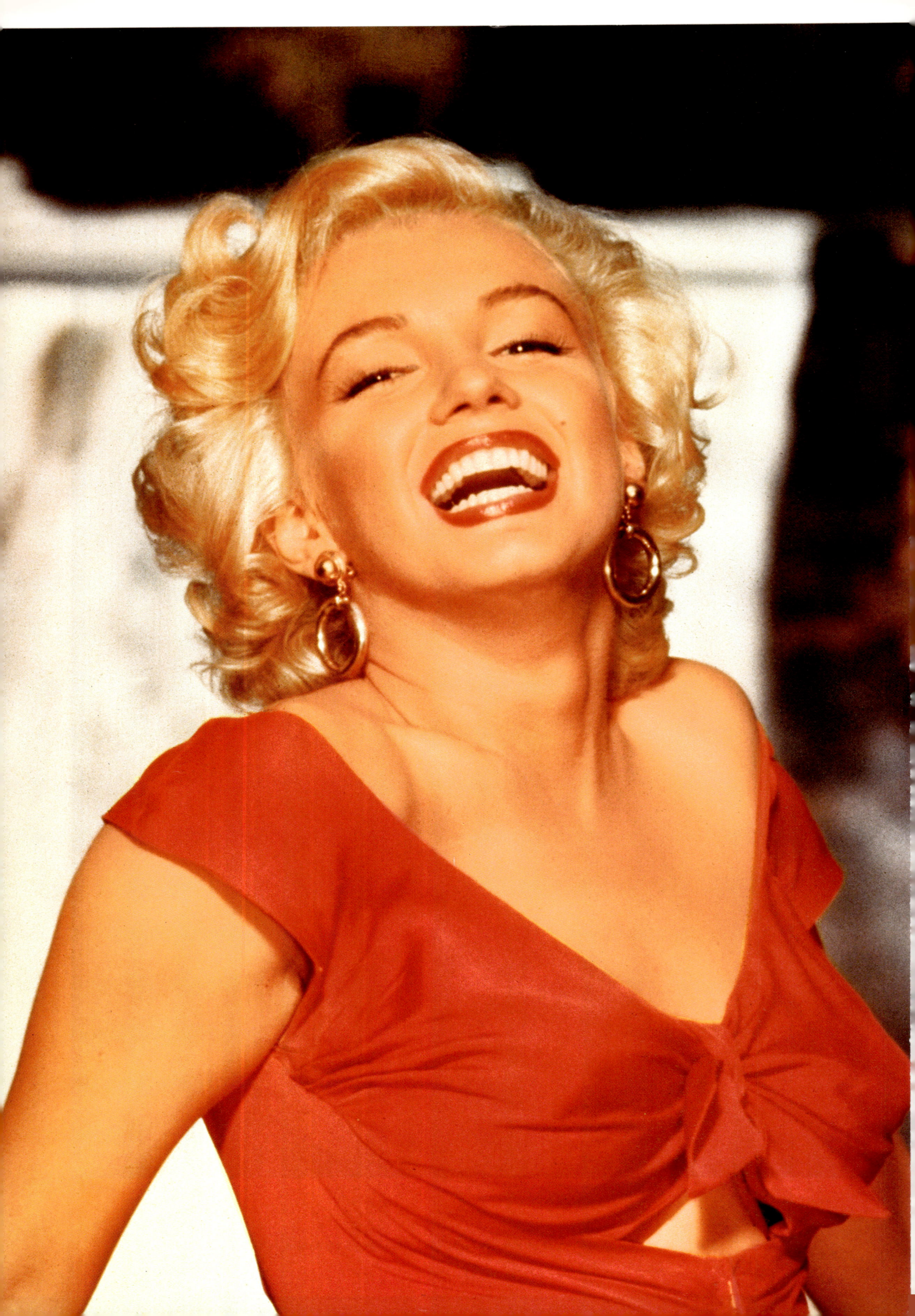

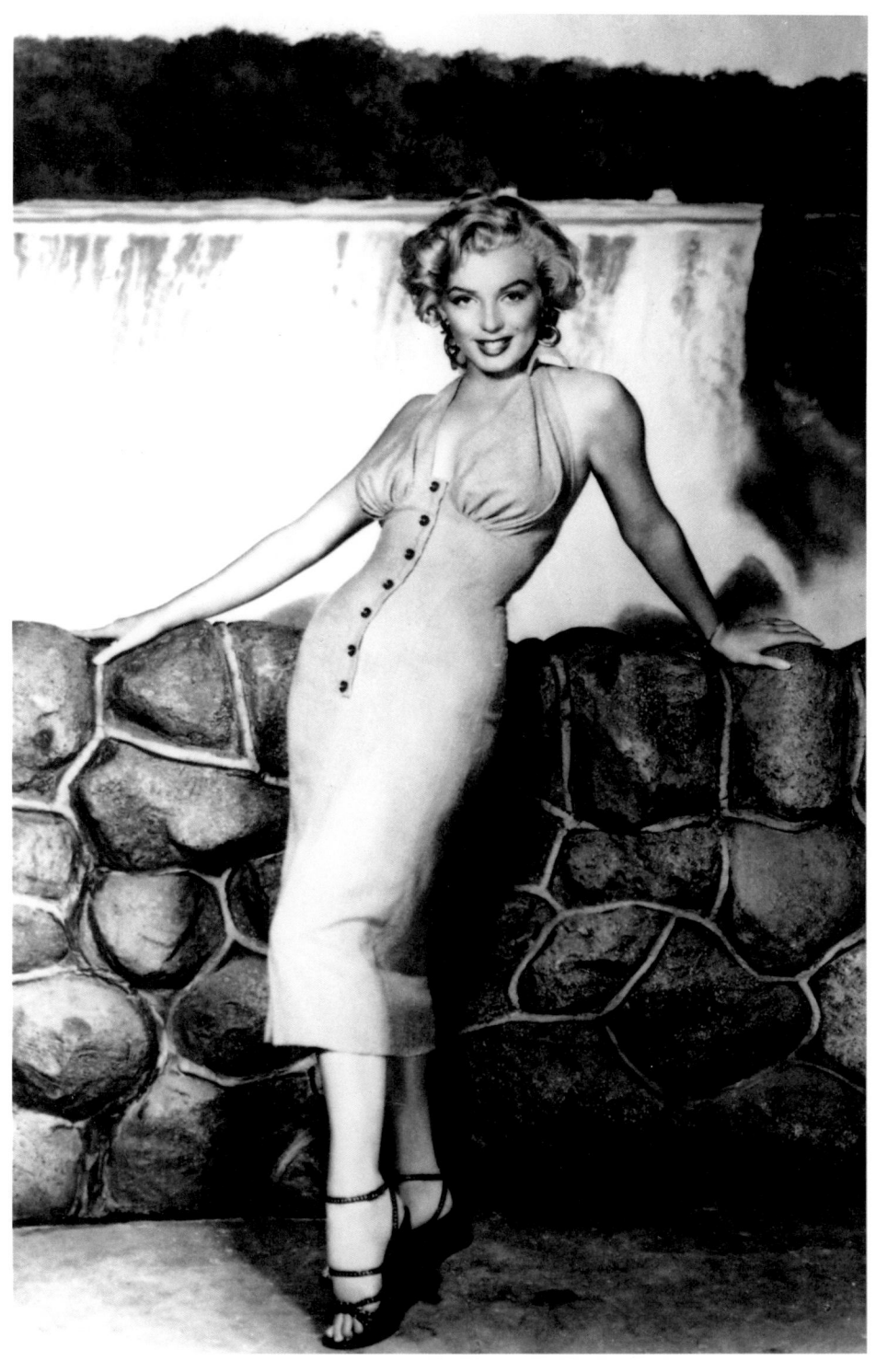

Two publicity stills for *Niagara*, 1953. Rarely in any film
has an actress been so beautifully directed and photographed as Marilyn
was by director Henry Hathaway and cameraman
Joe MacDonald. The color portrait is from Bernard of Hollywood.

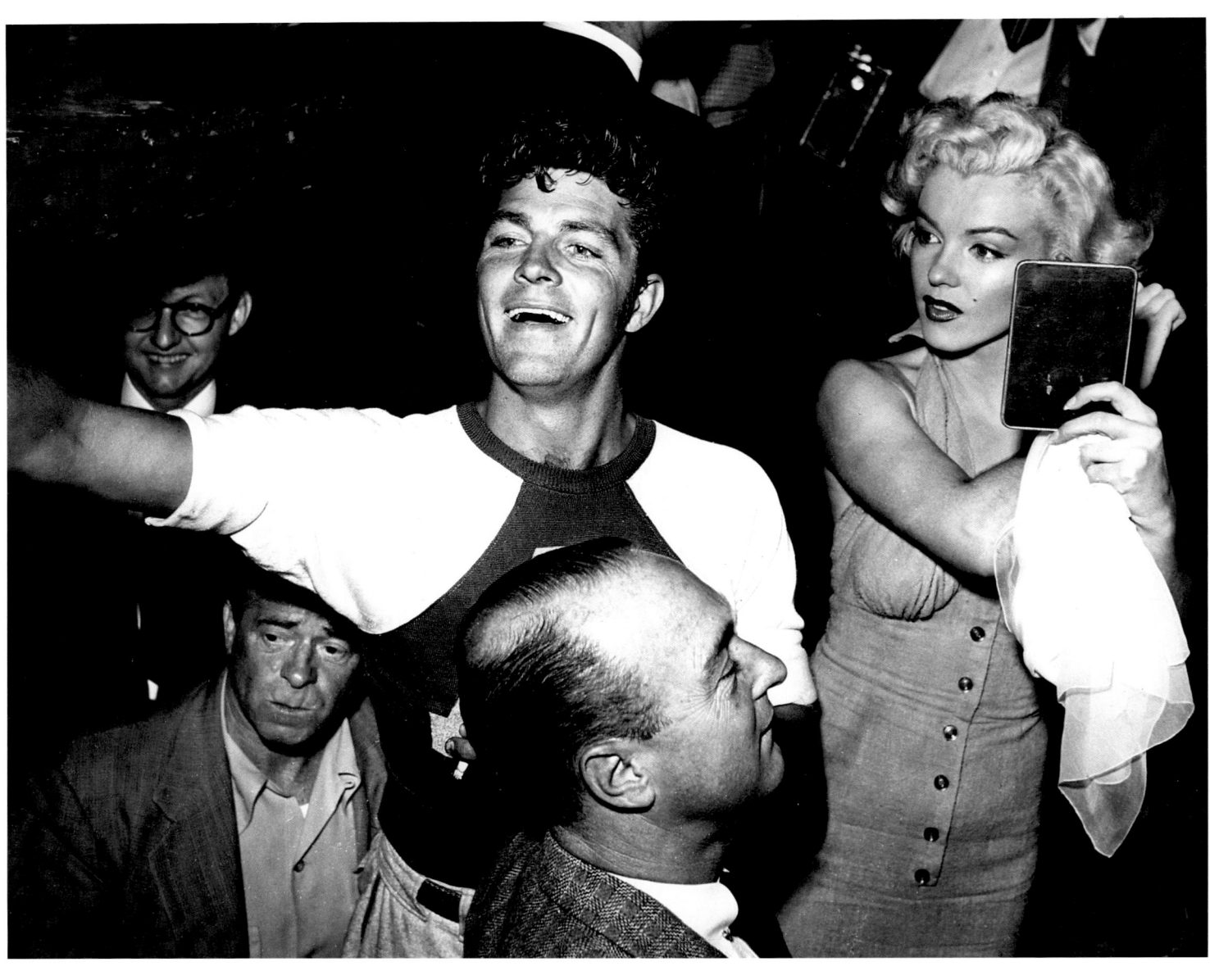

Marilyn Monroe during the shooting of *Niagara;* on the left is the actor Dale Robertson.

Publicity still for *Niagara.* The movie, filmed in Technicolor,
received glowing reviews. The *New York Times* wrote: "Obviously ignoring the idea that
there are seven wonders of the world, 20th Century-Fox has discovered
two more and enhanced them with Technicolor in *Niagara,* which descended on the Roxy
yesterday. For the producers are making full use of both the grandeur
of the Falls and its adjacent areas as well as the grandeur that is Marilyn Monroe."

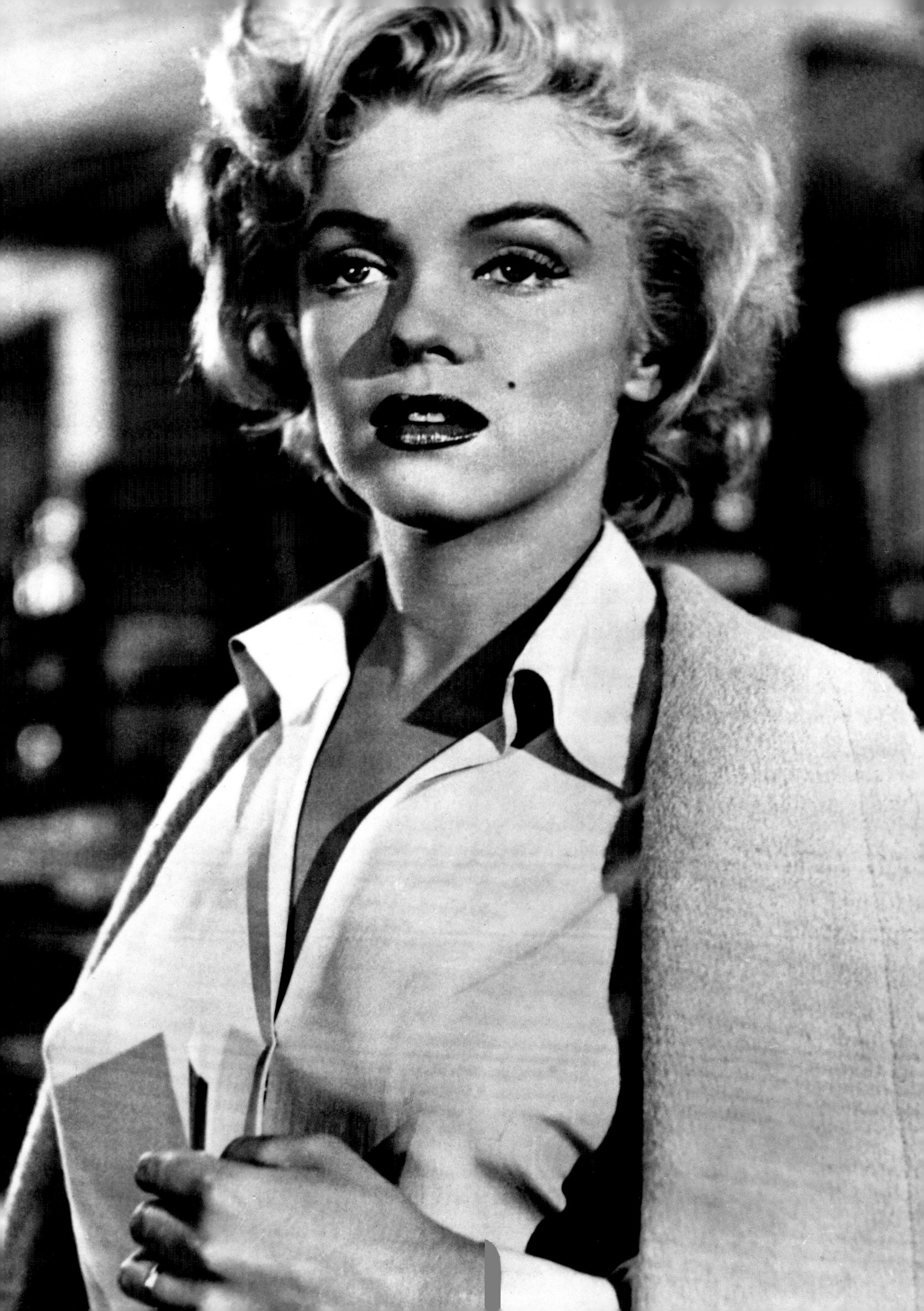

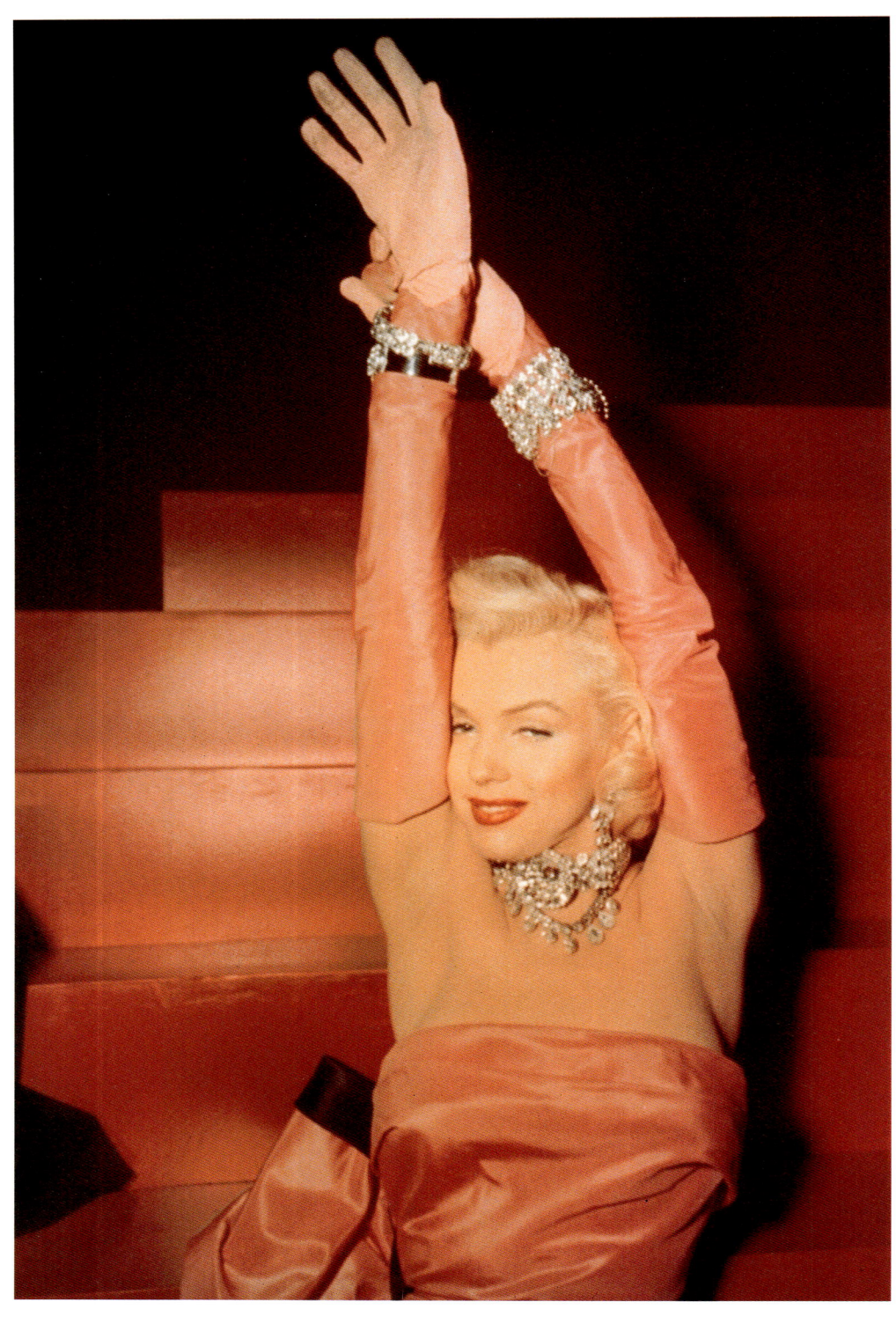

Publicity stills for *Gentlemen Prefer Blondes,*
the film most people associate Marilyn Monroe with. Although she was paid the
mini-stipend of $1500 a week, whereas costar Jane Russell
received several times that amount, Marilyn remained self-assured: "It is
Gentlemen Prefer Blondes, and I am the blonde."

Pages 100/101

Ronald Reagan, who as an army officer unwittingly had advanced
Marilyn's career with his commission to David Conover in 1945, meets the star at a
Hollywood banquet. Photograph by Bernard of Hollywood, about 1953.

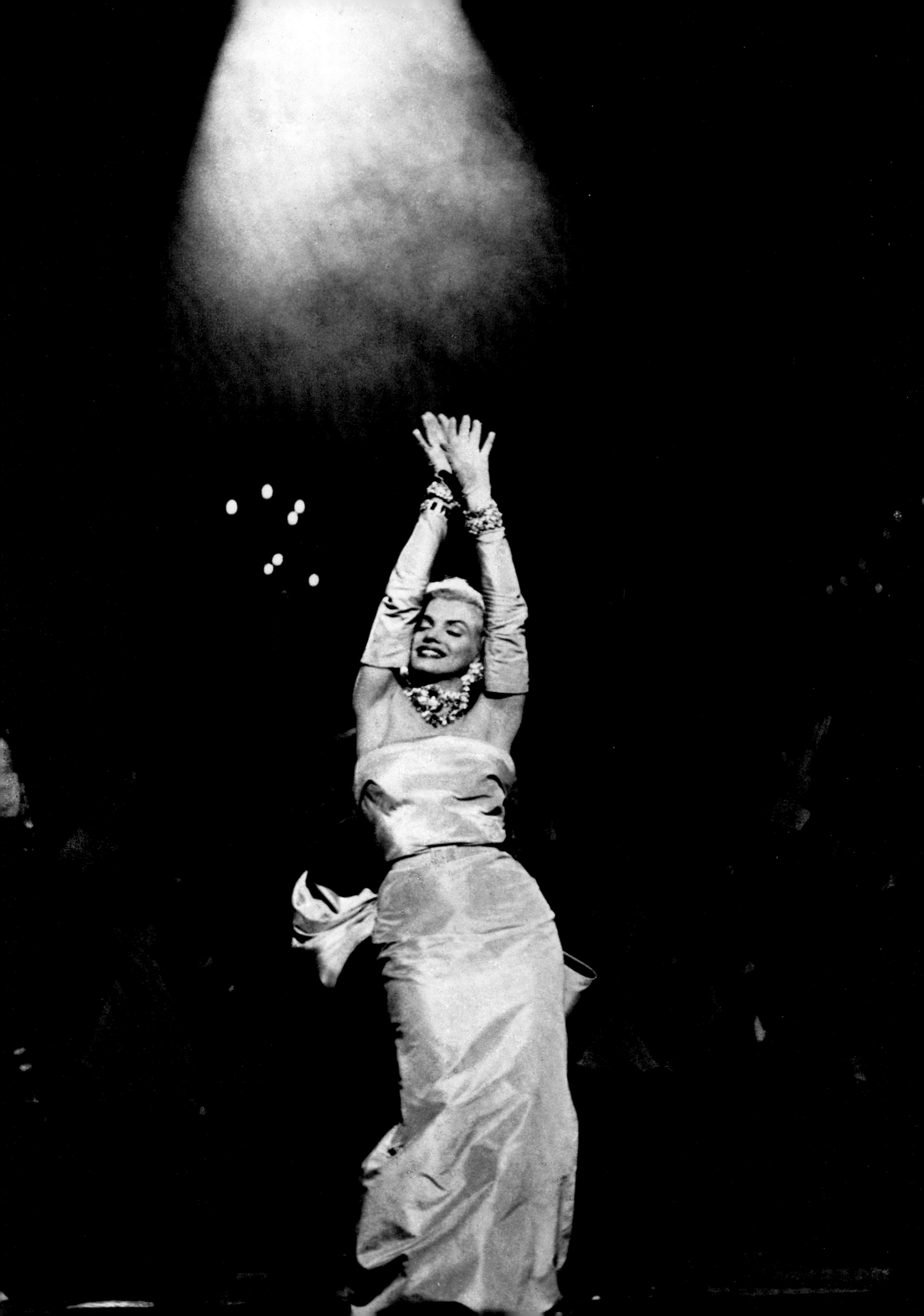

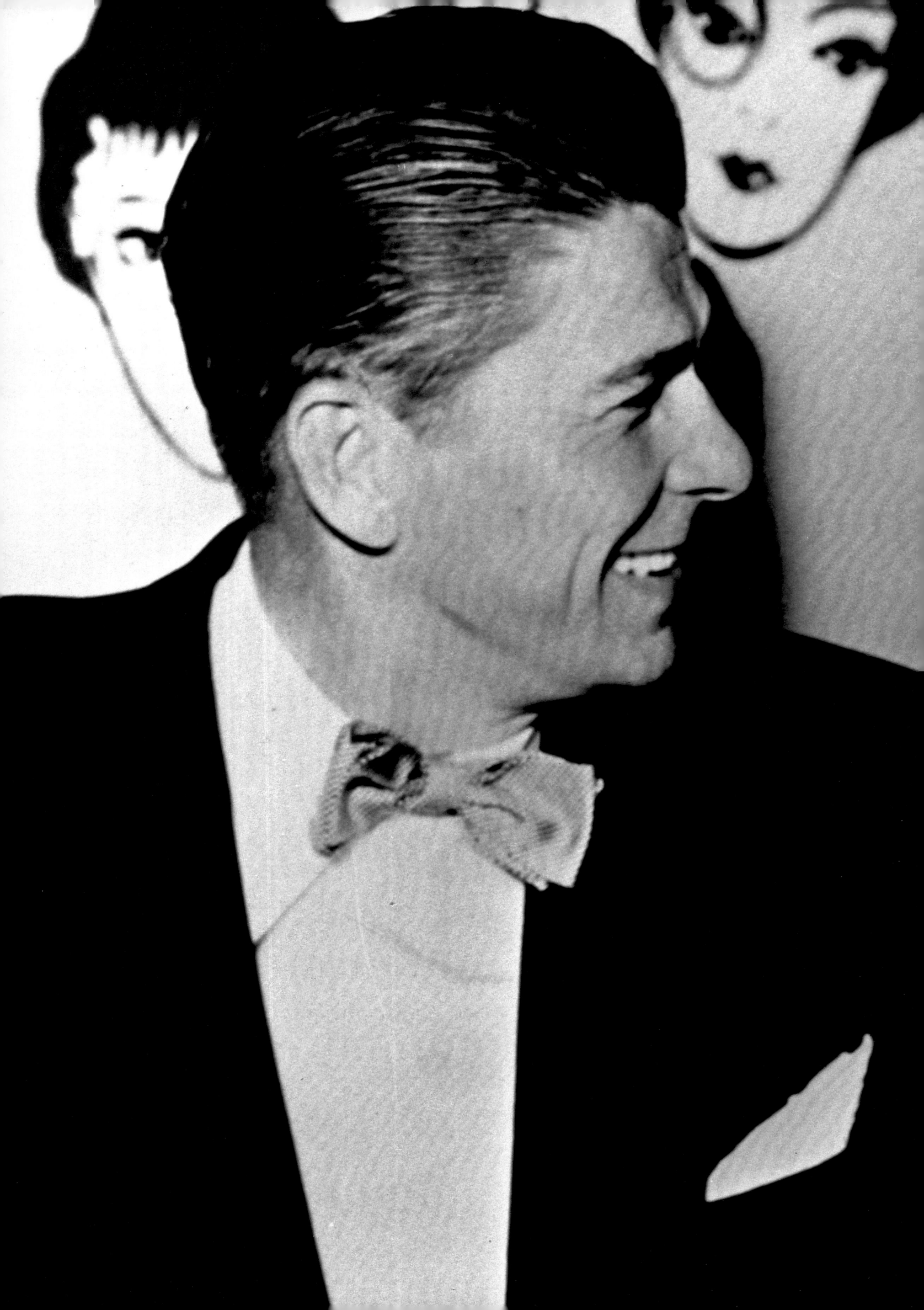

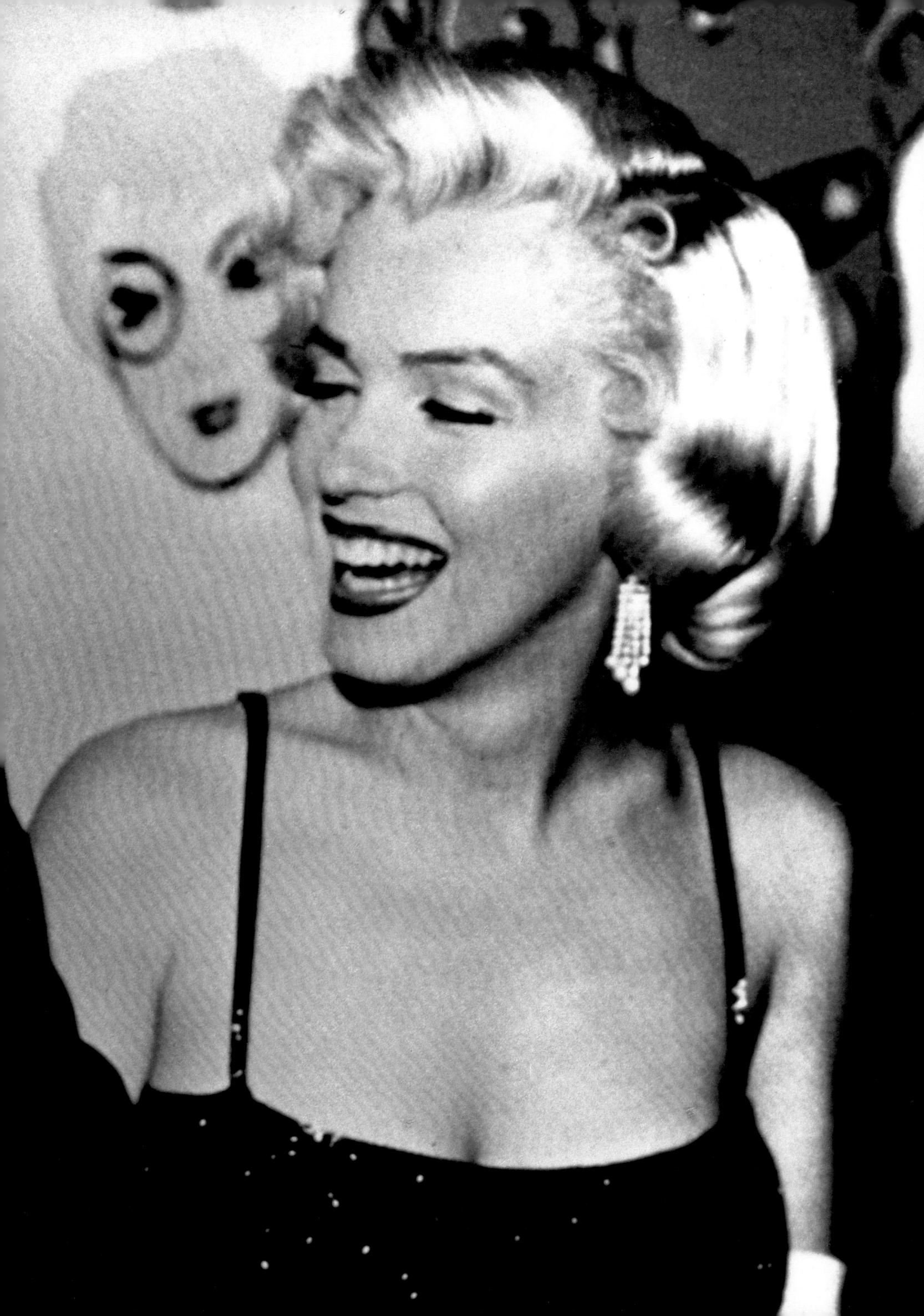

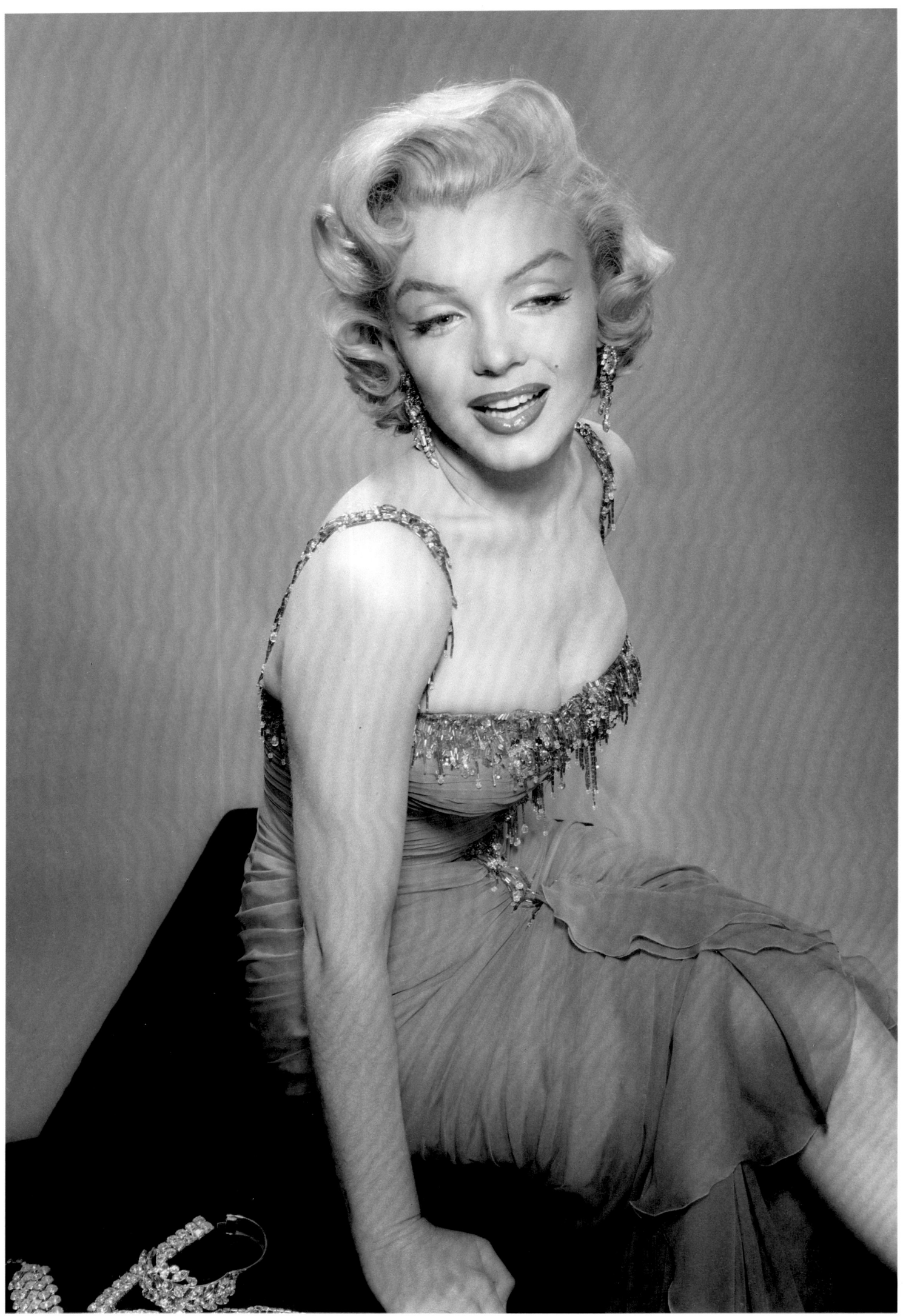

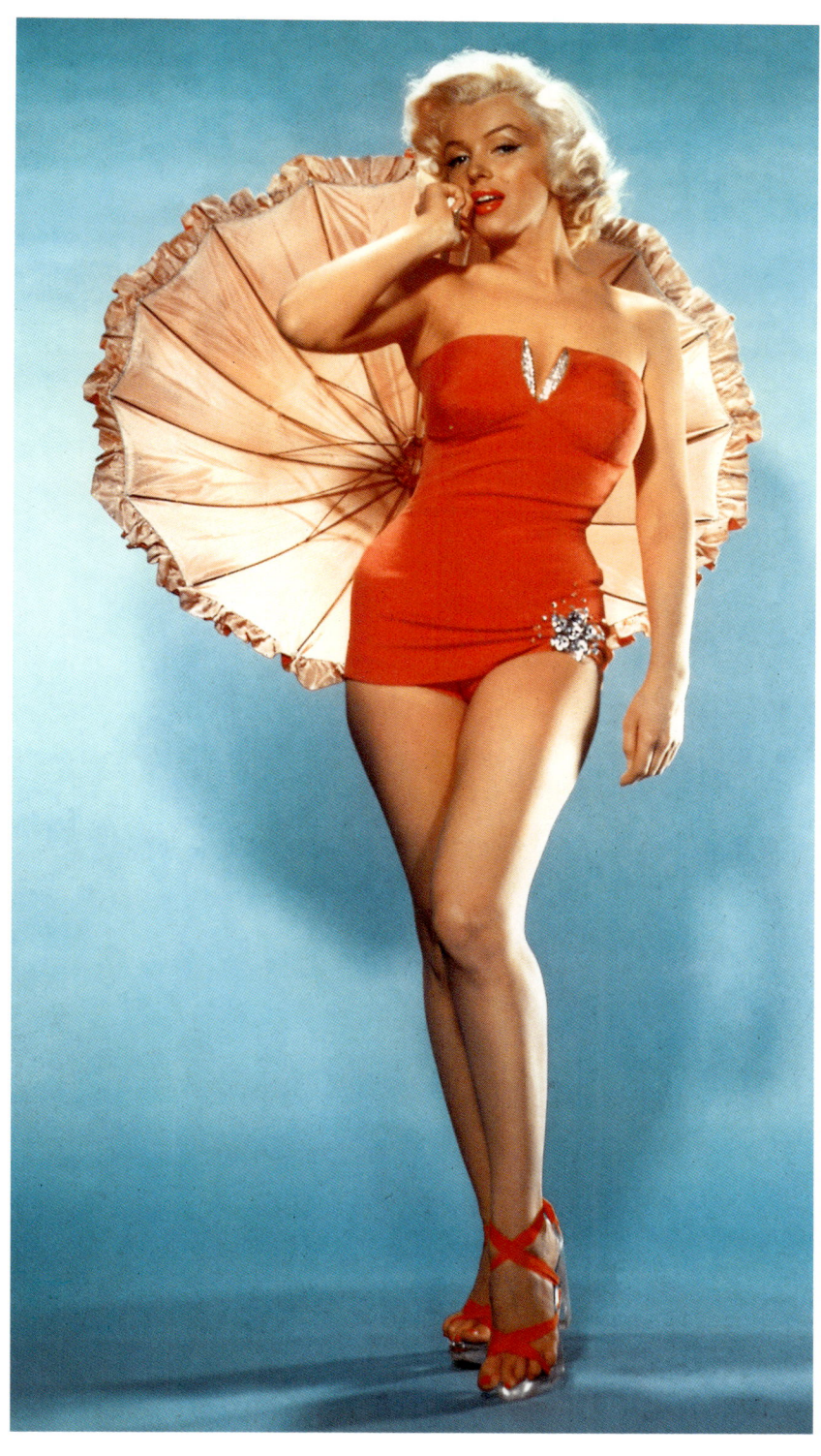

Page 102

The photographer John Florea took this picture of Marilyn Monroe during the
shooting of *How to Marry a Millionaire,* 1953. It is in the 20th Century-Fox Portrait Gallery.

Page 103

Publicity still for *How to Marry a Millionaire,* 1953.
Photograph by Bert Reisfeld.

Pages 104/105

Marilyn in a particularly seductive pose, taken by John Florea, 1953.

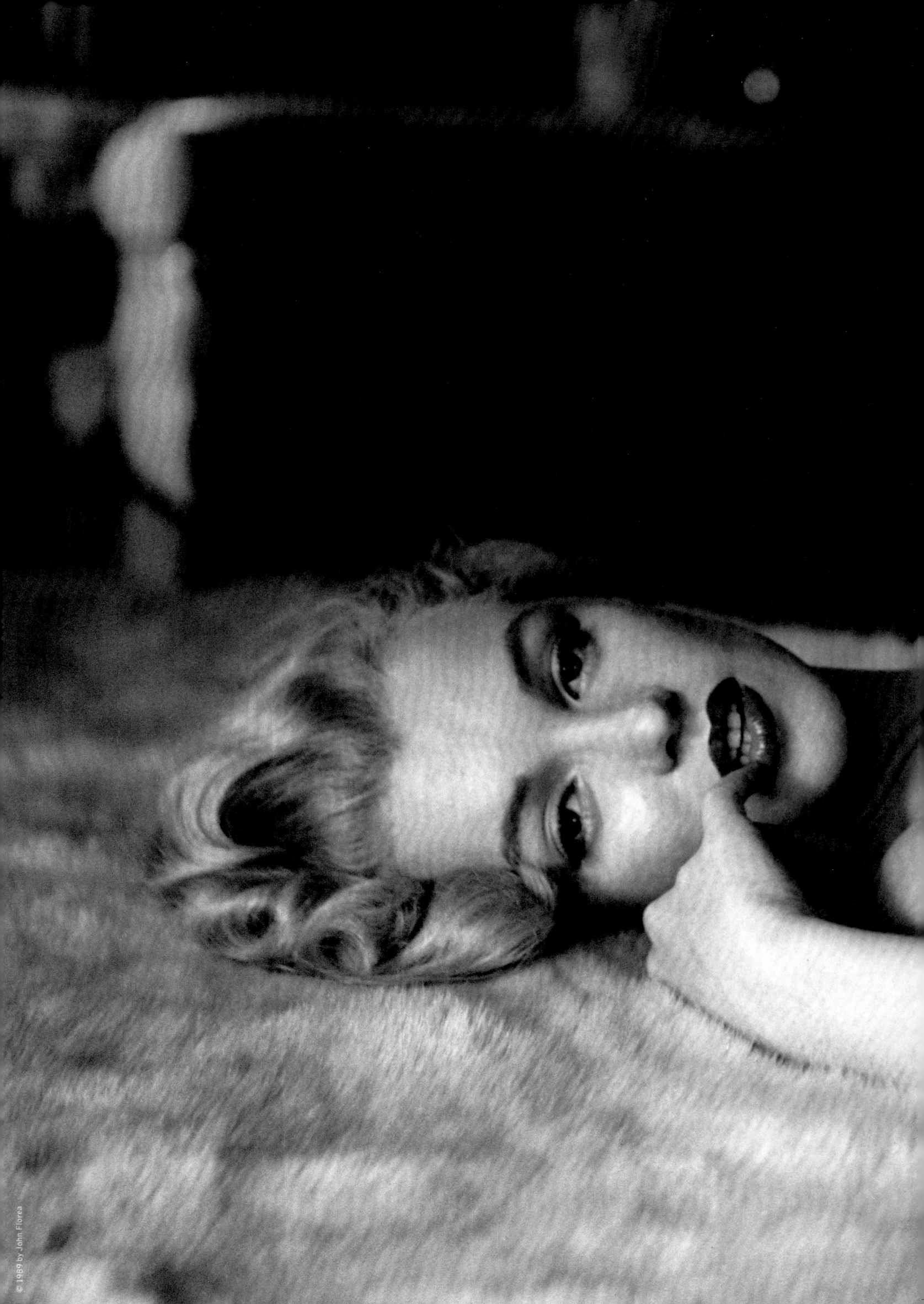

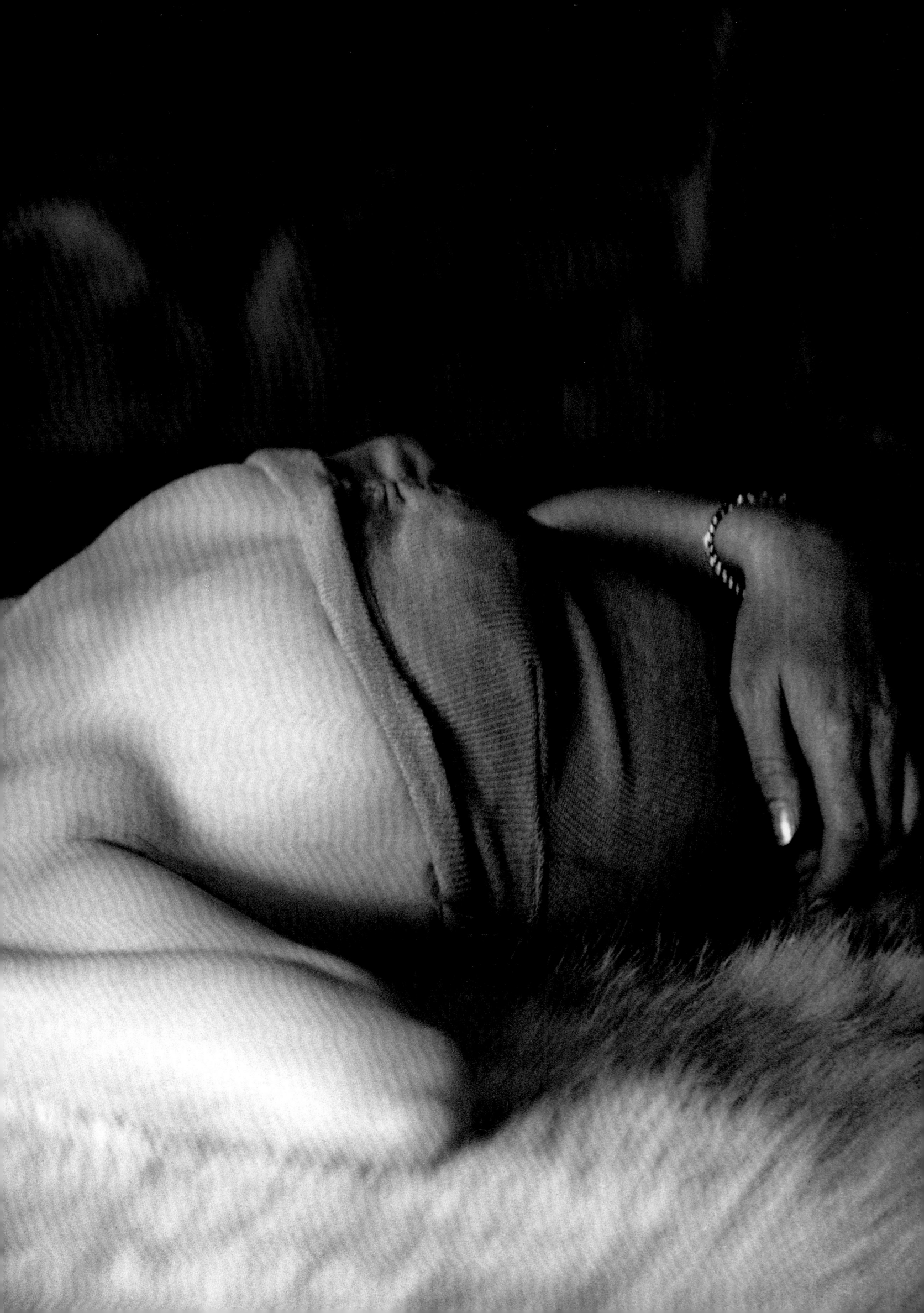

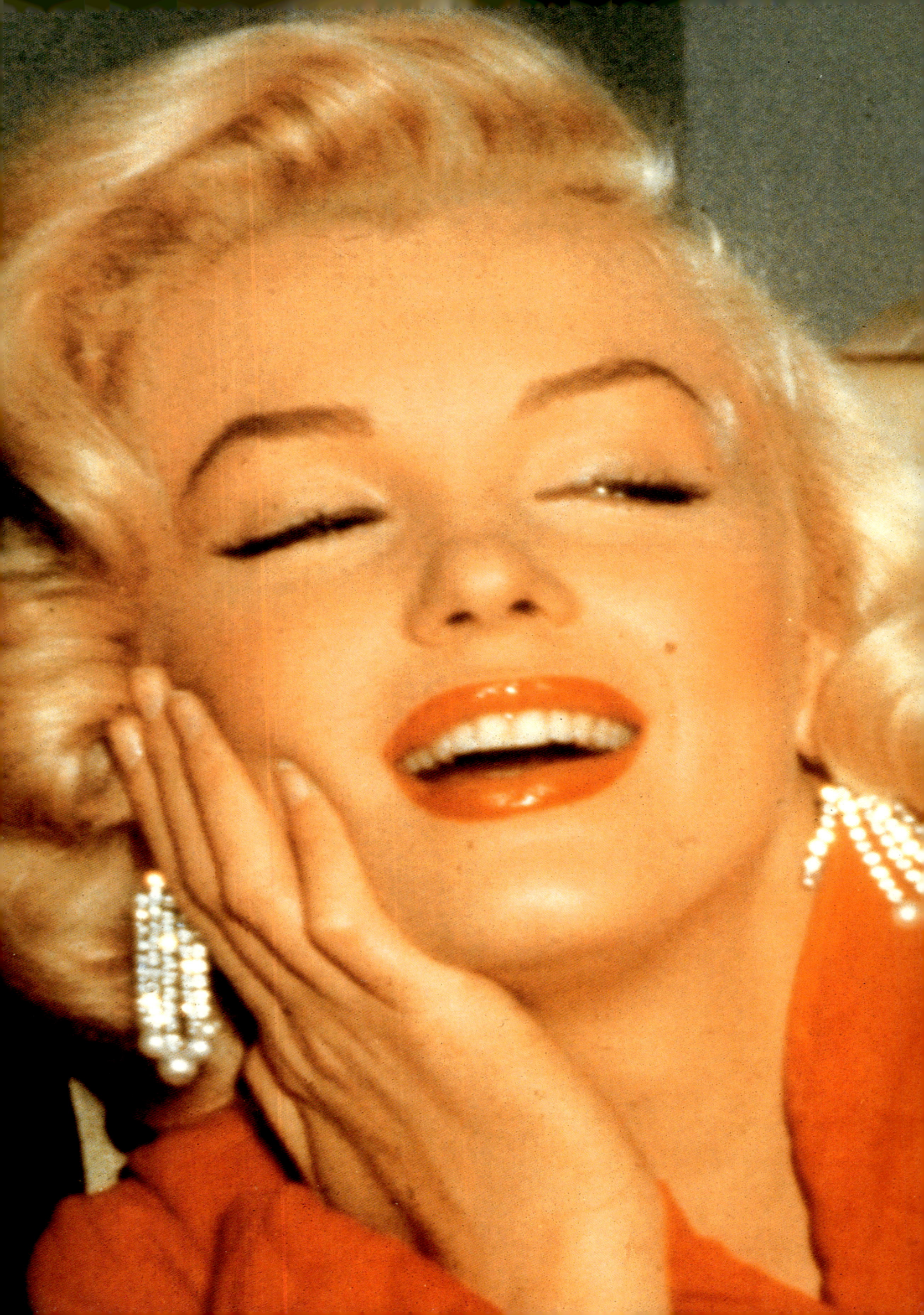

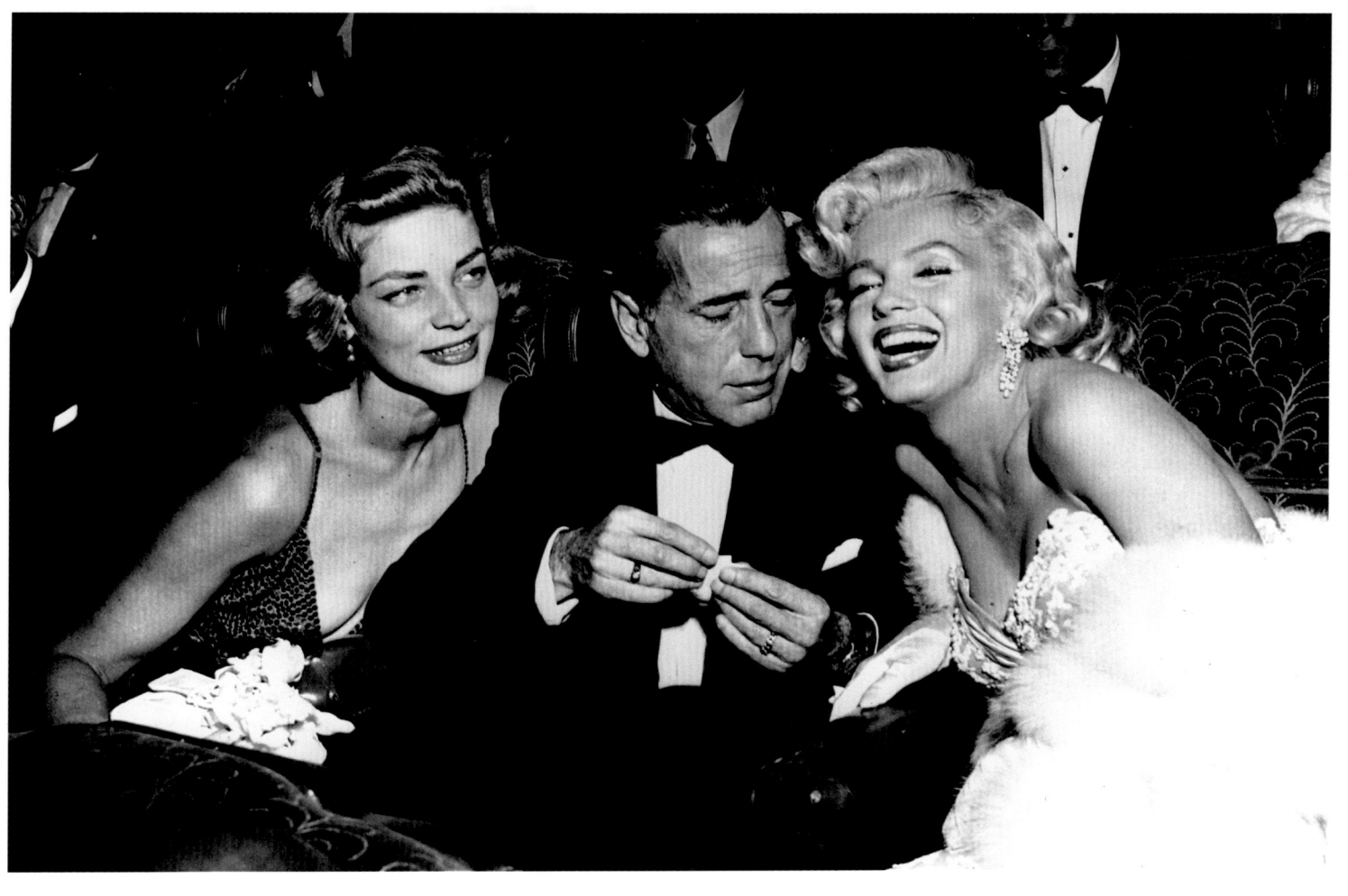

Page 106

During the shooting of *How to Marry a Millionaire,* 1953.

Page 107

At the premiere of *How to Marry a Millionaire,* with
Lauren Bacall and Humphrey Bogart, 1953. The film, which followed immediately
on the success of *Gentlemen Prefer Blondes,* considerably advanced Marilyn's
fame as a star. In the ads for the film, Marilyn was listed
before Betty Grable and Lauren Bacall.

Pages 108/109

Publicity still for *How to Marry a Millionaire.*

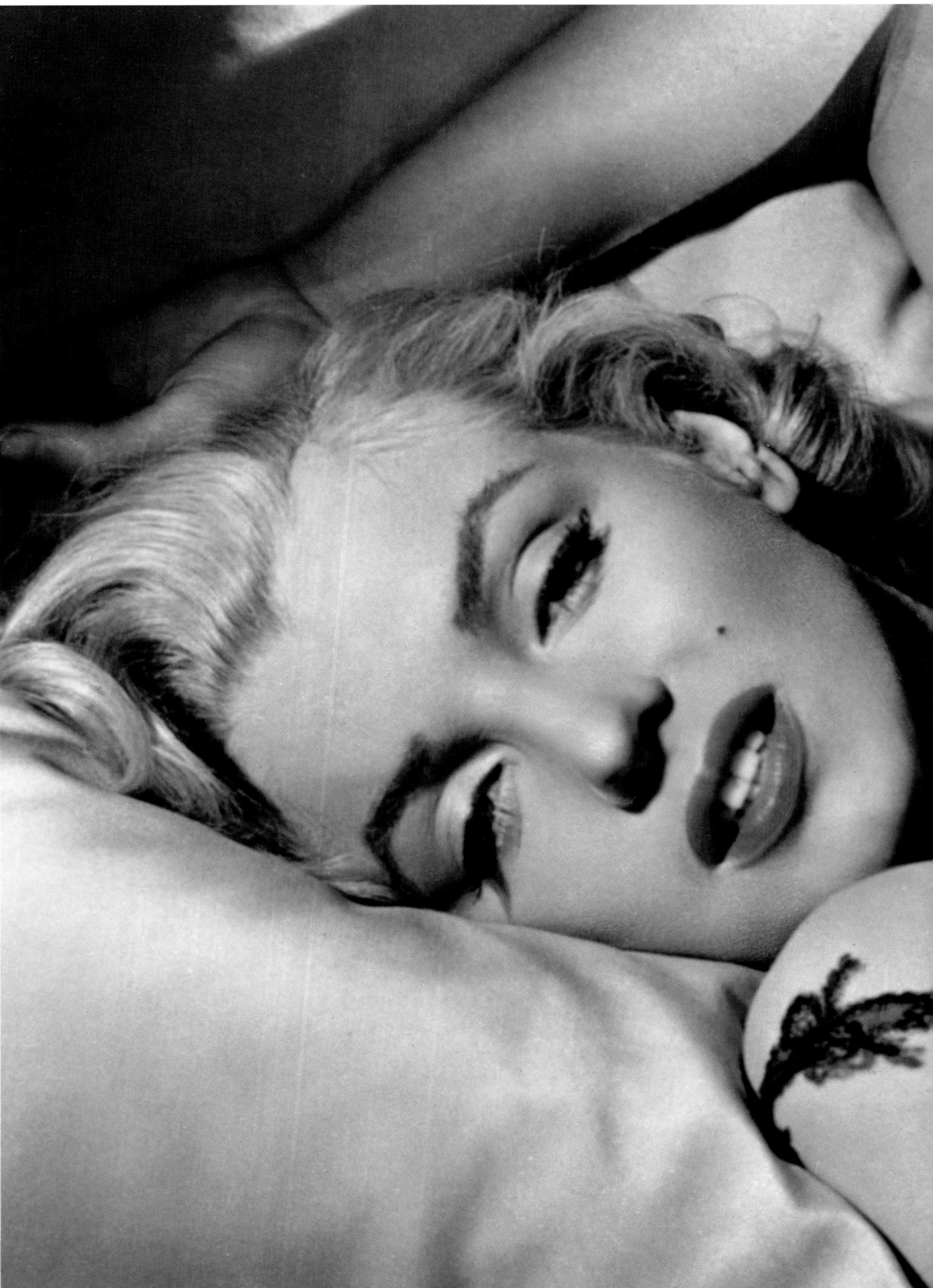

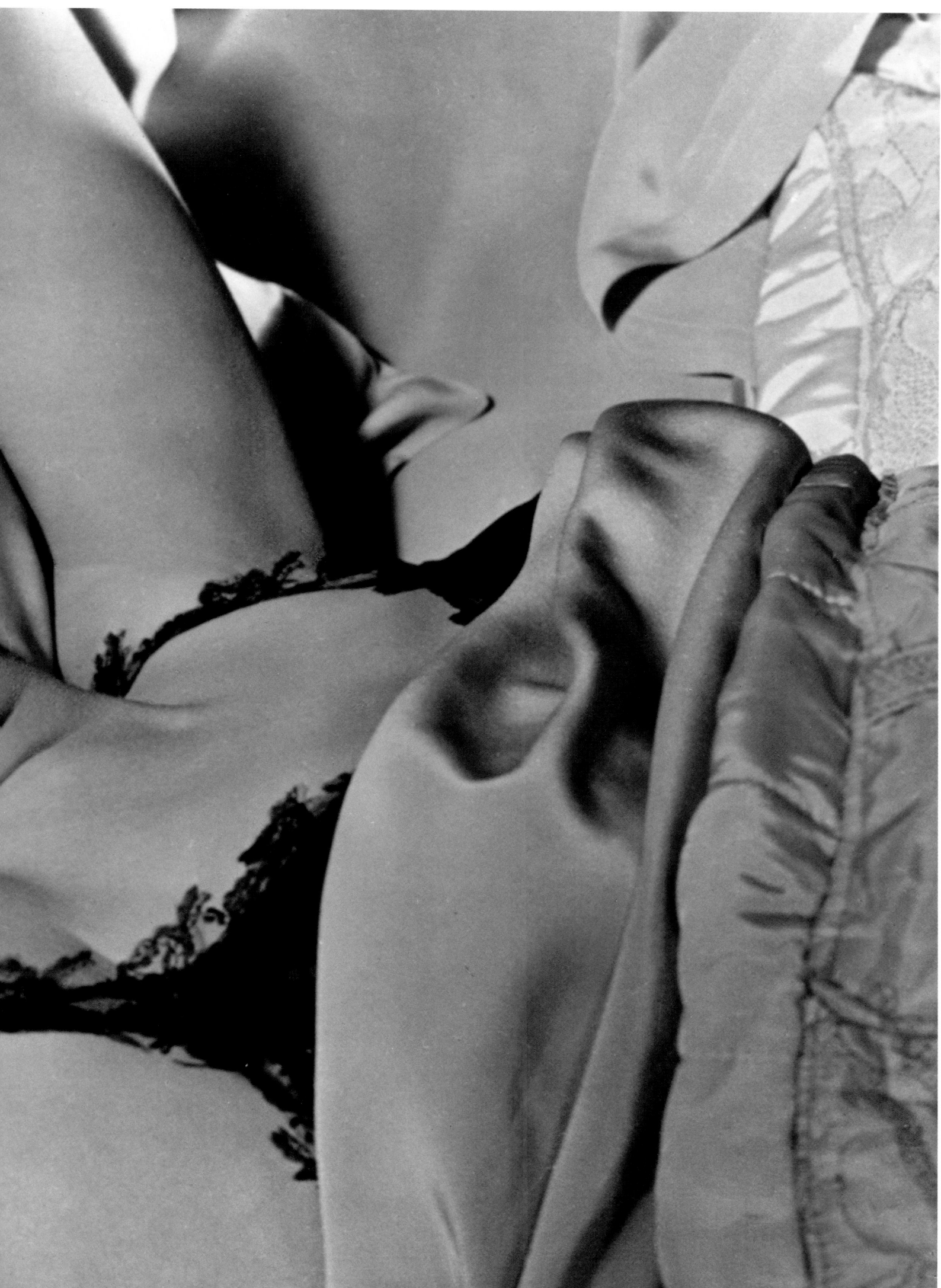

In the spring of 1953 Marilyn Monroe received *Photoplay* magazine's plaque
for "the fastest rising star of 1952." For the award ceremony she borrowed this spectacular
gold lamé gown that designer Bill Trevilla had created for
Gentlemen Prefer Blondes and that literally became Marilyn's own. After the ceremony,
for which she appeared two hours late, her hip-swinging
departure was so provocative that pandemonium broke out in the audience.

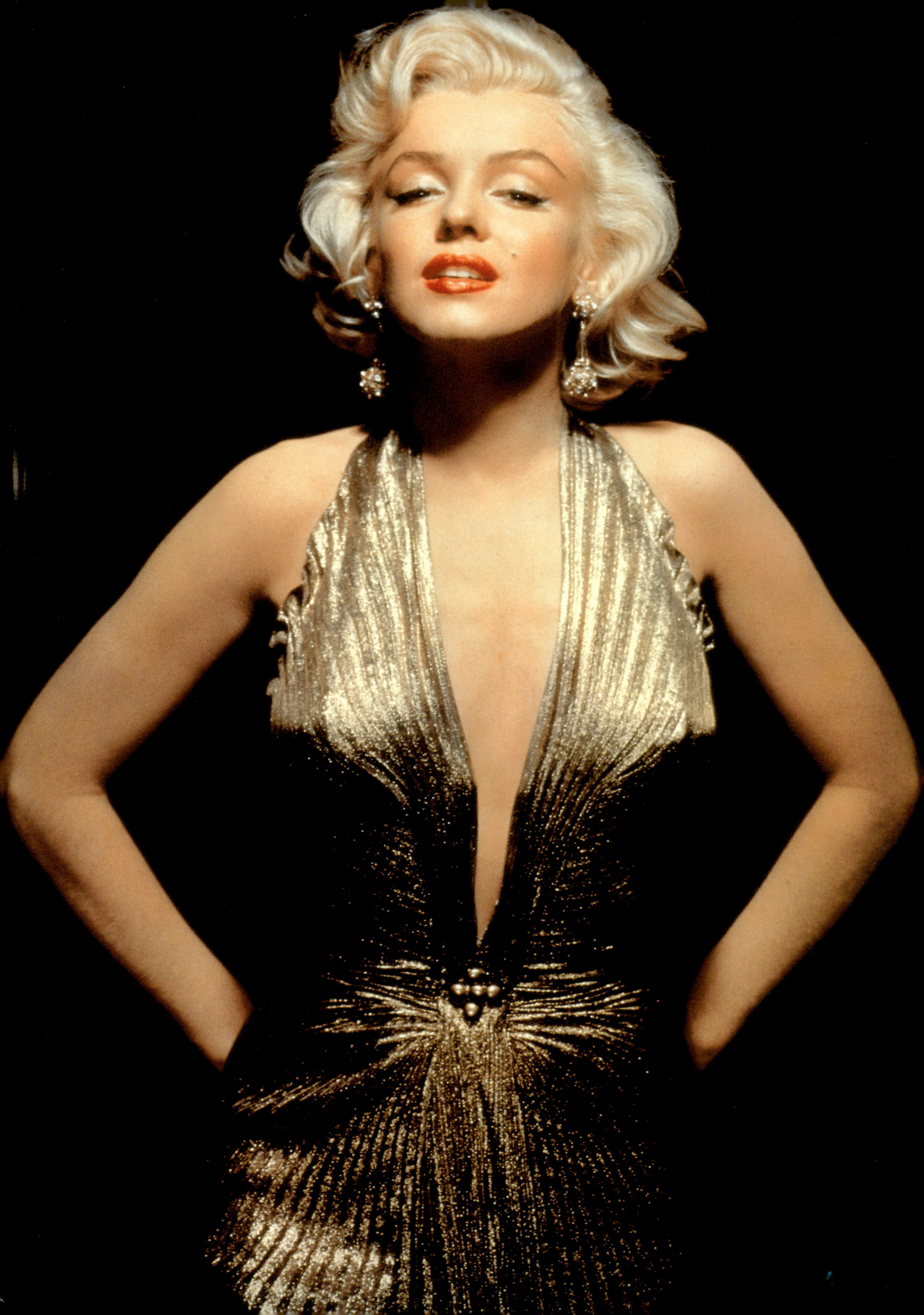

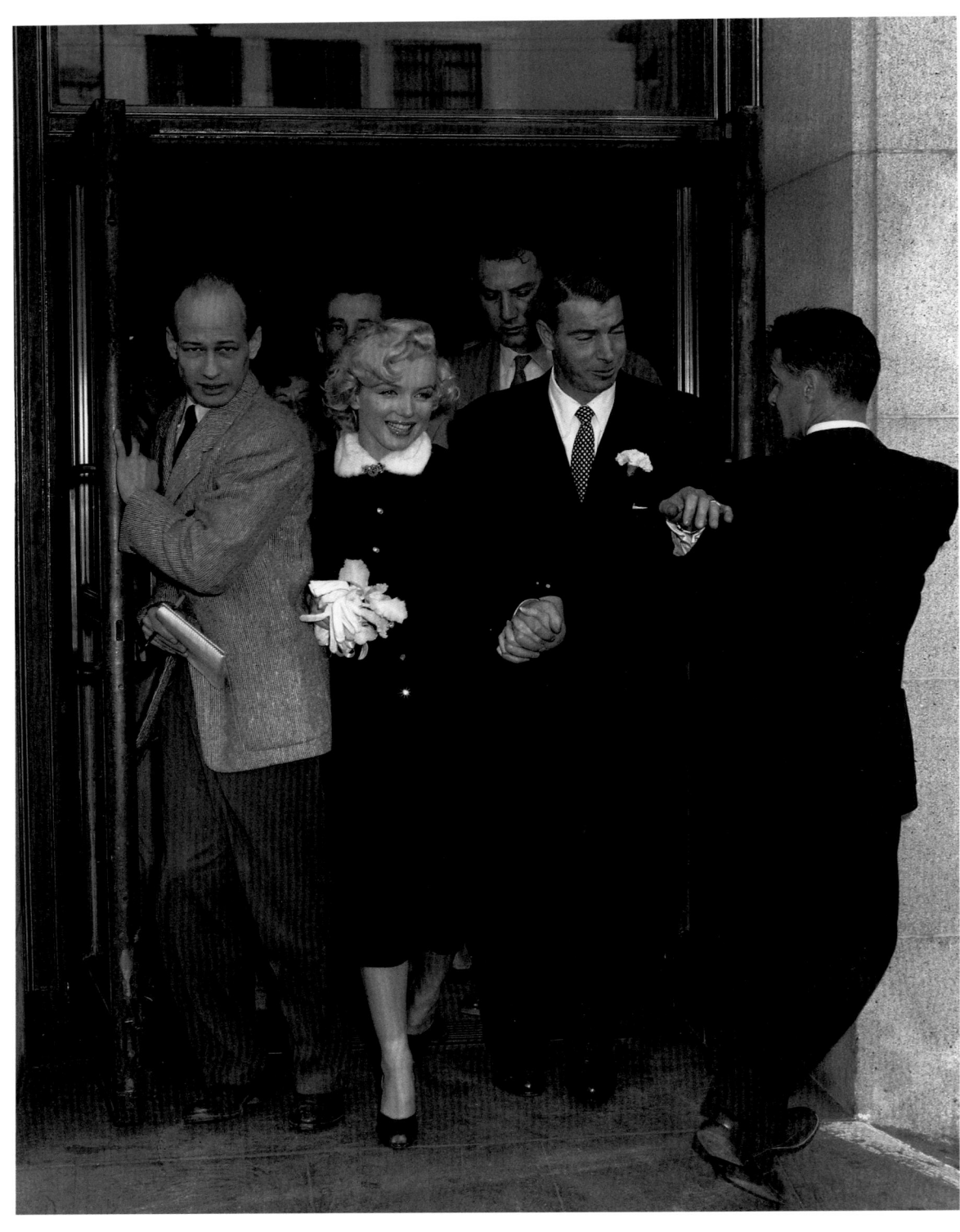

The bride was on time. On January 14, 1954, at one o'clock,
Marilyn Monroe, twenty-seven years old, married Joe DiMaggio, thirty-nine, in the
San Francisco City Hall. The ceremony, which lasted all of three minutes,
was performed by Municipal Court Judge Charles Peery. The *Los Angeles Herald Express*
commented sarcastically on the marriage that shook the nation:
"It could only happen here in America, this story-book romance.... Both of them ... had
to fight their way to fame and fortune and to each other.
One in a birthday suit, as a foundling and later as a calendar girl, the other in a ...
baseball suit." Photographs from UPI.

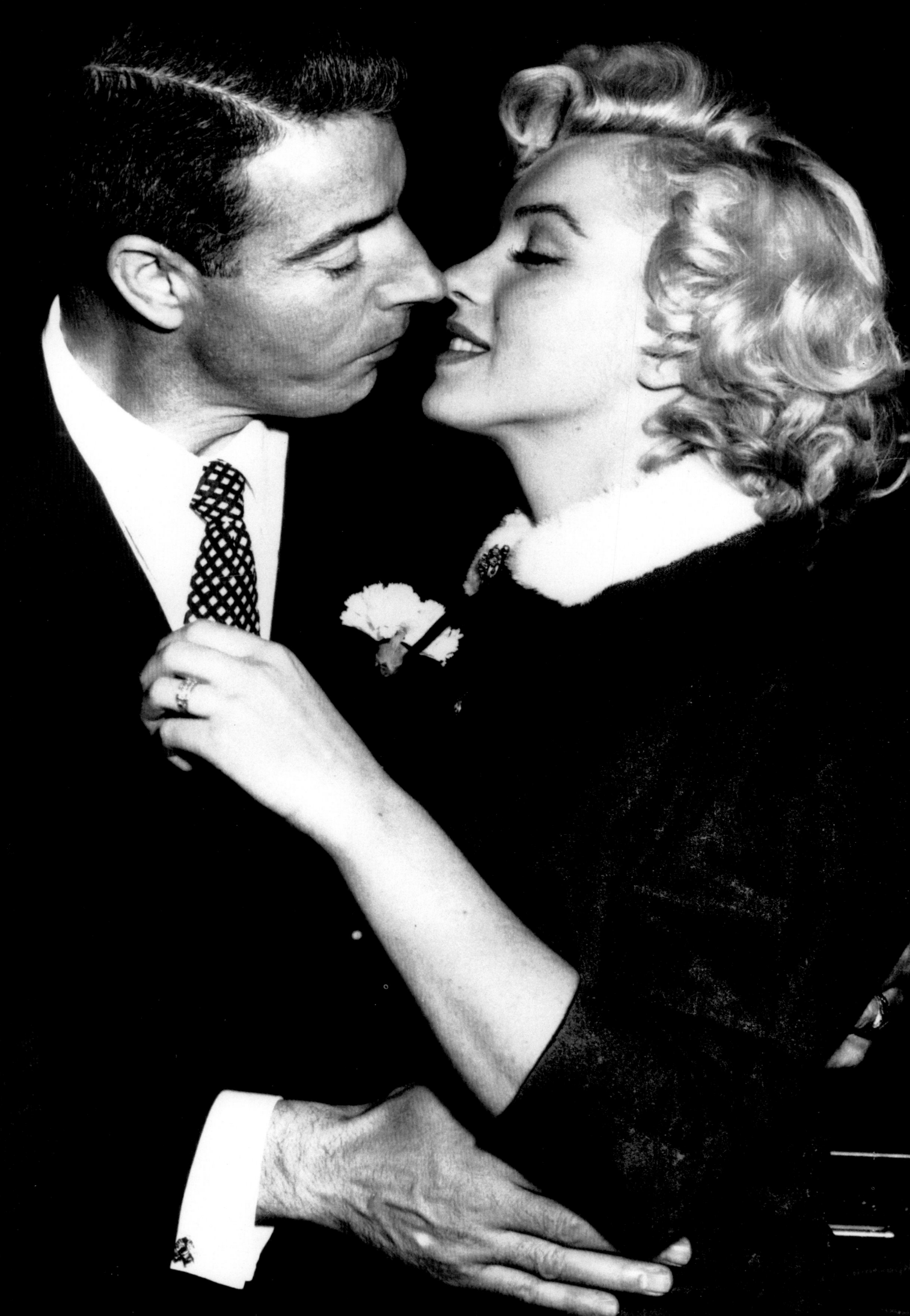

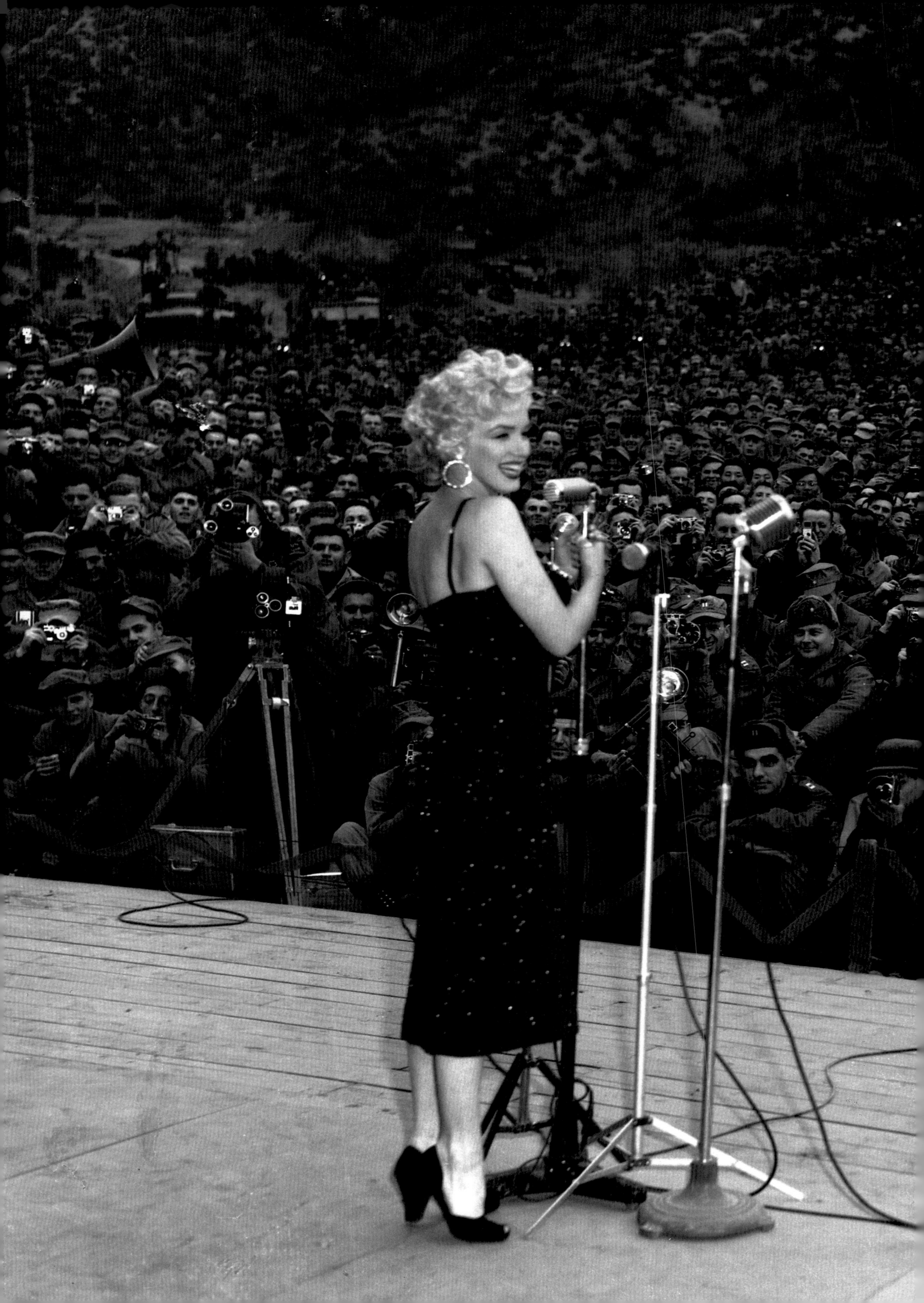

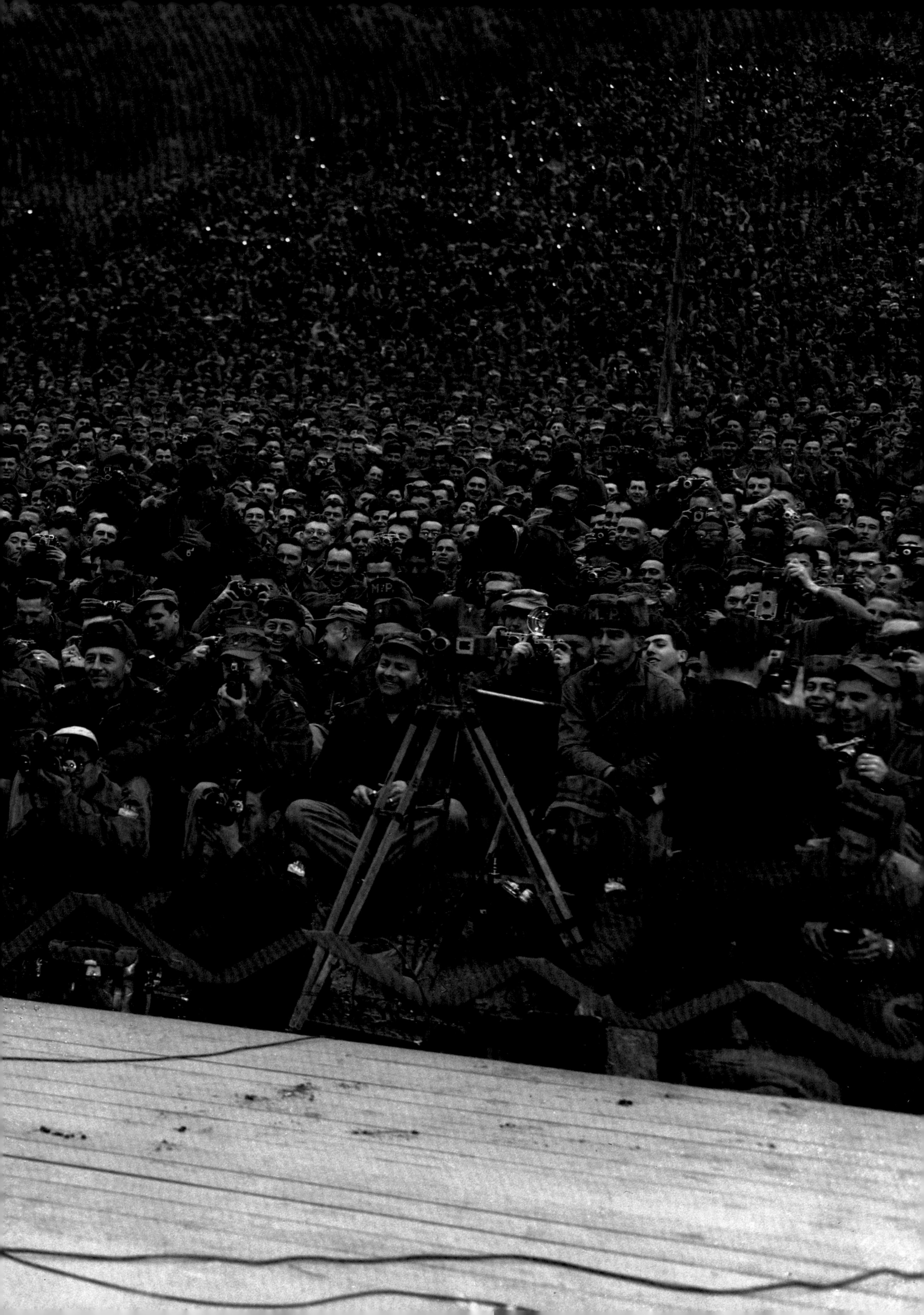

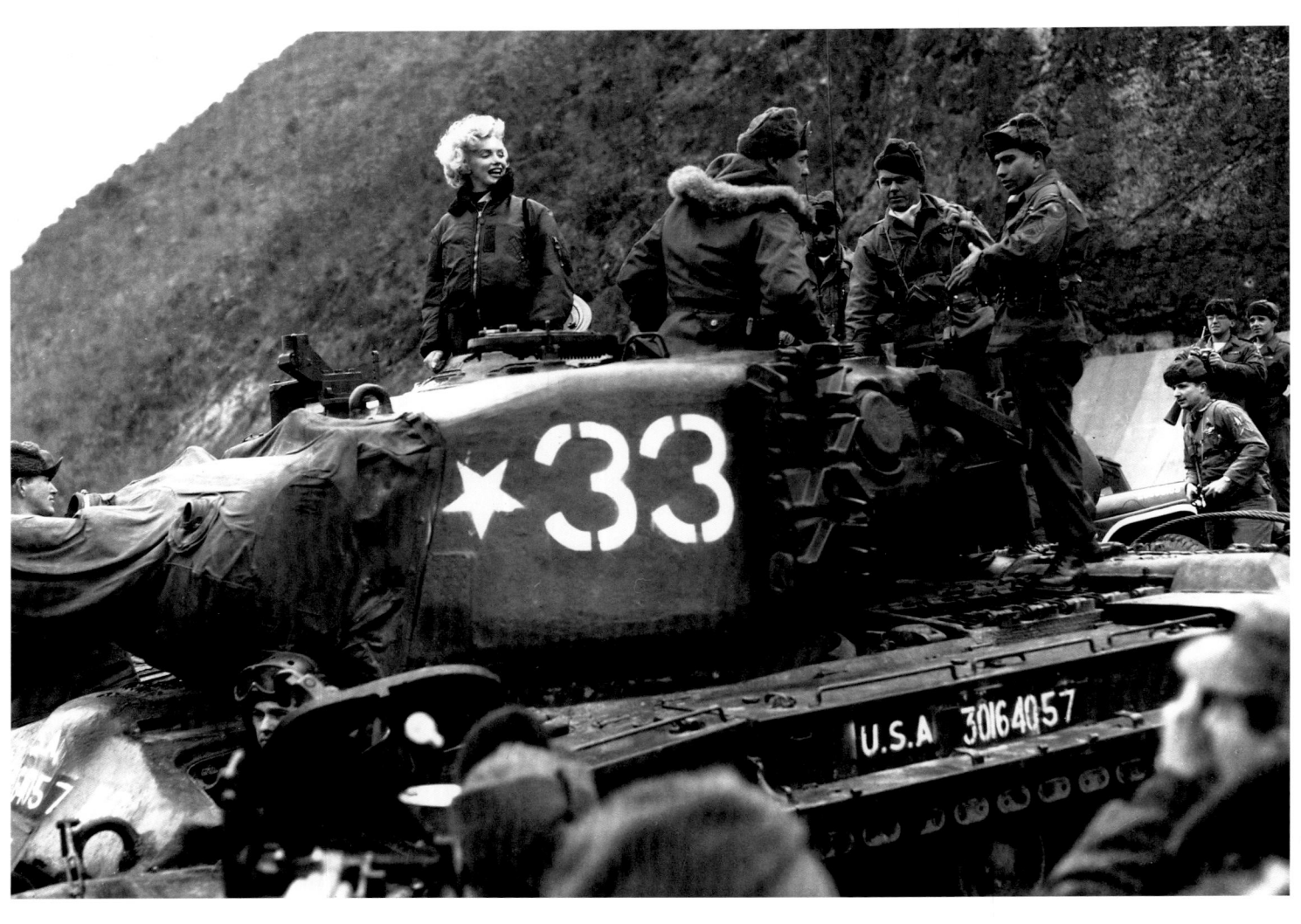

The honeymoon brought Joe DiMaggio and Marilyn to Japan.
The crowd of fans greeting her on their arrival at the Tokyo international airport was so huge
that the couple had to leave the airplane through the cargo hatch.
At this time Marilyn was the most popular foreign film star in Japan. Then, interrupting
her visit to Japan, Marilyn flew to Korea, where she performed
for the American troops stationed there. For the soldiers she sang songs like
"Diamonds Are a Girl's Best Friend," "Bye Bye Baby,"
"Somebody Loves Me," and "Do It Again." Within four days, she gave ten shows to more
than a hundred thousand soldiers who came from all parts
of the Korean peninsula. The enthusiasm was mutual. Marilyn said: "This was the best thing
that ever happened to me," and, "I never felt like a star before in my heart."

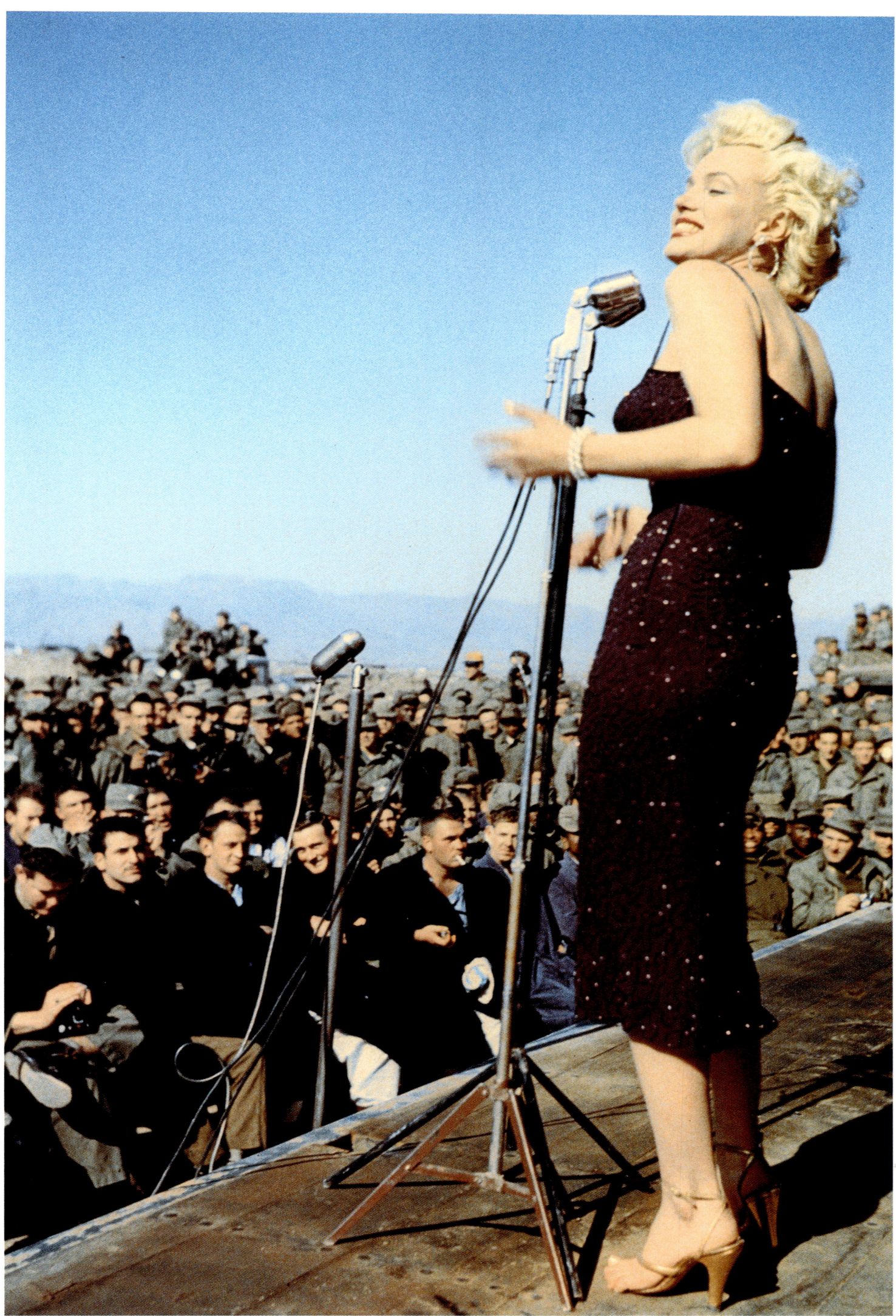

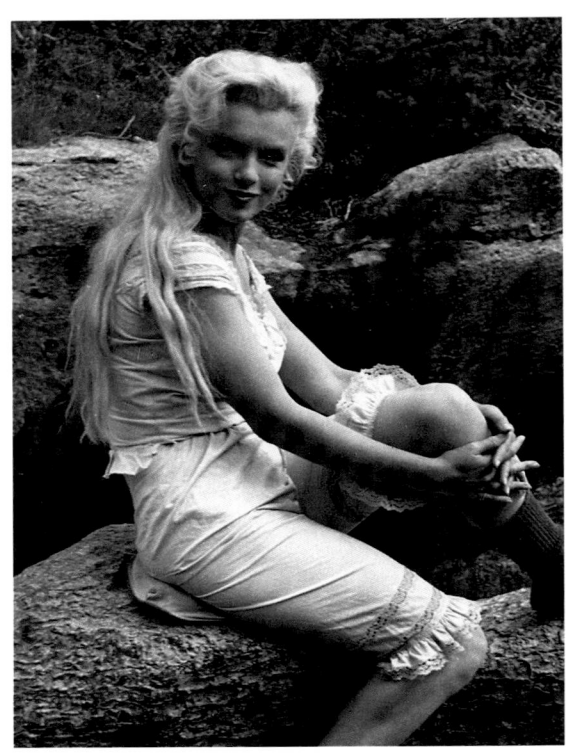

Snapshot taken during the shooting of *River of No Return,* 1954.

Publicity still for *River of No Return.* Under the direction of
Otto Preminger, Marilyn played the bar singer Kay, who starts a new life after many
adventures with the widowed Matt Calder (Robert Mitchum)
and his ten-year-old son Mark (Tommy Rettig). It was Marilyn's first western.

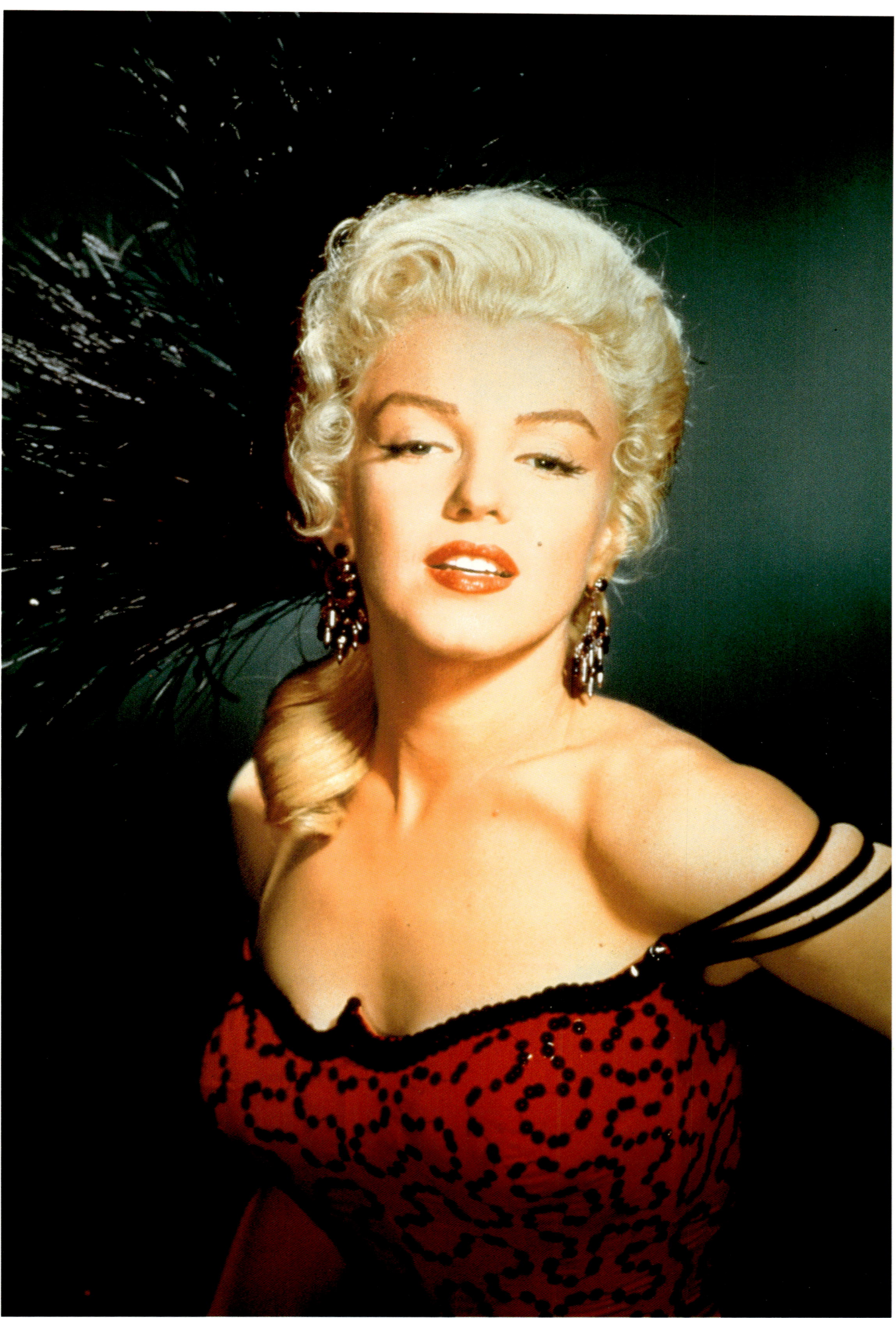

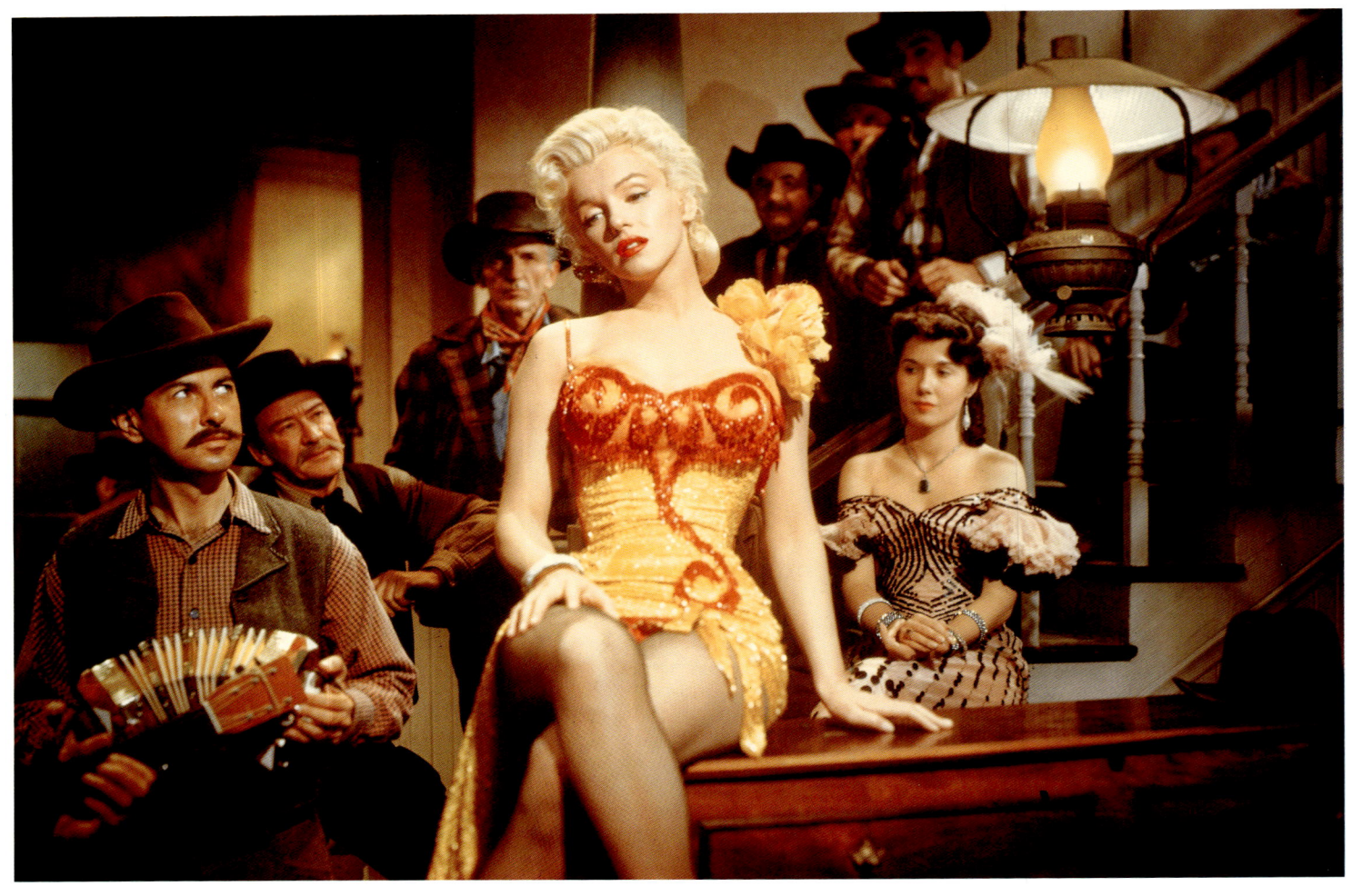

Publicity stills for *River of No Return,* in which Marilyn sang
"River of No Return," "I'm Gonna File My Claim," "One Silver Dollar," and "Down in the
Meadow." She herself was very unhappy with the film
and blamed it on 20th Century-Fox: "I think I deserve a better deal than a 'Z' cowboy movie
in which the acting finishes third to the scenery and cinemascope."

Page 121

In a limousine during the shooting of *River of No Return.*
Photograph by John Florea, 1954.

Pages 122/123

A happy Marilyn Monroe posed for the British photographer
Baron in the summer of 1954.

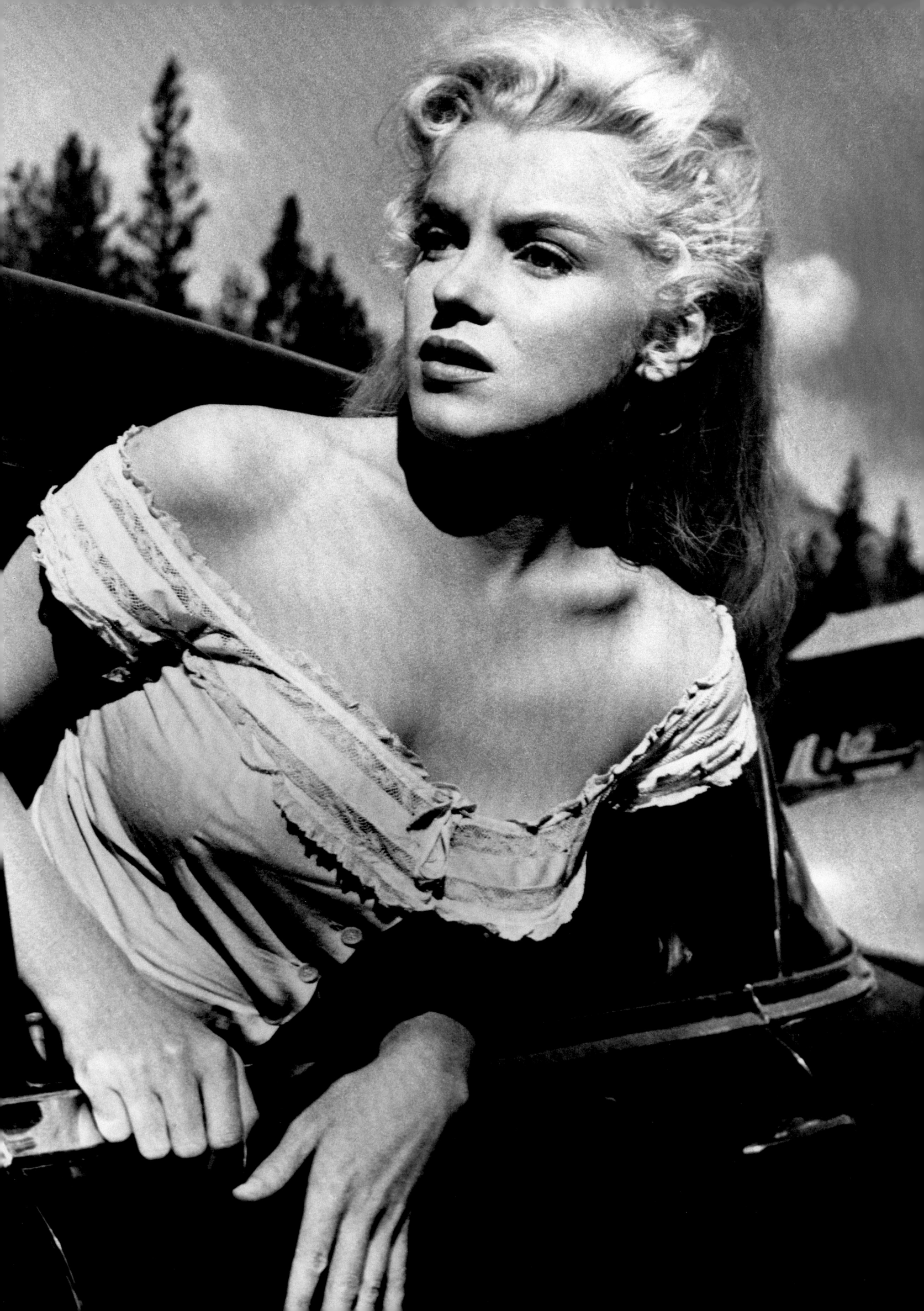

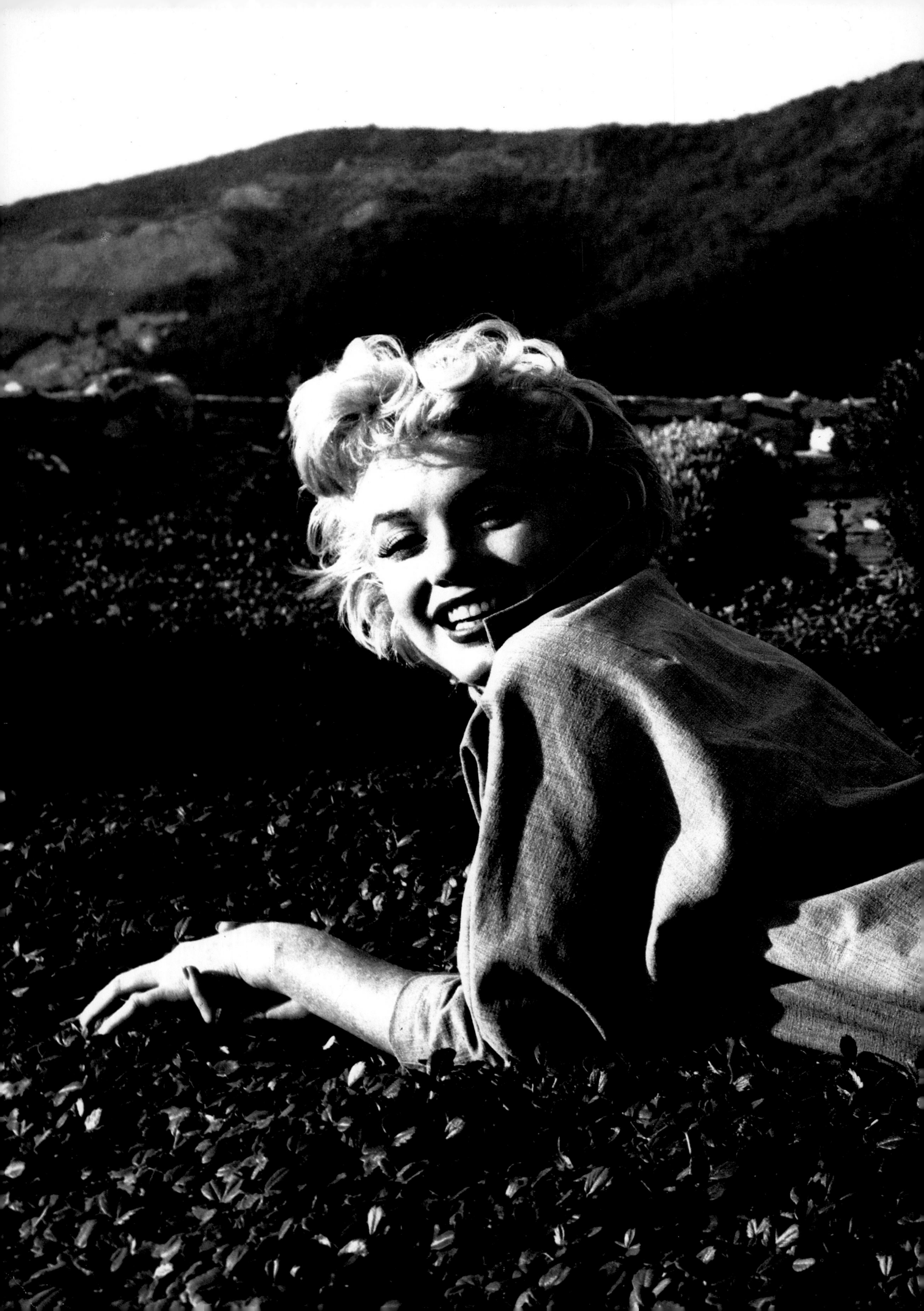

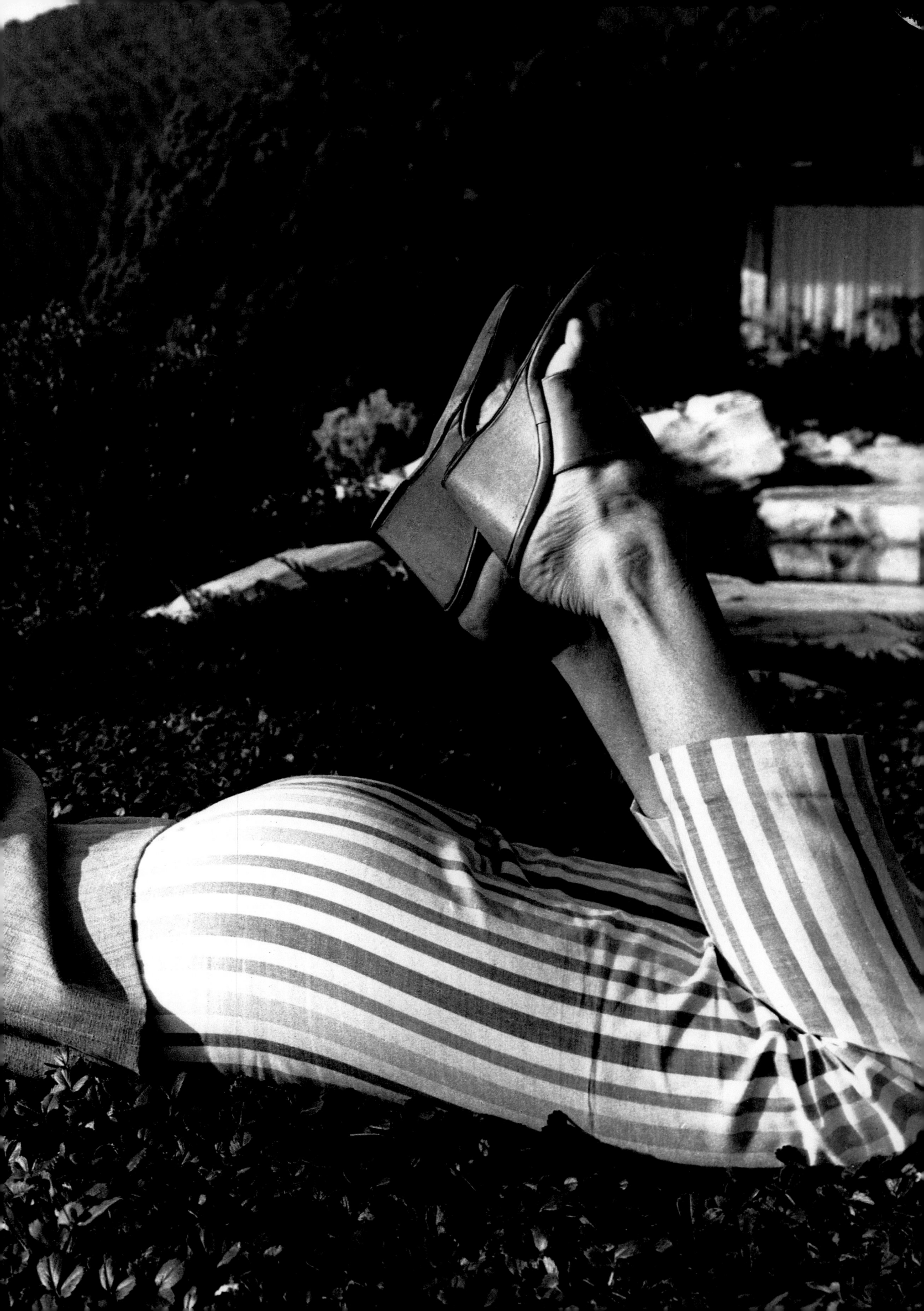

Publicity still from *There's No Business Like Show Business,*
in homage to the great Irving Berlin. Marilyn accepted the rather weak script on the promise
of being able to star in the filming of the Broadway comedy
The Seven Year Itch. The film turned out to be somewhat of a flop and Marilyn became
determined to accept only artistically demanding material.

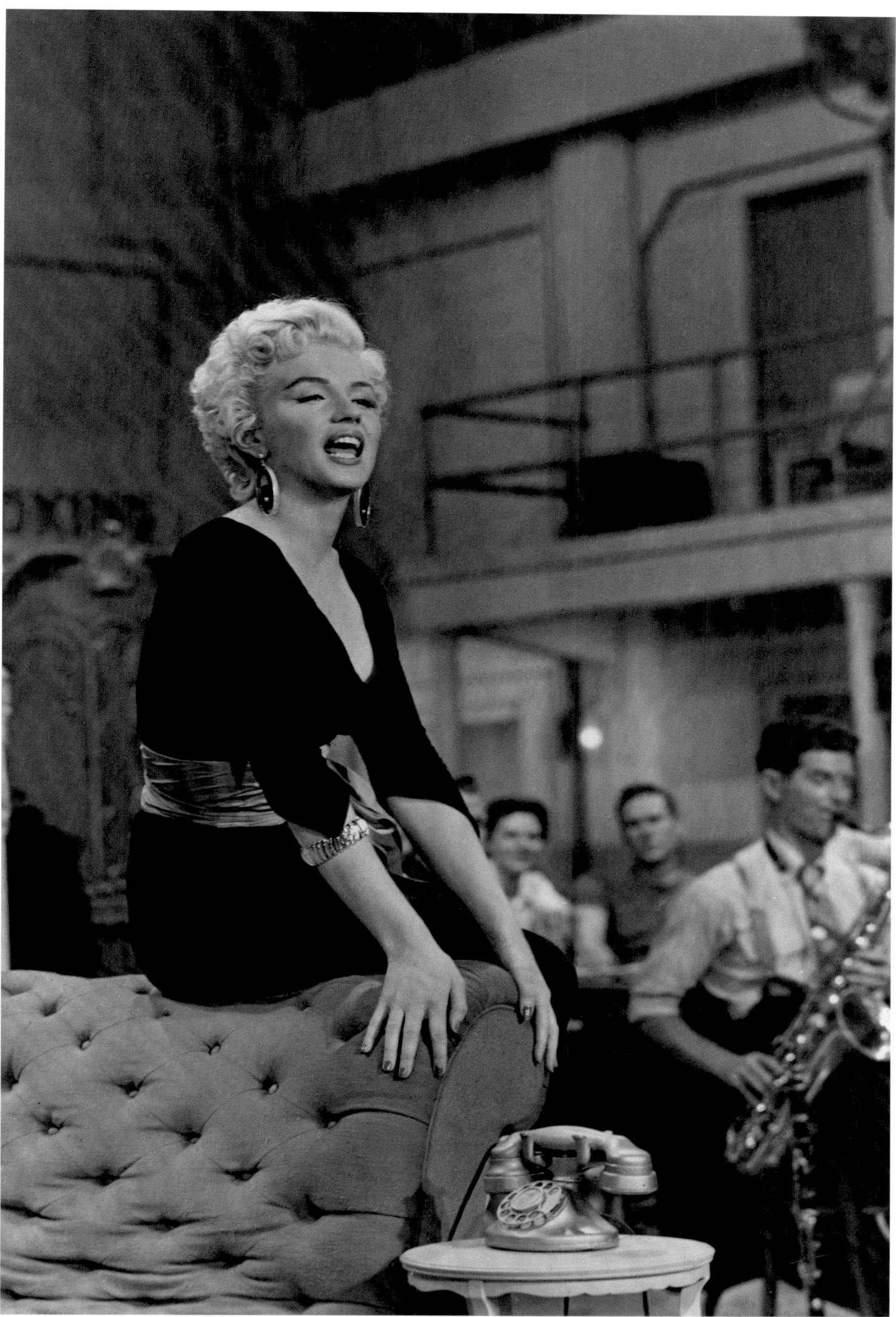

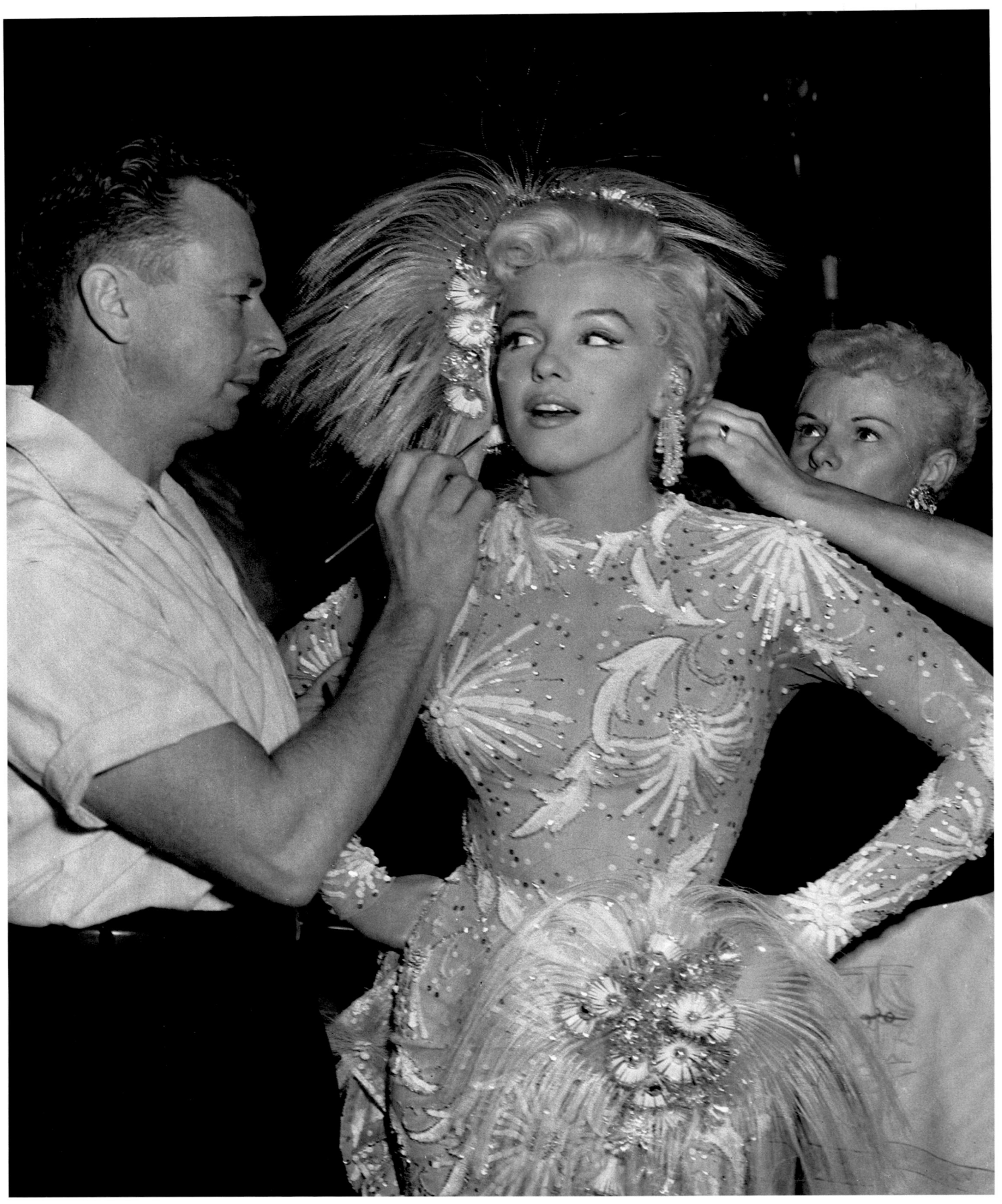

Pages 126/127

Marilyn Monroe "getting good and ready" for her performance in
There's No Business Like Show Business (above). In this film Marilyn sang three songs,
"After You Get What You Want, You Don't Want It," "Heat Wave," and "Lazy."

Pages 128/129

Film still from *How to Marry a Millionaire.*

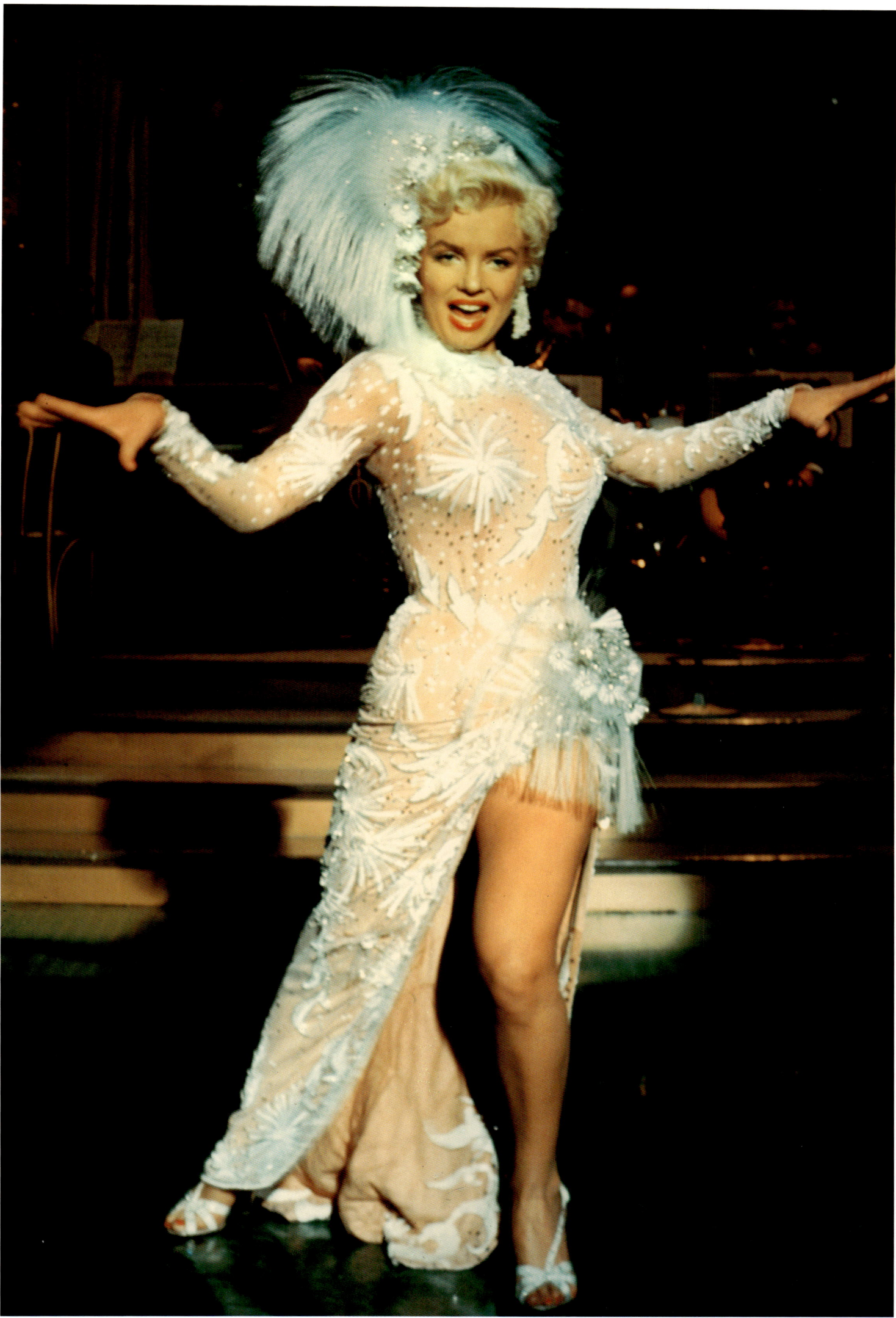

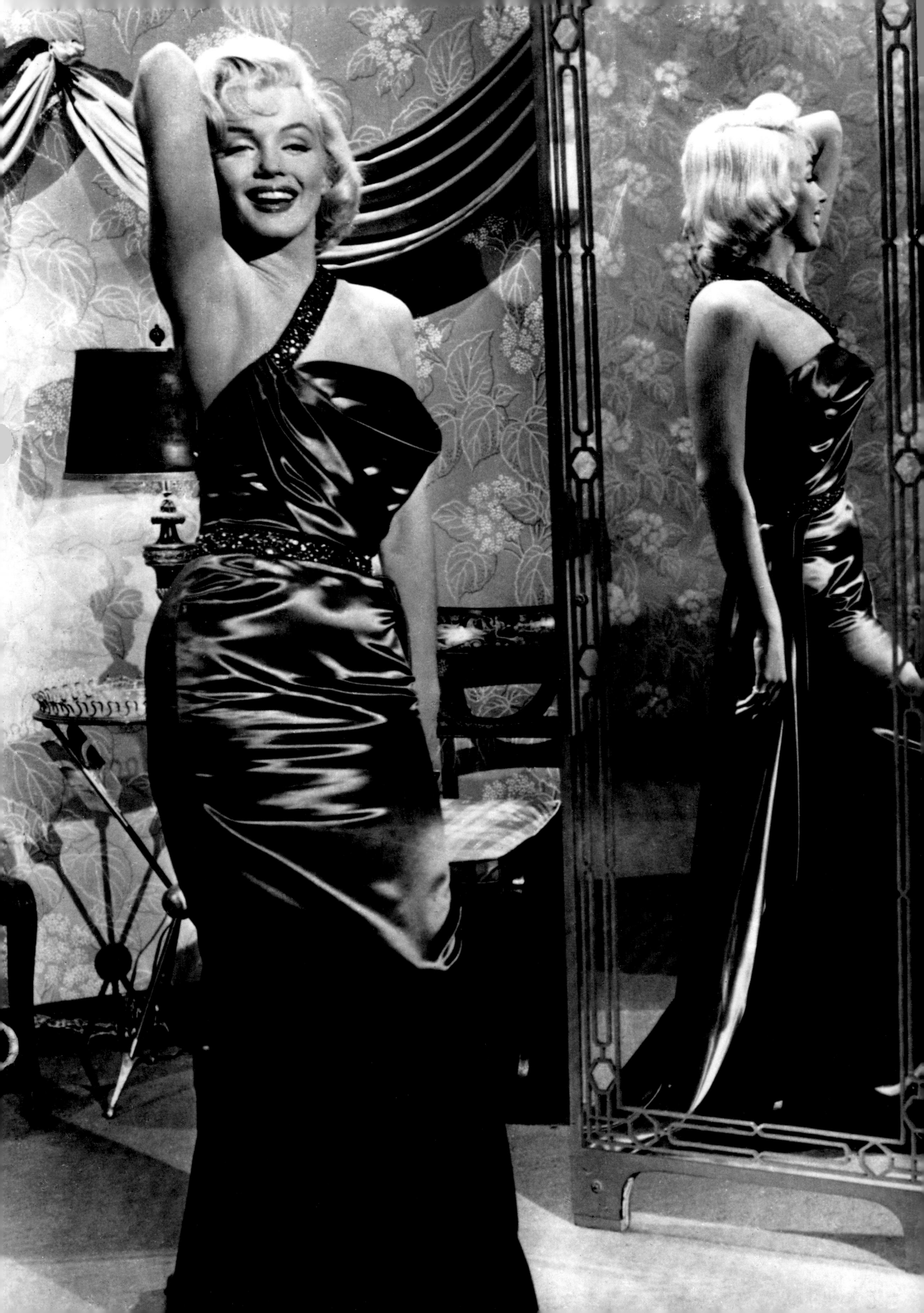

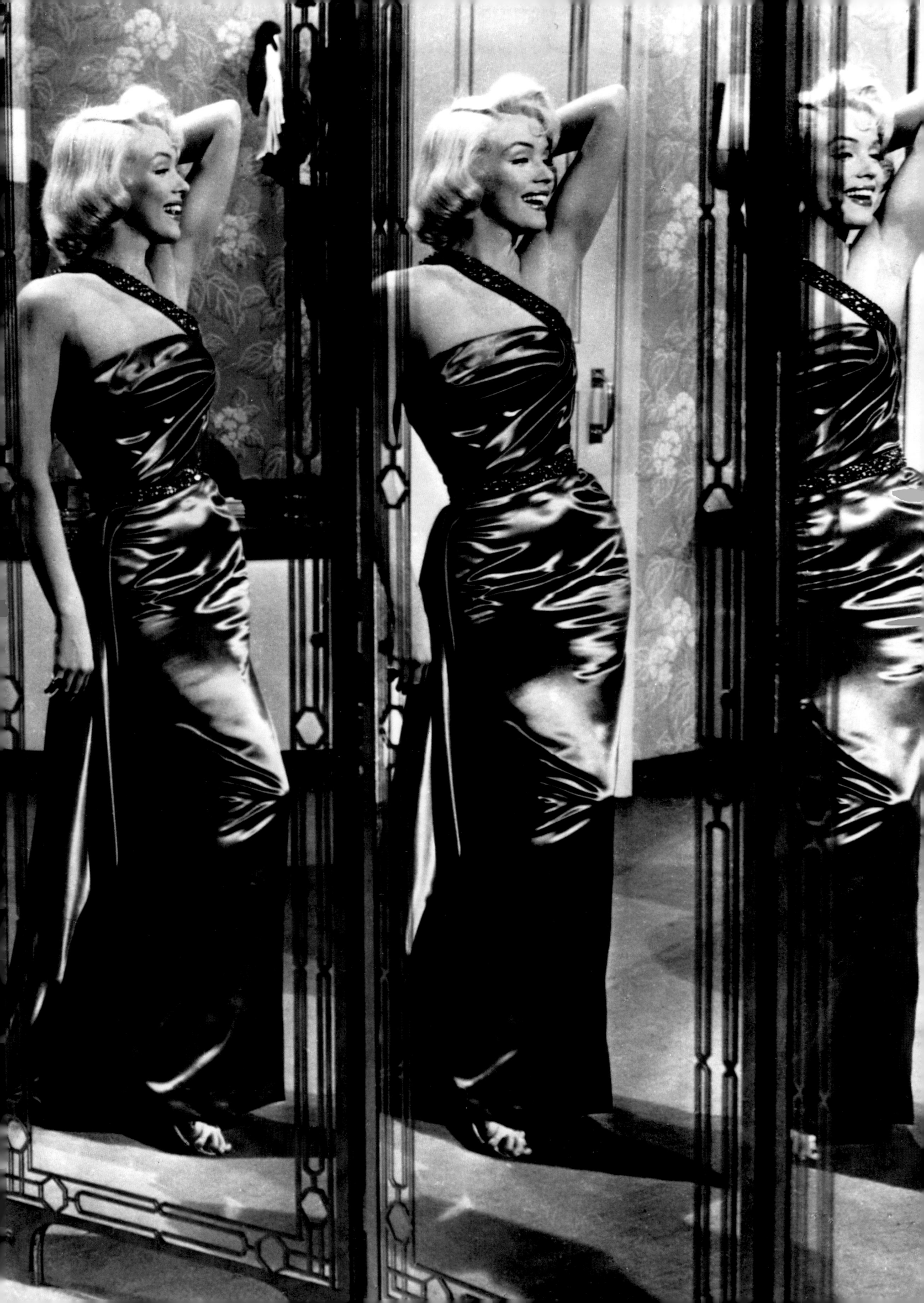

Arrival at Idlewild (later John F. Kennedy) Airport, for the shooting of
The Seven Year Itch. The puckered lips were for the photographer Weegee, the craftiest of all
New York's fleet-footed reporters. Photograph by Weegee, 1955.

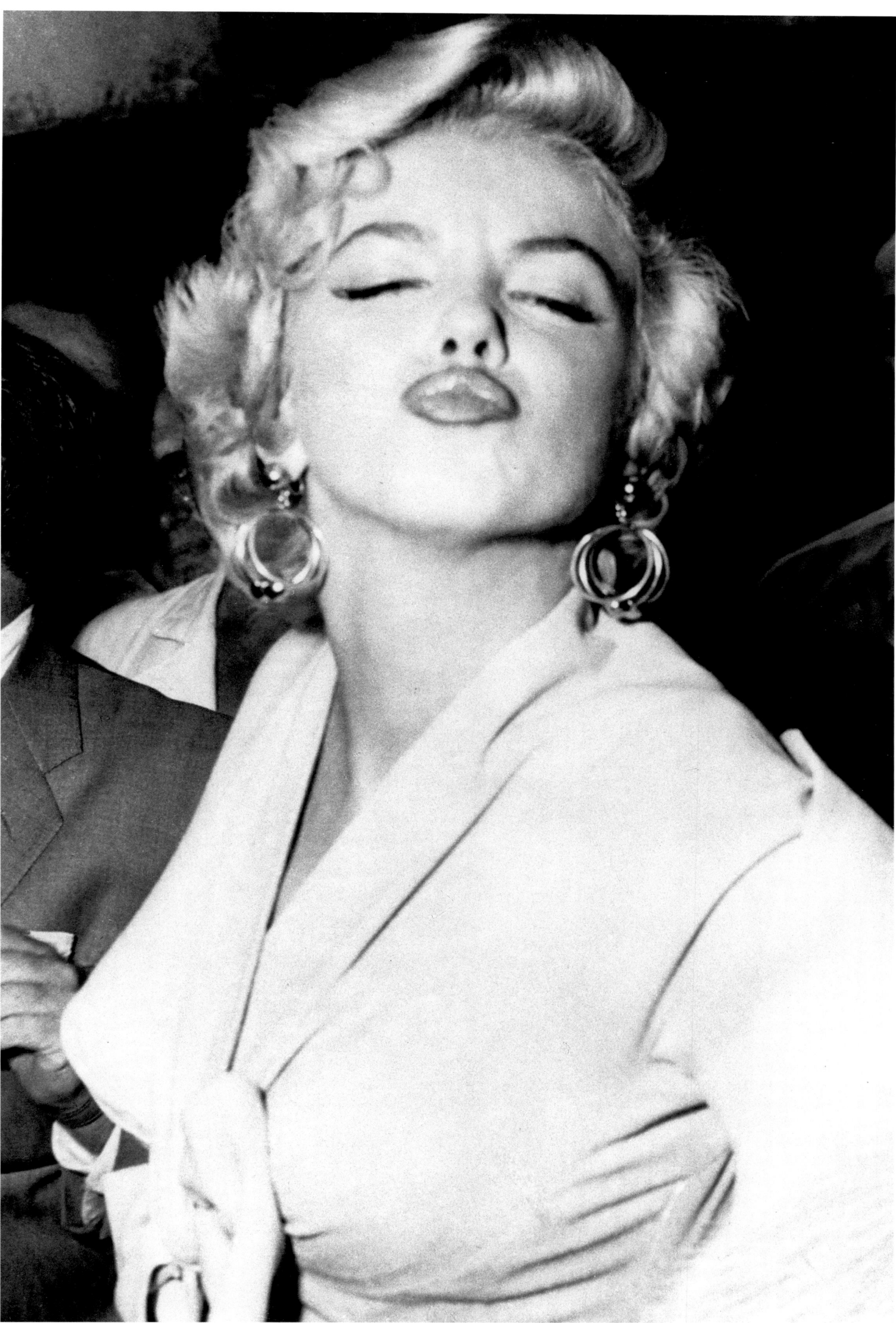

The shooting of *The Seven Year Itch* took place in New York.
The location was a brownstone on East Sixty-first Street in Manhattan. During the breaks,
Marilyn laughed and waved to her numerous fans assembled in front of the house.

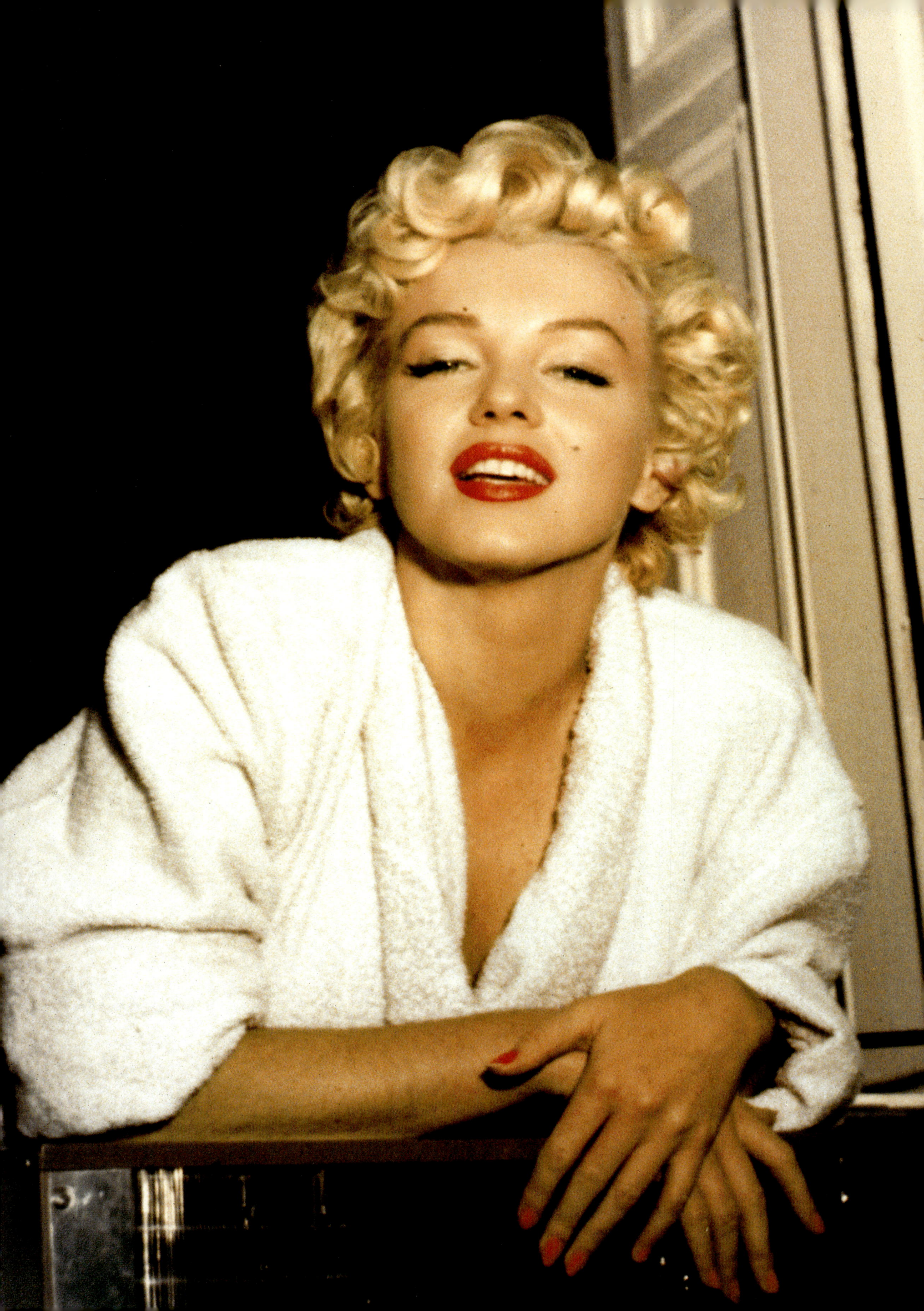

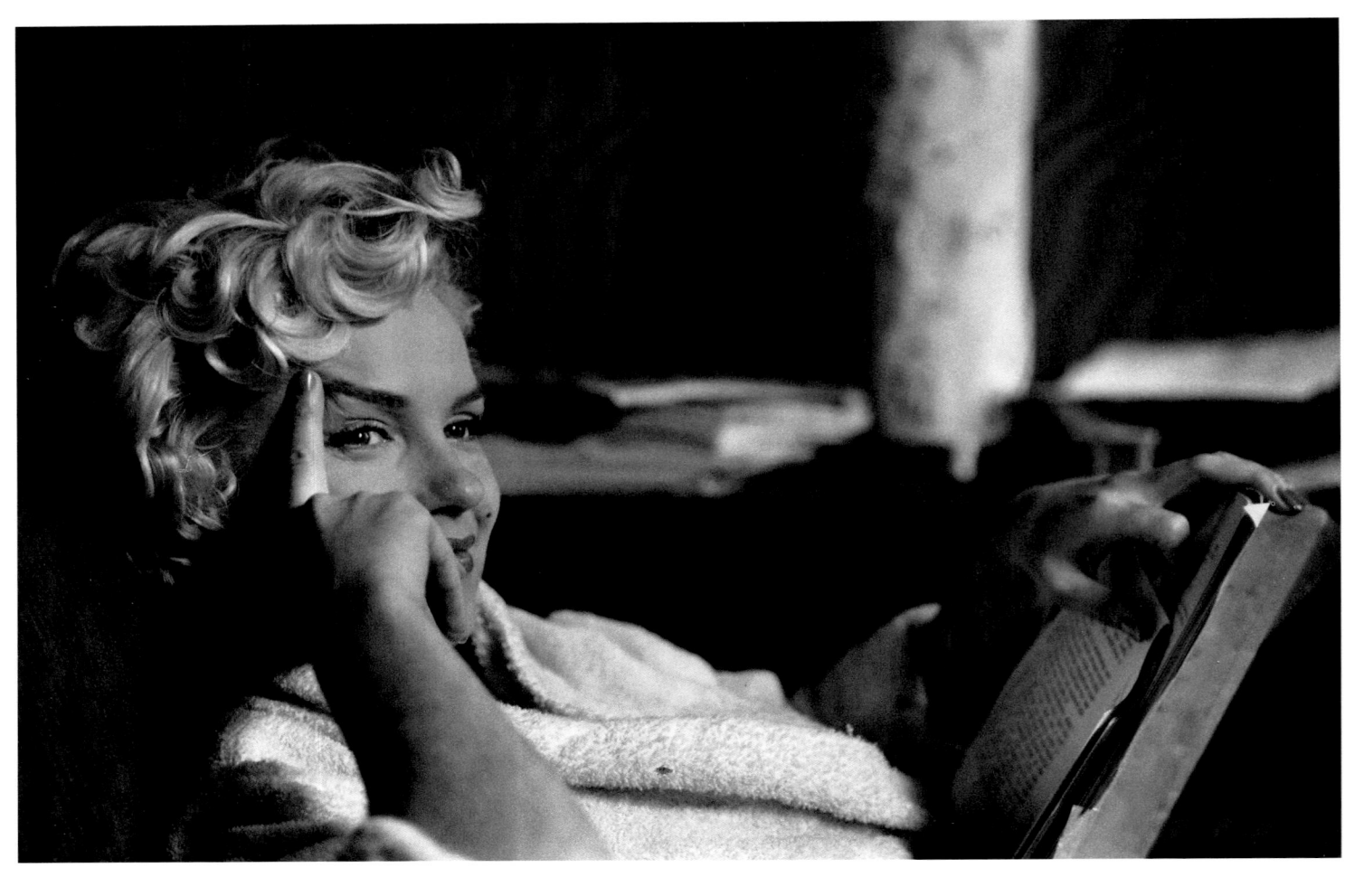

An ever-increasing number of photographers followed the shooting
of *The Seven Year Itch*. These two shots of Marilyn Monroe, taken during a break, are by
Elliott Erwitt (right) and Bob Henriques (left), two photographers from the famous
picture agency Magnum.

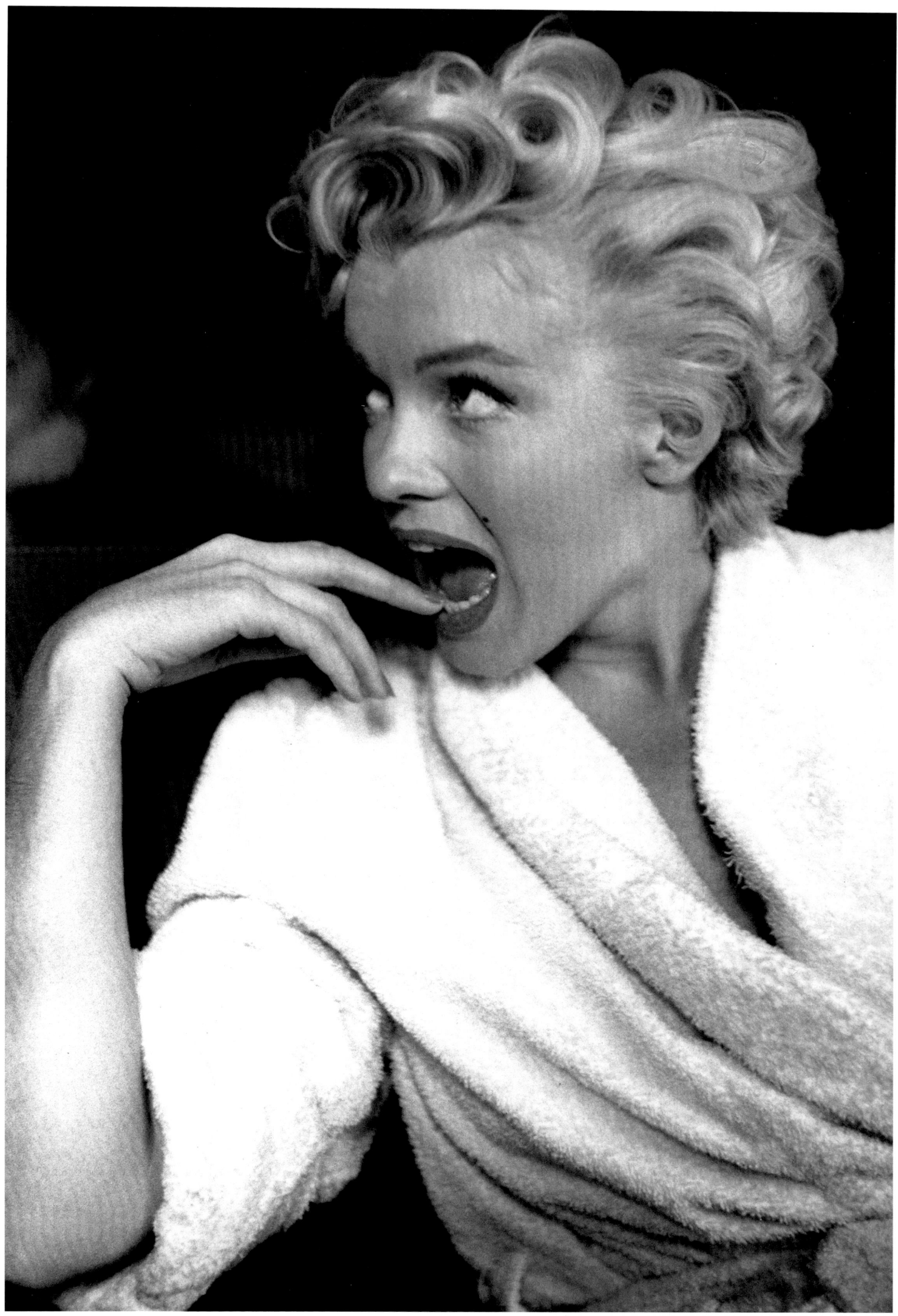

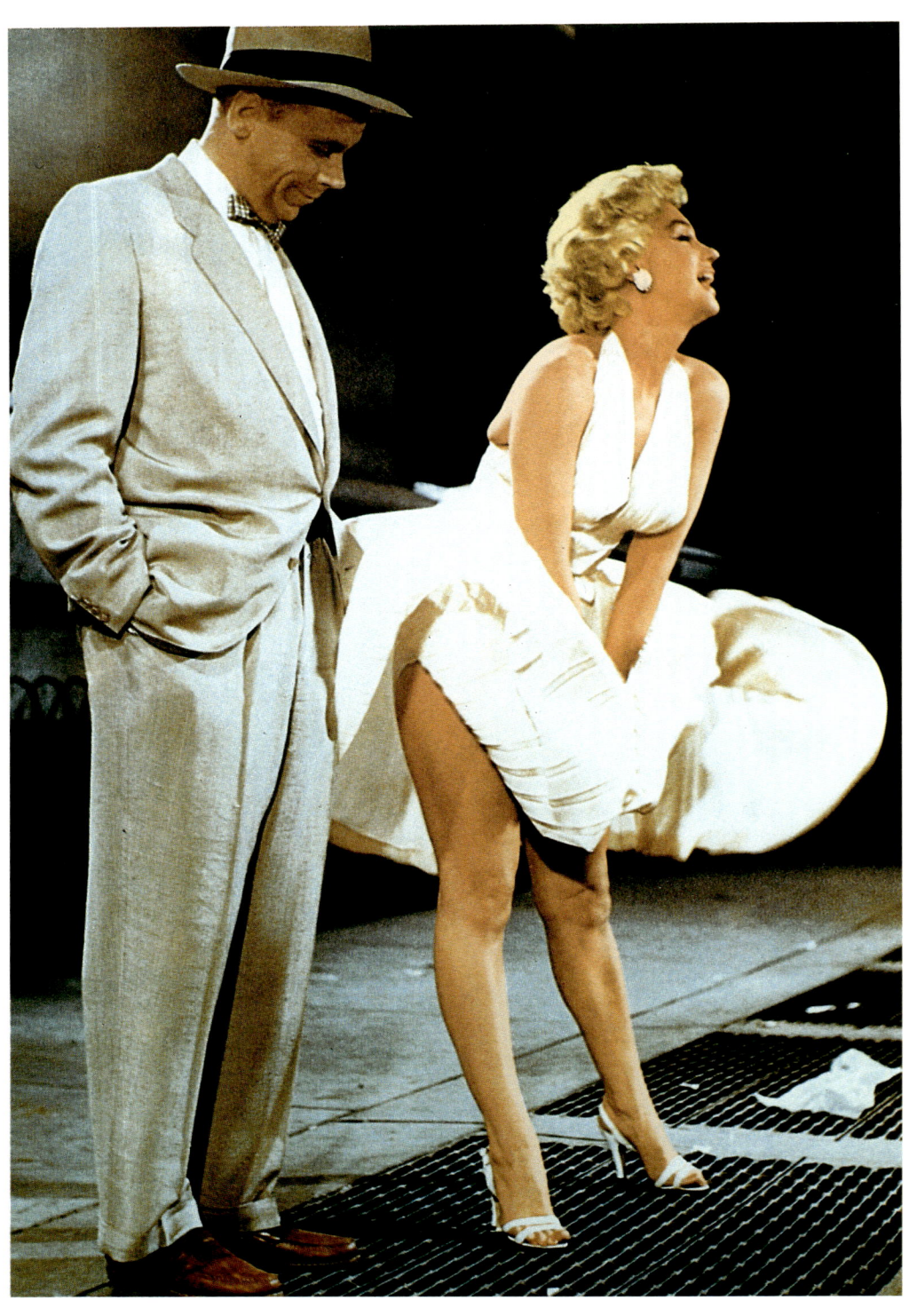

Pages 136/137

Surely the most famous scenes from *The Seven Year Itch,*
photographs of which went around the world like wildfire, show Marilyn on a subway grate
with her skirt flying up. More than four thousand fans,
including many reporters, arrived on location (Lexington Avenue and Fifty-second Street),
in the early-morning hours of September 15, 1954, to witness the spectacle.
Billy Wilder repeated the scene, which gave the film international publicity, more than
fifteen times before he was satisfied. Bruno Bernard
was among the photographers and is responsible for these two extraordinary classics
of all the Marilyn photos.

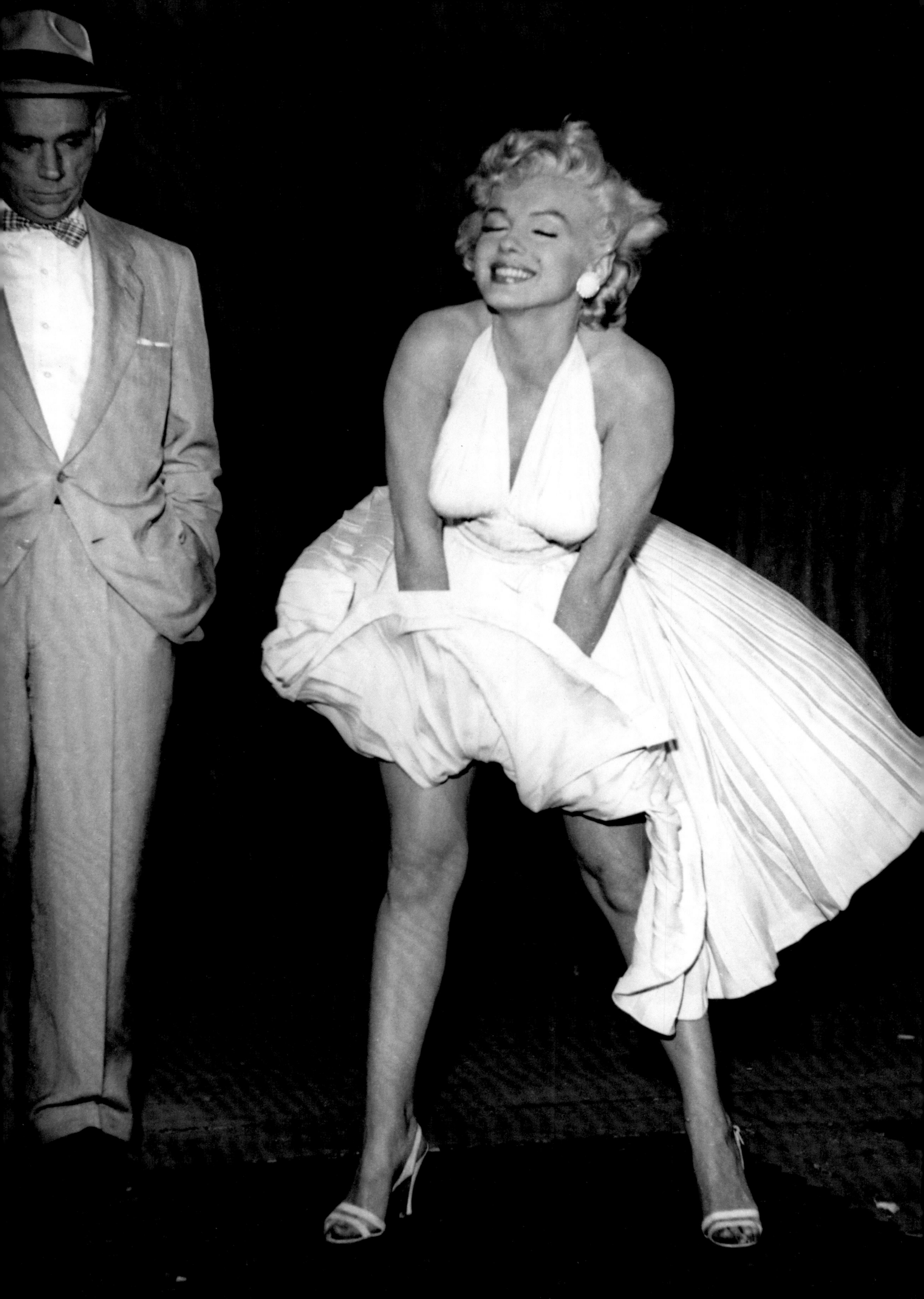

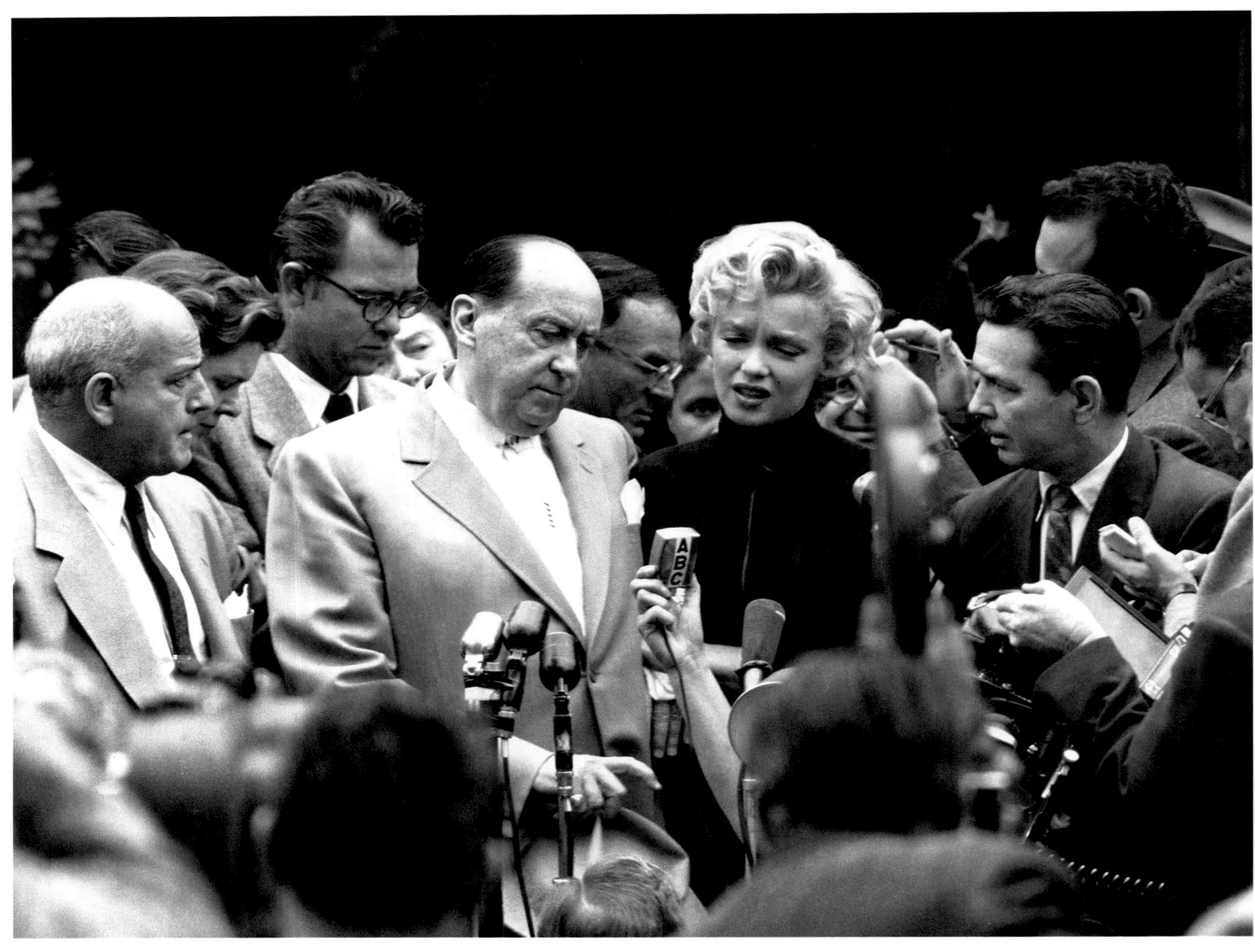

During the shooting of *The Seven Year Itch,* rumors about a marriage crisis began to intensify.
On October 6, 1954, Marilyn, accompanied by her lawyer, Jerry Geisler, appeared before the reporters
who had gathered in front of Marilyn and Joe DiMaggio's house in Beverly Hills. Geisler announced
that a suit for divorce had been filed. Marilyn herself was silent, but she sobbed and burst into
tears before they all drove away. Geisler remarked: "She had nothing to say except that her
application for a divorce is based on a matter of conflicting careers." A witness described the scene and
Marilyn's appearance as "worthy of an Oscar." Again, it is Bruno Bernard (right) who captured the
climax of the scene in a memorable photo. Picture above is from UPI. One day later Marilyn was
back on location for *The Seven Year Itch,* in pink pajamas, shooting one of the funniest scenes
in the movie. This movie was the biggest box-office hit of 1955.

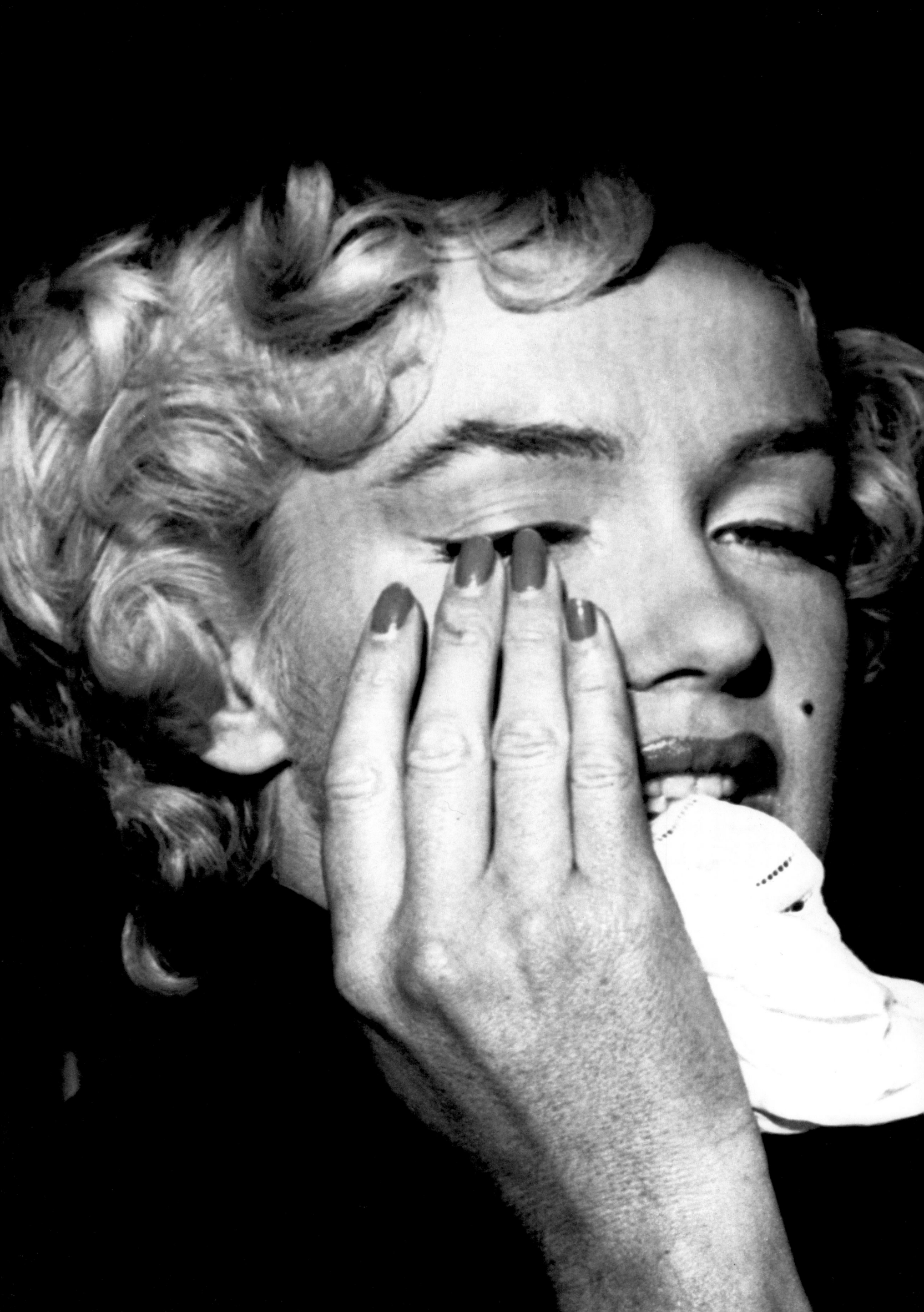

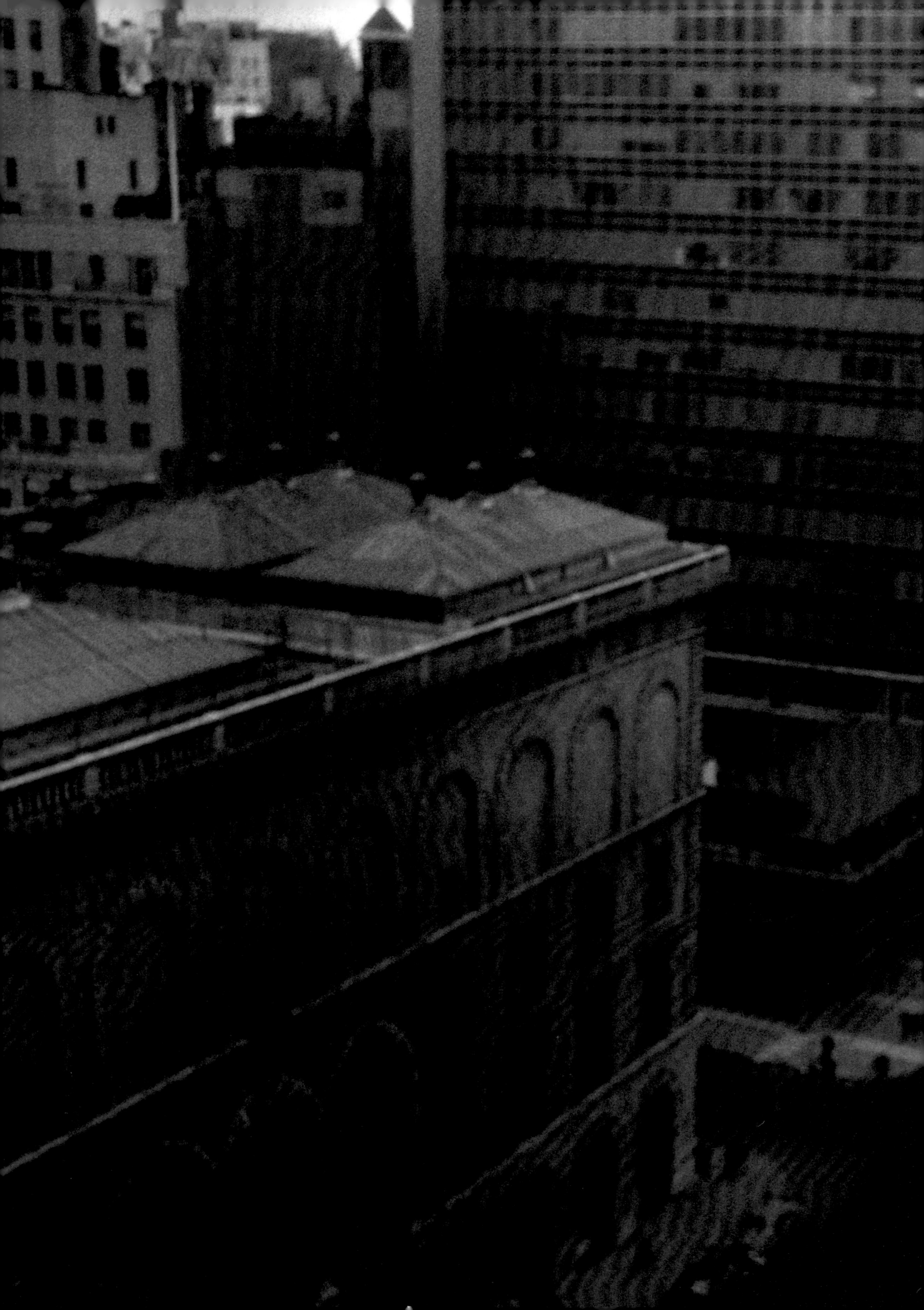

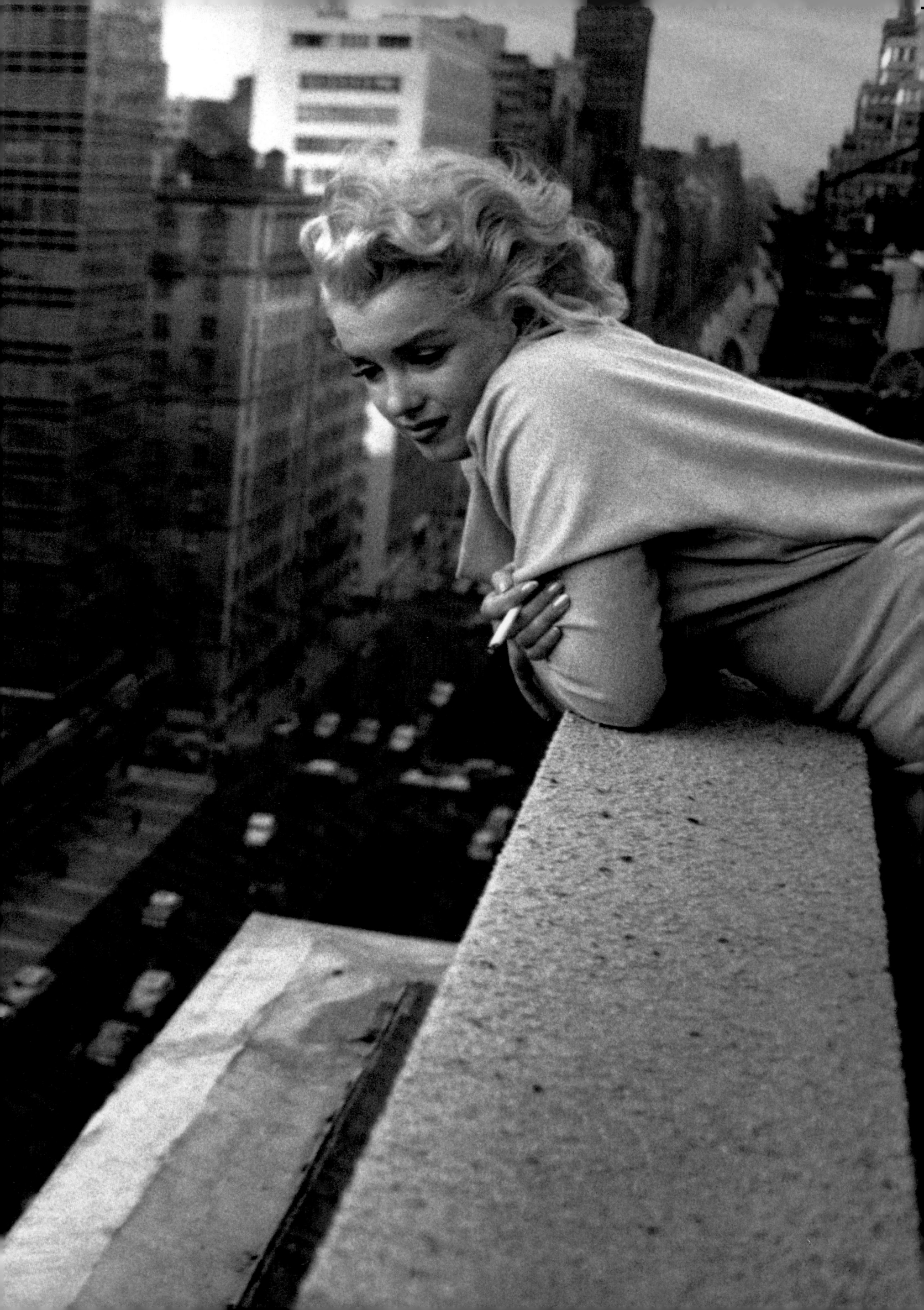

Pages 140/141

After the divorce Marilyn left Hollywood and moved back to New York
accompanied by the photographer Milton H. Greene, who now looked after her personally
and professionally. Commissioned by Greene, the photographer Ed Feingersh
took several pictures of Marilyn in the summer of 1954. This photograph shows a pensive
Marilyn on the balcony of her hotel room.

Page 143

Marilyn in a pose that could illustrate one of her oldest bons mots:
when asked by a journalist what she wore in bed, she answered, "Chanel Number Five."
Photograph by Ed Feingersh, 1955.

Pages 144/145

On March 9, 1955, Marilyn Monroe took the part of an usherette
at the Astor Theater, New York, for the charity premiere of the film *East of Eden,* directed by
Elia Kazan for Warner Bros. James Dean, the star of the film,
died six months later. The proceeds of the benefit went to the Actors Studio.
Marilyn devotedly posed for the crowd of photographers.
Picture left is by Frank Maestro of UPI.

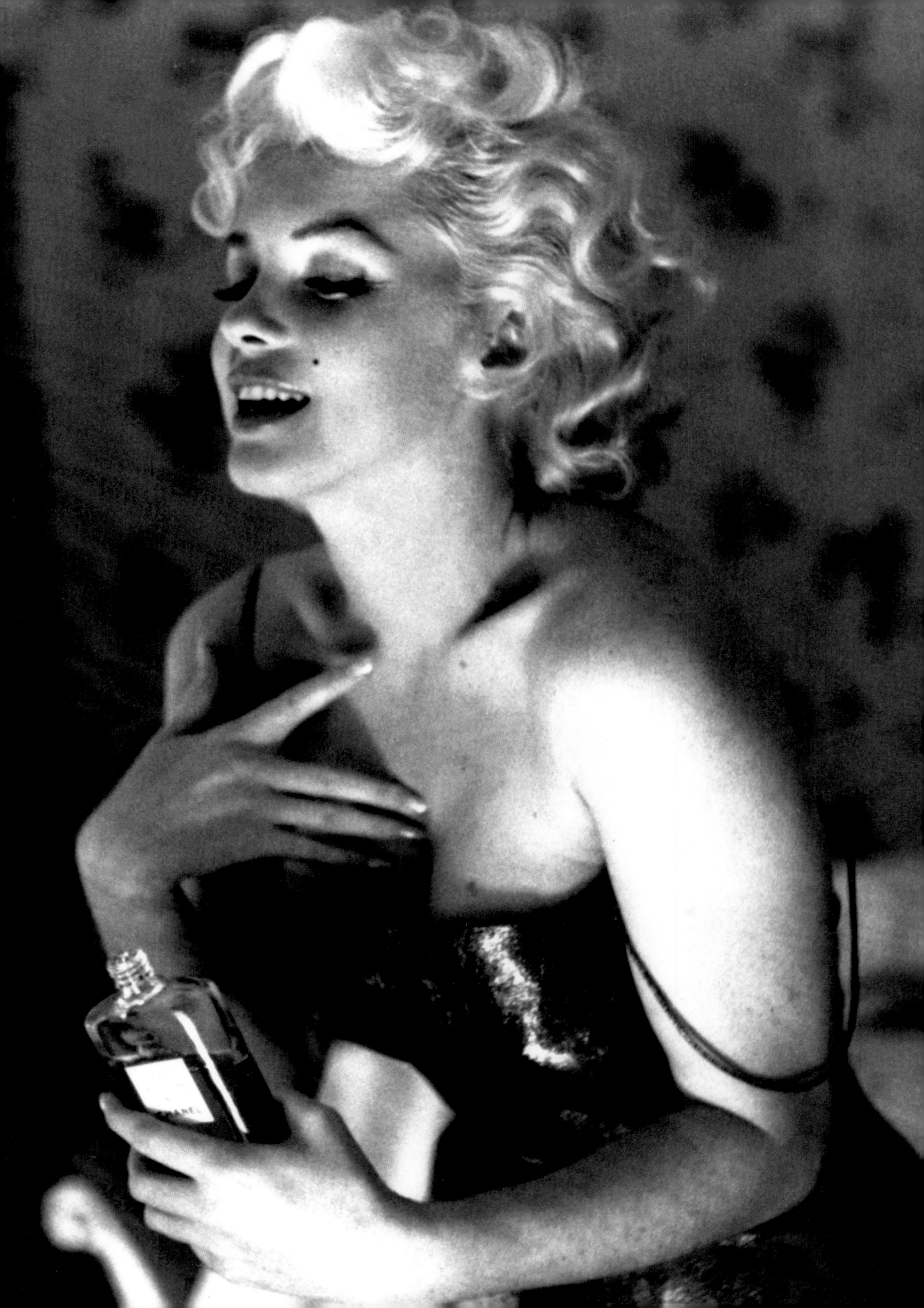

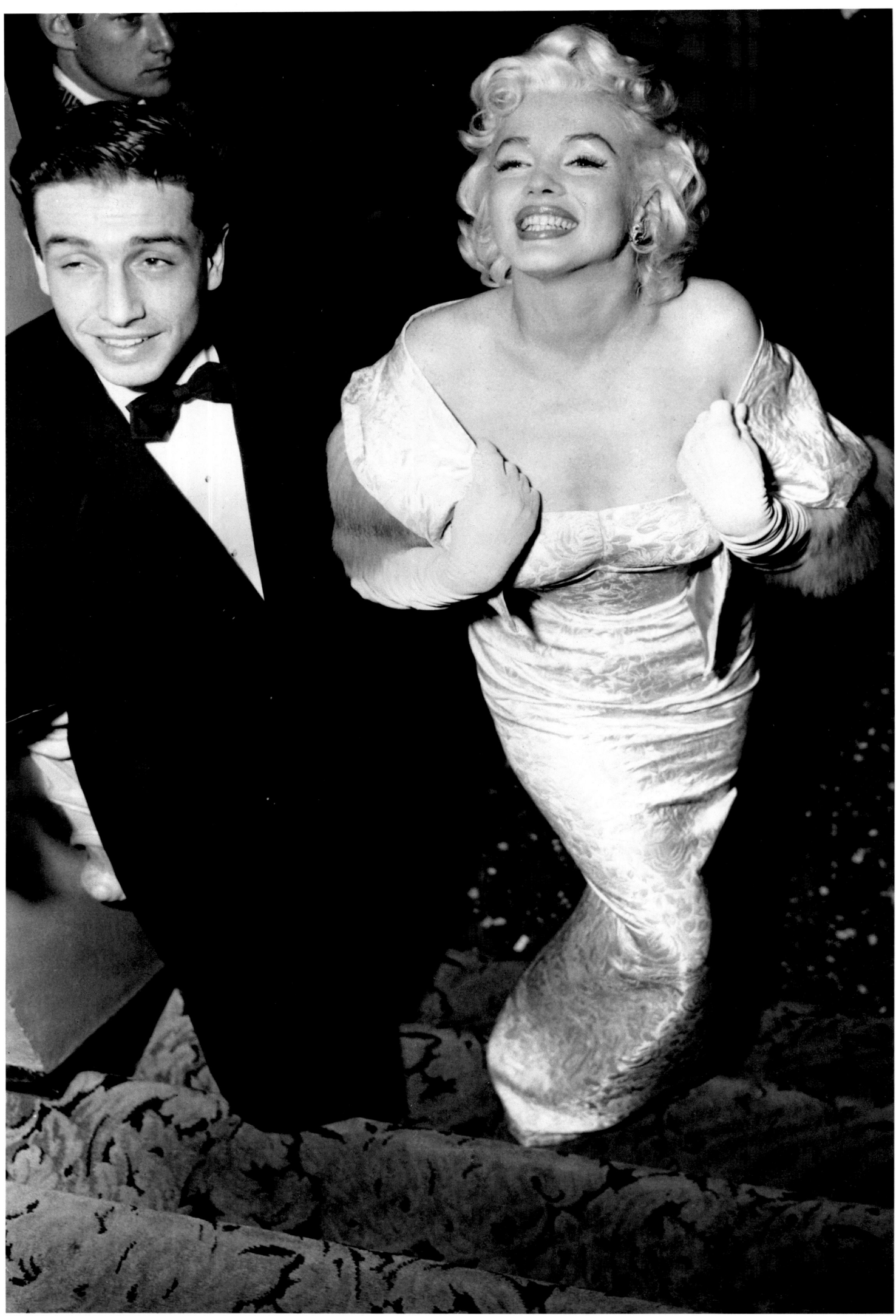

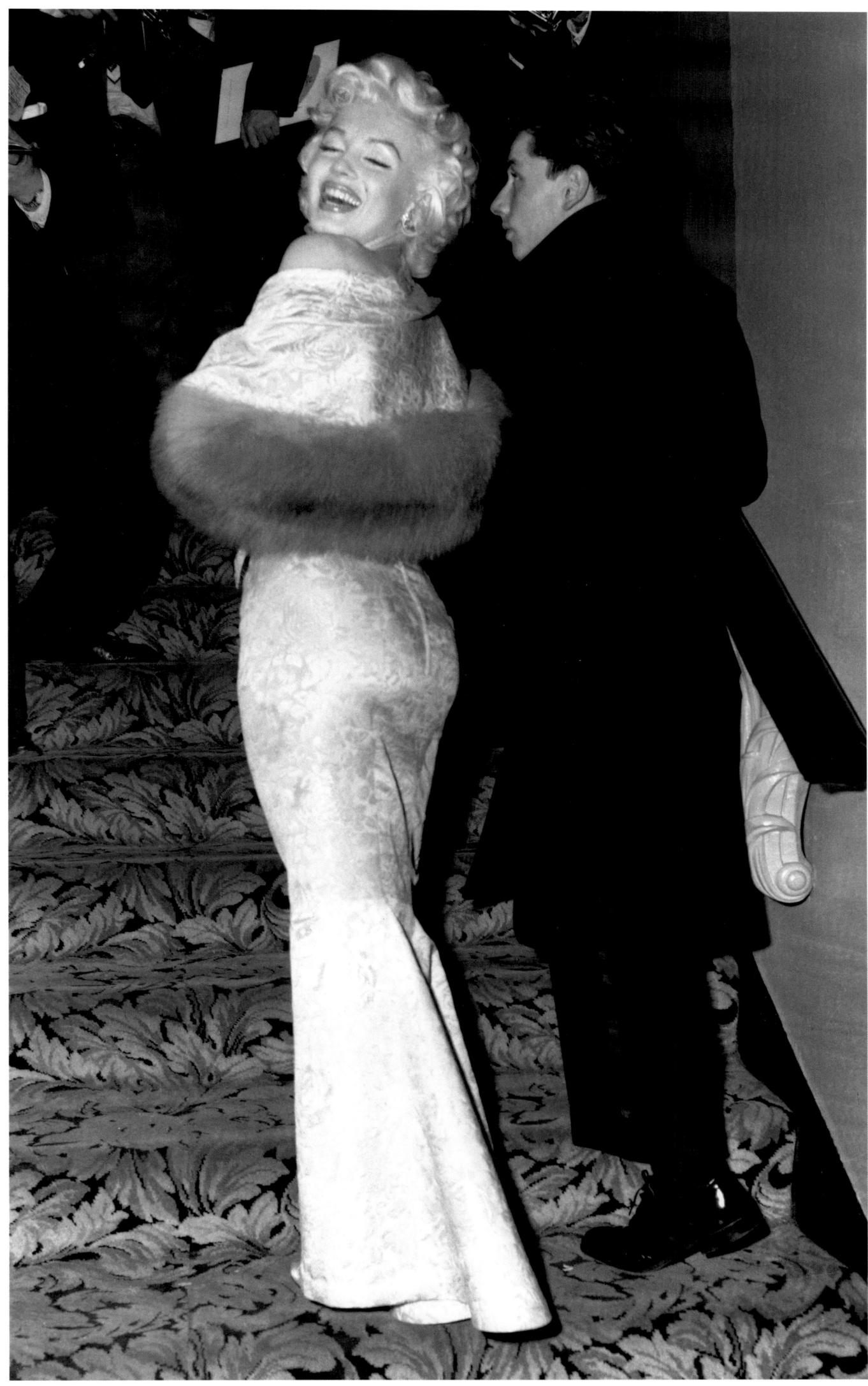

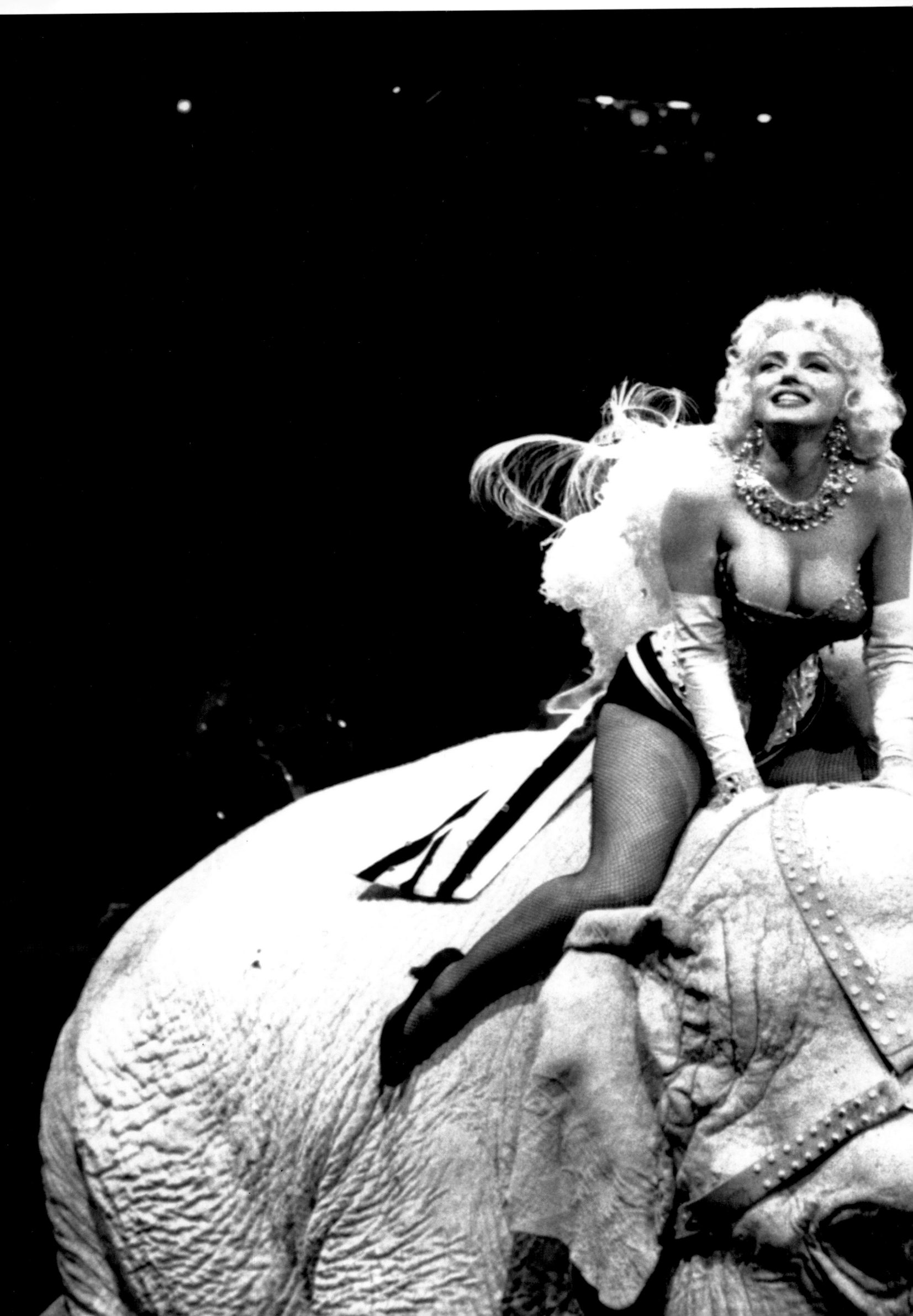

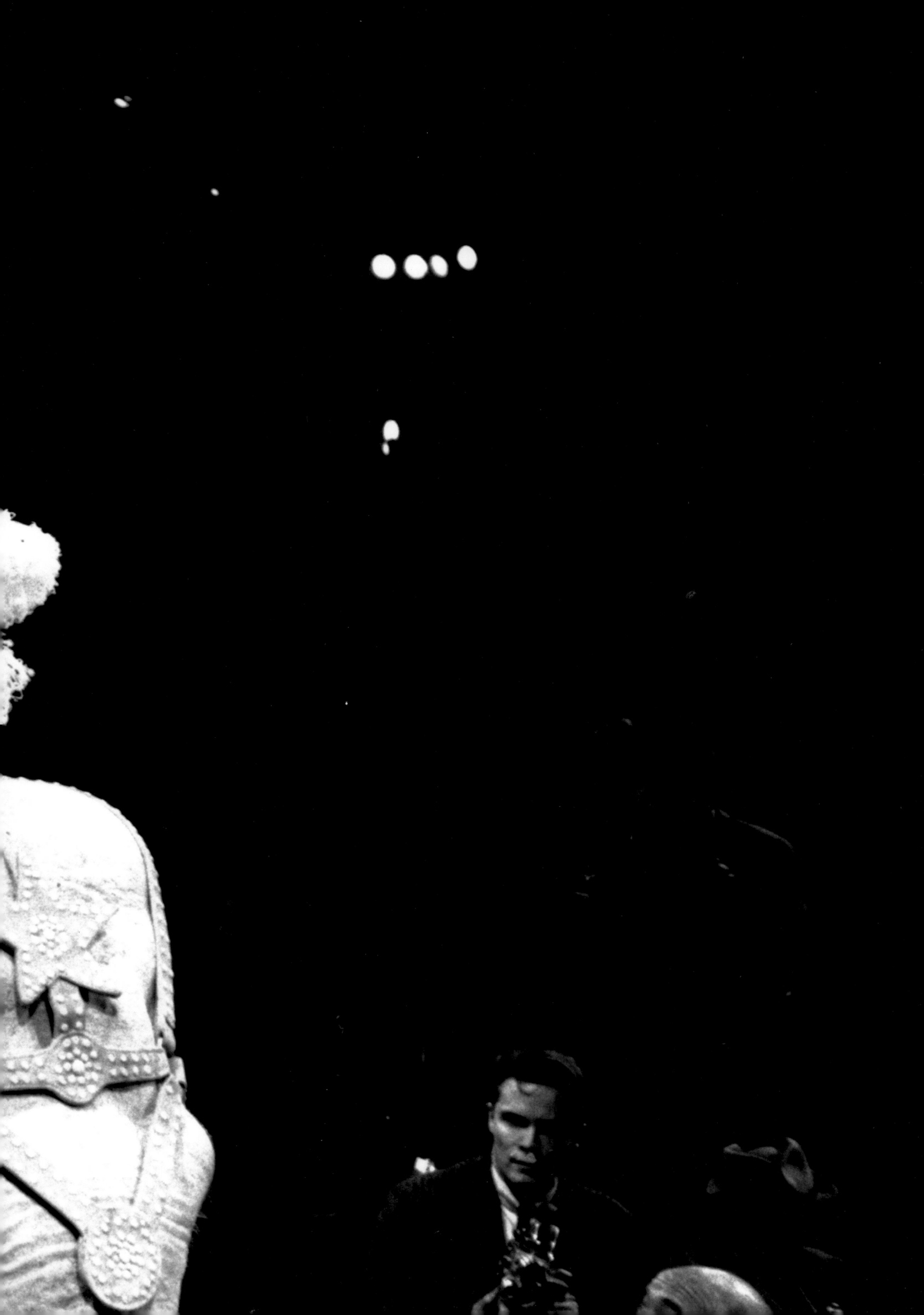

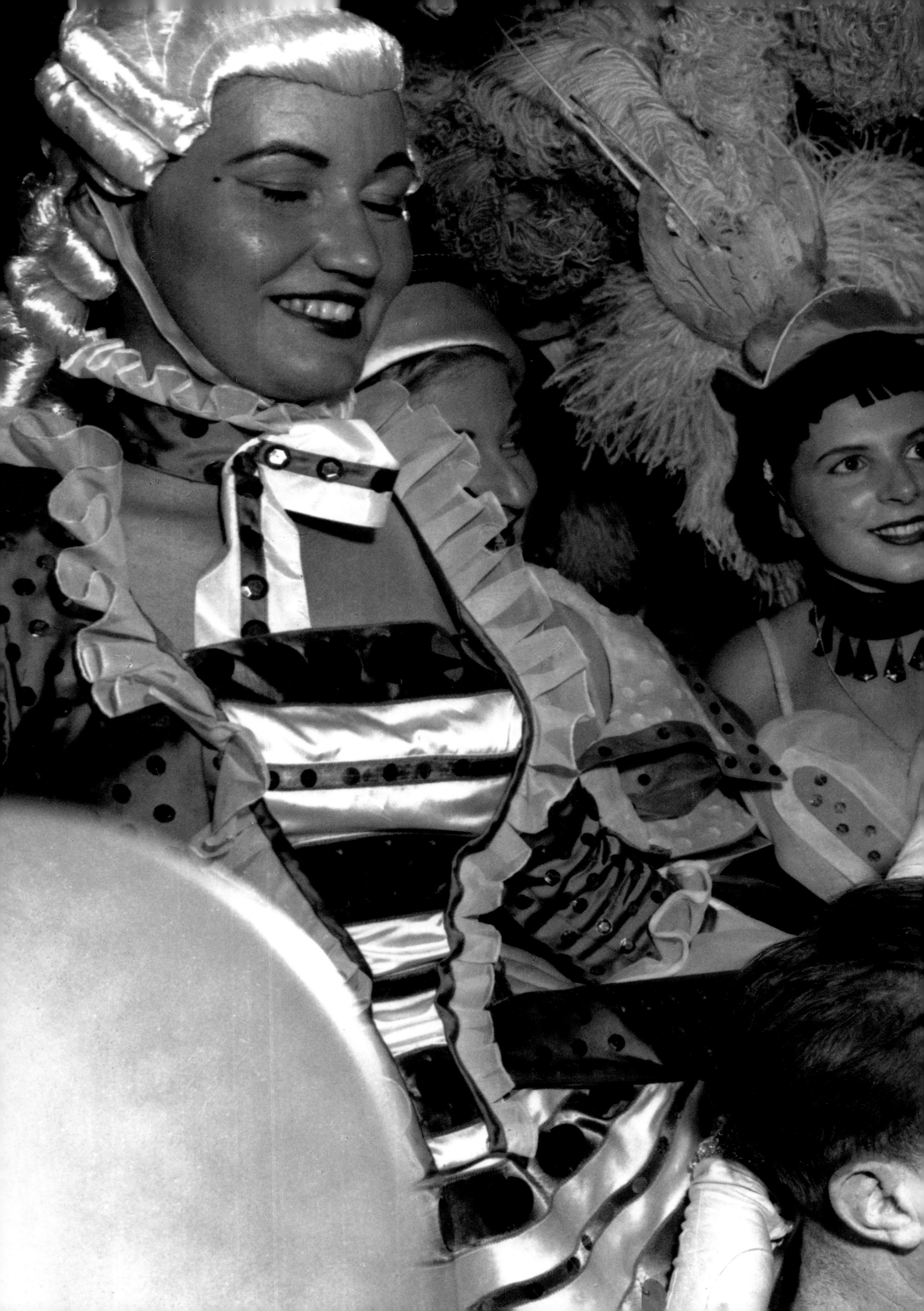

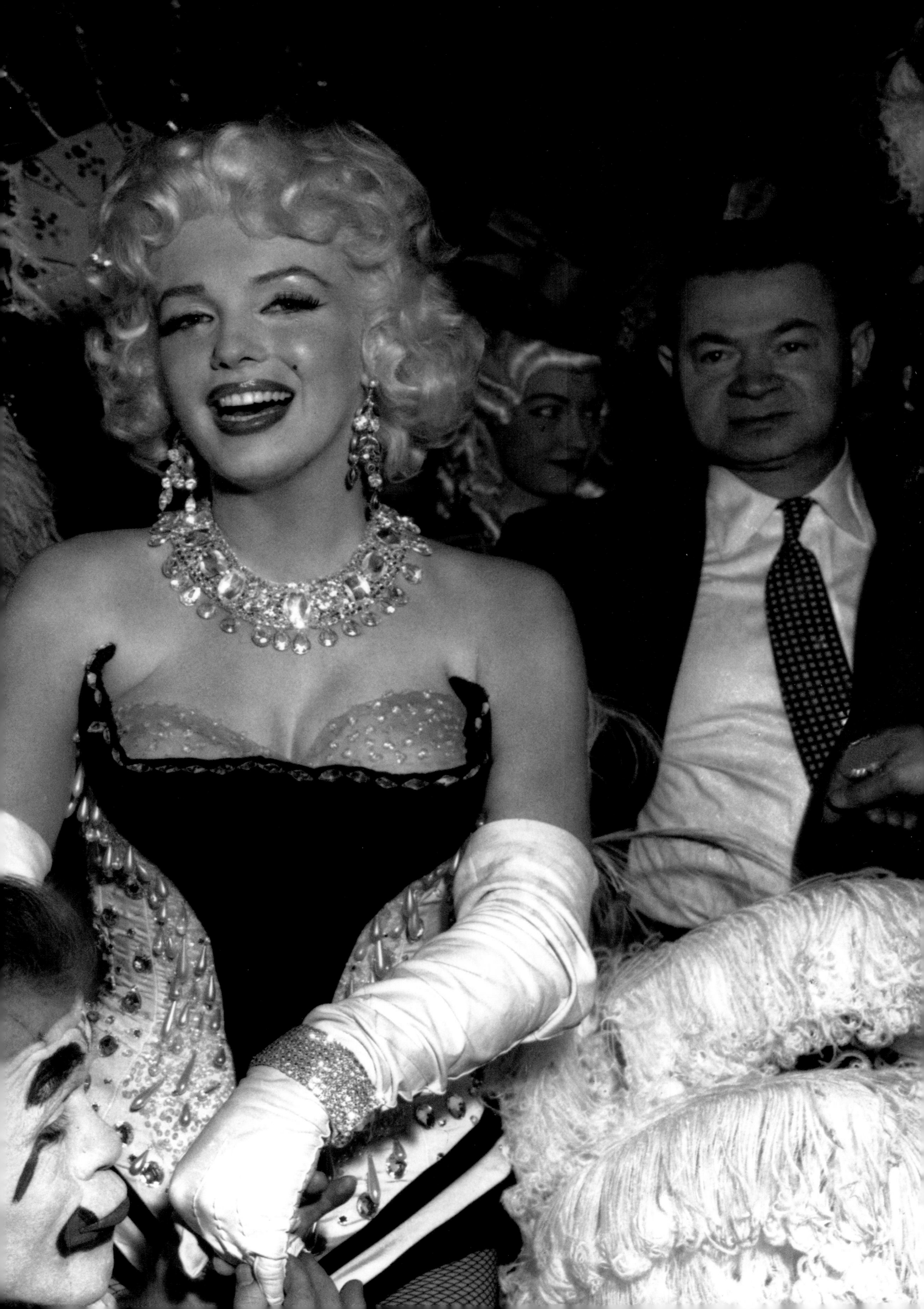

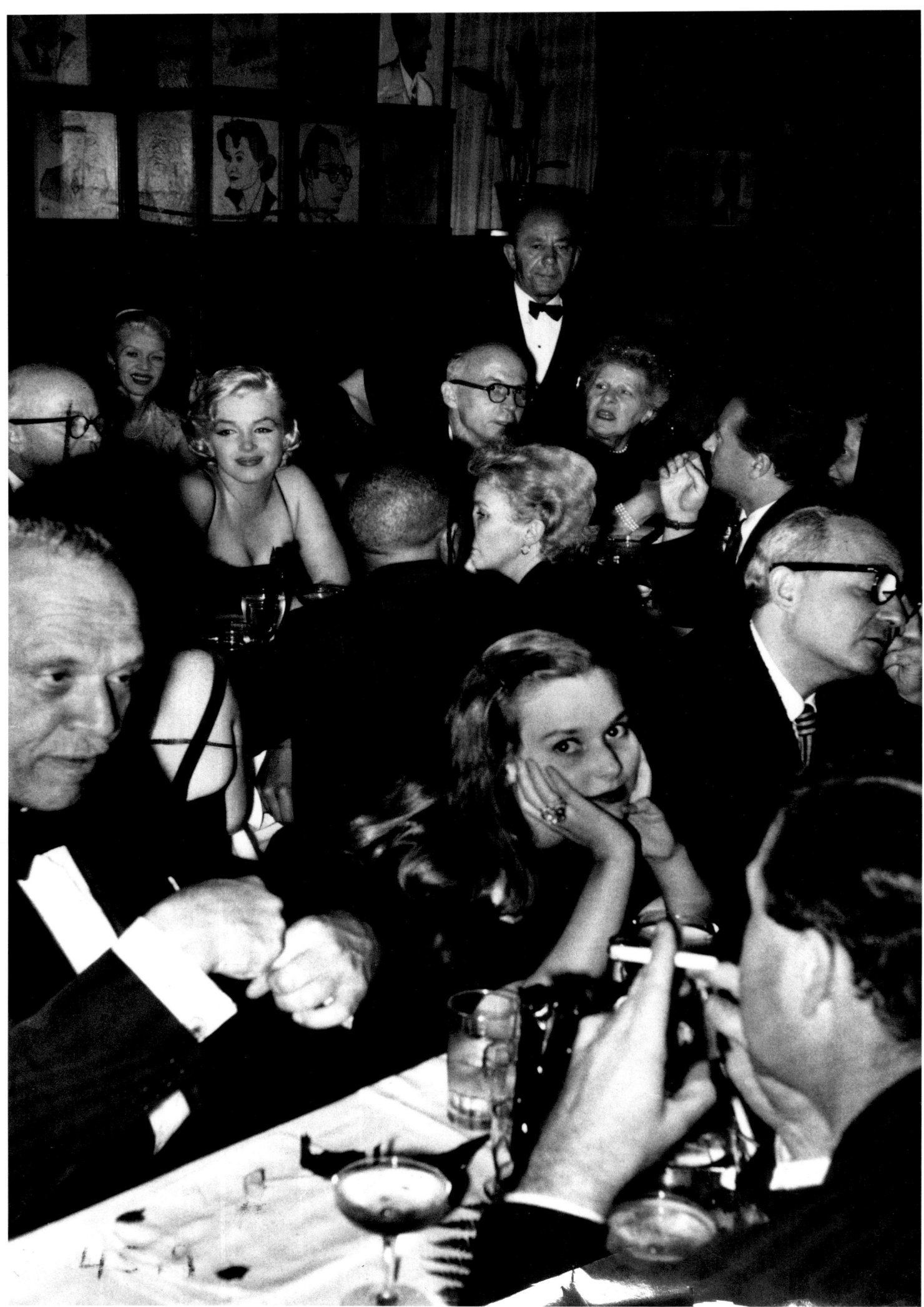

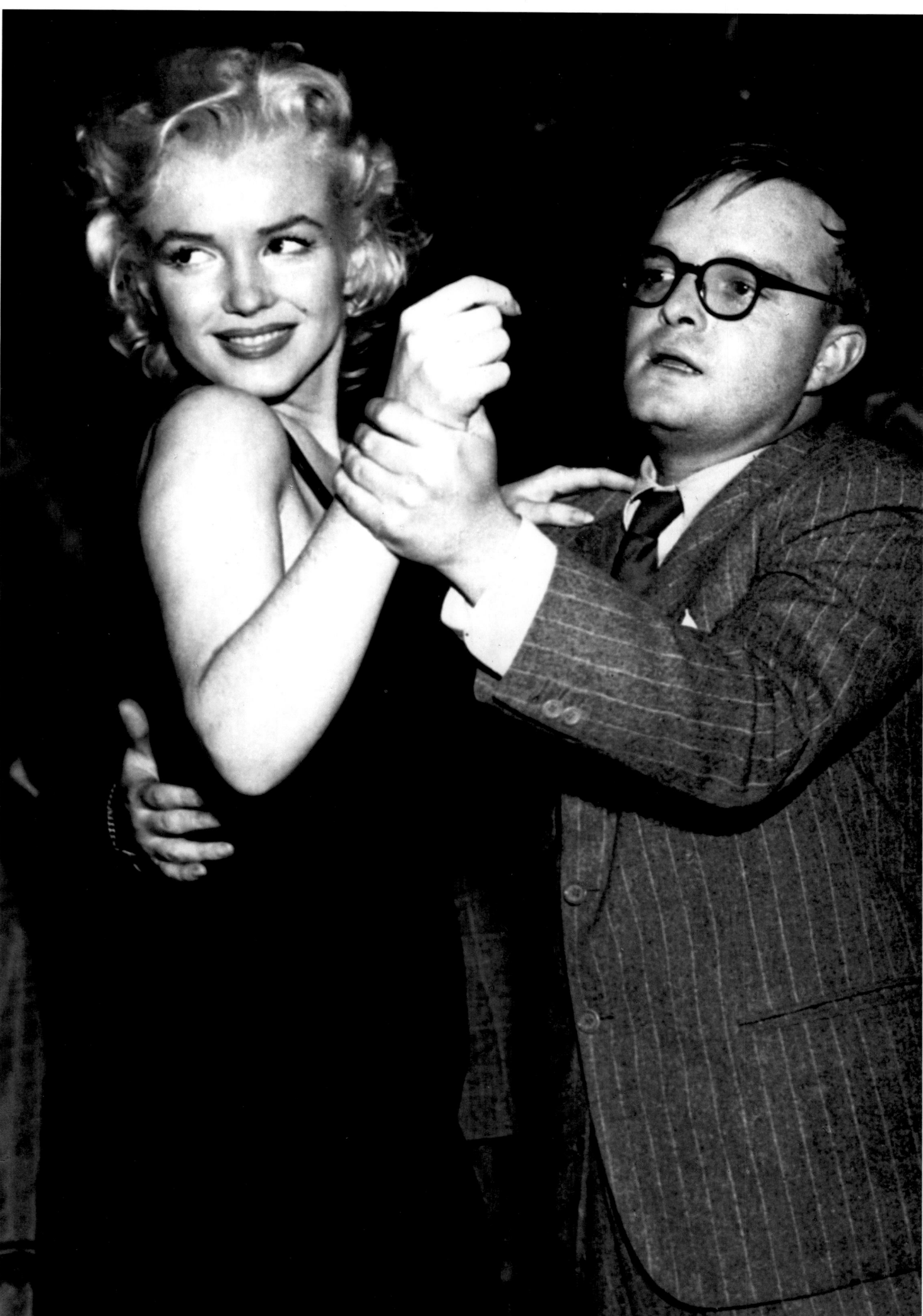

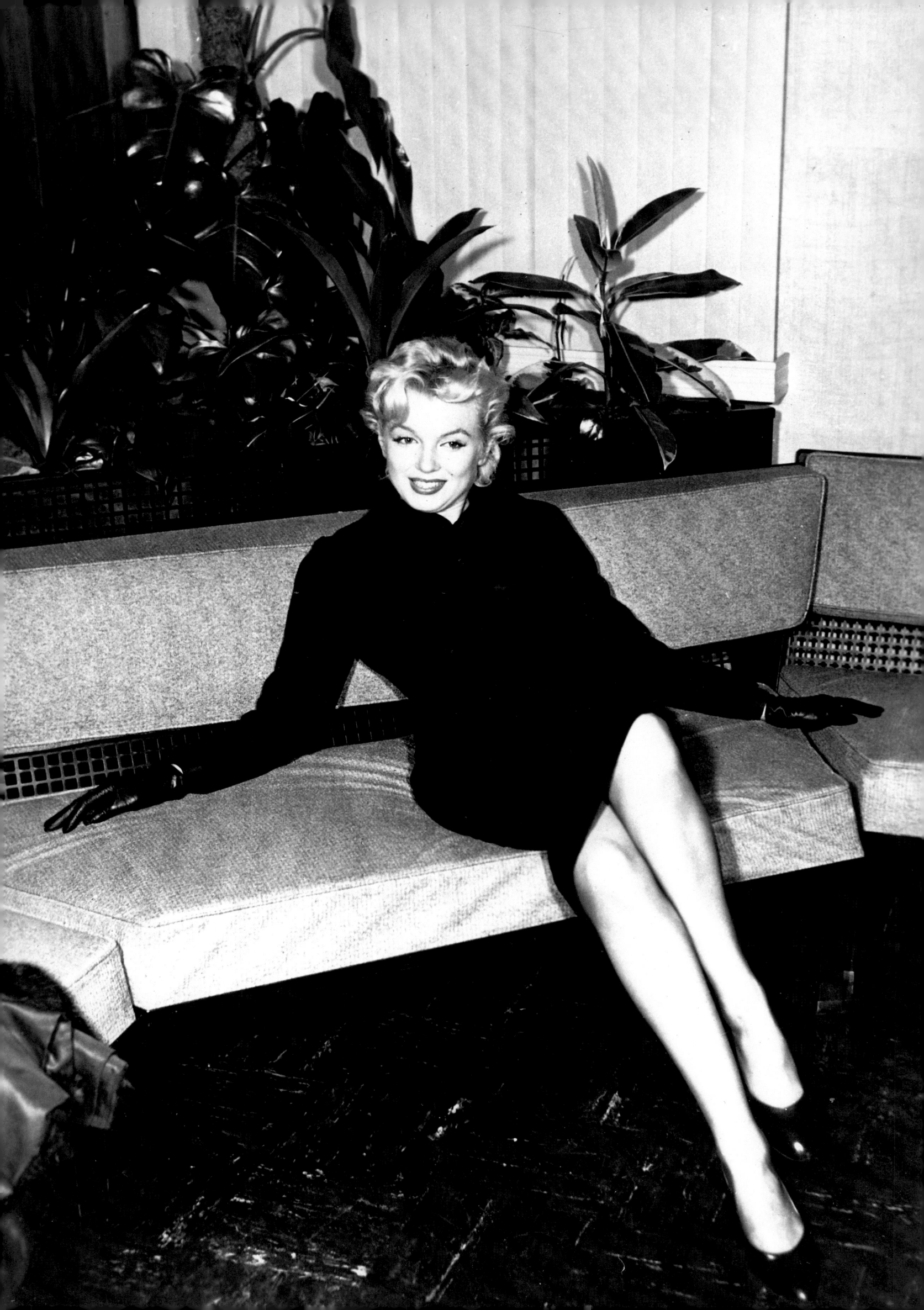

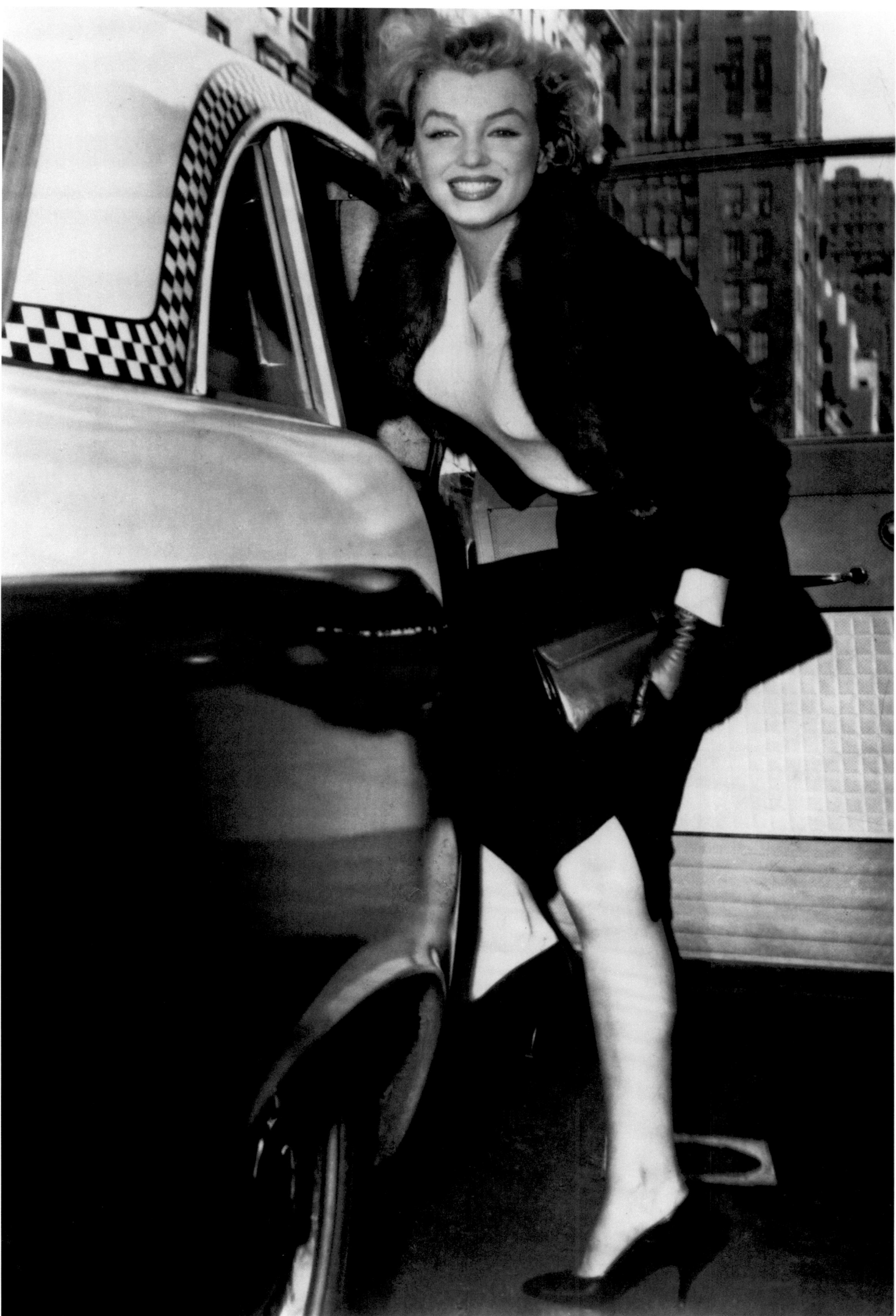

Page 154

One of the many publicity events that Milton H. Greene
arranged for Marilyn during her self-imposed exile from Hollywood was her big appearance
on Edward R. Murrow's television show "Person to Person,"
broadcast in April 1955 to more than fifty million viewers in the United States.

Page 155

Marilyn getting into a taxi in New York City. No opportunity seems too trivial for the photographers, and no photographer that Marilyn is not willing to grace with a beaming smile.
Photograph about 1955.

Page 157

Marilyn's move from Hollywood to New York, the phenomenal success of *The Seven Year Itch,* and
the founding of her own production firm, the first project of which was to be a film with Laurence
Olivier, all carefully managed by Milton H. Greene, strengthened her position vis-à-vis 20th Century-
Fox to such an extent that she was given a contract granting her extensive rights in selecting
future film projects. In February 1956 shooting began for the 20th Century-Fox production *Bus Stop.*
Marilyn chose the story herself, as well as the director for it. The publicity stills were taken by
Greene. During the shooting a cover story in *Time* appeared, which spoke of Marilyn's wish "to be a
real actress" and added: "In *Bus Stop* she has the chance to show what she can do with the first part
she has ever played that is any deeper than her makeup." For many critics, Marilyn's portrayal of
Cherie in *Bus Stop* was her most significant accomplishment as an actress.

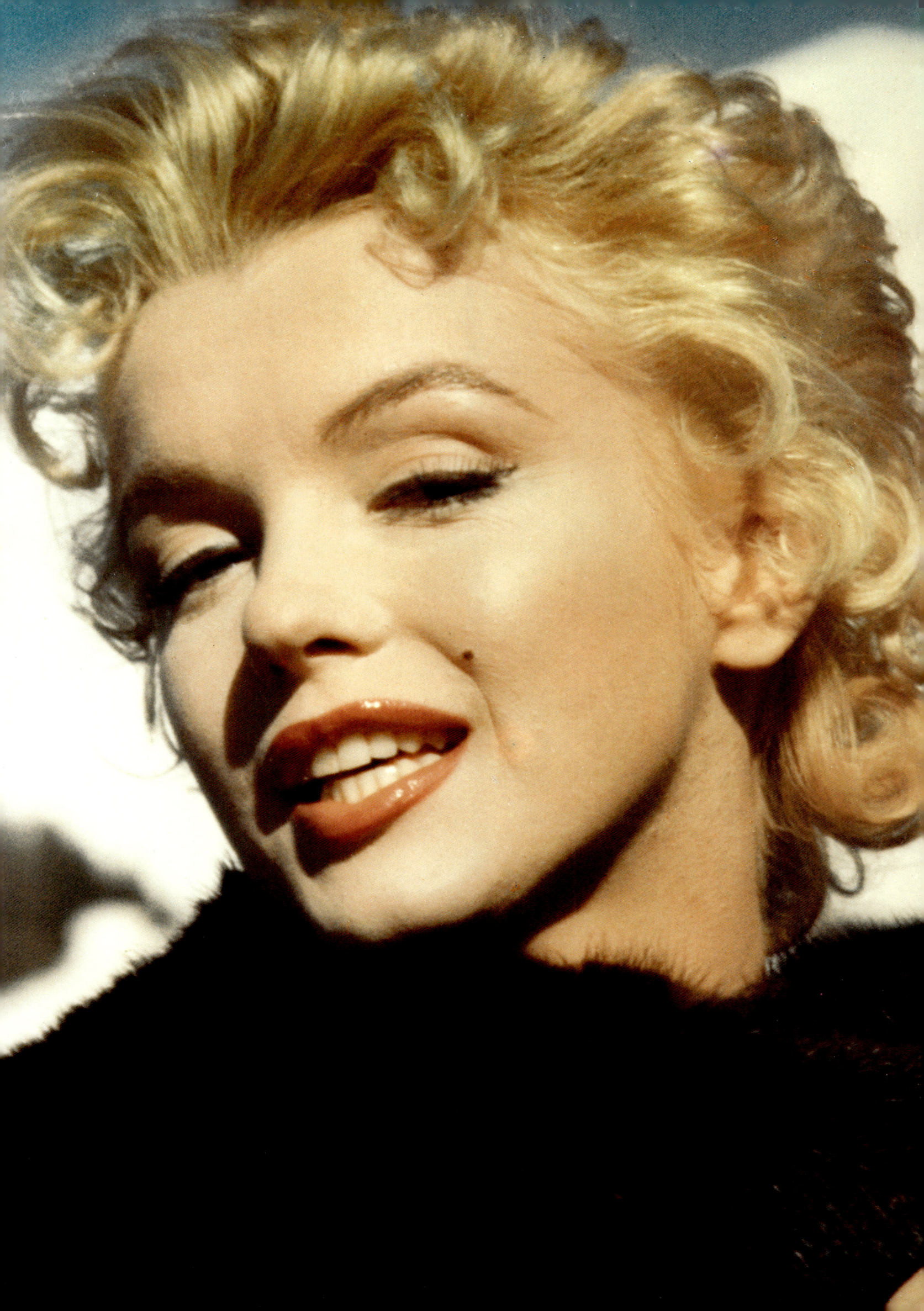

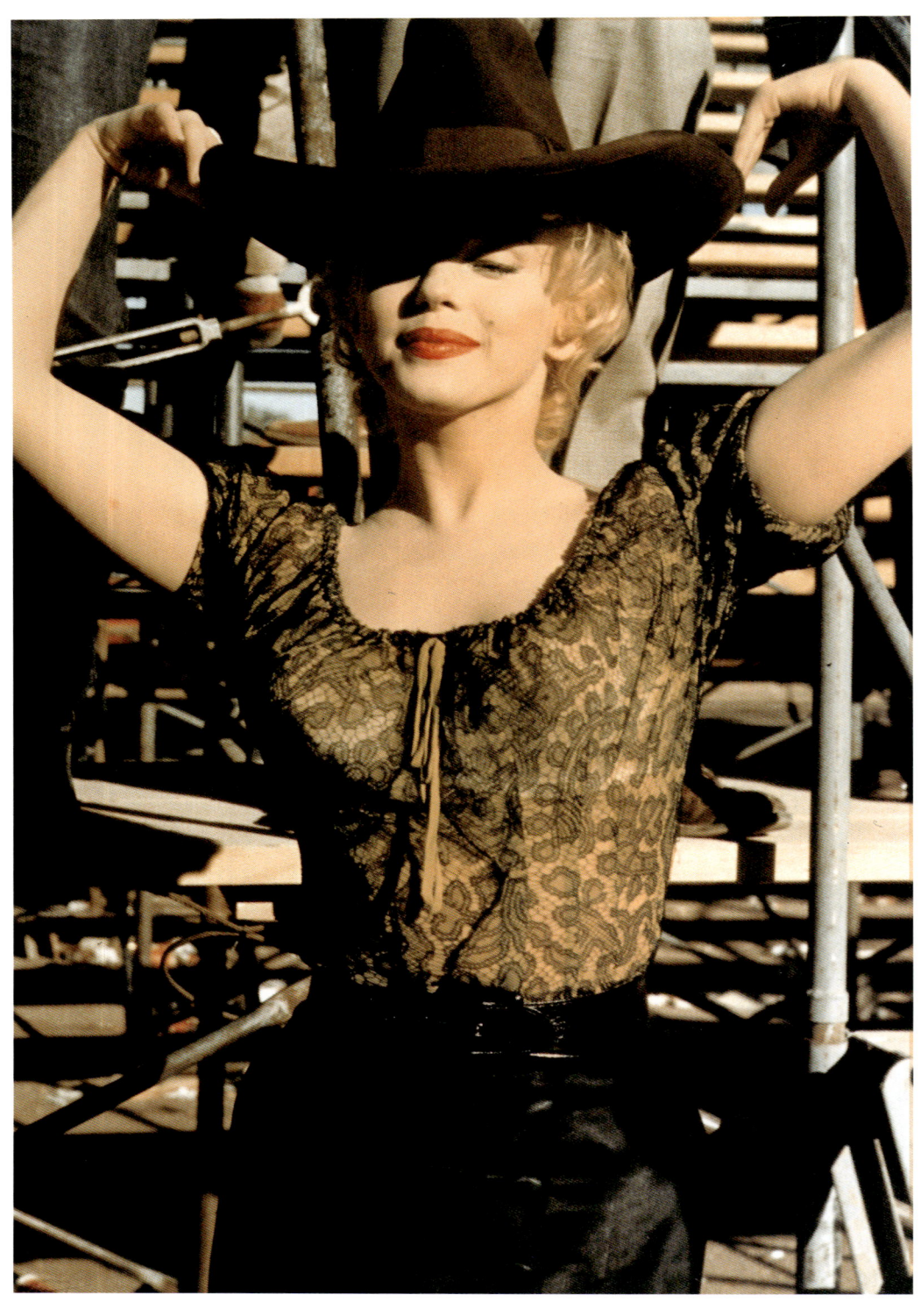

Pages 158–161

Publicity stills for *Bus Stop* by Milton H. Greene.

Pages 162/163

After the filming of *Bus Stop* was completed,
and one day after her thirtieth birthday, Marilyn and Milton Greene returned to New York
from the West Coast. Both the photo at Idlewild Airport and the portrait
in the backseat of her limousine show a confident young woman at the pinnacle of her
artistic, personal, and financial success. Photographs by UPI.

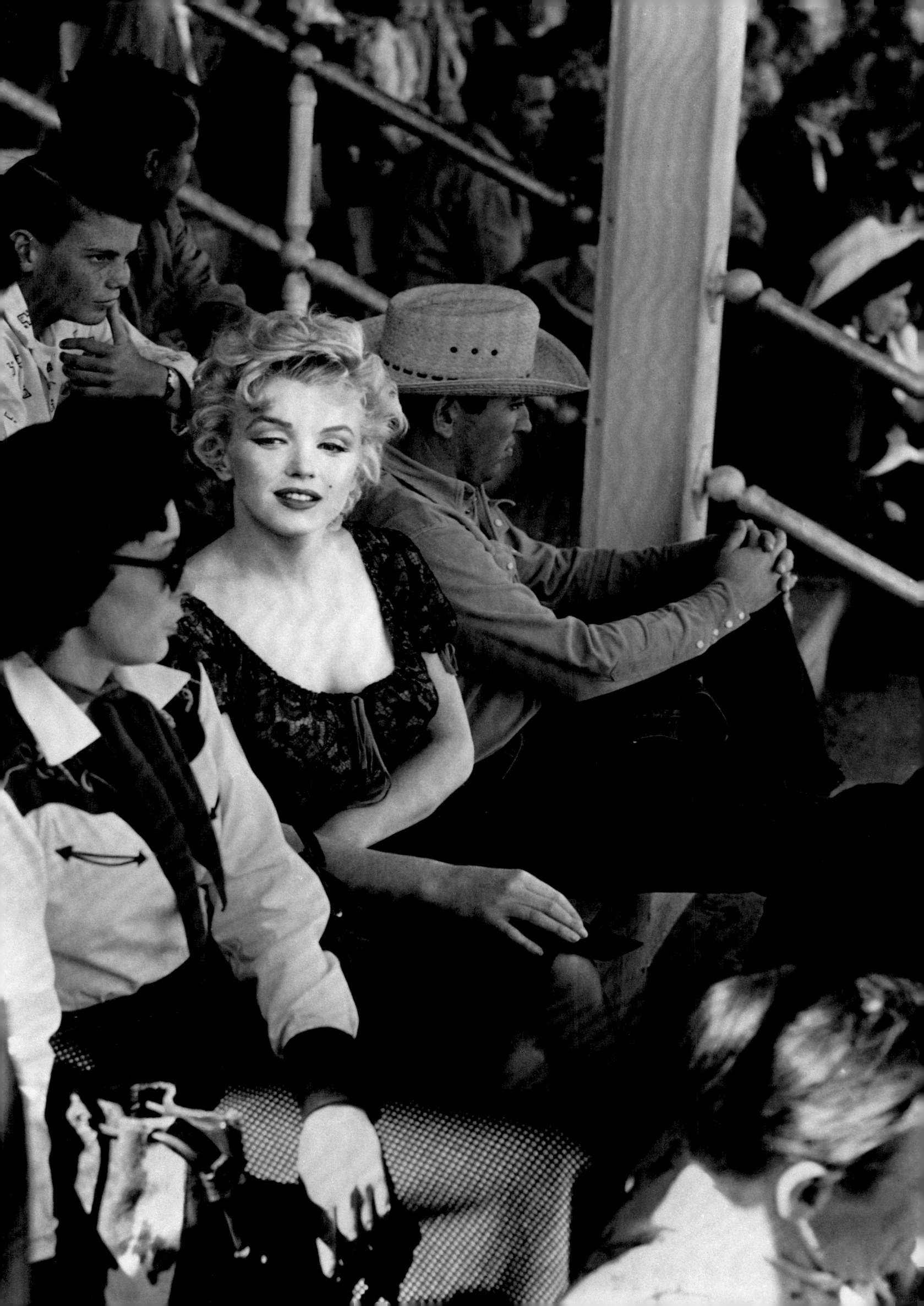

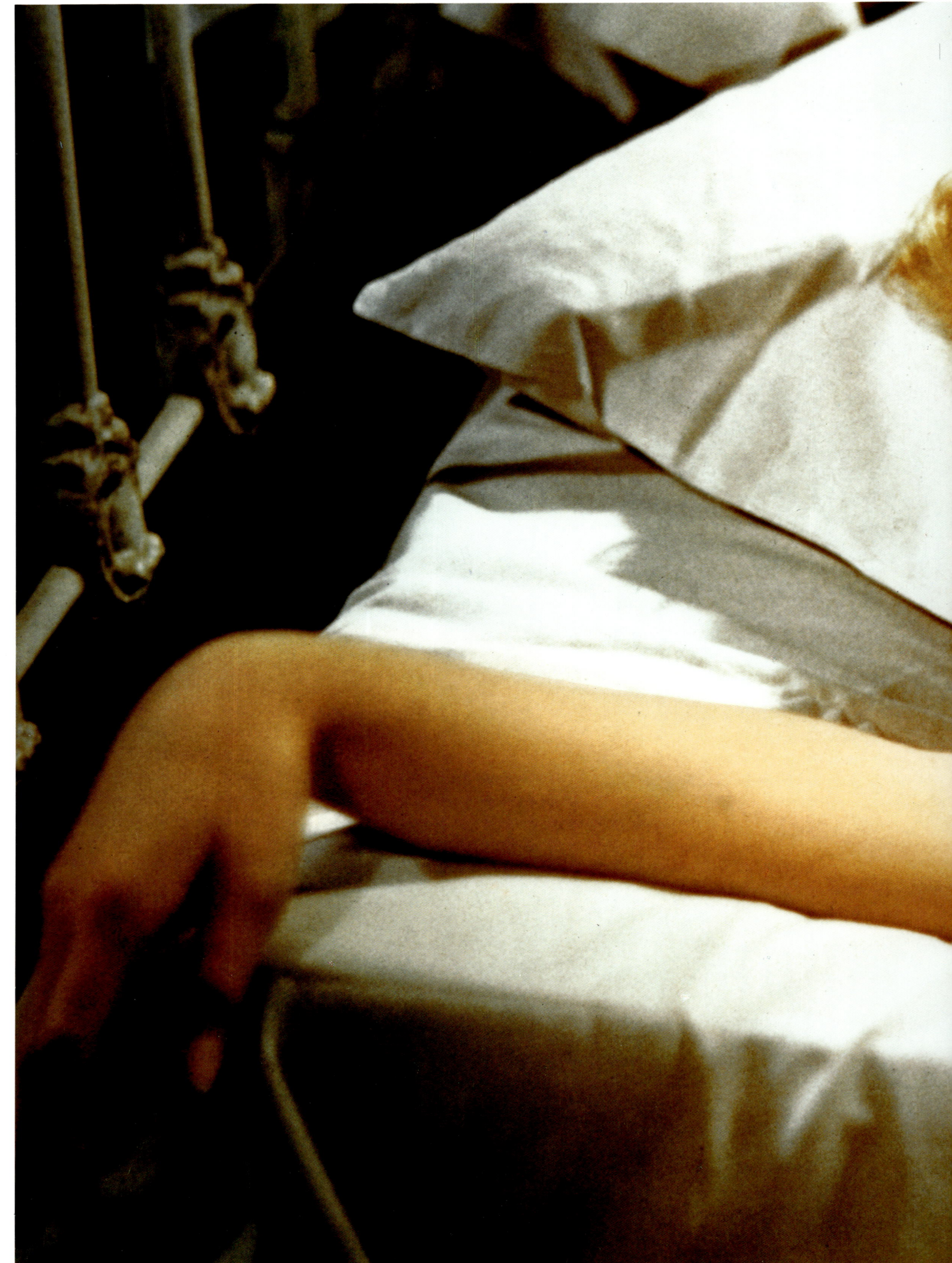

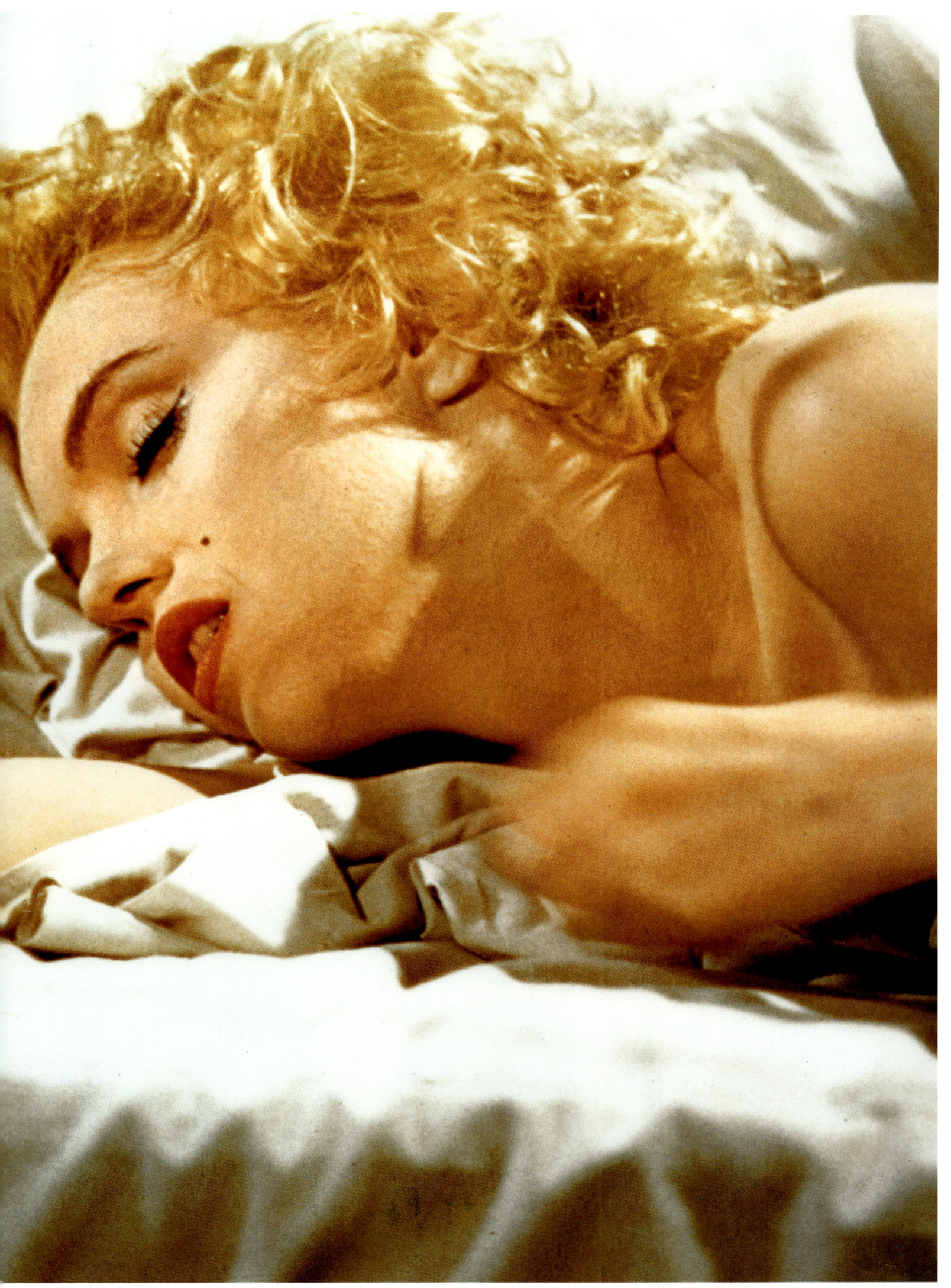

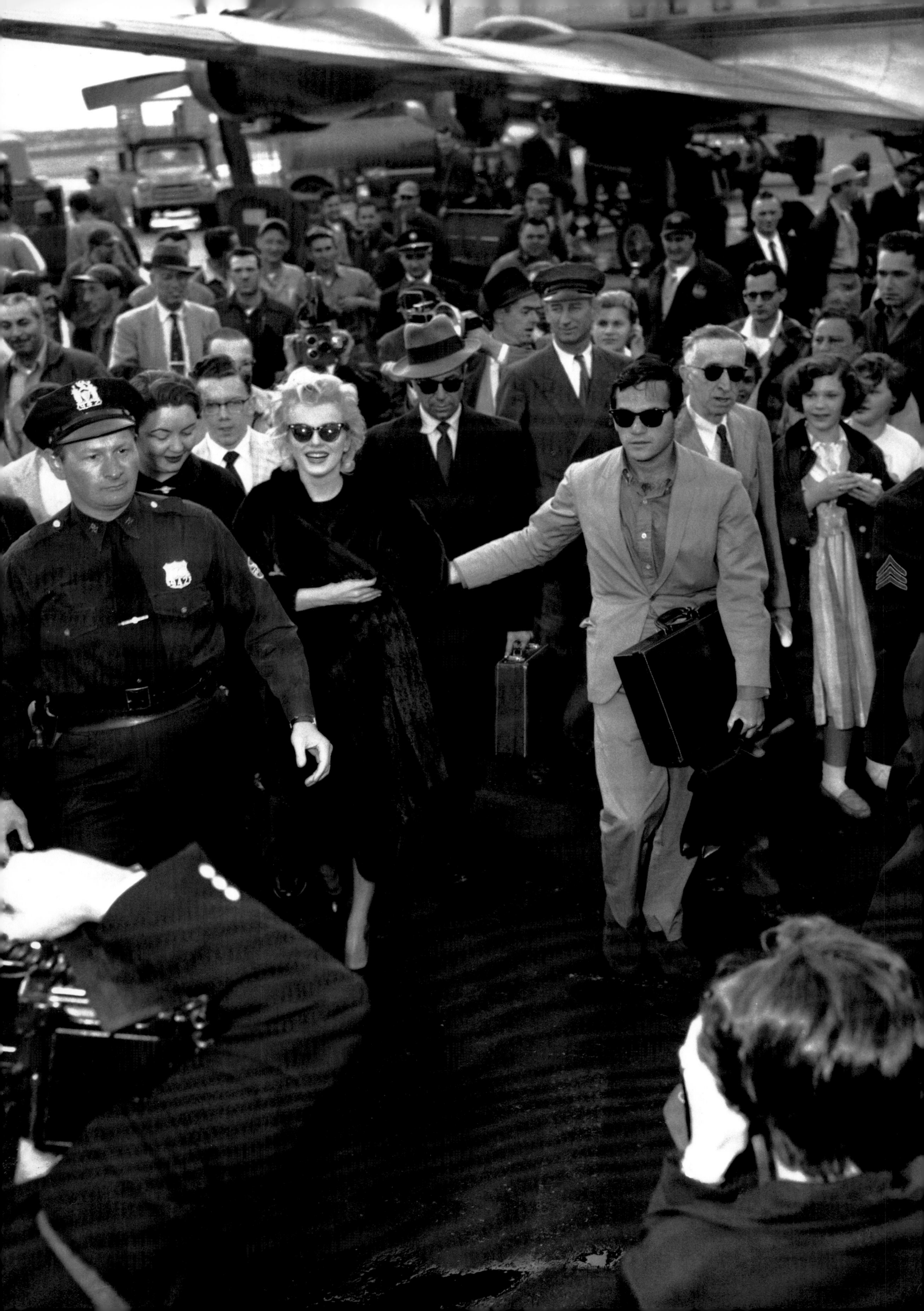

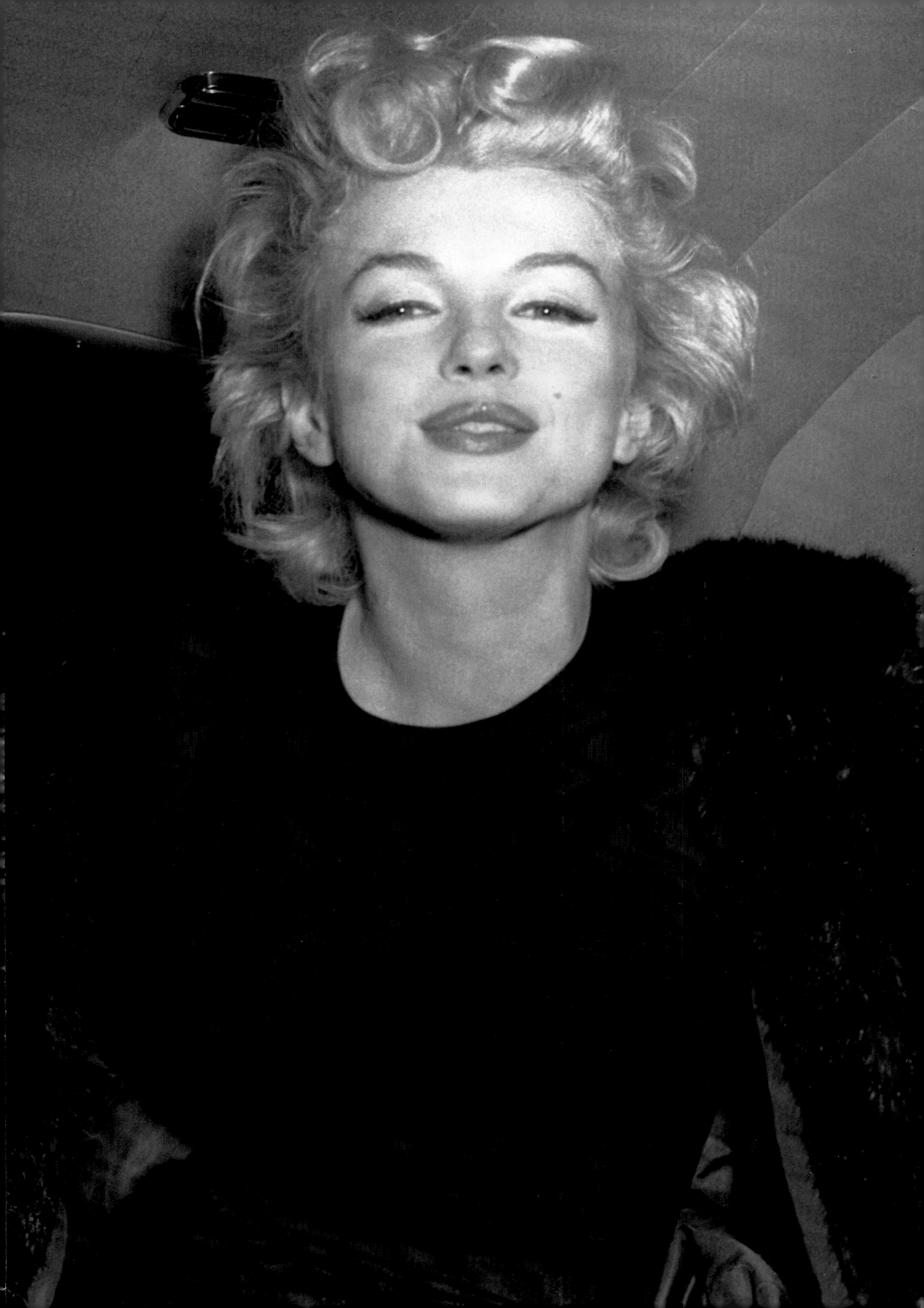

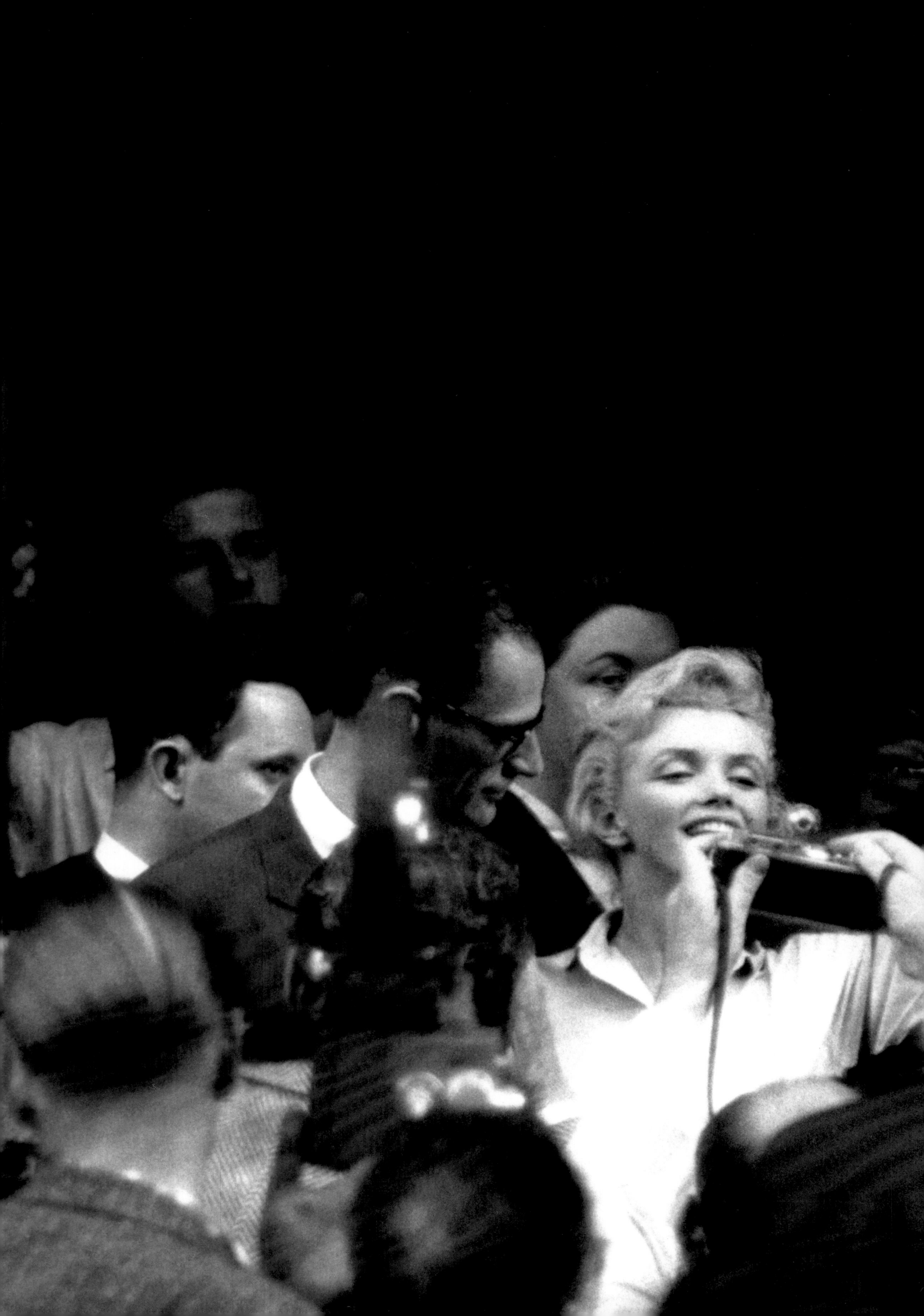

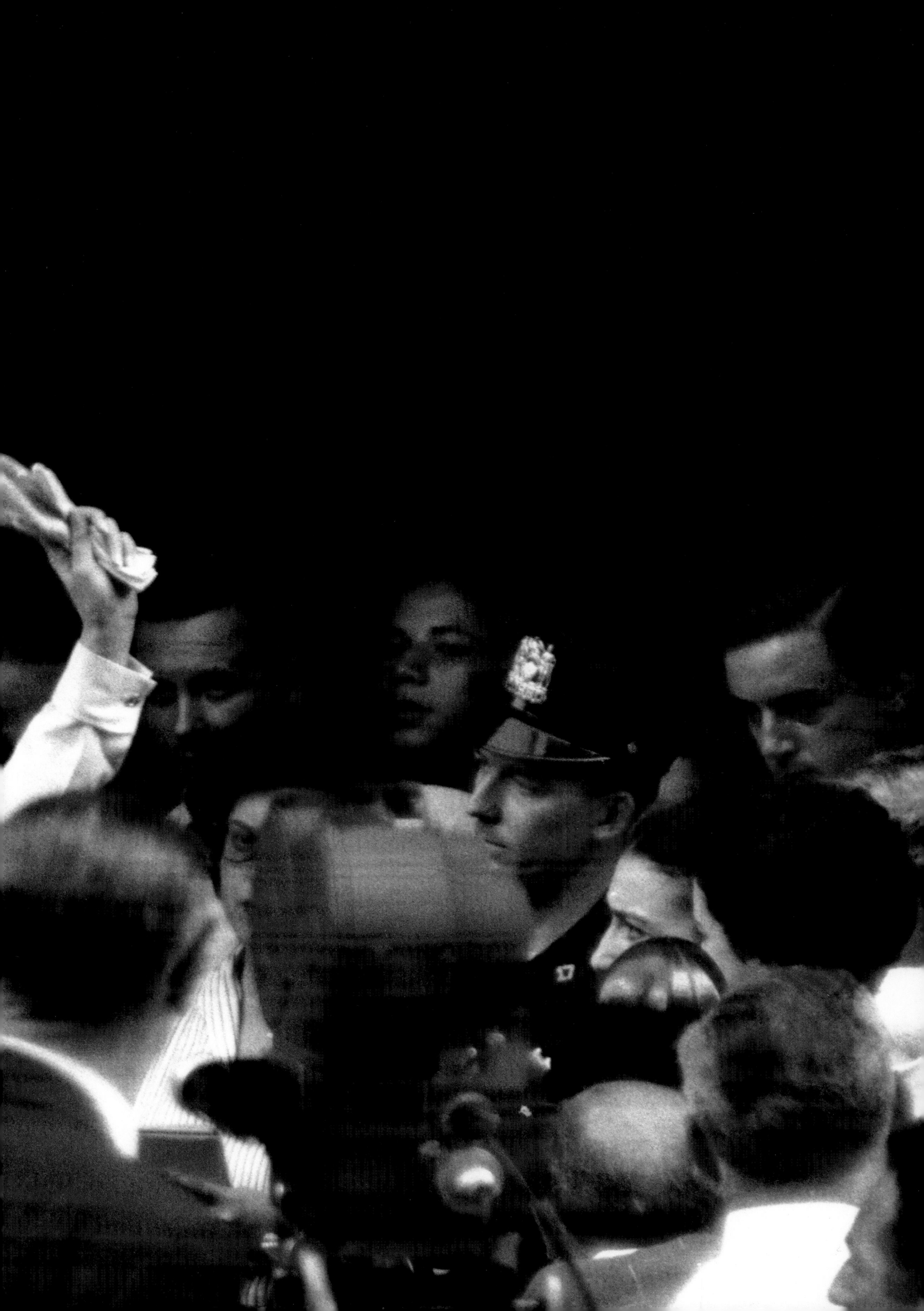

Pages 164/165

On June 20, 1956, the *New York Post* ran the story
of the imminent marriage between Marilyn and Arthur Miller. The civil ceremony was on
June 29, followed by the wedding according to Jewish ritual on July 1,
for which Marilyn had converted to Judaism. The marriage of America's most famous
contemporary playwright to the film star was an eruptive publicity event
and made headlines around the world. The picture shows Marilyn and Arthur Miller at the
turbulent press conference in front of their house
in New York, where they officially announced their wedding plans.

Page 167

After the marriage ceremony at the court house in White Plains,
New York, Marilyn and Arthur Miller withdraw to Miller's summer house in Roxbury,
Connecticut. Here, too, they pose for the pursuing reporters.

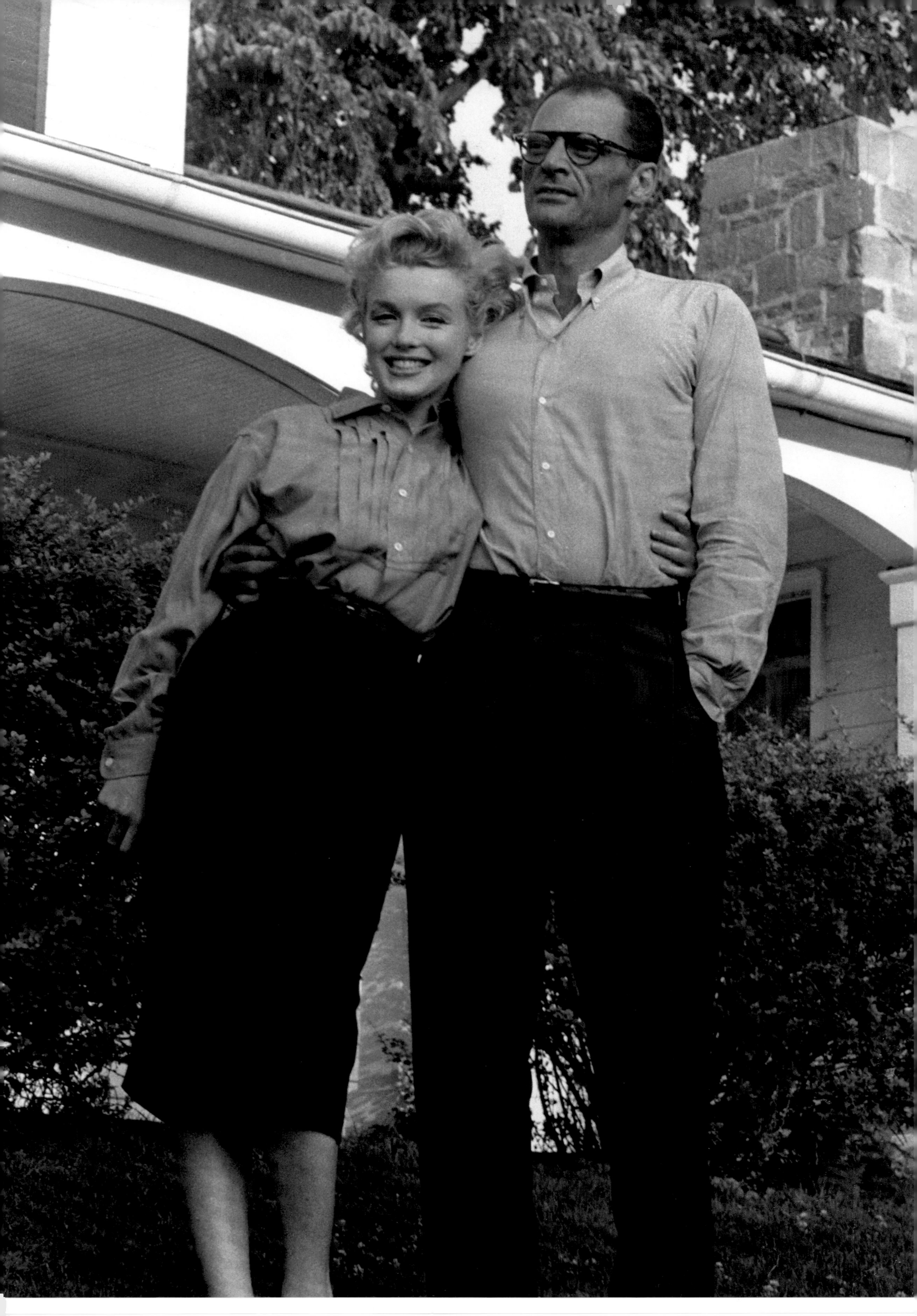

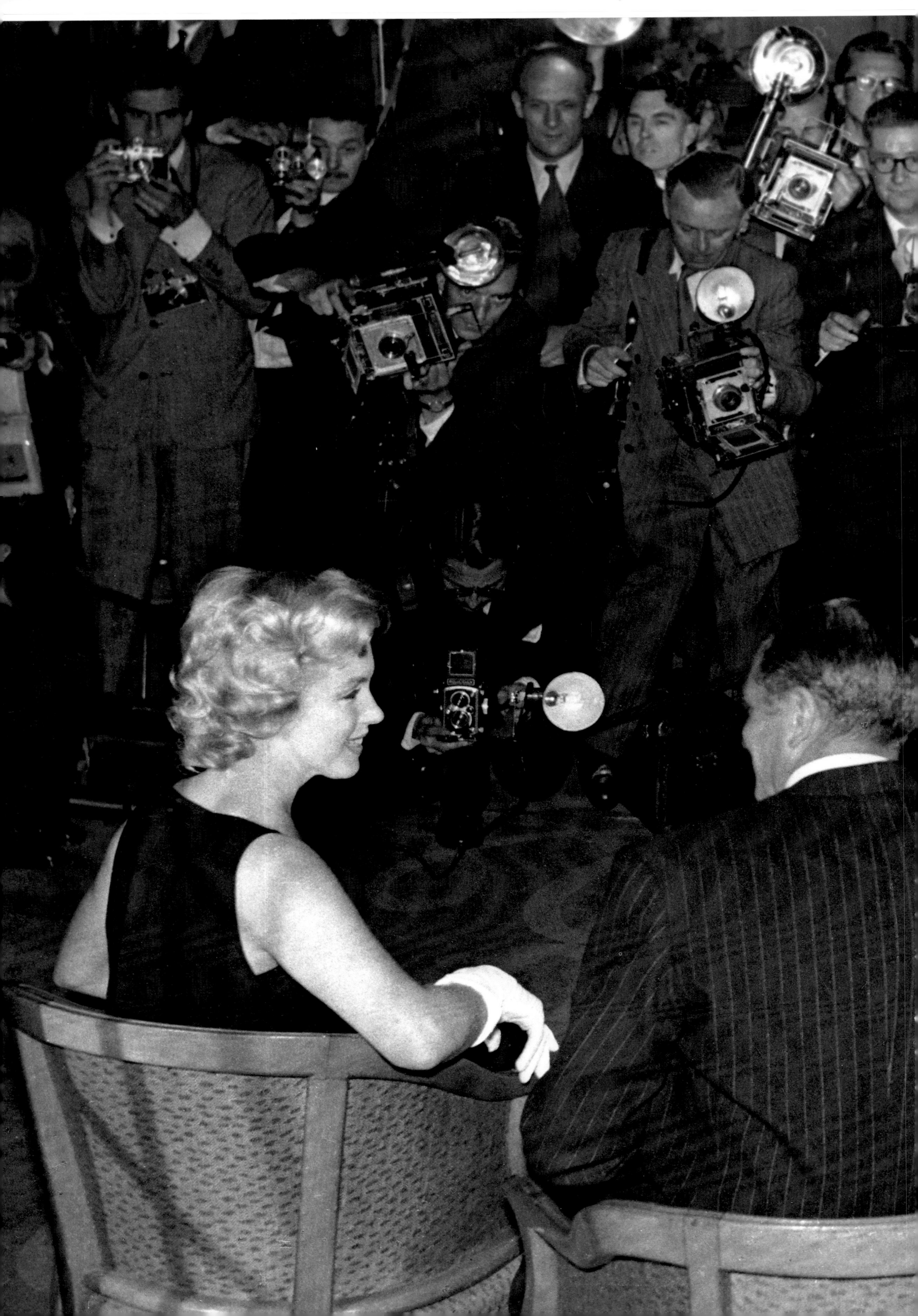

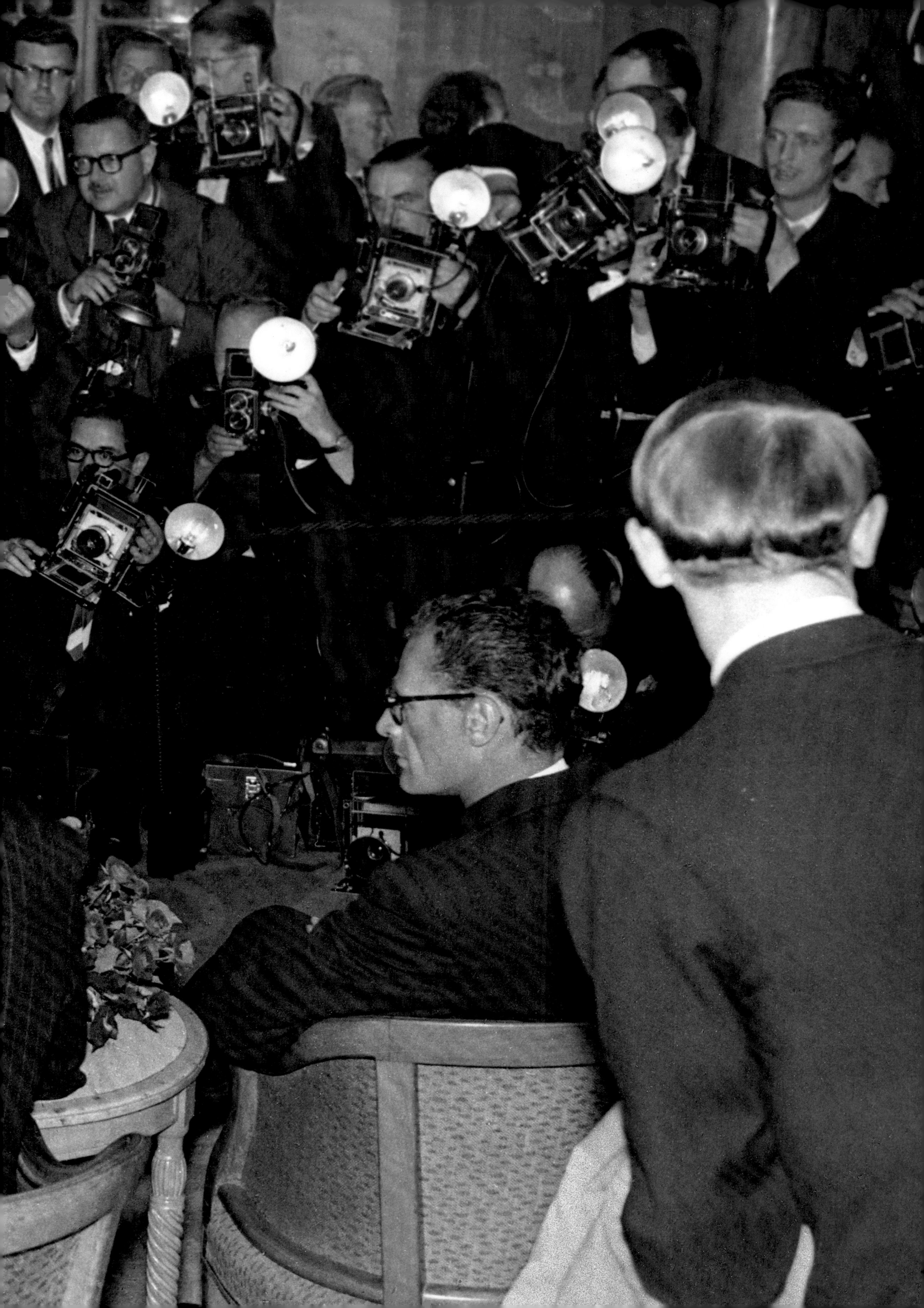

Pages 175 and 176/177

Stills from *The Prince and the Showgirl,* taken by Milton H. Greene. Laurence Olivier later
described his work with Marilyn: "It can be no news to anyone to say that she was difficult to
work with. The work frightened her, and although she had undoubted talent, I think she
had a subconscious resistance to the exercise of being an actress. But she was intrigued by the
mystique and happy as a child when being photographed; she managed the business of
stardom with uncanny, clever, apparent ease."

Pages 178/179

The Queen and the showgirl. At a Royal Command film performance
on October 29, 1956, Marilyn Monroe and other actors were presented to Queen Elizabeth II.

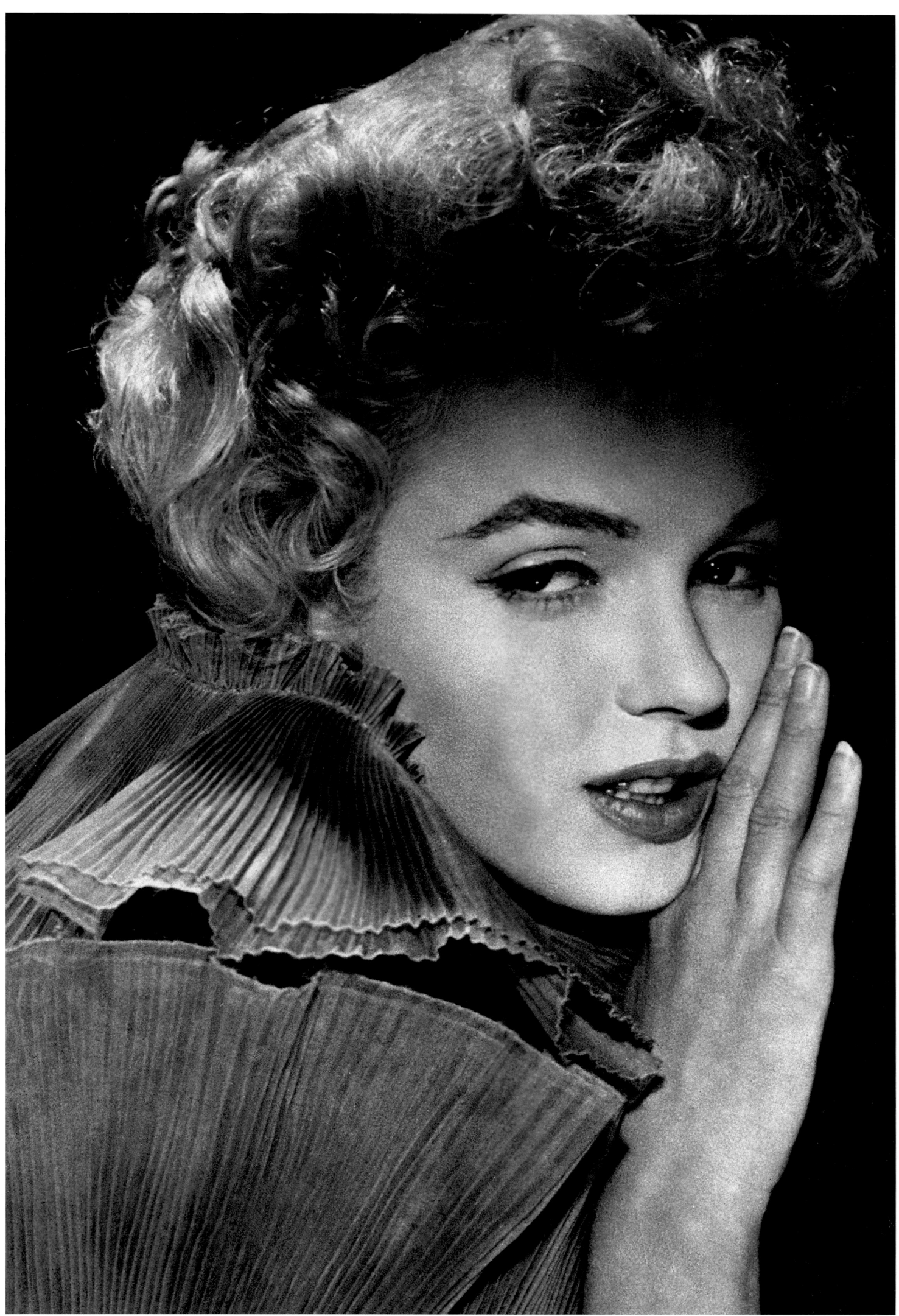

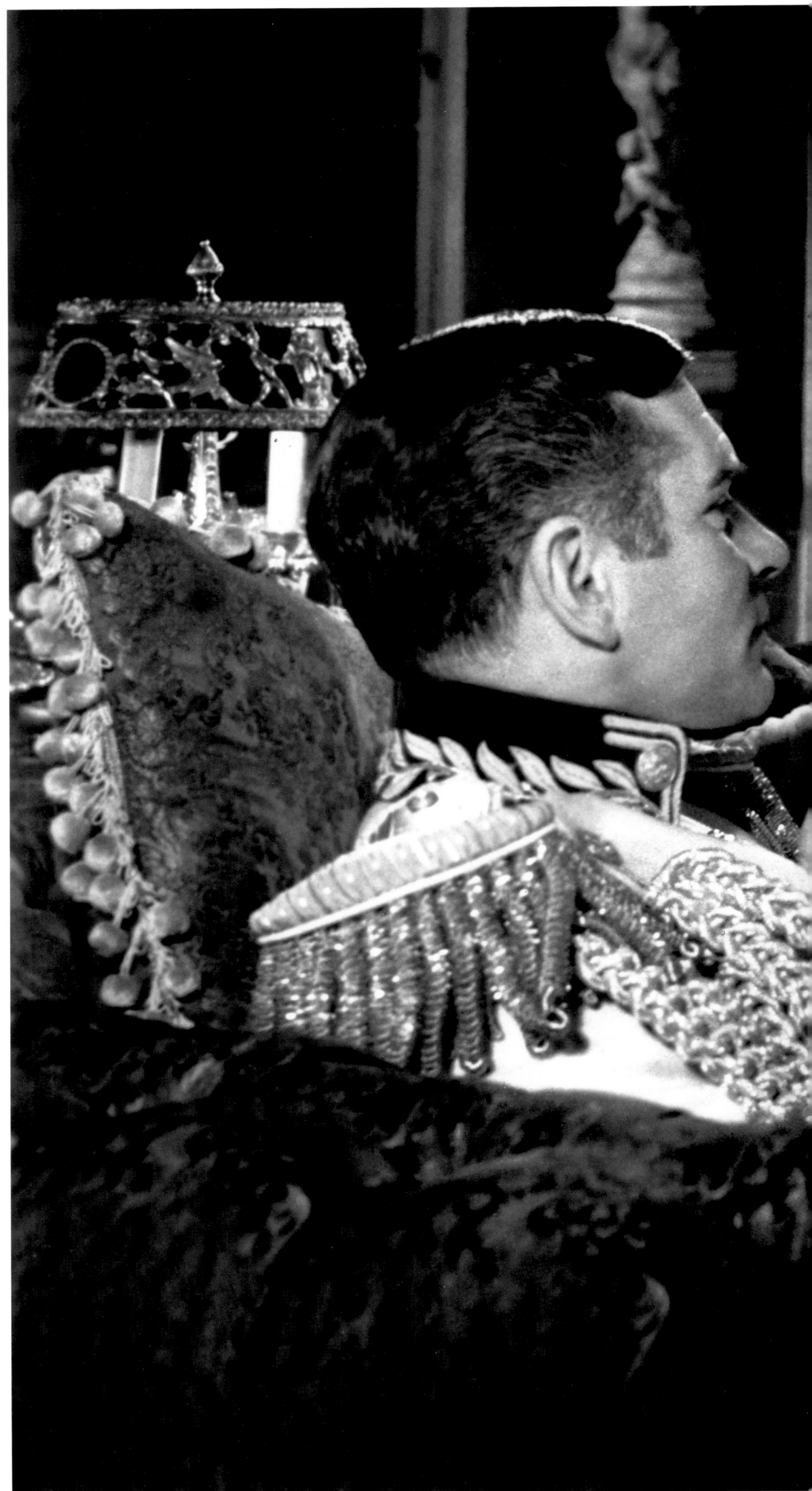

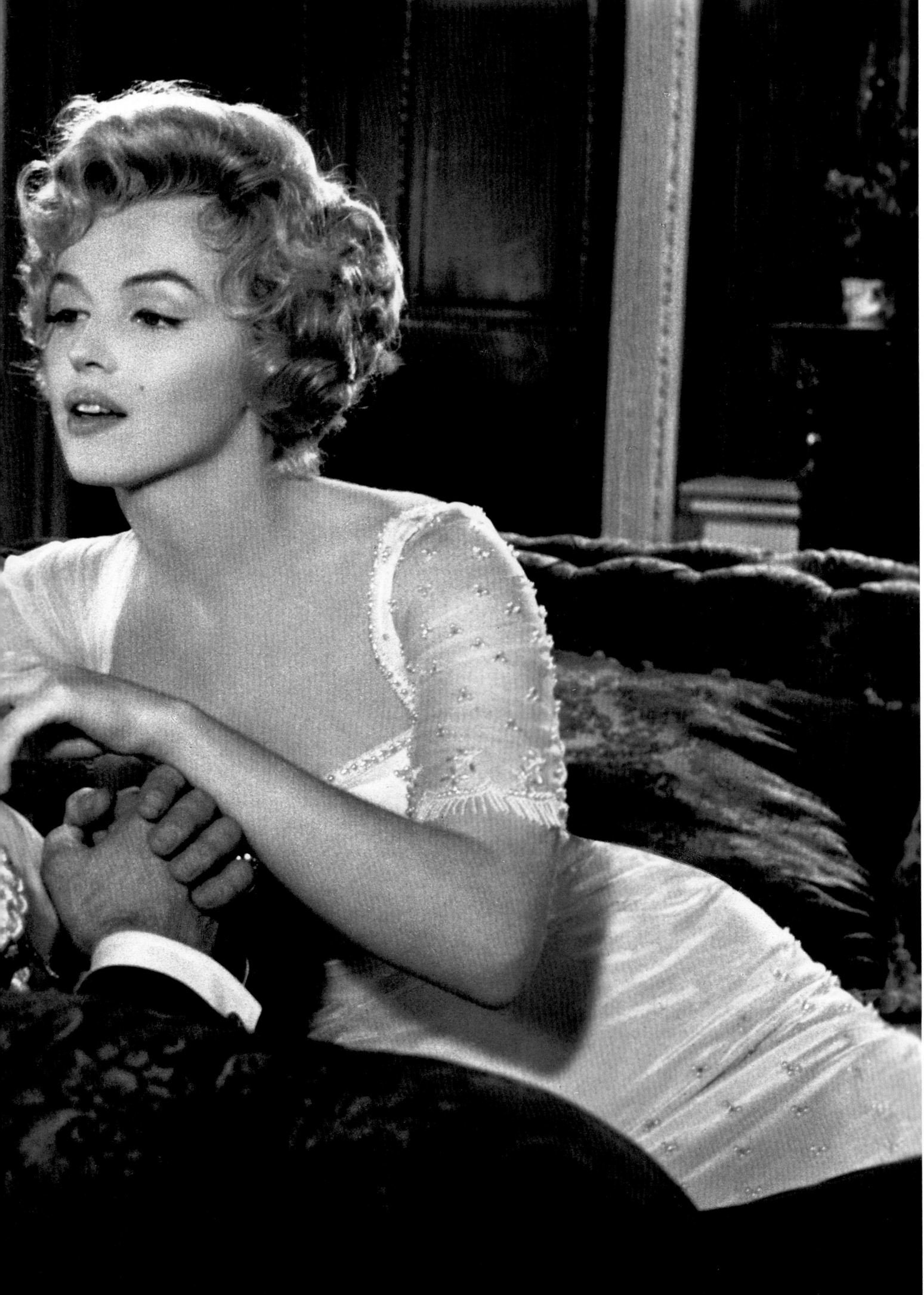

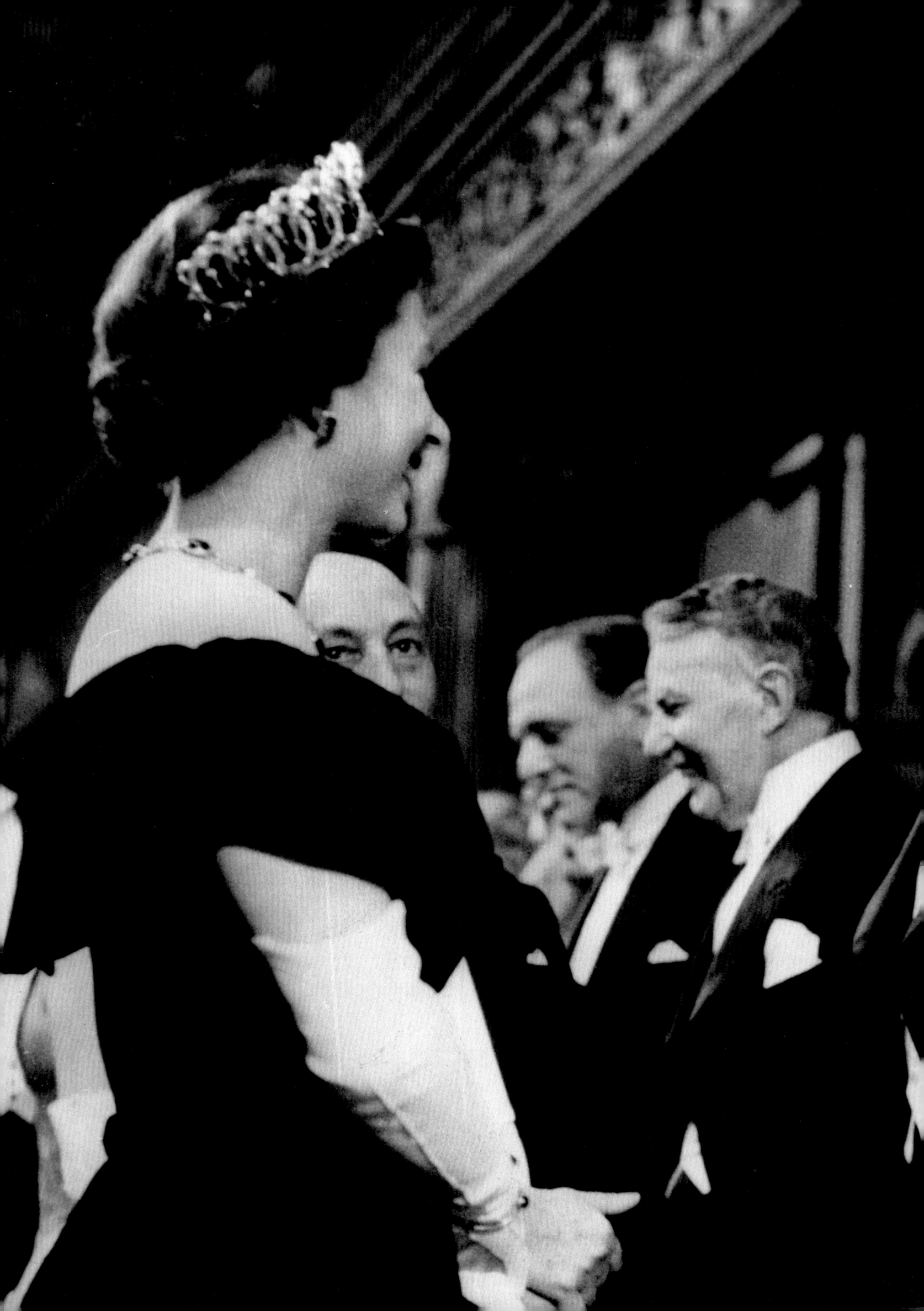

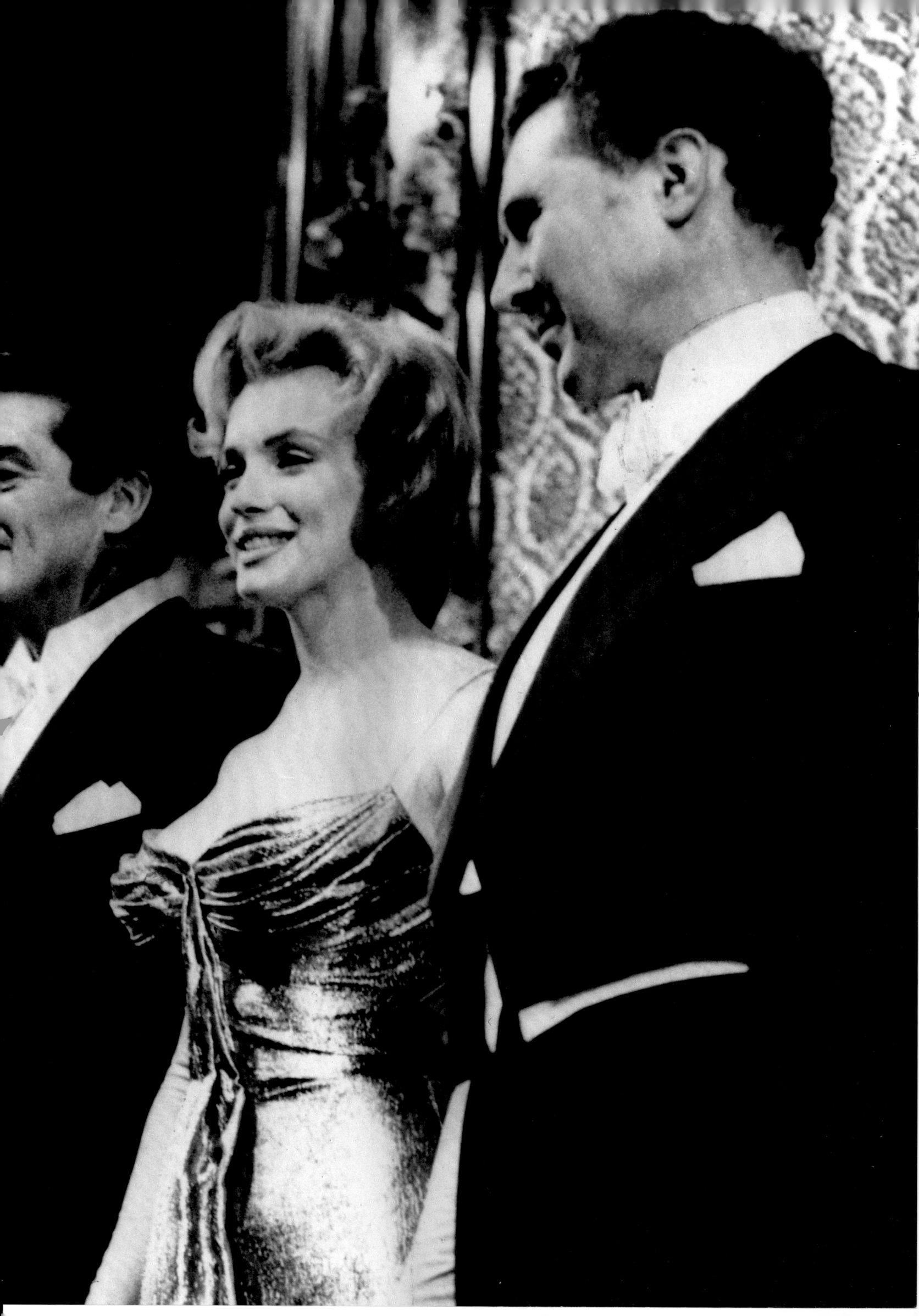

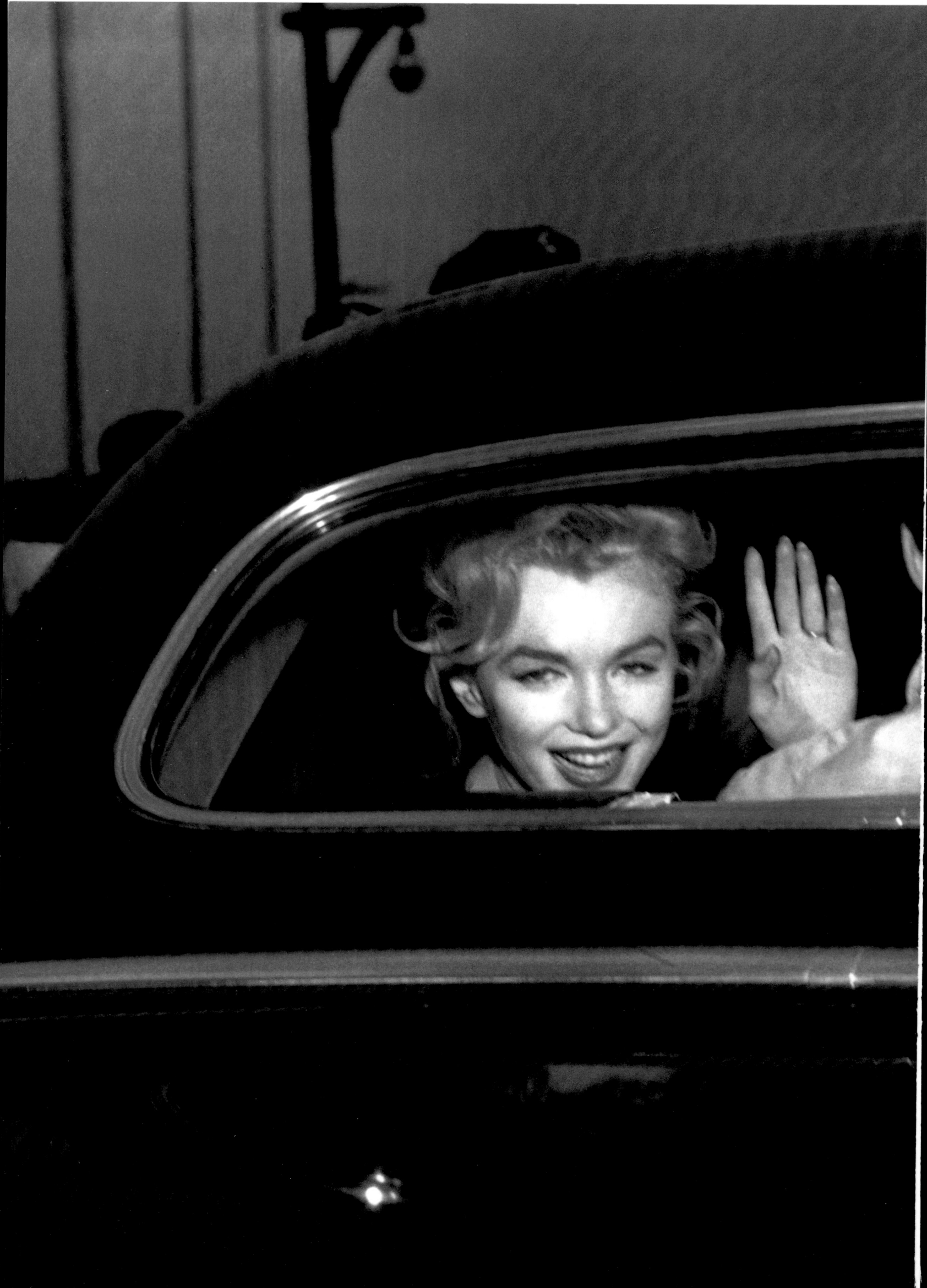

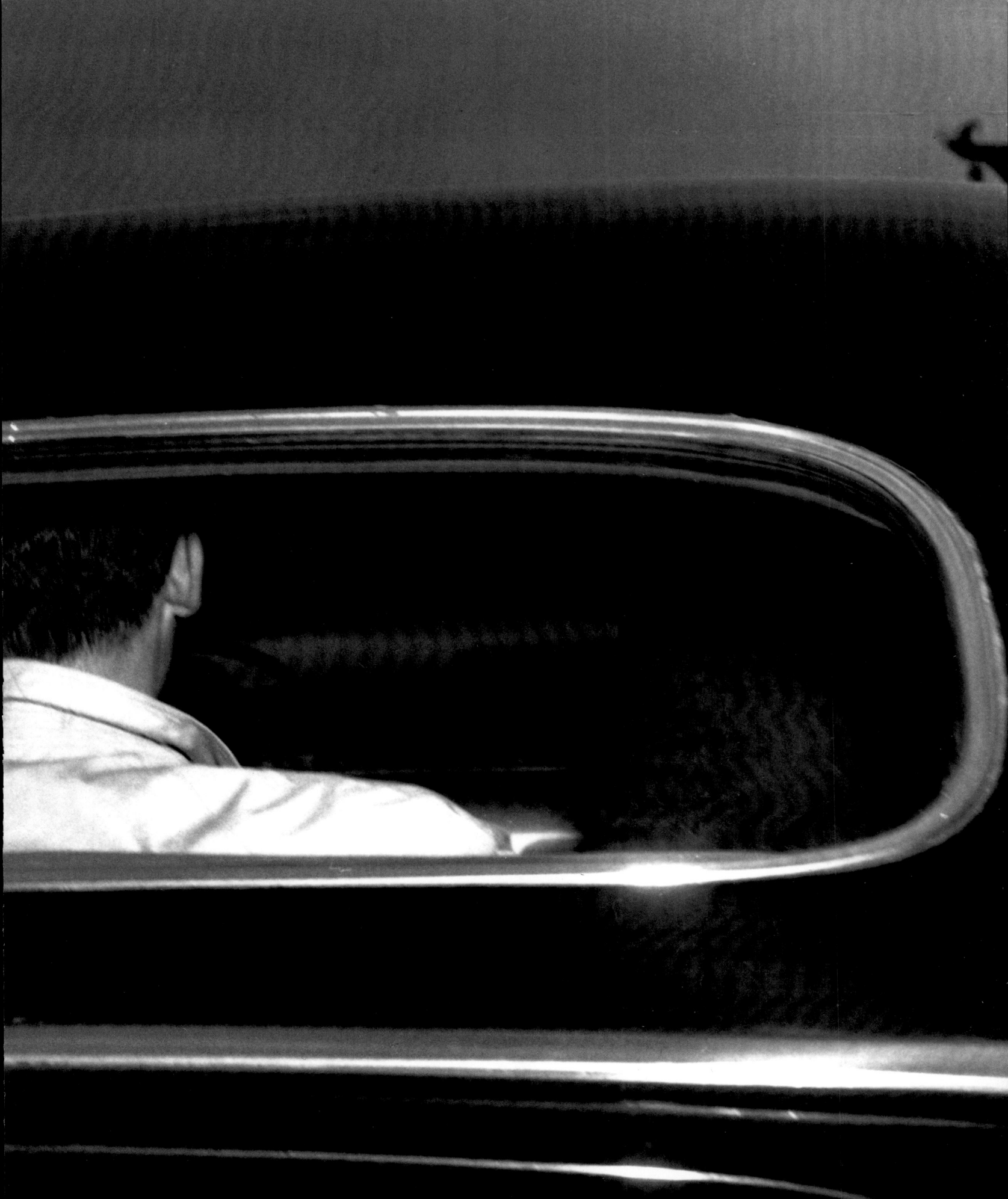

Pages 185 and 186/187

Publicity stills for *The Prince and the Showgirl,* taken by Richard Avedon.

184

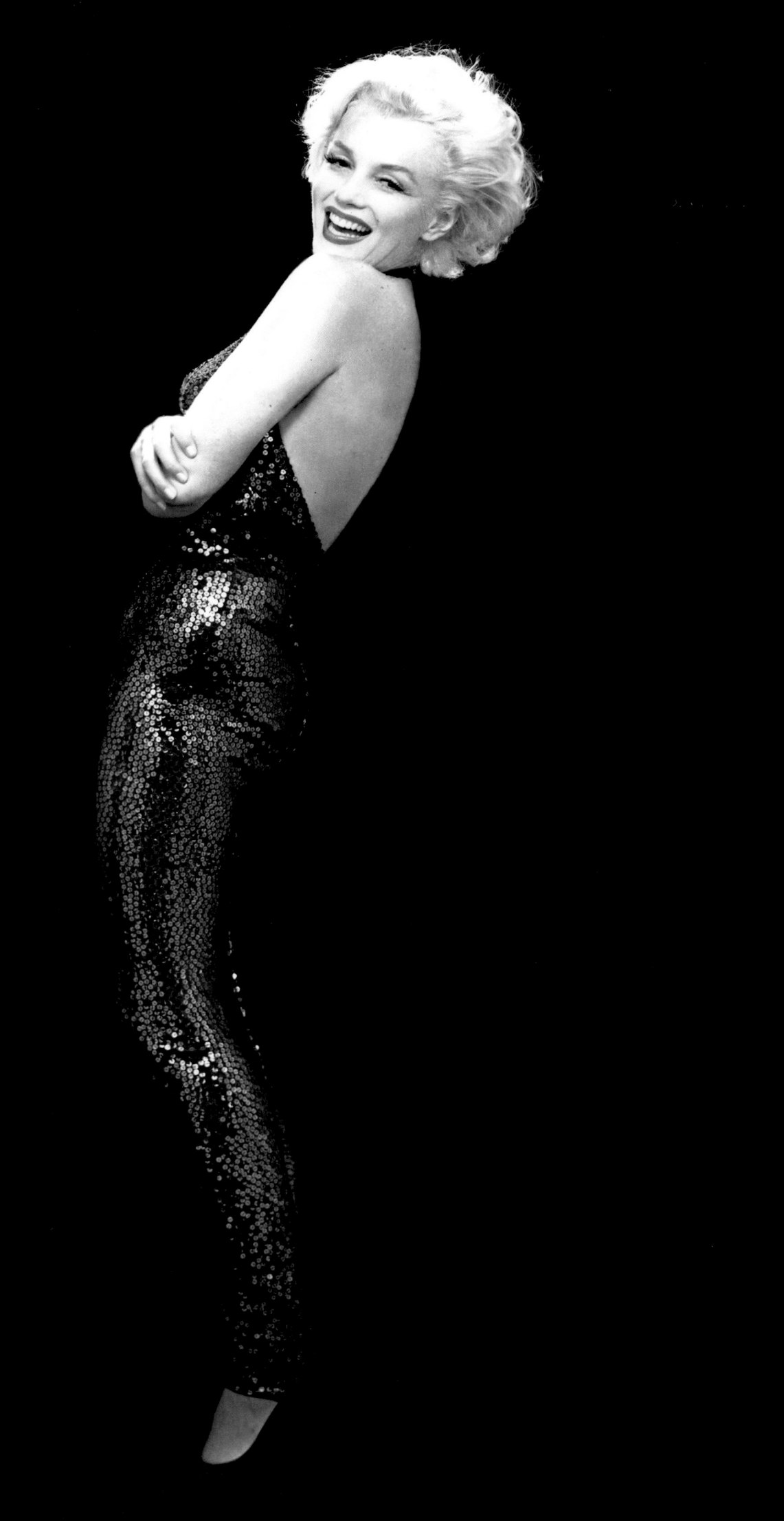

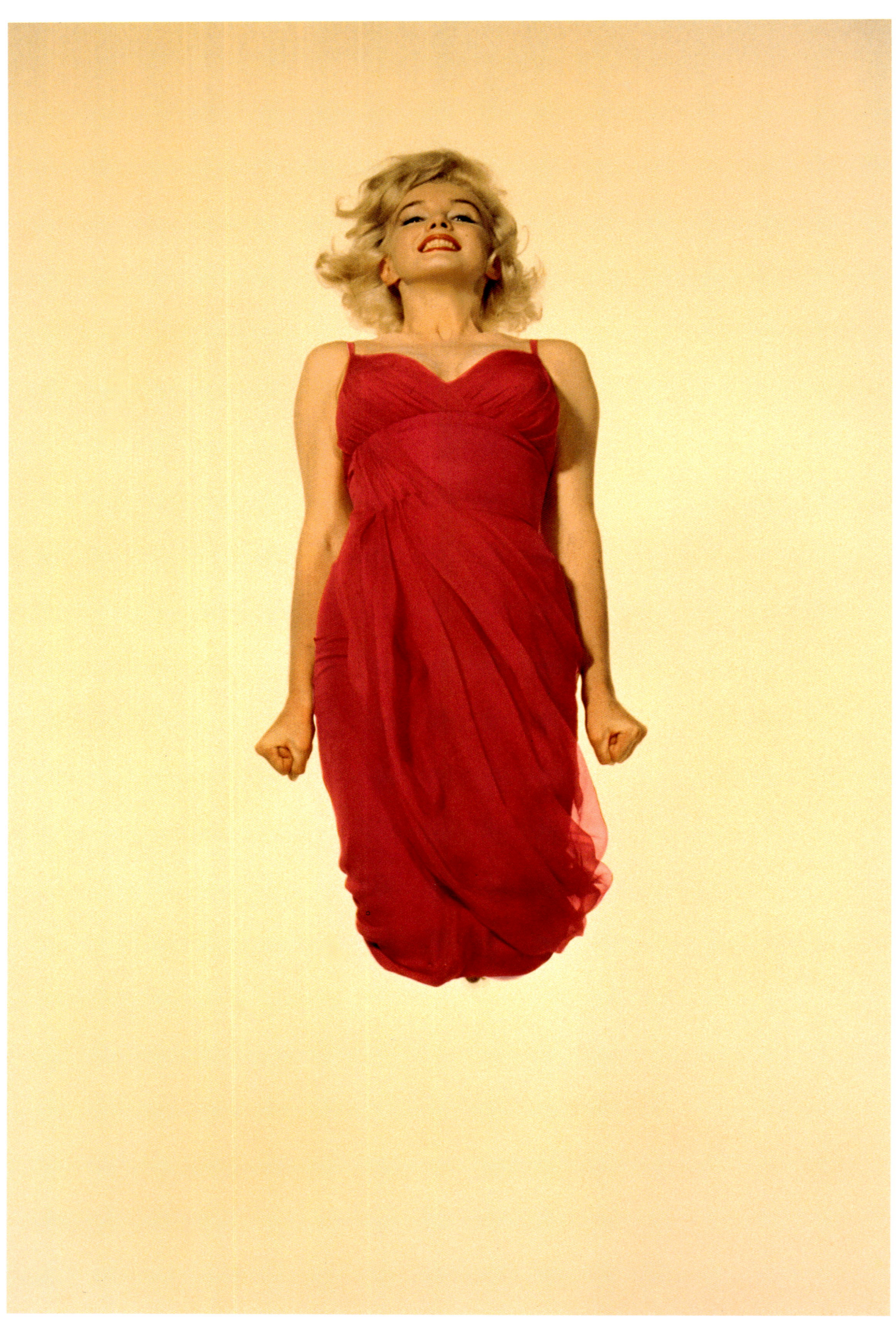

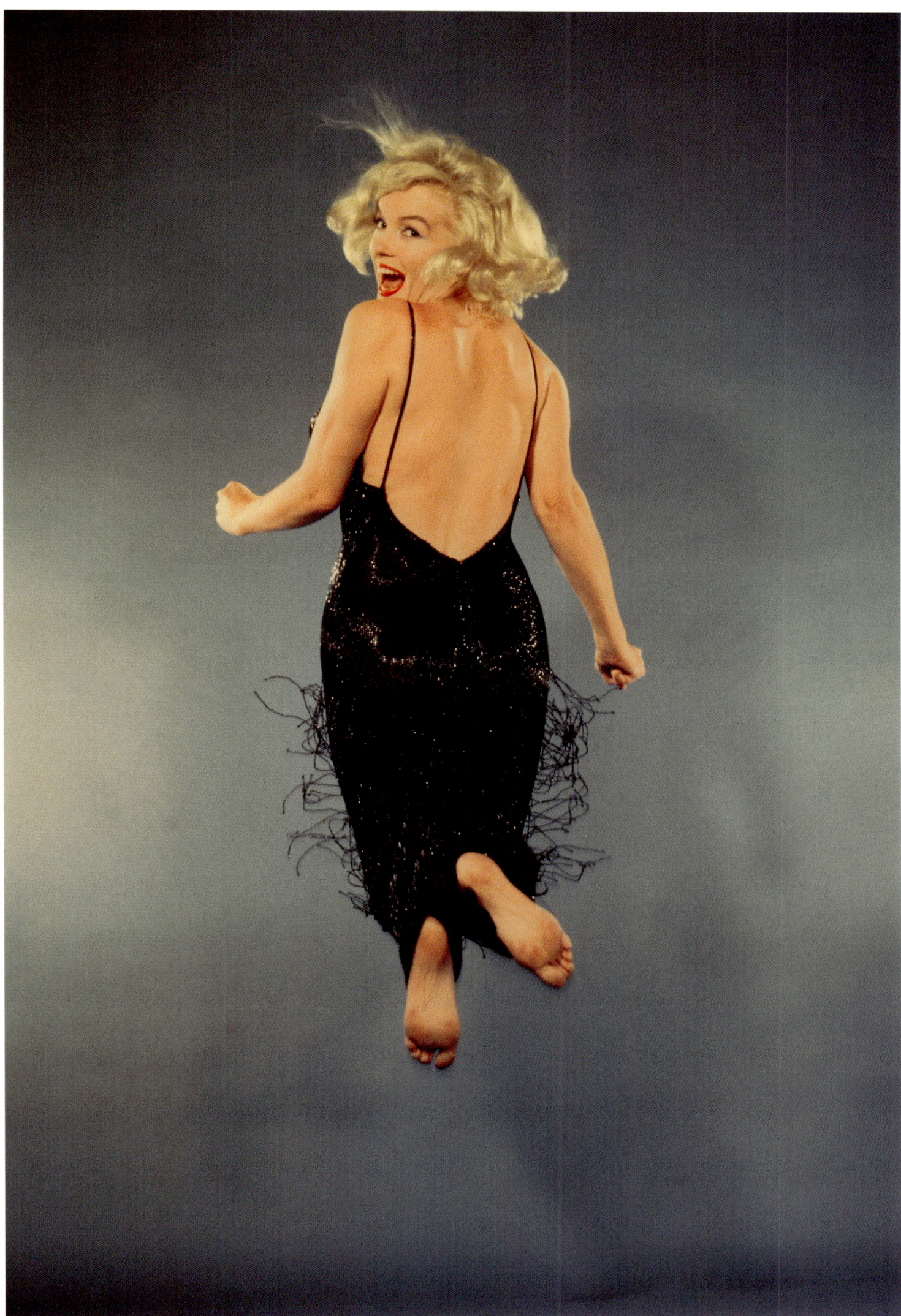

After a break of two years, Marilyn appeared before the camera
as Sugar Kane in the film *Some Like It Hot* in the summer of 1958. Her partners were
Jack Lemmon and Tony Curtis; the director, Billy Wilder.
This picture, which was taken during the filming, shows Marilyn in an unusual pose
as a diva with wind-touseled hair.

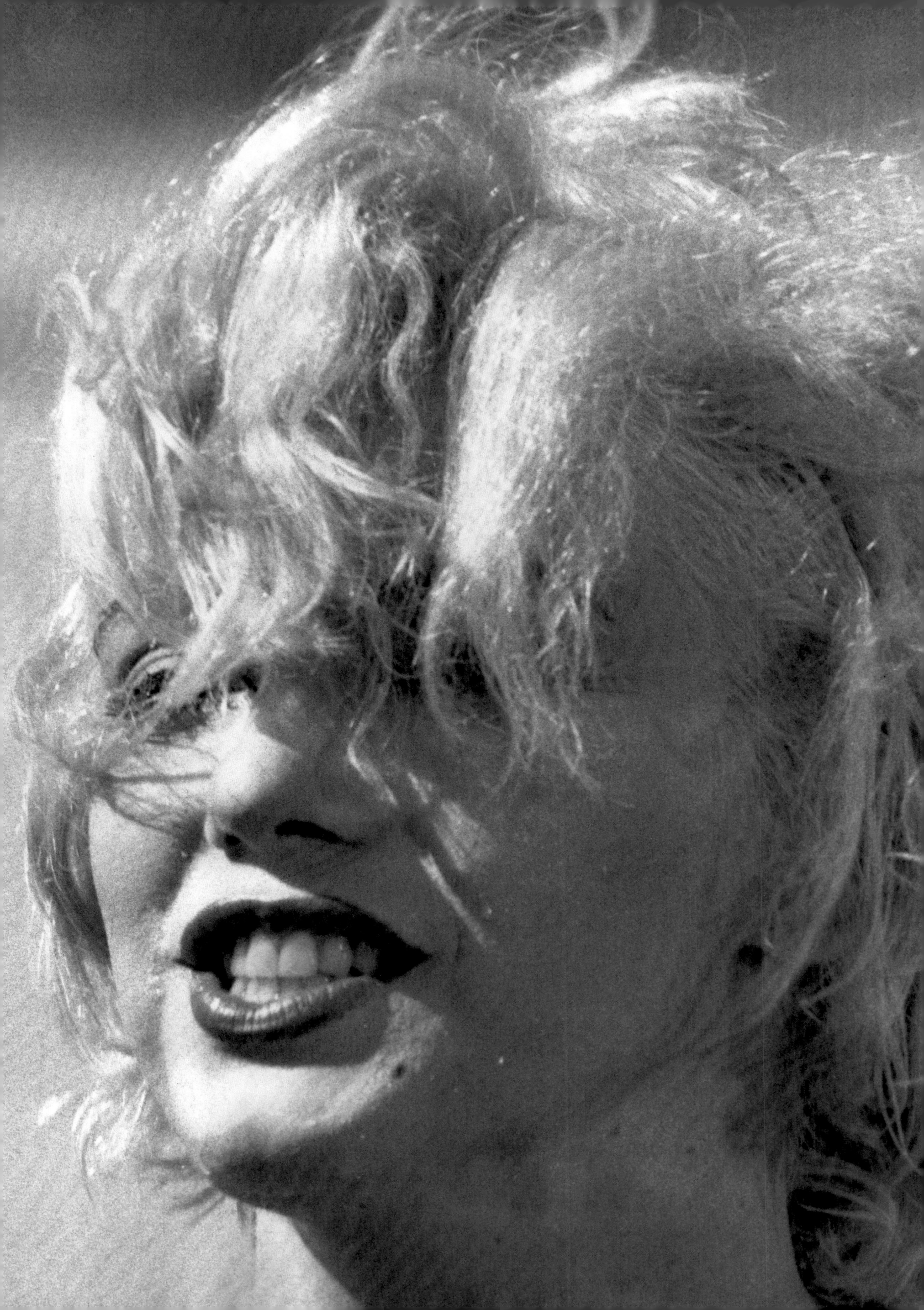

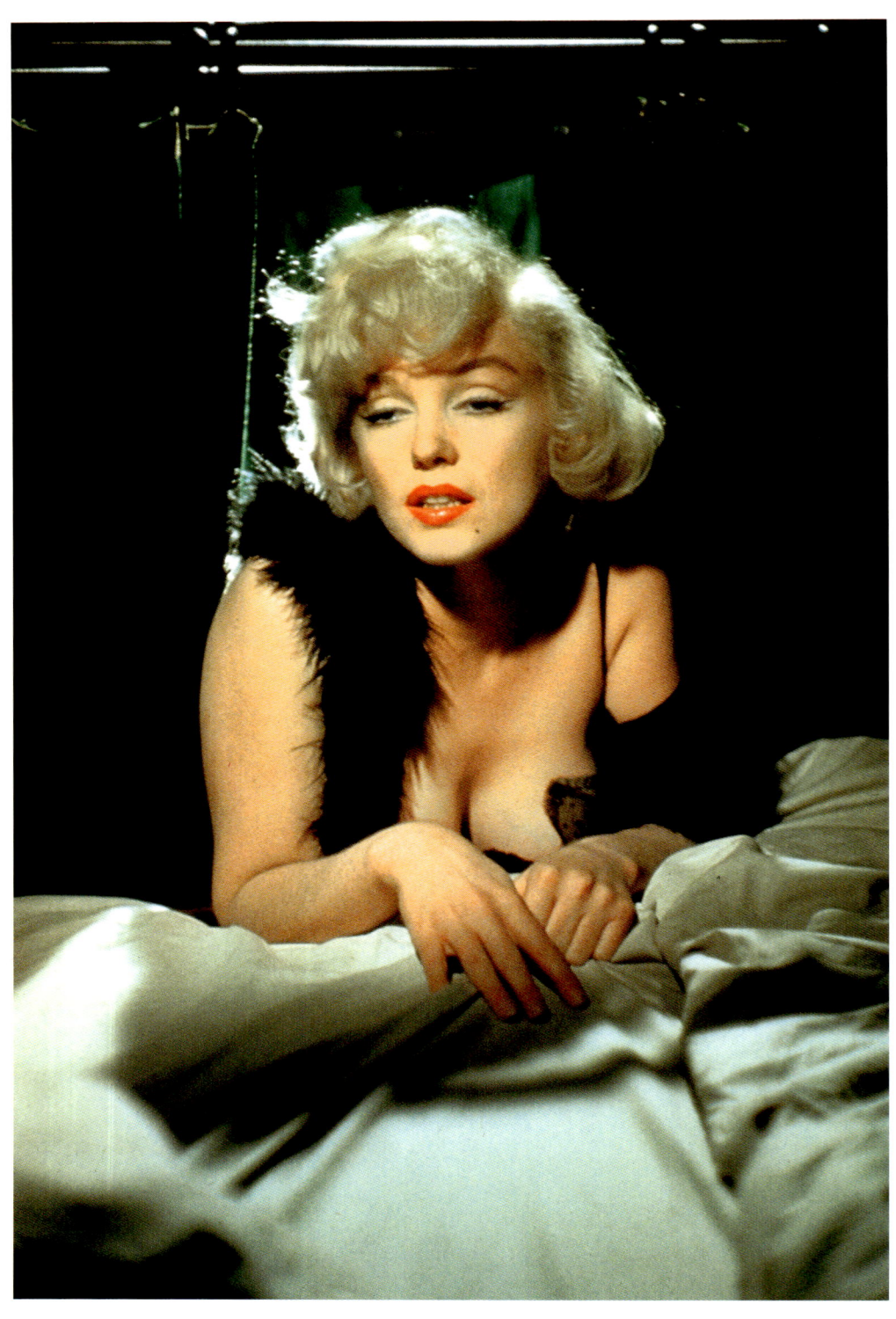

A still from *Some Like It Hot* by Richard C. Miller, for whom Marilyn
had already posed for photo ads in 1946. During the filming, which had to be interrupted
several times, Marilyn was so difficult that Miller asked director Billy Wilder
why he put up with Marilyn if she only caused trouble. Wilder's reply: "It's like somebody
who can play one note on an instrument. They play it perfectly,
though they cannot play anything else." Wilder's inexhaustible patience paid off; *Some Like
It Hot* was his most successful film.

A still from *Some Like It Hot*.

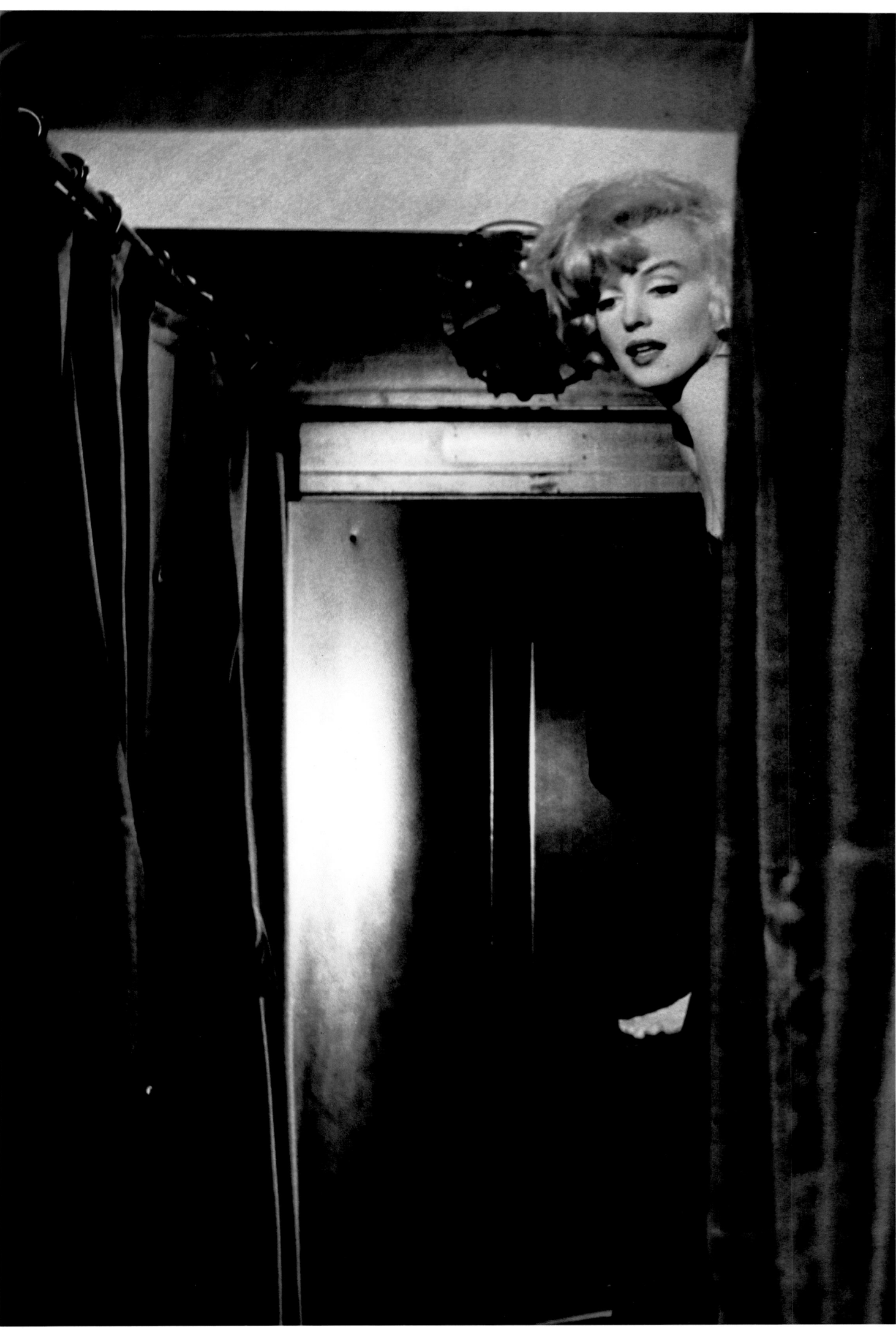

Henri Dauman photographed a beaming Marilyn Monroe
on her arrival for the premiere of *Some Like It Hot* in New York on March 29, 1959.

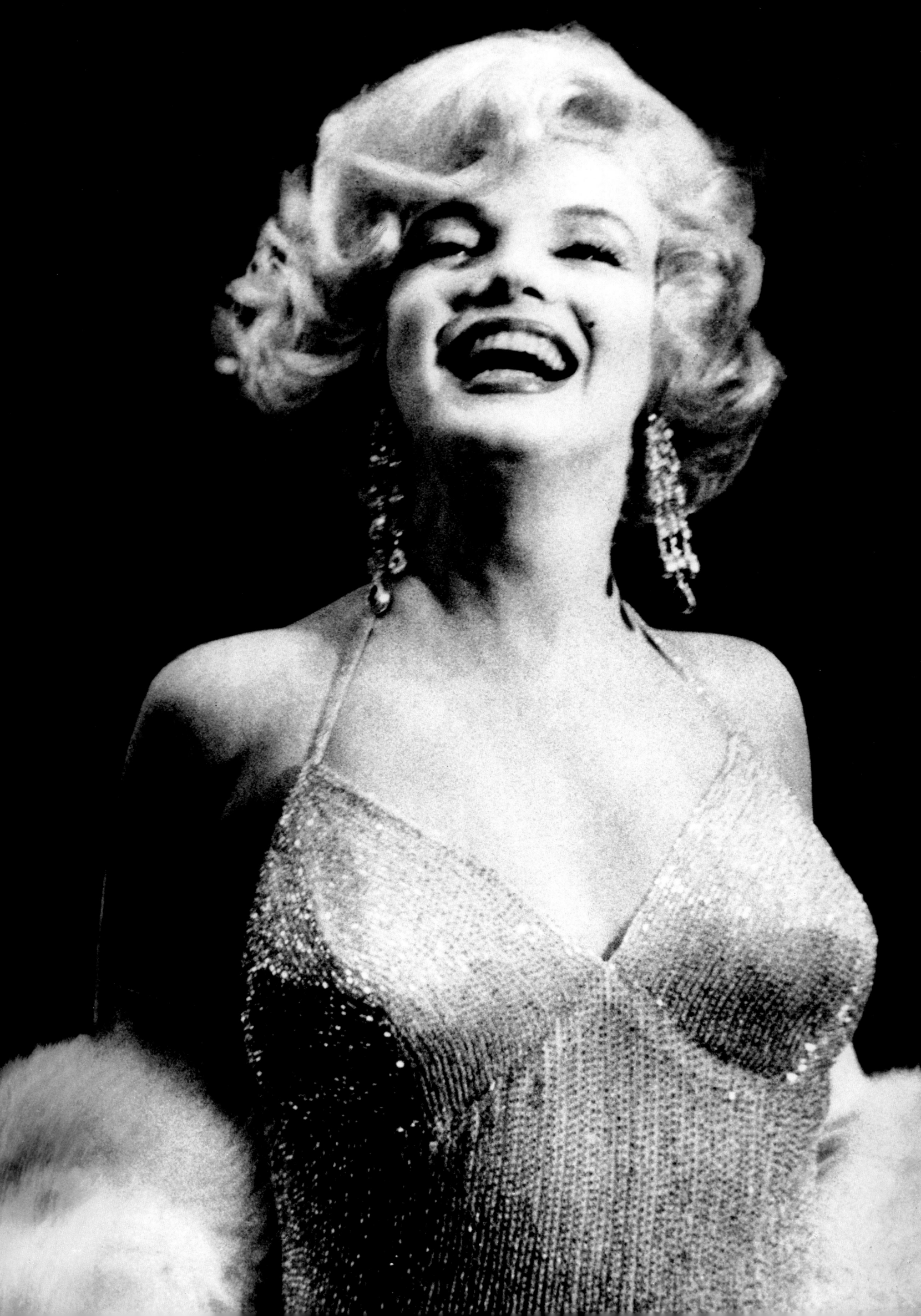

A publicity still with Yves Montand for the film *Let's Make Love,* 1960.
Yves Montand was given the part at the last minute after both Gregory Peck and
Rock Hudson had declined. Montand and his wife, Simone Signoret, had already
appeared in plays by Arthur Miller. The love affair that obviously unfolded between the two
leading actors during the course of the filming evoked this reaction
from Simone Signoret: "If Marilyn is in love with my husband, it proves she has good taste."

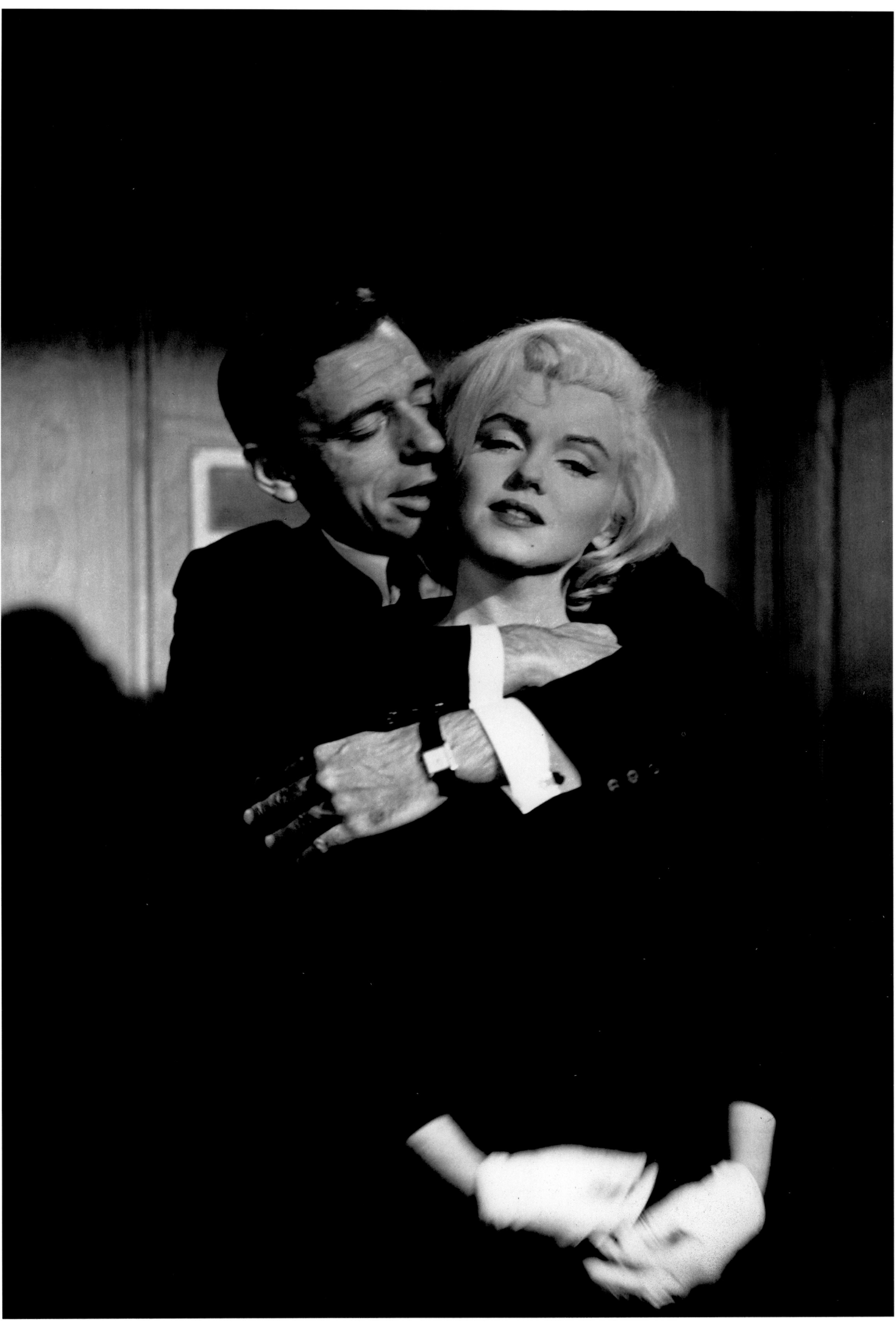

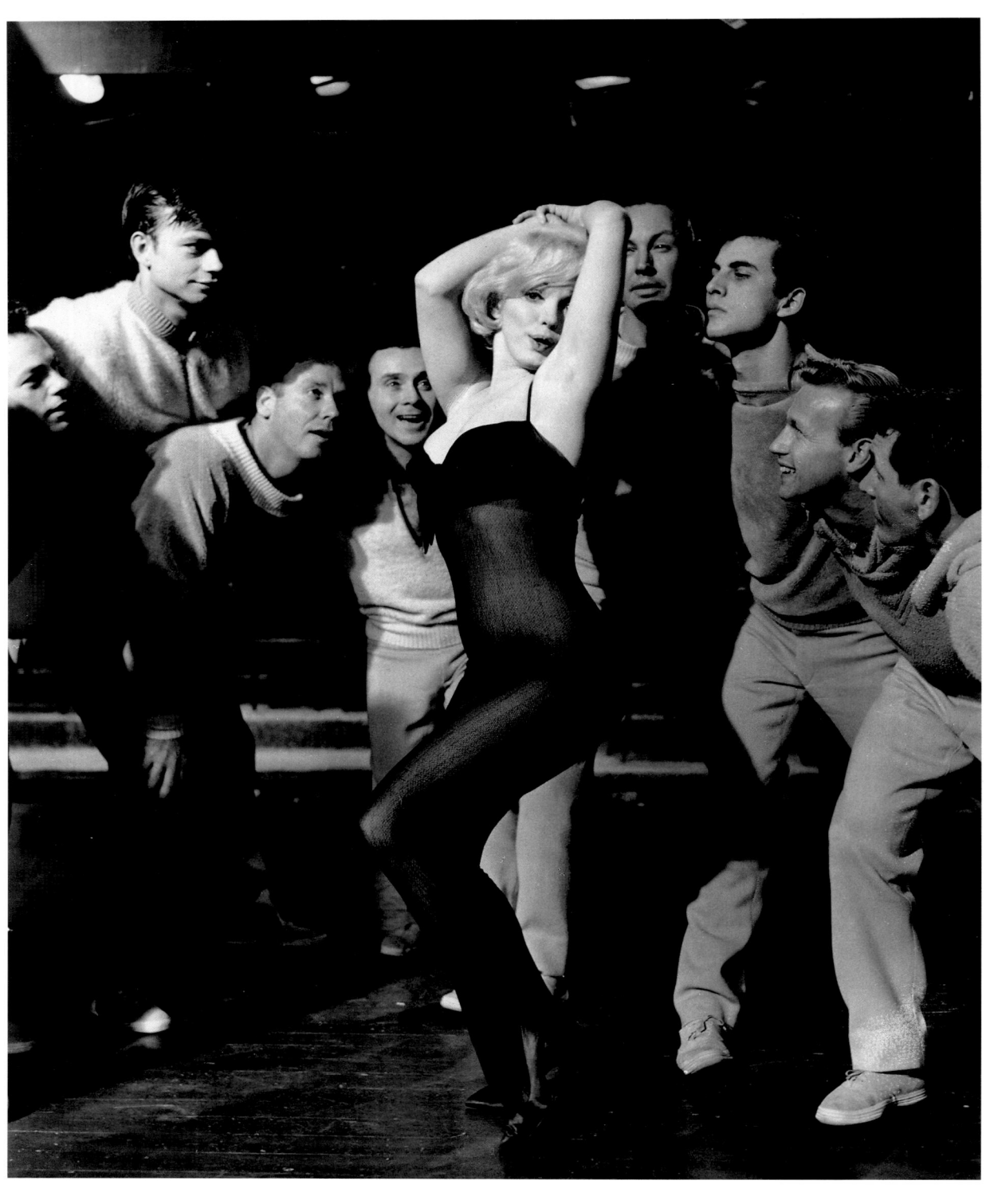

Publicity stills for *Let's Make Love*.
The choreographer Jack Cole was responsible for the numerous dance numbers in the film.

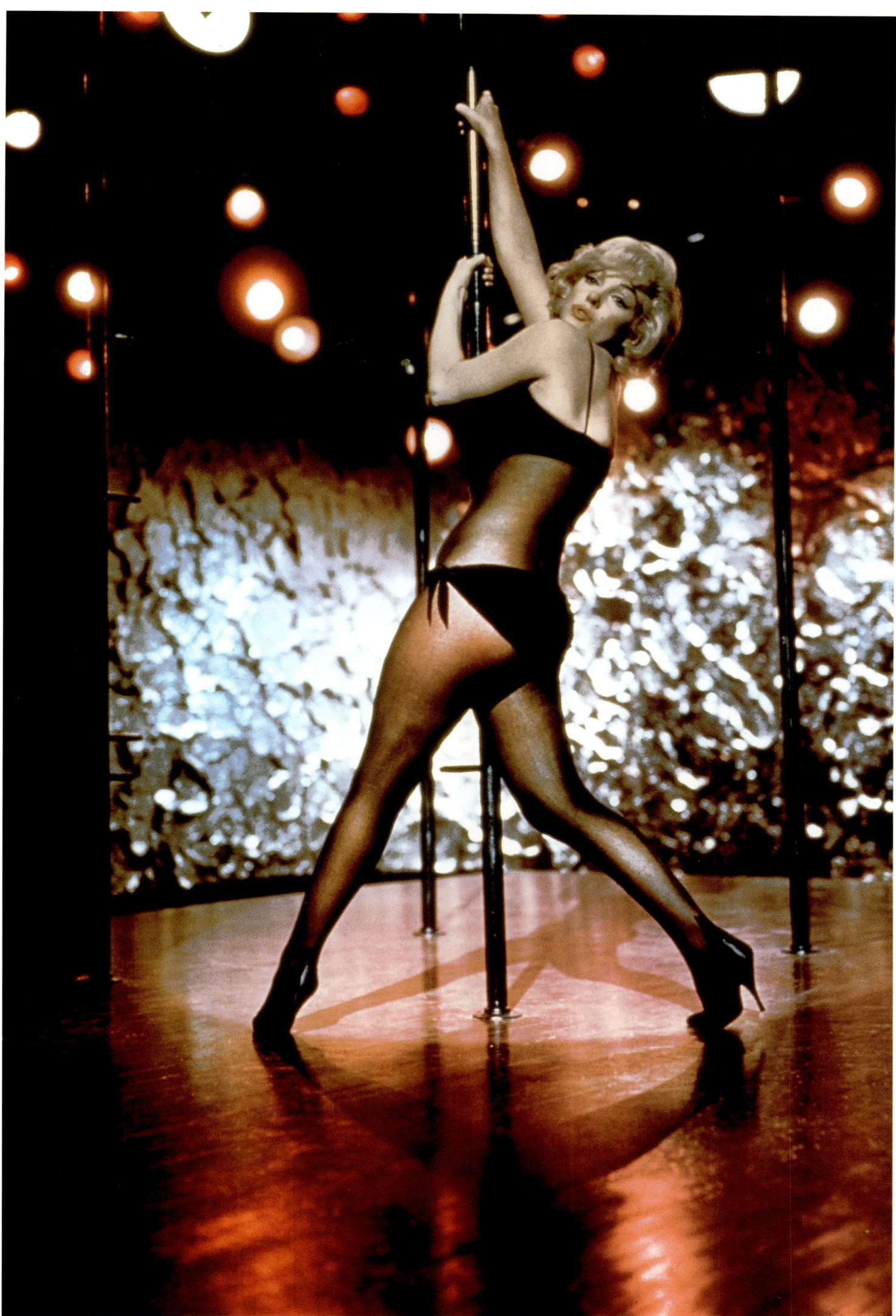

This impressive portrait of Marilyn lost in herself was taken on the set for
Let's Make Love. Photograph by Bob Willoughby.

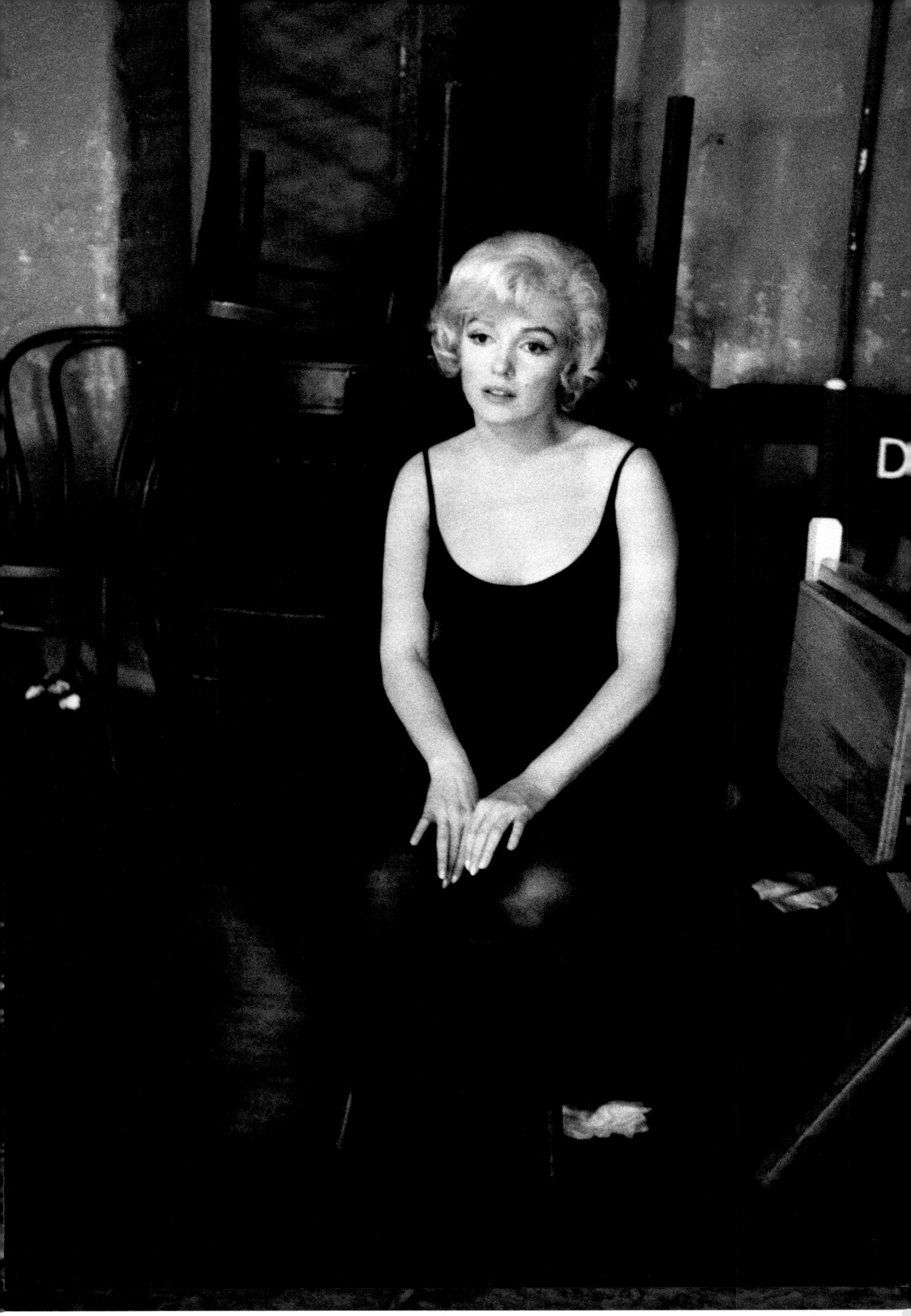

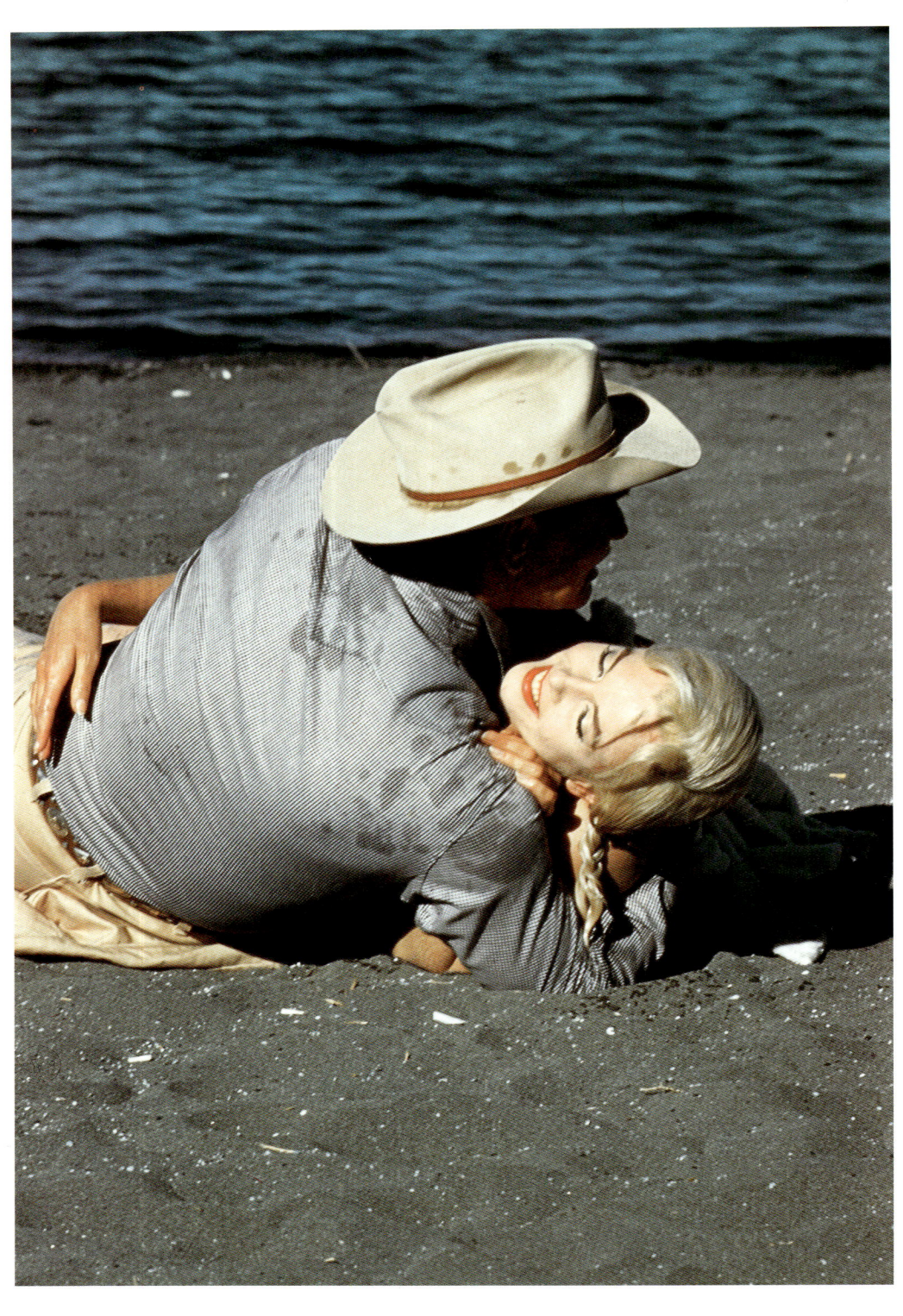

With Nevada's magnificent scenery in the background,
Marilyn in a flesh-colored bikini emerges like Botticelli's Venus from the waters of Pyramid
Lake. A passionate love scene with Clark Gable follows.
Photographs by Eve Arnold.

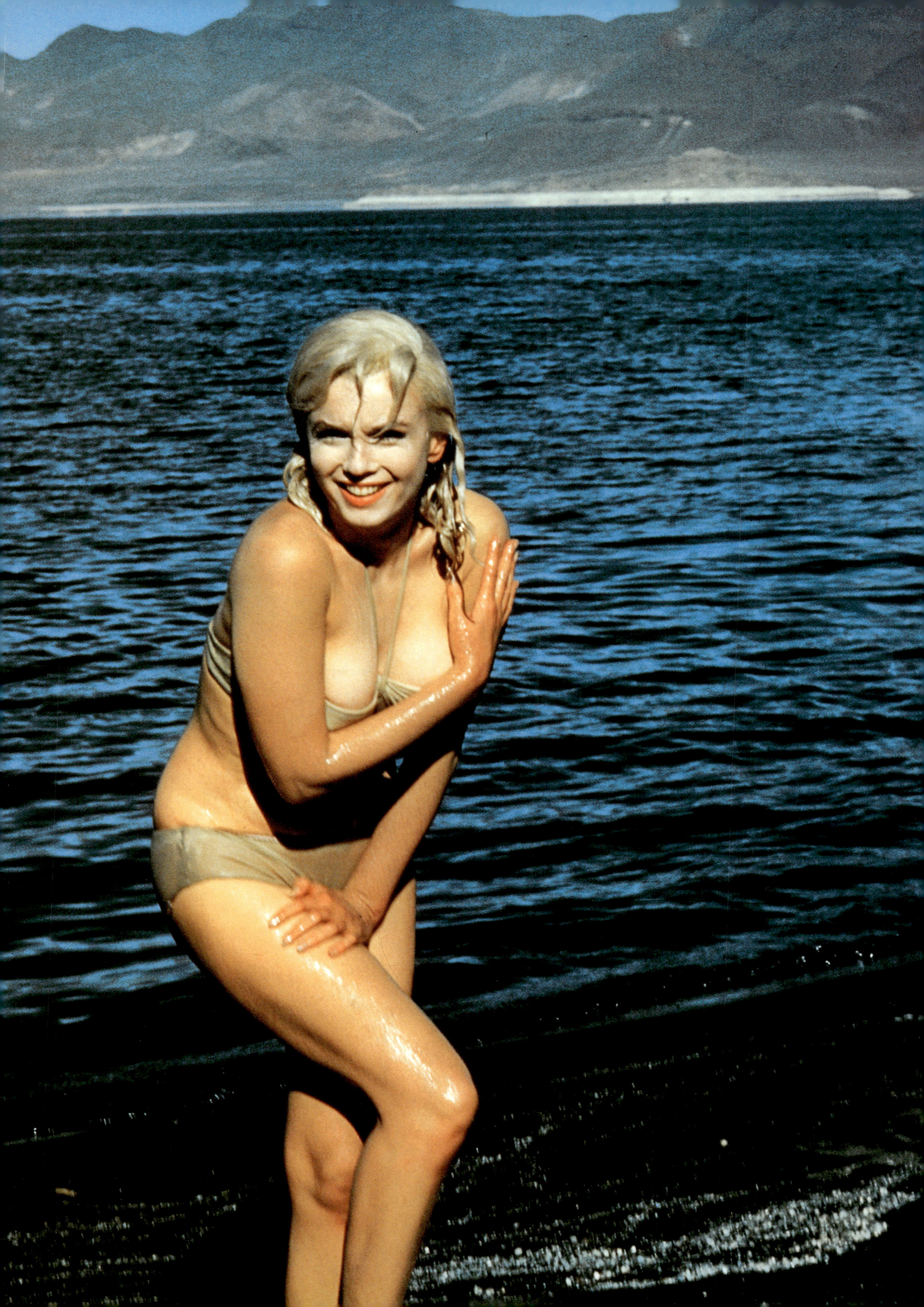

Page 211

The great French photographer Henri Cartier-Bresson, who with
Inge Morath (later to become Arthur Miller's wife) was sent by Magnum for the first two
weeks of filming for *The Misfits,* took this picture of Marilyn Monroe.

Pages 212/213

Ernst Haas, another Magnum photographer, was responsible for this shot,
which best expresses Marilyn's attitude toward *The Misfits*. Marilyn saw the film as a
men-and-mustang story and felt more and more neglected the longer the filming stretched on.

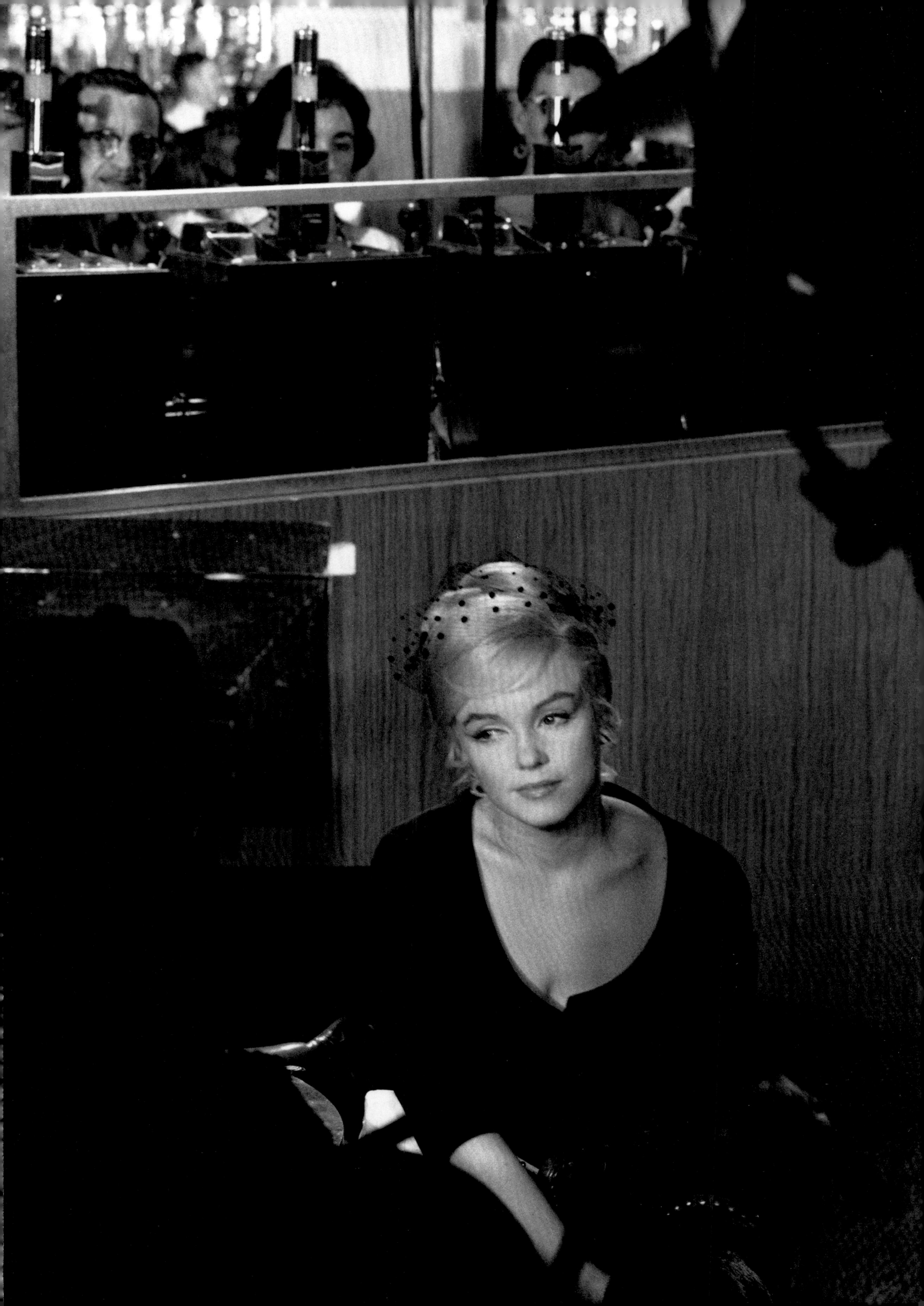

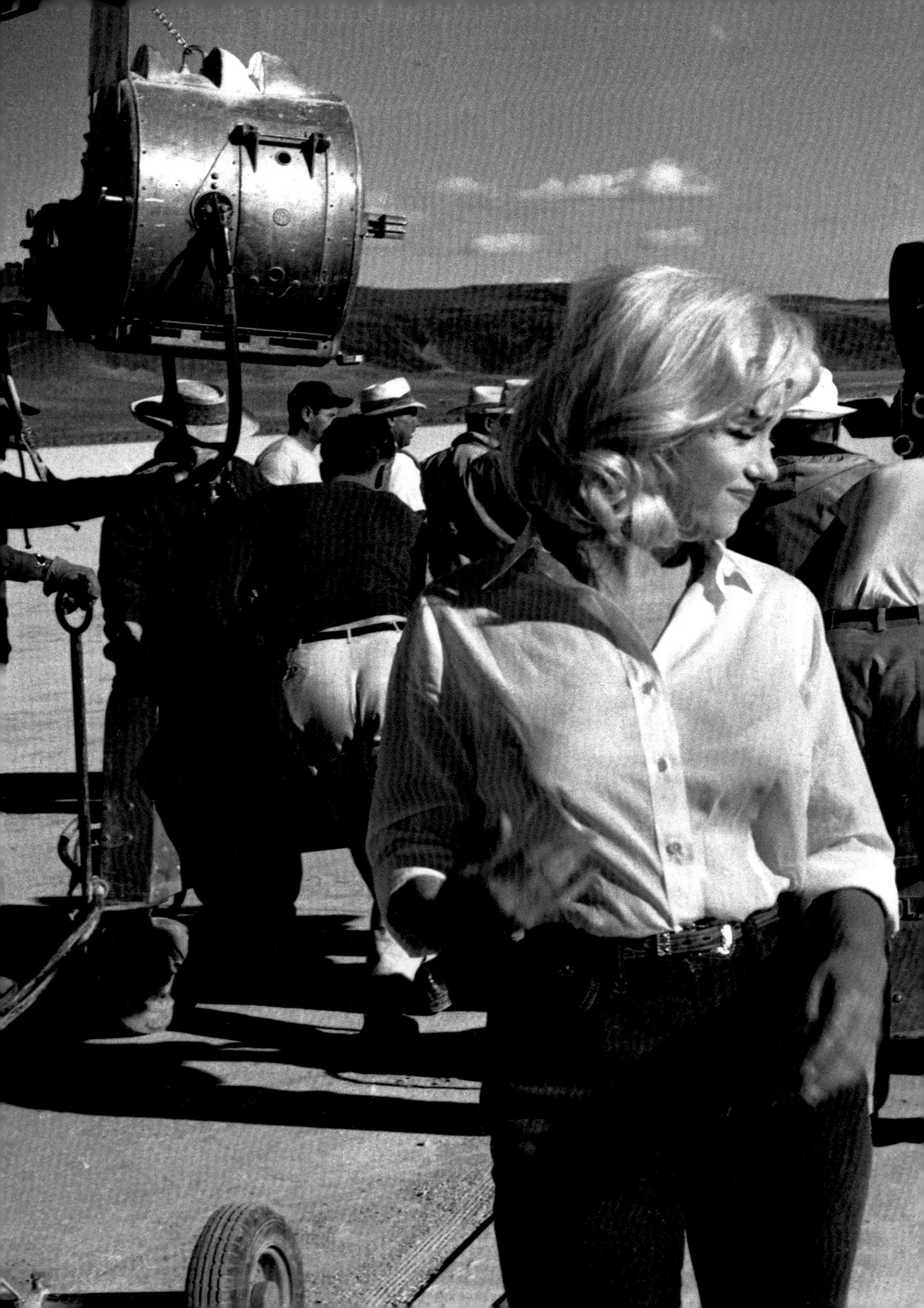

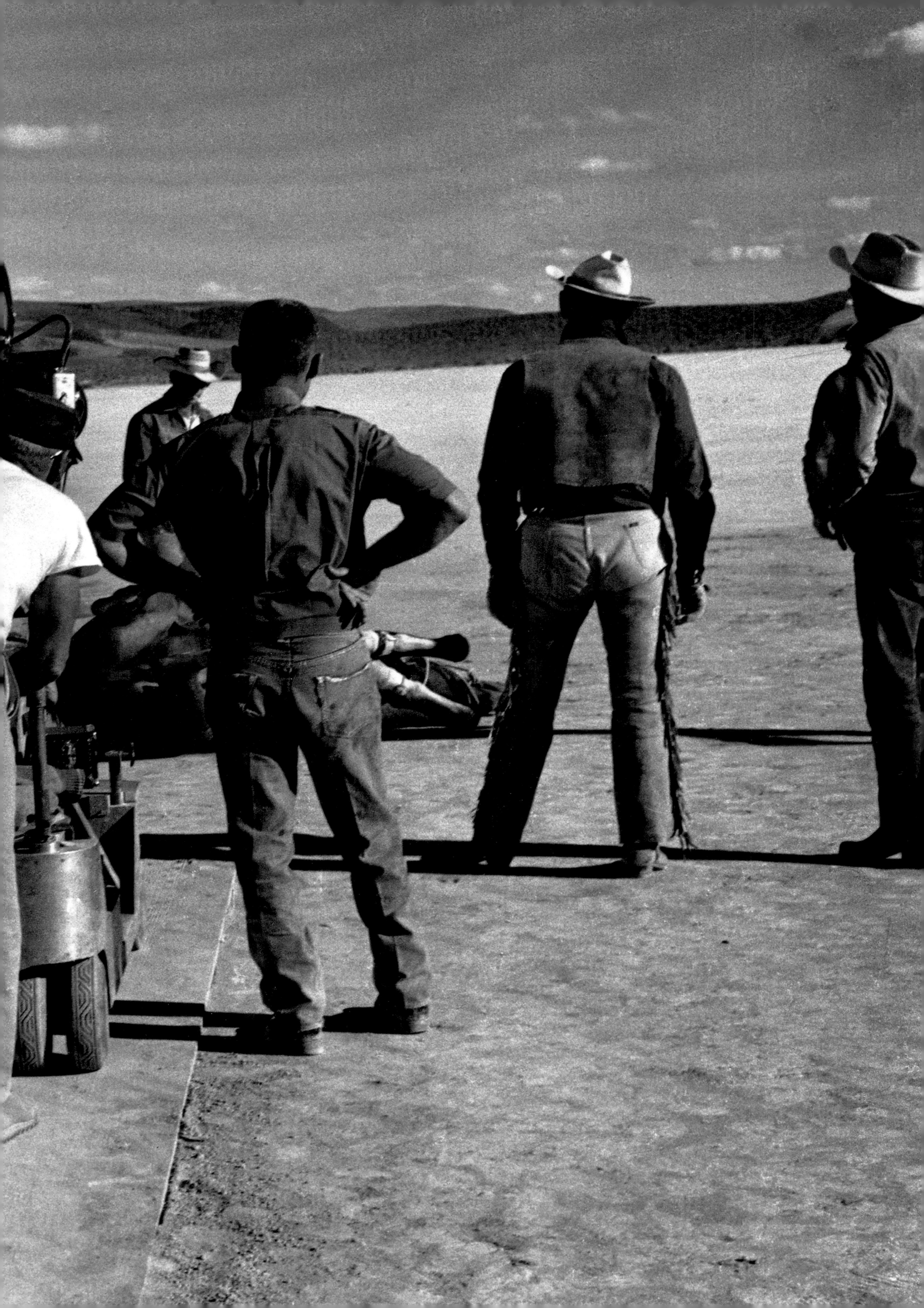

The star and the floodlights:
Marilyn, thoughtful and alone, with the set equipment. Photograph by Ernst Haas, 1960.

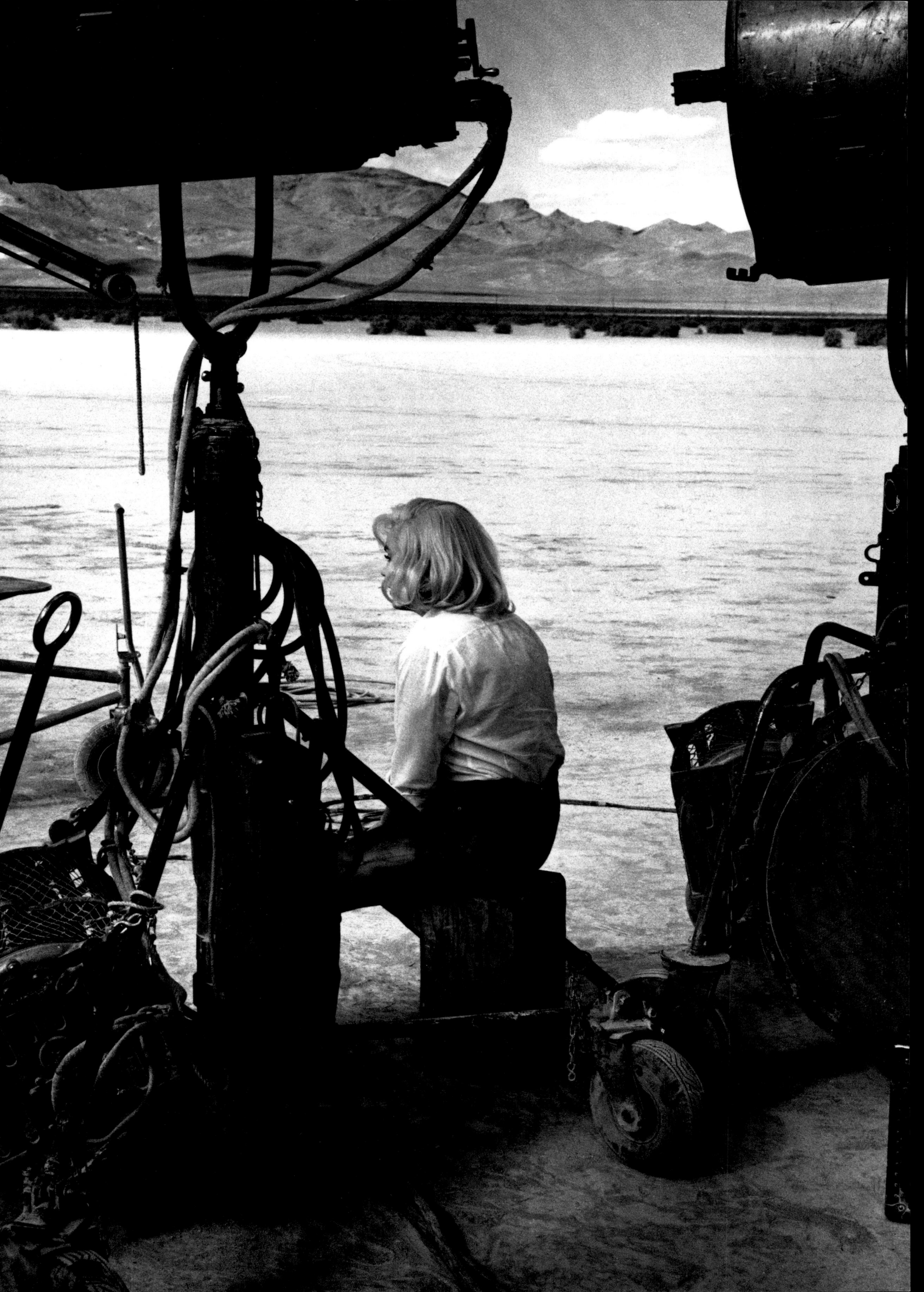

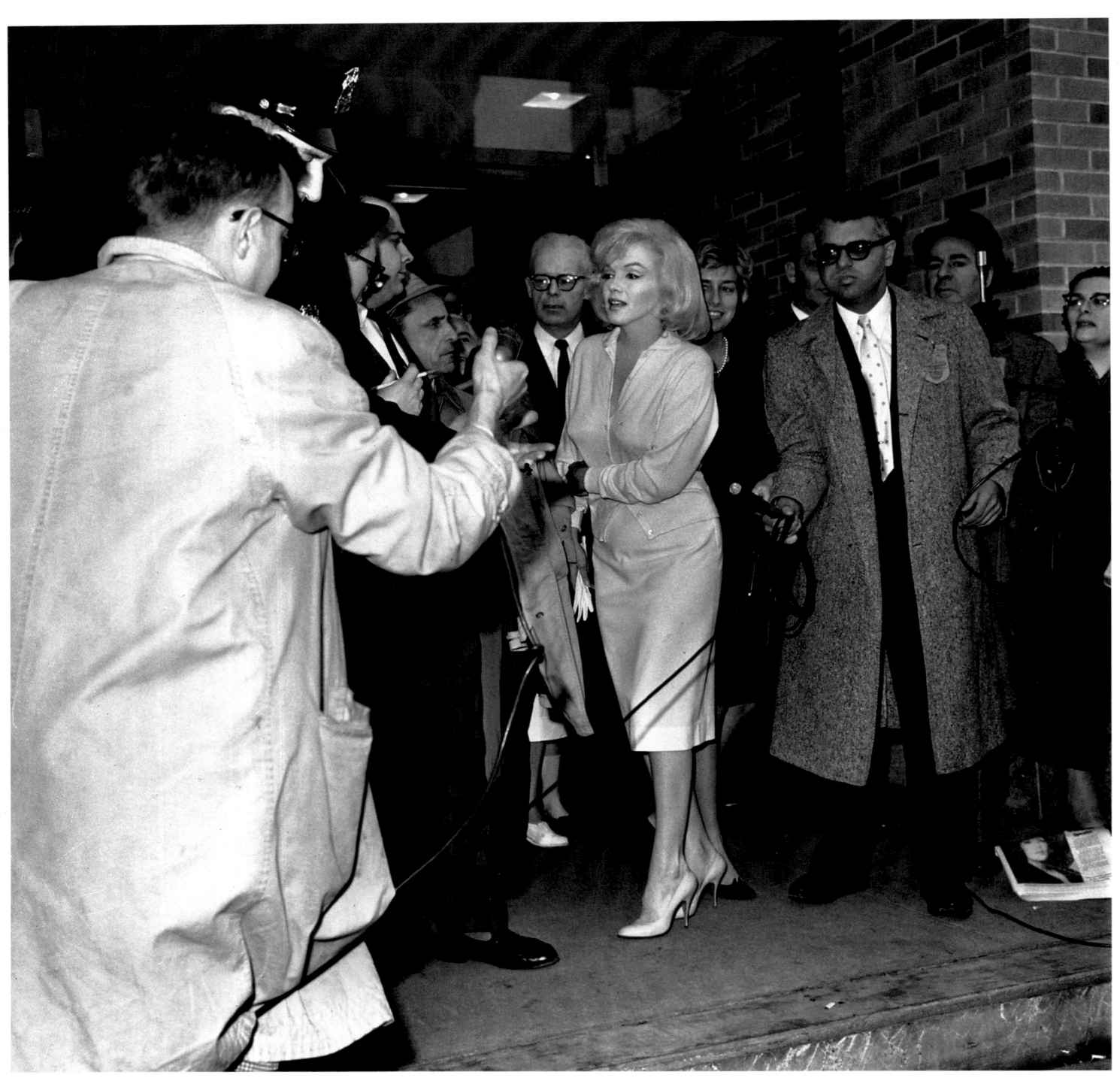

On March 7, 1961, Marilyn Monroe was accosted by reporters
while leaving Columbia Presbyterian Medical Center. Although she had spent a month in
psychiatric treatment, and in spite of the unusually noisy hounding by the reporters,
Marilyn still found enough time and energy for a smile.

Pages 218/219

After Marilyn's divorce from Arthur Miller and her release
from the psychiatric clinic, Joe DiMaggio once again looked after her. This snapshot taken
through a windshield by a paparazzo shows an alert and harassed-looking Marilyn.

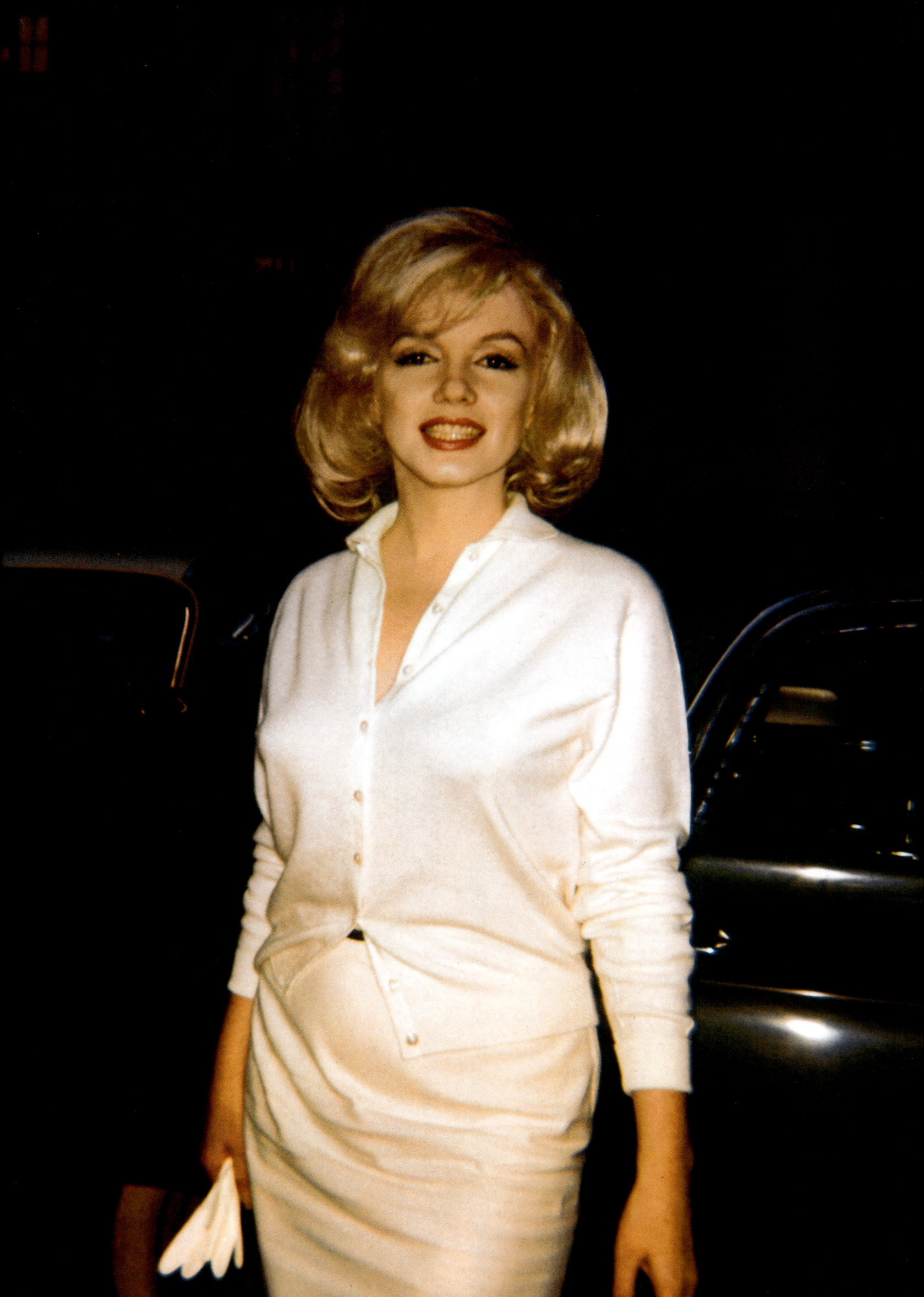

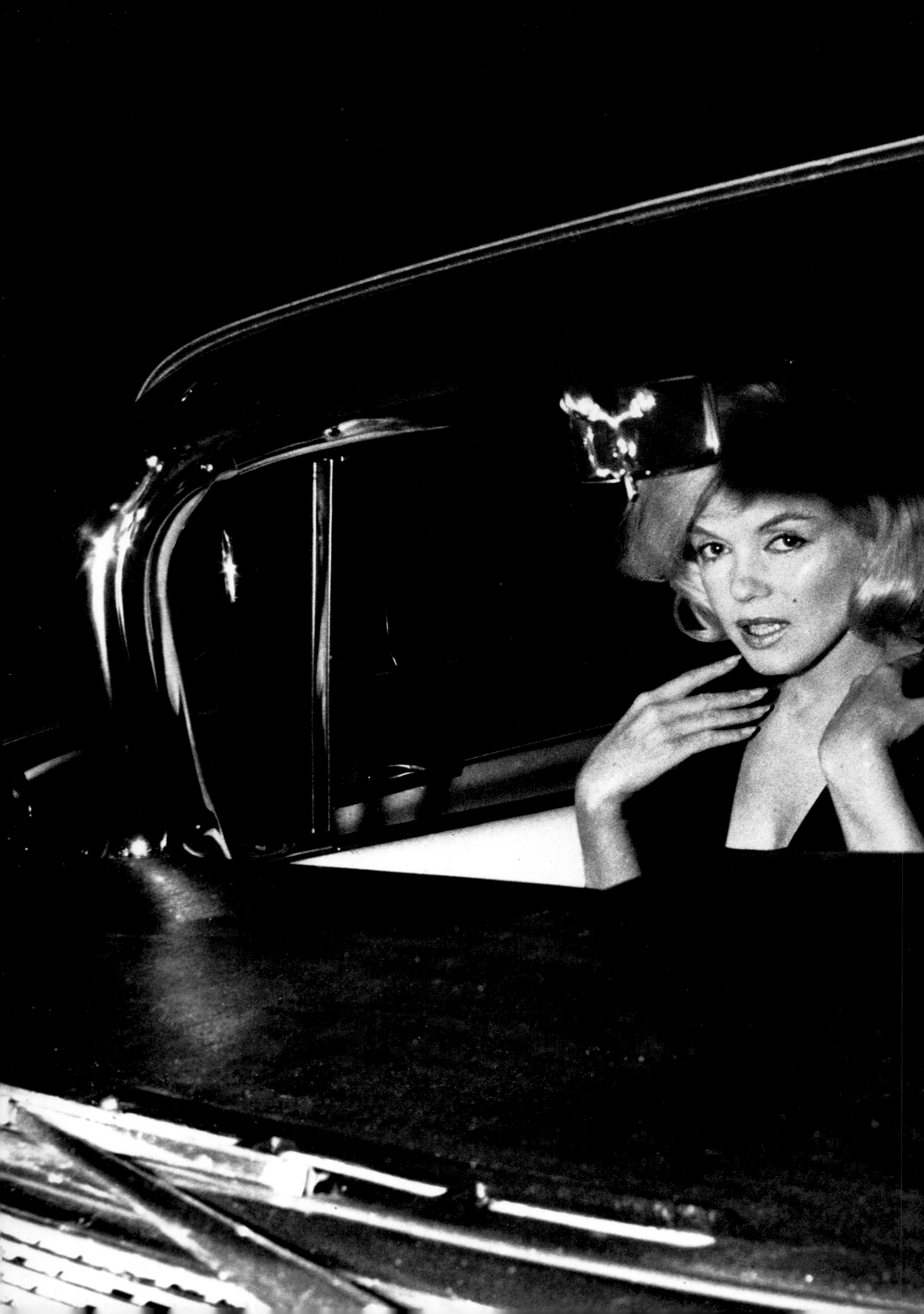

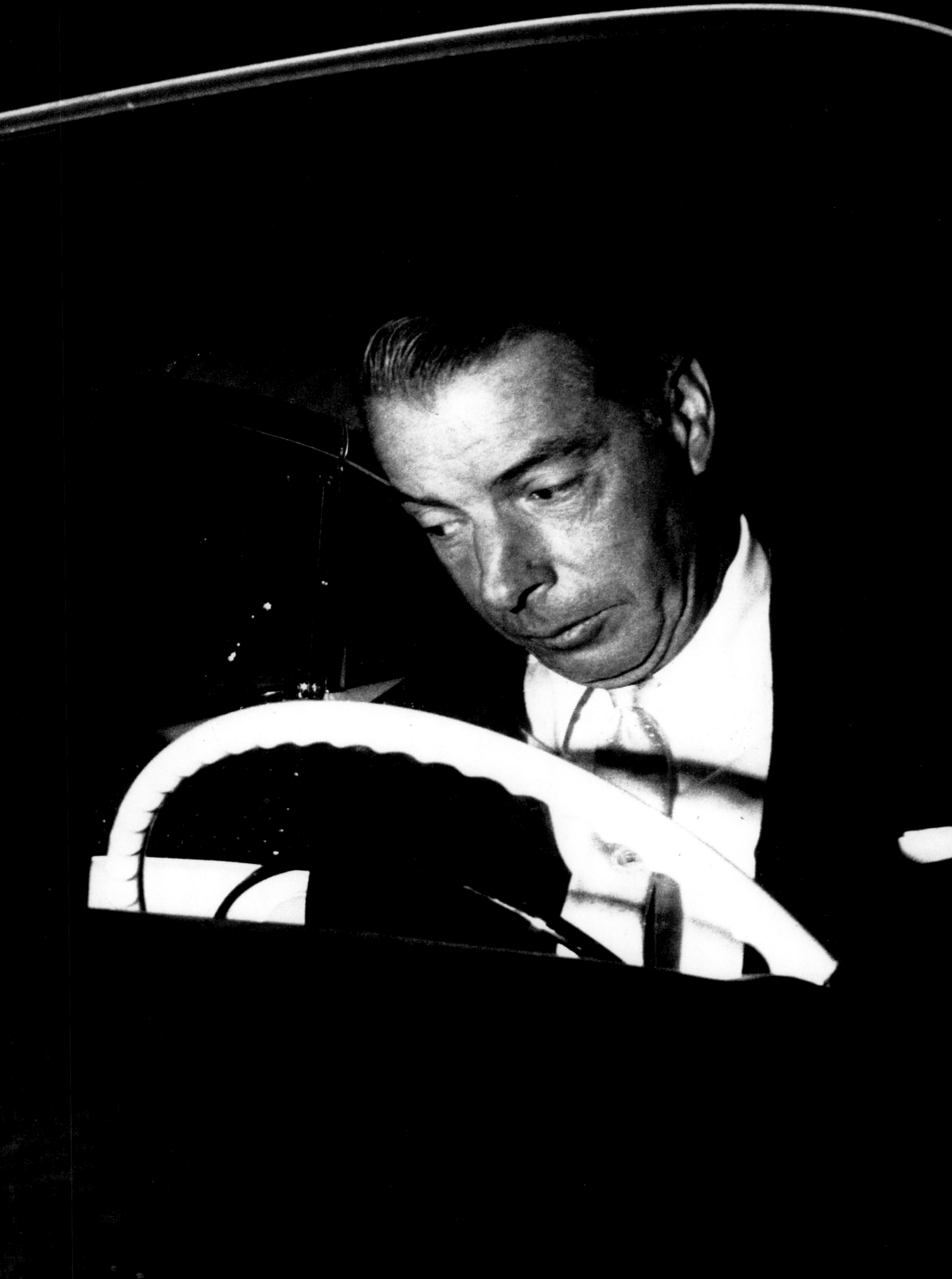

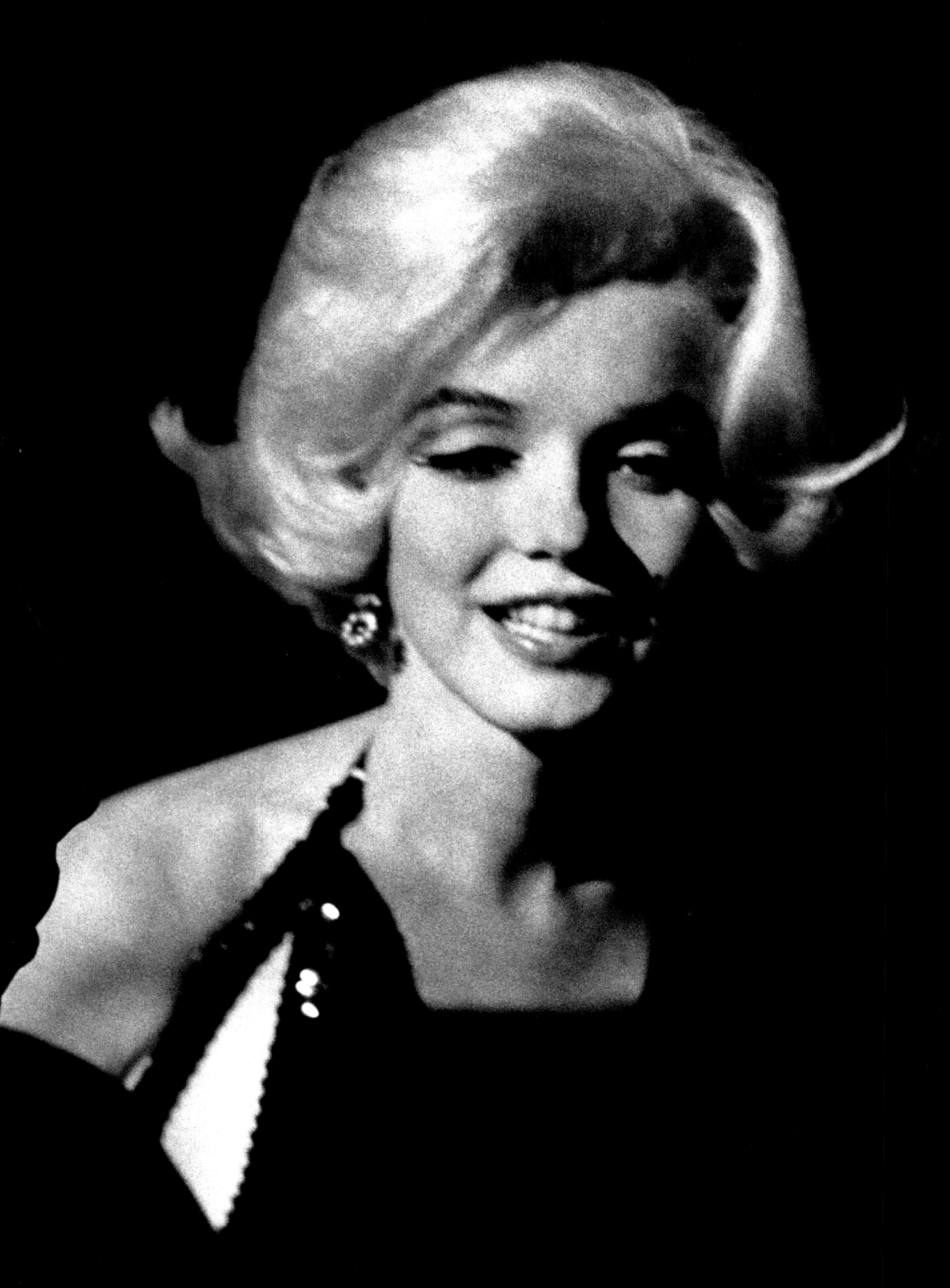

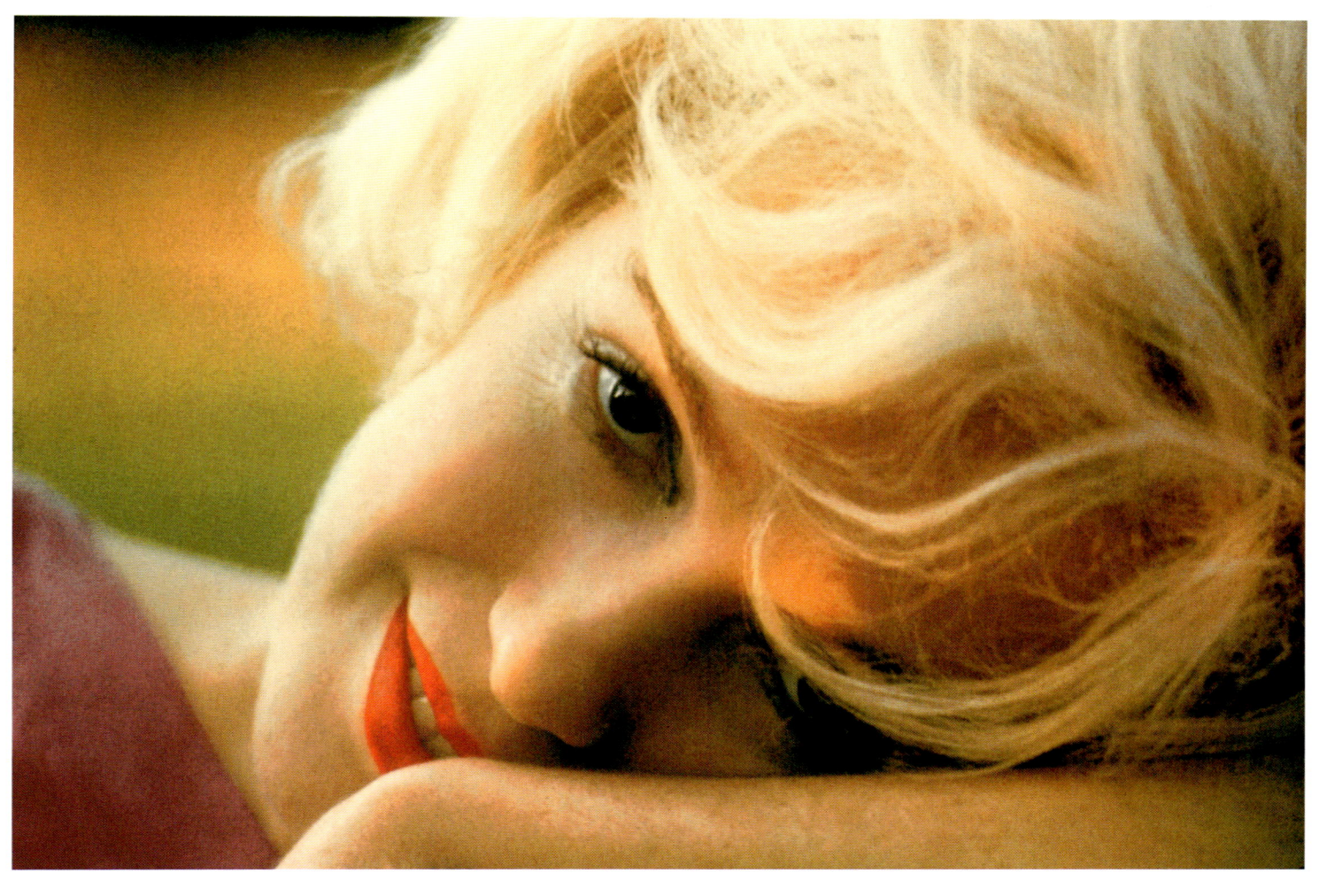

On March 5, 1962, Marilyn received the Golden Globe Award as
"the world film favorite of 1961." At the presentation her companion was José Balanos,
a Mexican scriptwriter.

Portrait study by Willy Rizzo for *Paris Match,* spring 1962.

Publicity still for *Something's Got to Give.*
Filming was suspended on June 8, 1962, because Marilyn was perennially late and finally
did not show up at all on the set.

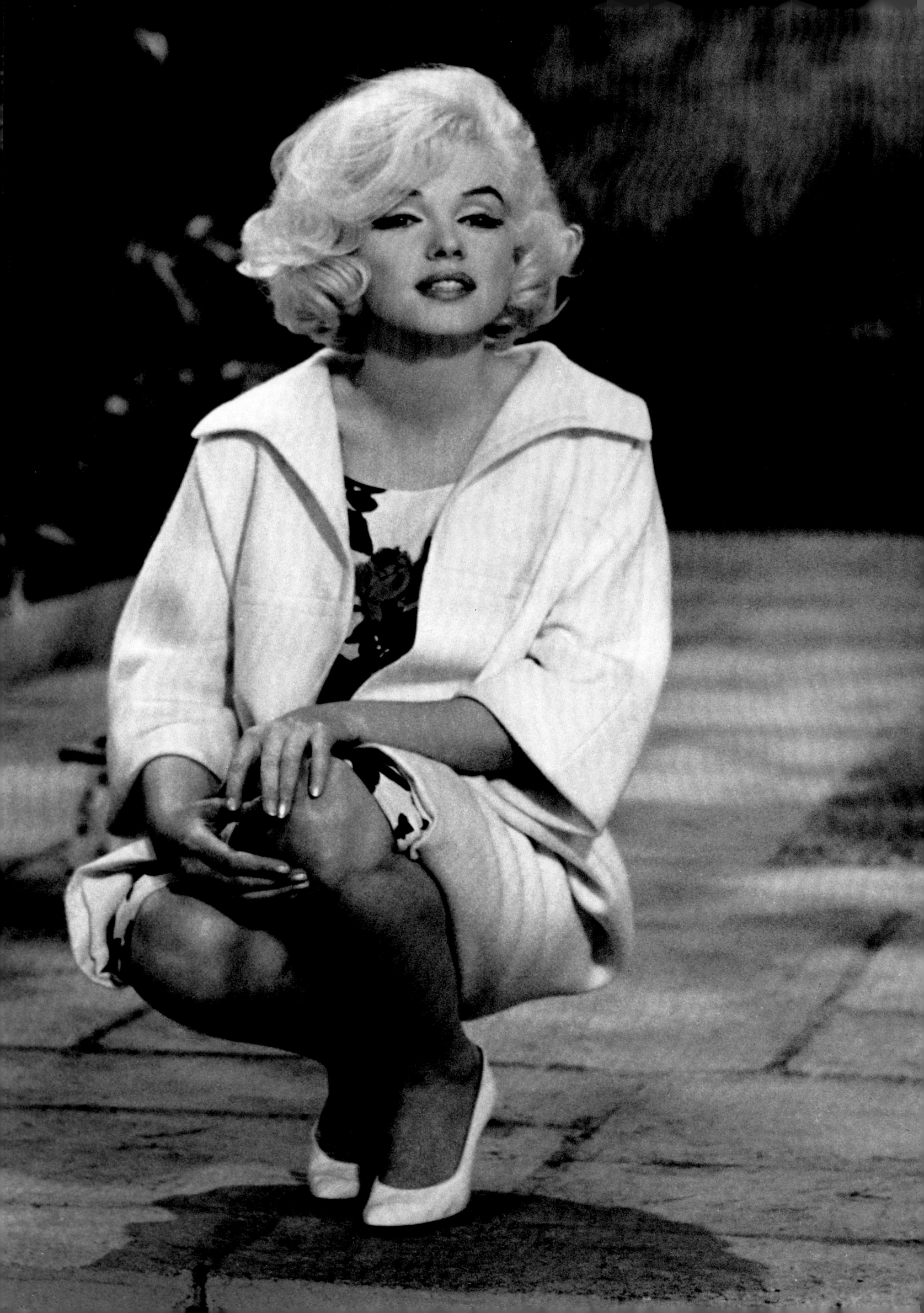

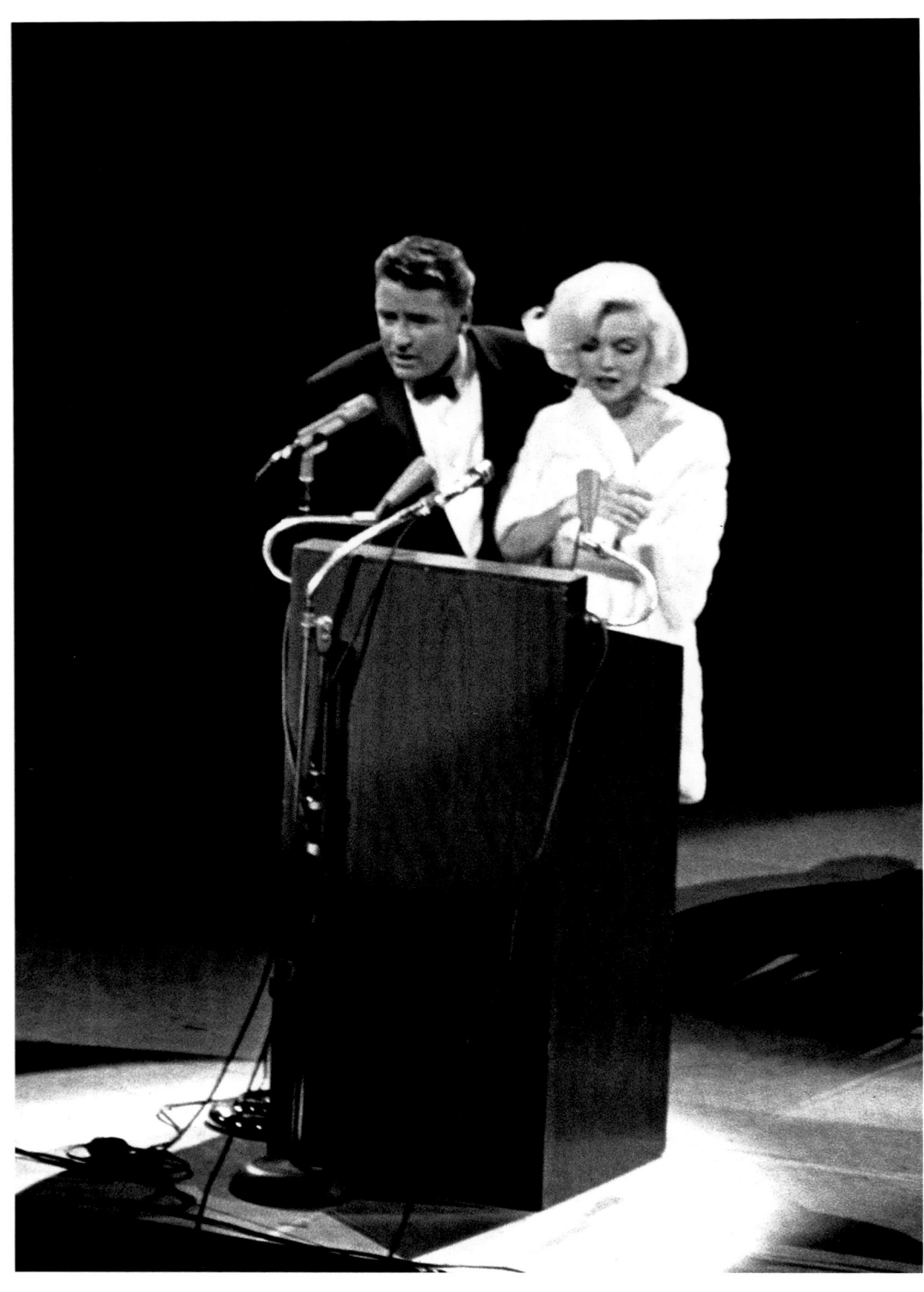

On May 19, 1962, Marilyn had left the filming of *Something's Got to Give*
without permission to appear at the birthday gala for John F. Kennedy
in New York's Madison Square Garden. Here, too, she arrived about
forty minutes late. Peter Lawford's ambiguous introduction was: "Mr. President, the late
Marilyn Monroe . . ." John F. Kennedy thanked her for the song by saying,
"I can now retire from politics after having had 'Happy Birthday' sung to me in such a sweet,
wholesome way."

224

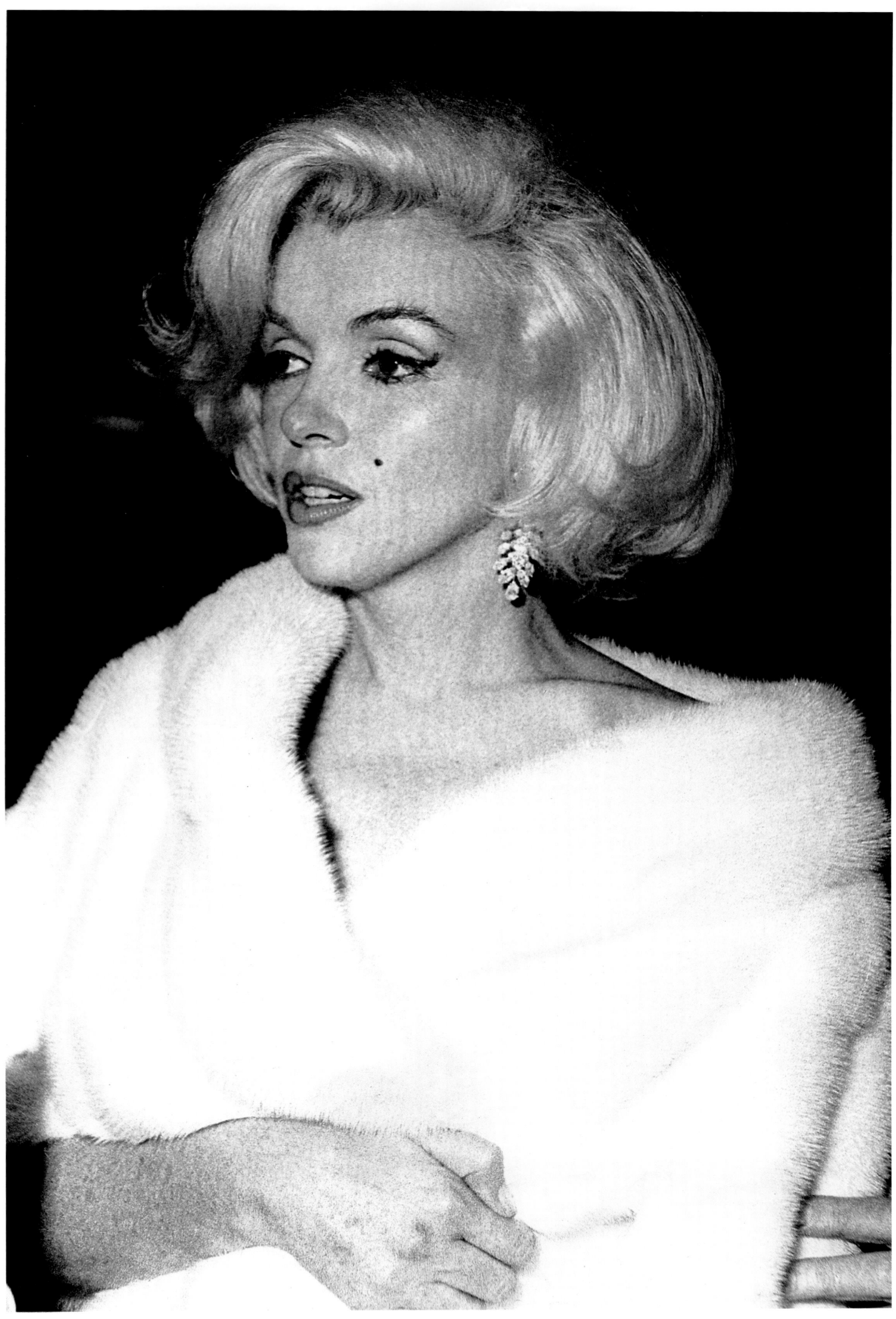

225

Pages 227 and 228/229

On June 23, 1962, a three-day sitting began with Bert Stern
at the Los Angeles Bel Air Hotel, arranged by *Vogue*. Nearly twenty-seven hundred pictures
were taken, from which *Vogue* editors decided to publish eight.
This was the first time that *Vogue* reported on Marilyn Monroe.

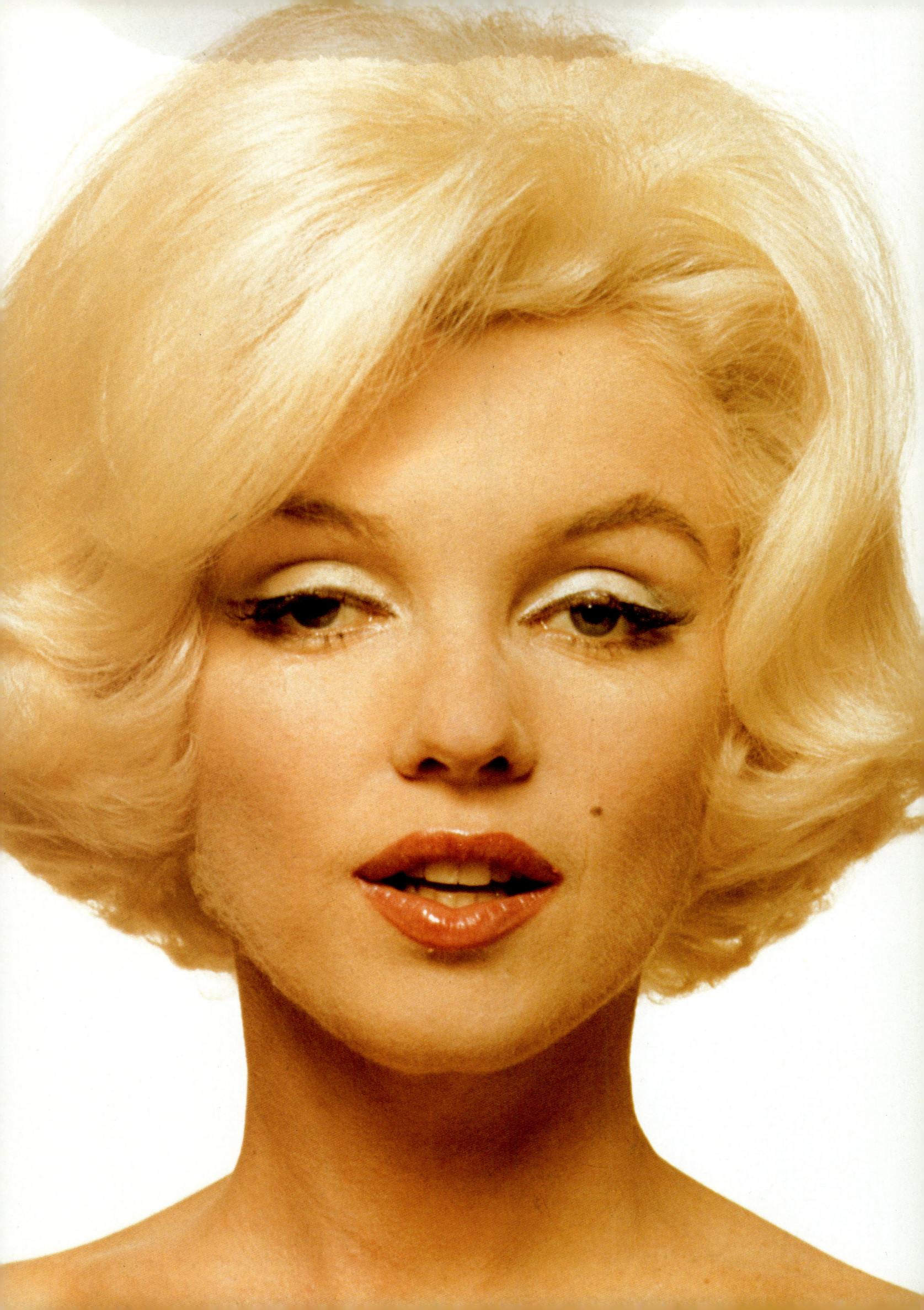

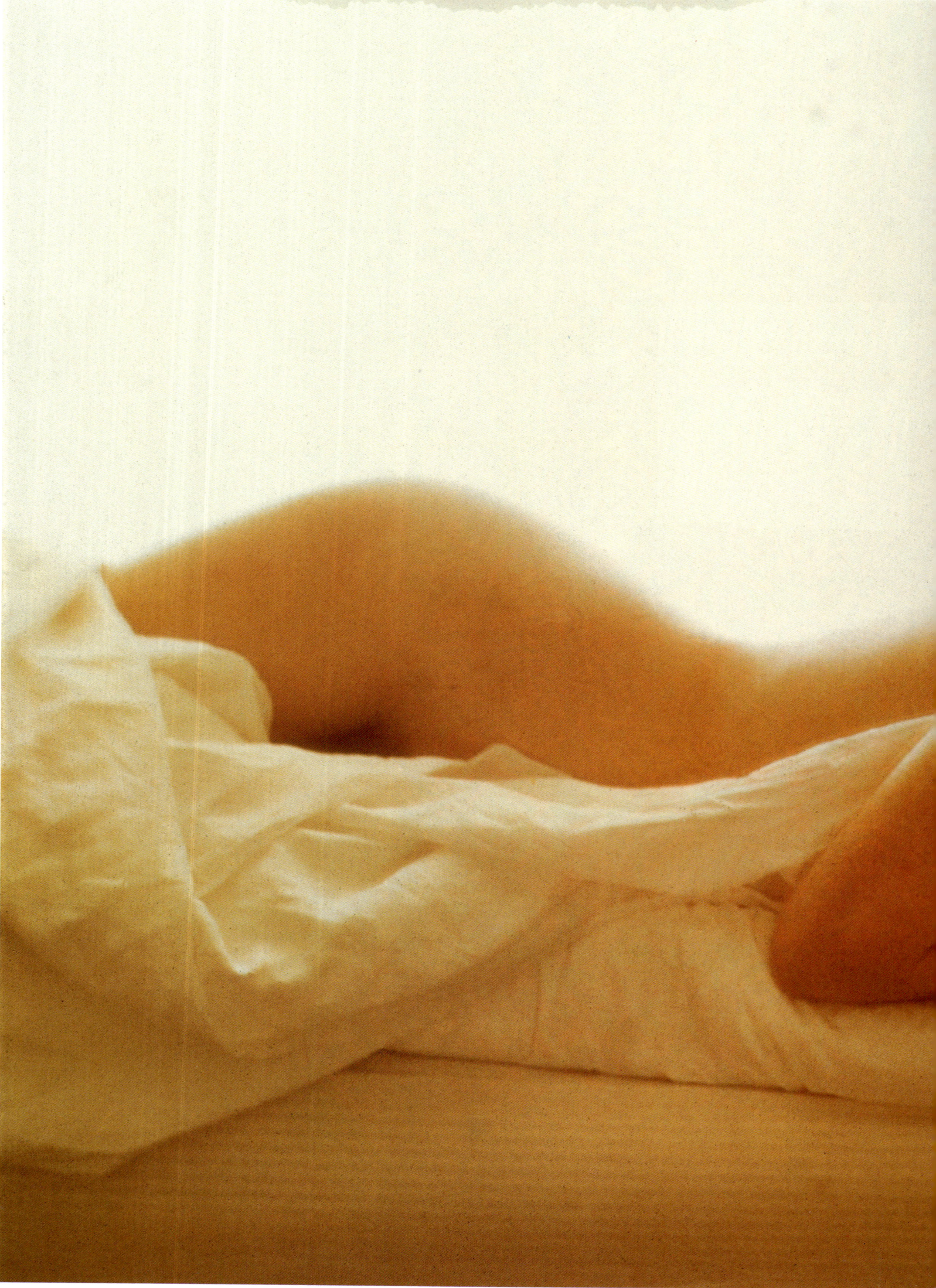

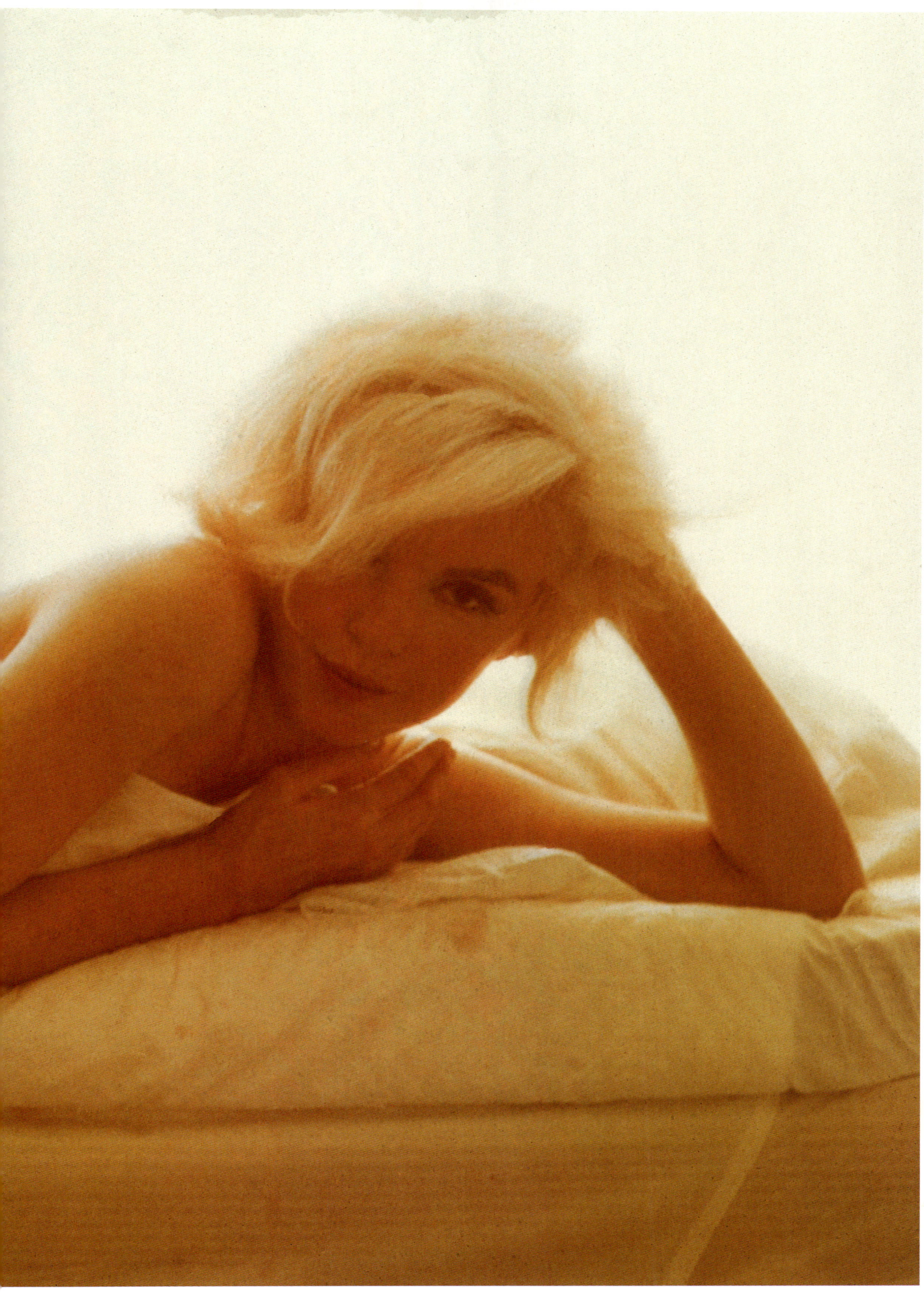

Page 231

The agreement between Bert Stern and Marilyn Monroe stipulated
that all pictures be presented to her for her approval. When Stern received the pictures from
her, more than half were crossed through, including this shot.
Bert commented that it was as if she had crossed out herself and not the pictures.

Pages 232/233

This fashion photograph by Bert Stern for *Vogue* shows a pensive Marilyn.
In her last interview, which *Life* published a week before her death, a strong detachment
came through: "Fame to me is only a temporary and partial happiness,
that's not what fulfills me. It warms you a bit, but the warming is temporary. It might be kind
of a relief to be finished. It's sort of like you don't know what kind of yard dash
you're running, and then you're at the finish line and you sort of sigh – you've made it. But
fame will go by – and so long. I've had you, fame. I've always known it was fickle."

Pages 234/235

August 5, 1962. The sign on the building of the
New York Times at Times Square flashed news of the death of Marilyn Monroe.

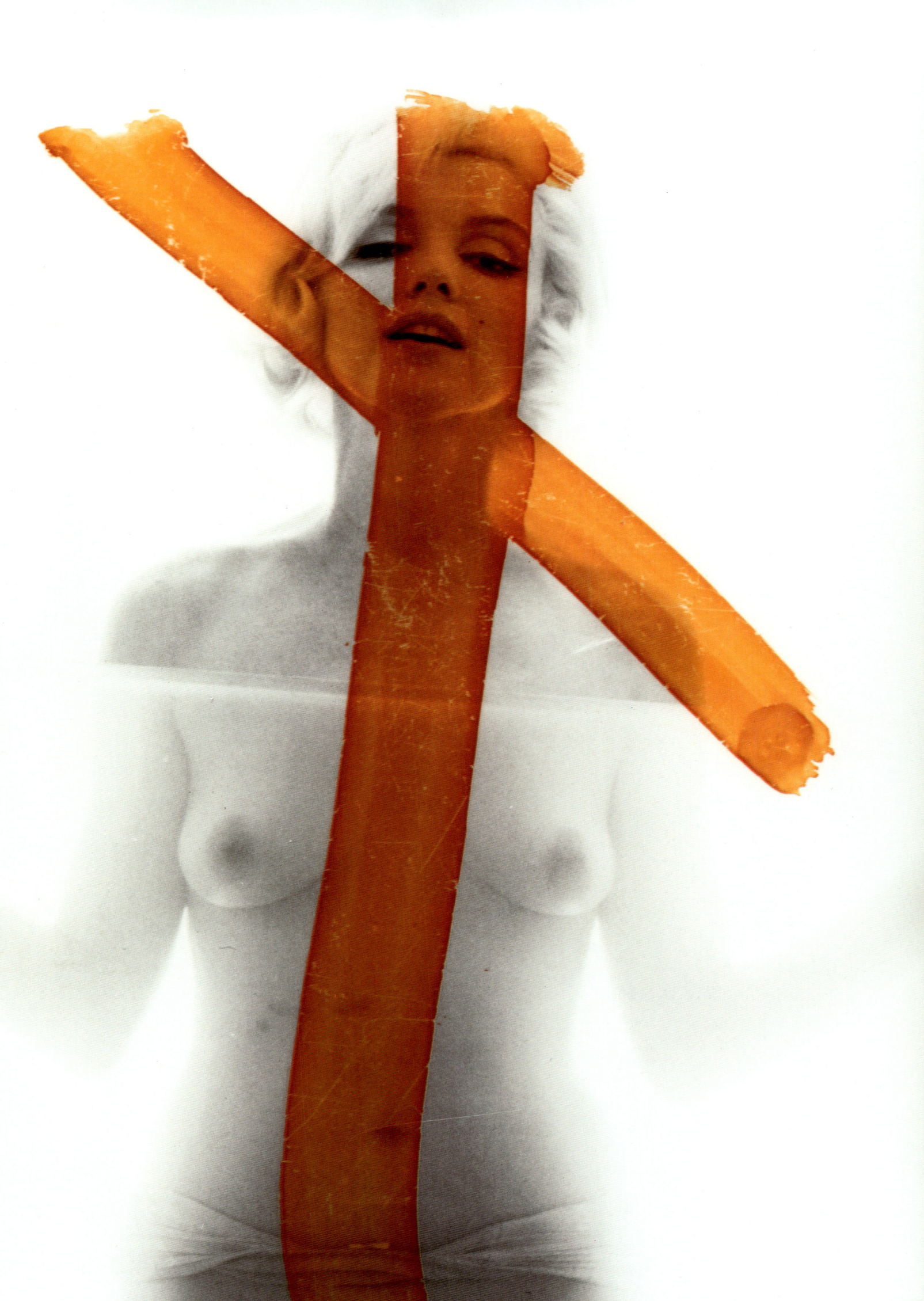

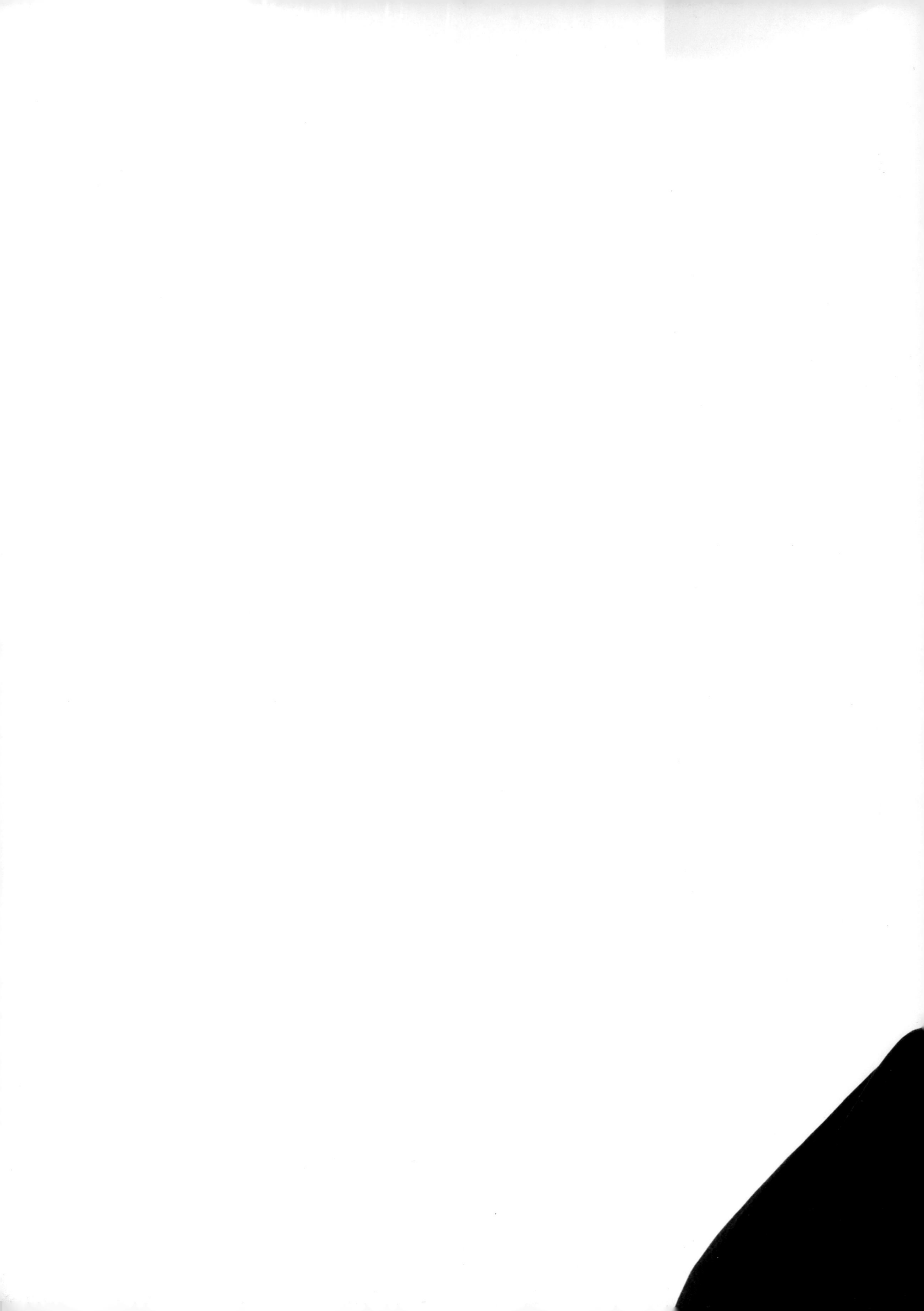

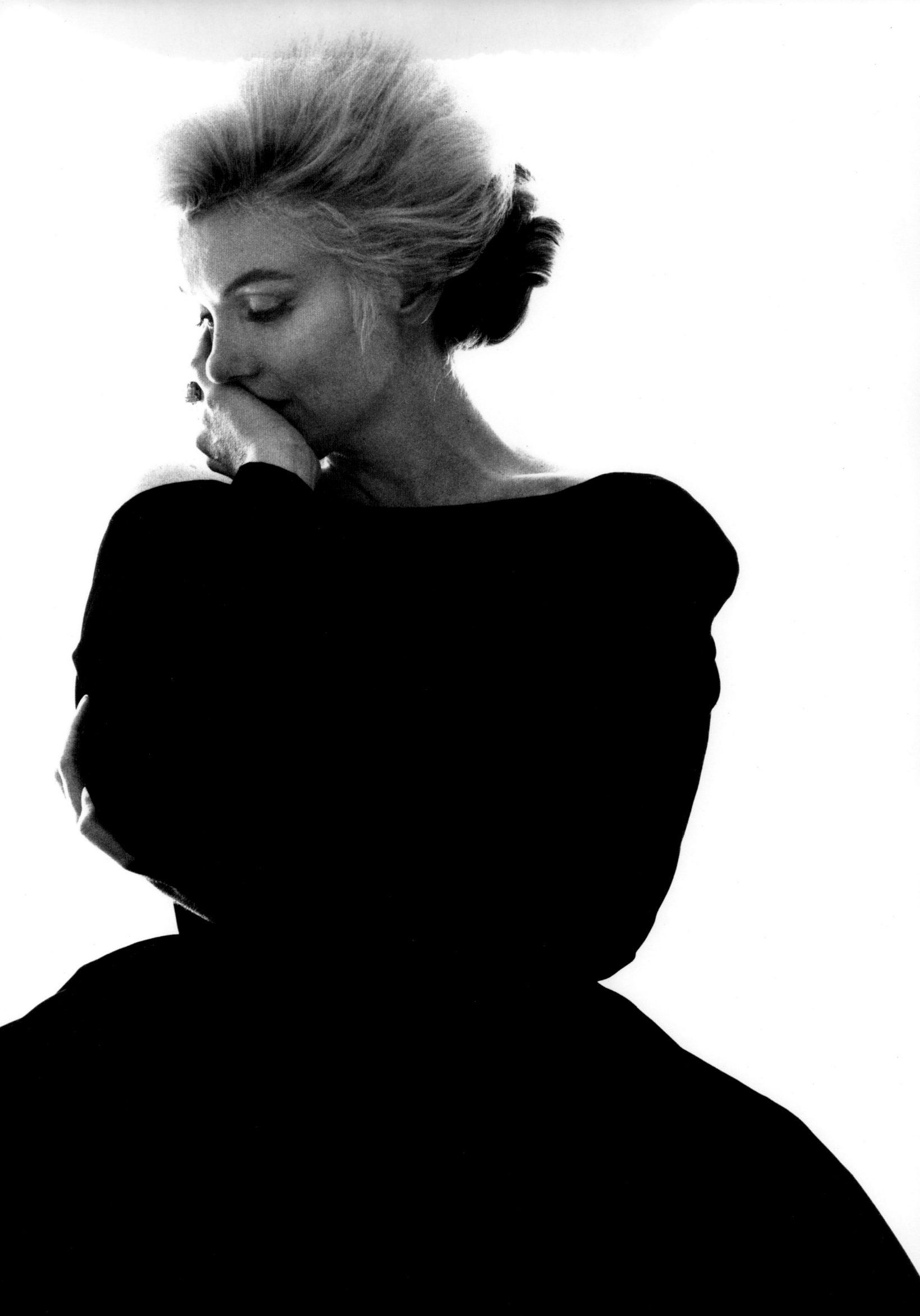

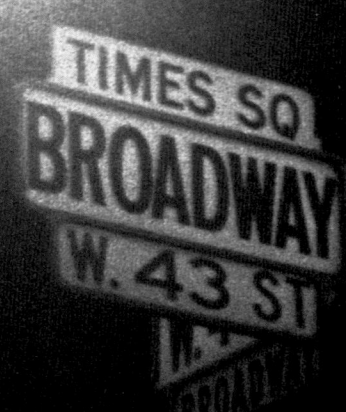

TIMES SQ
BROADWAY
W. 43 ST

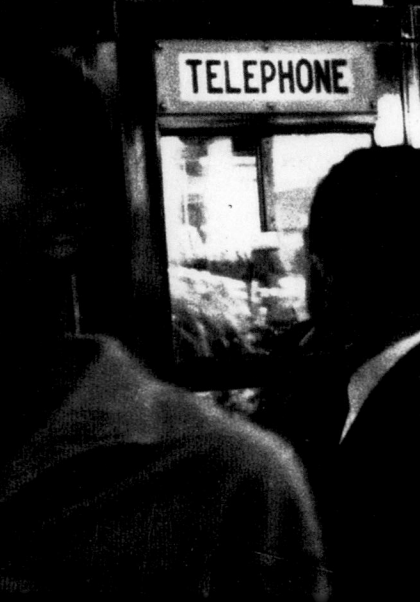

TELEPHONE

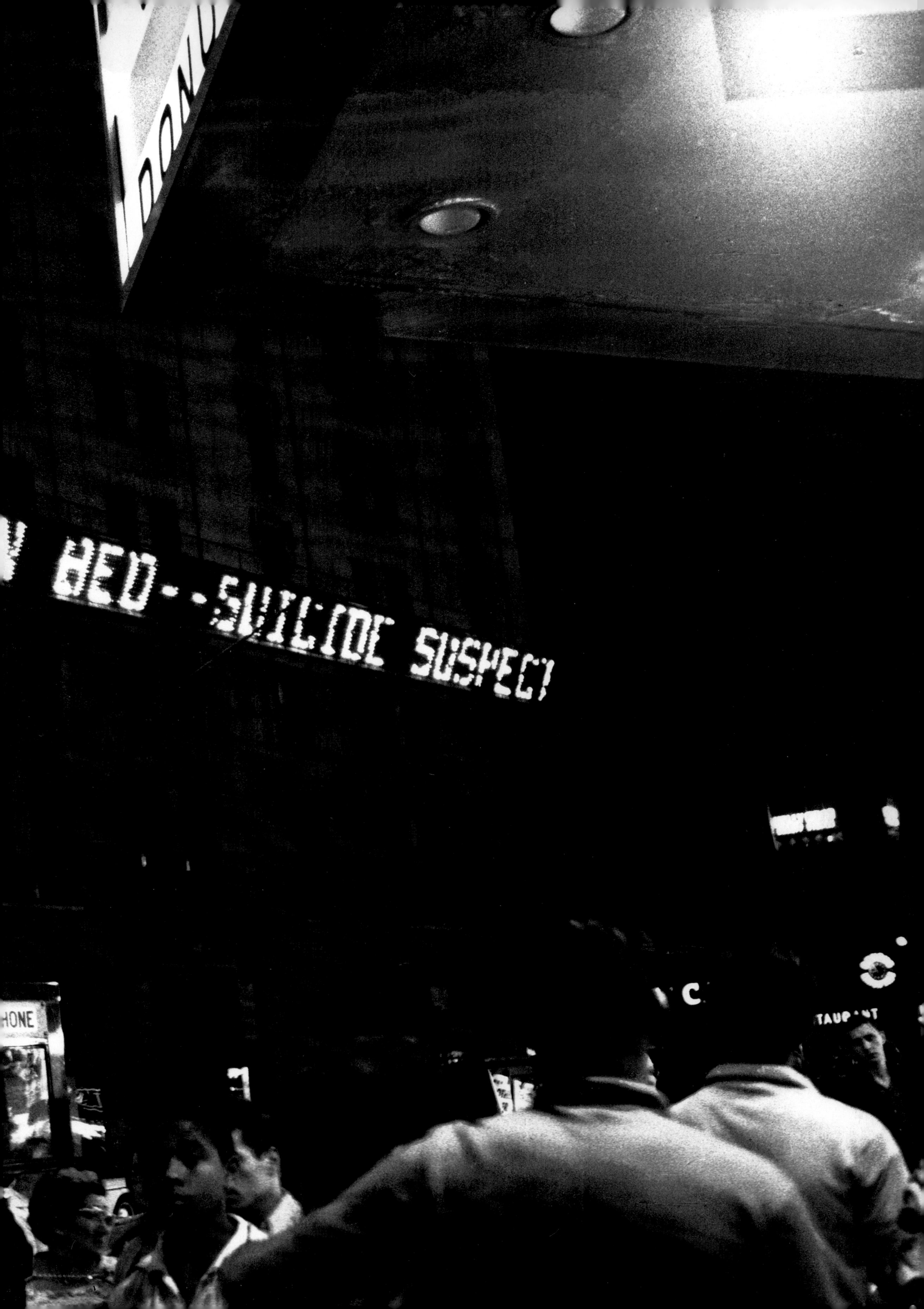

-SUICIDE SUSPECT
HONE
TAURANT

Biography

June 1, 1926   Marilyn Monroe is born in Los Angeles General Hospital, the third child of Gladys Pearl Baker, née Monroe (May 25, 1900–March 11, 1984). She is named "Norma Jeane" (later Marilyn often left off the *e* in Jeane.) The father remains unknown. The name "Edward Mortensen" is given on her birth certificate, since Gladys was married to a man of this name two years before the birth. Although Marilyn often uses this name for official documents, in numerous private conversations she denies that he was her real father. In one interview Marilyn mentions that her real father lived in the same apartment building as her mother did and that he left her during the pregnancy. This reference led to a man named Stanley Gifford, who worked for Consolidated Film Industries, where Marilyn's mother was employed as a cutter. Rumors have it that Gifford was Gladys's lover when her second marriage with Mortenson broke up. In 1962, the year of her death, Marilyn gives the name of her father as "unknown" on an official questionnaire.

January 1935   Norma Jeane's mother goes into a deep depression and is sent to Los Angeles General Hospital; diagnosed as a paranoid schizophrenic, she is later committed to Norwalk State Asylum. Gladys's best friend, Grace McKee, is declared Norma Jeane's guardian. Gladys, who lives alone, on September 9, 1935, takes the young Norma Jeane to the orphanage of the Los Angeles Orphans Home Society.

June 26, 1937   Grace McKee marries "Doc" Goddard and time and again takes in Norma Jeane. In the following years Norma Jeane lives with many different foster families (who urgently need the five-dollar-a-week government allowance), spends two years in an orphanage, afterward is again in foster care, and finally lives for four years alone under an officially appointed guardian.

June 19, 1942   On a Friday, Norma Jeane Baker marries Jim Dougherty. The marriage was arranged by Grace Goddard because she and her husband were moving east and didn't want to take Norma Jeane with them. Jim Dougherty, a neighbor's son, is taken completely by surprise when he hears that he is to marry the pretty Norma Jeane. A talented football player, he decided not to go to college and first worked as an embalmer in a mortuary, later as a mechanic for Lockheed Aviation. The marriage is scheduled for June, after Norma Jeane's sixteenth birthday. No honeymoon is possible: Monday morning Jim returns to work at the airplane factory. In fall 1943 Jim joins the Merchant Marine and spends most of his marriage as a soldier abroad.

June 26, 1945   David Conover, an army photographer for a military film unit, takes pictures of Norma Jeane for *Yank,* an army magazine. His task, which his commanding officer, later U.S. President Ronald Reagan, had given him, was to take "morally uplifting snapshots of pretty girls" working on jobs vital to the war effort. At this time Norma Jeane is earning twenty dollars a week at Radio Plane Corporation for ten hours' work a day. The offer to earn five dollars an hour as a model comes at just the right time, and she continues to work as a freelance model. David Conover offers some of her photos to the model agency Blue Book, and recommends her to them.

August 2, 1945   The name "Norma Jeane Dougherty" is placed in the files of the Blue Book Modelling Agency; this marks the beginning of Norma Jeane's phenomenal career as a cover girl and sex symbol. From now on she can talk only about her meteoric success, and this estranges her husband, who is at home only for a few weeks at a time. The well-known photographer André de Dienes courts the lonely young woman and wants to marry her. Although she poses for him extensively and goes on a photo excursion with him, which ends in an affair, she withdraws and turns her attention to other men. Her work with other famous Hollywood photographers such as Lazlo Willinger, Richard C. Miller, Earl Moran, Bruno Bernard, George Hurrel, and others begins to flourish. Her pictures soon appear on the covers of various magazines. This publicity leads to her first contact with the film world.

July 17, 1946   Marilyn has her first audition with Ben Lyon, her "discoverer," at 20th Century-Fox.

July 19, 1946   On the recommendation of Ben Lyon Norma Jeane is given her first film test at the 20th Century-Fox studios. His encounter with her convinces him of her talent and charisma, and he wants to put her under contract in spite of the reservations of Darryl Zanuck, head of 20th Century-Fox.

July 29, 1946   For the first time Norma Jeane Dougherty is mentioned in a *Los Angeles Times* gossip column.

August 24, 1946   Norma Jeane obtains her first studio contract with 20th Century-Fox. Ben Lyon finds the name "Norma Jeane Dougherty" completely inappropriate and calls her at first "Carole Lind" and then "Marilyn Miller." Finally, Norma Jeane recalls the name of her grandmother, and she and Lyon agree to the pleasing alliteration of "Marilyn Monroe." Years later, having achieved stardom, Marilyn sends Lyon a photo portrait with the dedication "You found me, named me and believed in me when no one else did. My love and thanks forever."

September 13, 1946   Marilyn divorces James Dougherty.

Early 1947   At twenty-one, Marilyn is an unnamed extra in the film *Scudda Hoo! Scudda Hay!* Her appearance ends up largely in the cutting-room wastebasket, but one scrap of dialogue survives, the word "hello," and a brief long shot where she can be seen paddling around in a canoe. *Scudda Hoo! Scudda Hay!* is the first film she appears in; it is shown in 1948, after the release of her second film, *Dangerous Years,* which premieres on December 8, 1947. In *Dangerous Years* she plays the minor role of Eve, a waitress in a bar. On her first year Marilyn remarks: "Most of what I did while I was at Fox that first time was pose for stills. Publicity made up a story about how I was a baby-sitter for a casting director.... You'd think they would have had me at least [be] a daddy-sitter." (M.M. to Pete Martin, *Will Acting Spoil Marilyn Monroe,* Doubleday, 1956)

August 25, 1947   After Marilyn has been with 20th Century-Fox for a year, Darryl Zanuck decides not to extend the contract of the blonde femme fatale, owing to "unsatisfactory dramatic performance." Marilyn and her mentor, Ben Lyon, are speechless.

March 9, 1948   Marilyn signs a half-year contract with Columbia Studios, which guarantees her $125 a week. Natasha Lytess, head drama coach at Columbia, gives her drama lessons for several months. The first movie in which M.M. is allowed to talk, sing, and dance is a low-budget production entitled *Ladies of the Chorus.* A passionate affair begins with Fred Karger, the studio's vocal coach. "A new life began for me.... I had always thought of myself as someone unloved. Now I know there had been something worse than that in my life. It had been my own unloving heart.... When he said 'I love you' to me, it was better than a thousand critics calling me a great star." (M.M. to Ben Hecht) When her contract with Columbia expires in September 1948, it too is not extended.

Early 1949   Marilyn is unemployed and penniless again, and about to leave Fred Karger, the first man she really gave her heart to, as she often confesses. But that spring Groucho Marx gets her a small role in the Mary Pickford production of *Love Happy.* She was chosen from three actresses auditioning for a small gag in the film. Groucho, a private detective, is approached by her, a young, curvaceous beauty: Marilyn: "Mr. Grunion. I want you to help me ... Some men are following me." Groucho: "Really? I can't understand why." In the credits to the movie, which premiered in 1950, her name is listed separately: "Introducing Marilyn Monroe."

May 27, 1949   In Tom Kelley's studio, the first nude photographs are taken. Their publication in a calendar leads to a "scandal" three years later.

July 24, 1949   Marilyn has her first interview with the gossip columnist Earl Wilson in connection with a promotion tour for *Love Happy* in the New York Sherry Netherland Hotel. Wilson writes: "Over the years Hollywood has given us its 'It Girl,' its 'Oomph Girl,' its 'Sweater Girl,' and even 'The Body.' Now we get the 'Mmmmmmm Girl.'" During this tour the famous photo series by André de Dienes on Tobey Beach, Long Island, is taken.

August 15, 1949   The filming begins for *A Ticket to Tomahawk,* a trivial, not-so-entertaining western of limited dramatic quality in which Marilyn plays the role of Clara, a chorus girl. At the Racquet Club, an exclusive Palm Springs Tennis Club, Marilyn Monroe meets Johnny Hyde, a representative of the William Morris Agency, one of Hollywood's most influential theatrical agencies. Hyde is one of America's most successful talent scouts, fifty-three years old – thirty years older than Marilyn – very rich and with a heart condition. He promises to make Marilyn a star. During the day he extols Marilyn's talent; in the evenings he accompanies her to the houses of the famous, rich, and powerful. Marilyn turns down his proposal of marriage.

January 5, 1950   Shooting of *The Fireball,* in which she plays Polly, a roller-skating groupie, begins.

June 1950   The premiere of John Huston's *Asphalt Jungle* takes place. This film is the story of an aging gangster (Sam Jaffe) who, just released from prison, looks for a new gang for his last coup. Marilyn plays Angela Phinlay, the blonde, youthful lover of the gangster. *The Asphalt Jungle* is her first demanding script. In the same year Marilyn has a memorable part in the Academy Award-winning *All About Eve.* The public finally takes notice of Marilyn Monroe and admires her, and Hollywood producers present her with better offers.

December 10, 1950   Johnny Hyde negotiates a seven-year contract for Marilyn with 20th Century-Fox.

December 18, 1950   Johnny Hyde dies. Shortly thereafter, while filming *As Young As You Feel* at 20th Century-Fox, Marilyn meets two more influential men: Elia Kazan, one of the most distinguished stage and film directors; and Arthur Miller, Pulitzer Prize-winning playwright.

April 18, 1951   Shooting begins for *Love Nest,* the second production under Marilyn's new contract and one of the numerous films that called for a well-proportioned blonde. In this fairly mediocre movie, Marilyn plays Roberta Stevens, an ex-WAC. The premiere is held on October 10, 1951.

September 8, 1951   The first full-page feature about Marilyn appears in *Collier's.* Further cover stories in *Look* and *Life* follow.

March 13, 1952   The story of the nude calendar photos surfaces, and the public recognizes the connection between the new film star and the pinups that hung in many garages and barbershops. Marilyn, after many tears, refuses to deny that she made the photos. She pleads that they were taken when she was penniless so that she could pay for food and rent: "I was hungry," she tells reporters. Her touching story quickly turns the scandal into a gigantic publicity success. Later, in December 1953, a picture from the series appears on the cover of the newly founded *Playboy*.

June 1, 1952 On Marilyn's twenty-sixth birthday, she is told that she has been given the coveted role of Lorelei Lee in *Gentlemen Prefer Blondes*, one of the most important musicals of the fifties.

September 2, 1952 M.M. is the "Grand Marshal" for the Miss America contest.

October 4, 1952 An alleged, but somewhat uncertain, marriage to Robert Slatzer, an Ohio journalist, takes place in Tijuana, Mexico, marriage and divorce haven. According to rumors, the marriage lasts for three days. 20th Century-Fox insists on an immediate annulment. In the closing weeks of 1952 filming begins on *Gentlemen Prefer Blondes*. The movie is a smashing success for Marilyn in 1953 – the same year in which she achieves stardom in *Niagara*.

June 26, 1953 M.M. and Jane Russell (costar of *Gentlemen Prefer Blondes*) kneel on the sidewalk in front of Grauman's Chinese Theater, Hollywood's famous movie palace, in order to place for all time their handprints and their footprints in cement. Finally, they carve their names next to the imprints to the cheers of the surrounding crowd. Marilyn stresses the preeminence of her role in the movie: "It is *Gentlemen Prefer Blondes*, and I am the blonde." In the movie she sings the classic "Diamonds Are a Girl's Best Friend."

September 13, 1953 Marilyn makes her first TV appearance, on the Jack Benny show.

October 1953 Marilyn meets photographer Milton H. Greene at a party given for Gene Kelly. In the coming years Greene helps free her from the strictures of her contract with 20th Century-Fox. She signs a recording contract with RCA.

November 4, 1953 Premiere of *How to Marry a Millionaire*. Three women – M.M. as Pola Debevoise, Lauren Bacall, and Betty Grable – rent an exclusive apartment in New York and try to land a trio of millionaires. This successful comedy enhances Marilyn's fame as a star and ranks with the success of *Gentlemen Prefer Blondes*.

December 15, 1953 Shooting for *The Girl in Pink Tights* begins, after Darryl Zanuck refuses her the leading role in *The Egyptian*. Frank Sinatra takes on the leading male role. Although Marilyn is the greater box-office attraction, Sinatra receives $5,000 a week to Marilyn's $1,500, a result of her seven-year contract. M.M. protests by not showing up and is suspended by 20th Century-Fox on January 4, 1954.

January 14, 1954 Marilyn Monroe marries former baseball champion Joe DiMaggio, a "living legend" of American sports, in San Francisco. He has courted her assiduously for a year. The marriage receives worldwide publicity, and Marilyn is able to get 20th Century-Fox to drop the disciplinary measures resulting from her breach of contract. The newlyweds' honeymoon begins in Japan.

February 16, 1954 Marilyn interrupts her honeymoon and flies to Seoul to entertain the troops stationed in Korea. She later calls her appearance before the soldiers one of the high points in her life. "I never felt like a star before in my heart. It was so wonderful to look down and see a fellow smiling at me," Marilyn admitted to her friend Amy Greene.

August 10, 1954 Filming for *The Seven Year Itch*, directed by Billy Wilder, begins. Marilyn plays the luscious blonde who lives in the apartment over that belonging to the conventional but susceptible costar Tom Ewell. When his wife goes on vacation, he is inspired to bold, erotic fantasies.

September 15, 1954 The famous scene on the subway grate from *The Seven Year Itch* is filmed in New York. Tipped off by the press through the studio's publicity department, thousands gather behind wooden police barriers to see the lovely young woman's snow-white skirt billow up to her shoulders – to the amusement of Marilyn and Tom Ewell. Less amused is Joe DiMaggio, who watches the scene in the crowd and thereafter engages in one of his and Marilyn's worst marital fights.

October 5, 1954 Marilyn and Joe separate officially. "Our marriage wasn't a happy one," she said later.

October 27, 1954 Marilyn files for divorce in Santa Monica.

November 6, 1954 Hollywood's film society celebrates Marilyn Monroe on the occasion of the completion of *The Seven Year Itch* at Romanoff's Beverly Hills restaurant. The signatures in her honor on the huge "Marilyn" souvenir portrait include those of Humphrey Bogart, Lauren Bacall, Claudette Colbert, William Holden, James Stewart, Susan Hayward, Gary Cooper, and Doris Day. Hollywood's film moguls, including Sam Goldwyn, Jack Warner, and Darryl Zanuck, pose for the cameras. For the first time Marilyn meets her childhood idol, Clark Gable.
Nevertheless, the celebrated star decides to turn her back on Hollywood. Shortly before Christmas 1954 she puts on a dark wig and sunglasses and, with a ticket in her pocket issued to the name of "Zelda Zonk," flies from Los Angeles to Connecticut, where she retreats to the house of photographer Milton H. Greene. Her self-imposed exile lasts a year.

December 31, 1954 With Milton H. Greene she founds Marilyn Monroe Productions, Inc. Her enthusiastic remarks about her companion: "I feel deeply about him. I'm sincere about his genius. He's a genius." As her mentor, partner, and impresario, he ensures that Marilyn's high cost of living of about $50,000 a year can be financed.

January 15, 1955 Marilyn's absence from Hollywood and her private initiative with Milton Greene lead 20th Century-Fox to announce another suspension. During a press conference in New York arranged by Milton H. Greene, Marilyn reveals her new dramatic ambitions, including the desire to play Grushenka in *The Brothers Karamazov*, a wish the press comments on sarcastically. 20th Century-Fox counters by pointing out that M.M. is bound to the studio until 1958, and that they see no necessity to honor her wishes for future roles. "In Hollywood last week Marilyn got a brusque reminder that she is firmly under contract to the studio until 1958. Fox issued a paper: '20th Century-Fox is very satisfied with both the artistic and financial results from the pictures in which Miss Monroe has appeared.... 20th Century-Fox has no intention of granting Miss Monroe's request that she play in *Brothers Karamazov.'"* (*Time,* January 24, 1955)

March 31, 1955 Marilyn Monroe rides on a pink-painted elephant in Madison Square Garden. The occasion is the benefit for the Mike Todd Foundation for victims of arthritis and rheumatism. Twenty-five thousand spectators enthusiastically applaud her appearance.

April 8, 1955 On Good Friday at breakfast time, Milton Greene and Marilyn's house in Connecticut is beseiged by several TV crews. M.M. appears on Edward R. Murrow's famous interview program "Person to Person," which is seen by more than fifty million viewers.

Spring 1955 Marilyn makes concerted efforts to fill in the gaps in her education, at least in the professional realm. She acquired Max Reinhardt's private library at an auction in December 1952 (and sold it shortly thereafter at cost to Reinhardt's son Gottfried). For seven years she has been taking drama lessons from Natasha Lytess and Michael Chekhov. Now she decides to switch to Lee Strasberg, breaking with Lytess. Strasberg's New York theater workshop, the Actors Studio, is of great benefit to Marilyn. In the 1950s, actors such as Marlon Brando, James Dean, Eli Wallach, Anne Jackson, Paul Newman, Montgomery Clift, Steve McQueen, and Tom Ewell are among the most prominent to attend the studio, which has become one of the most influential setups of its kind.
At this time, Marilyn's psychiatric treatment, which began around 1954, intensifies. She often goes five times a week to her female psychiatrist, Dr. Hohenberg, on the New York East Side.

June 1, 1955 On Marilyn Monroe's twenty-ninth birthday, *The Seven Year Itch* premieres.

November 1, 1955 Marilyn's divorce from Joe DiMaggio is granted.

December 31, 1955 On the basis of the phenomenal box-office success of *The Seven Year Itch,* Darryl Zanuck concludes a new contract with Marilyn, the best of her career. A clause very important for Marilyn gives her the right to reject any film that in her opinion is not "first class"; the same applies to directors and cameramen. This contract change, negotiated by Marilyn and Milton Greene, guarantees her a high level of artistic freedom, the prerequisite for her long-dreamed-of career as a serious actress. In addition, the clause gives her greater scheduling leeway to allow her to pursue projects in her own firm.

January 16, 1956 A press bulletin confirms that both parties have reached agreement on contested points in previous contracts. "Last week as the battle ended, the clear winner was Marilyn Monroe Productions, Inc." (*Time*) In 1970 Zanuck admits that he had underestimated Marilyn:
"One day, a great friend of mine, Joseph M. Schenck, brought over to my home in Palm Springs this very beautiful girl who was also on the plump side. I didn't jump up and say, 'Oh, this is a great star,' or anything like that. Later on, Joe said, 'If you can

work her in some role or something, some, you know, supporting role, do so.' I did, but I didn't think that I had found any gold mine. John Huston gave her a hell of a good role in 'The Asphalt Jungle' (1950). Jesus, she was good in it. I thought, it must have been the magic of Huston, because I didn't think she had all that in her. But then I put her in 'All About Eve' (1950), and she was an overnight sensation." (*Look* magazine, November 3, 1970)

February 1956 Marilyn's performance of a scene from *Anna Christie* at Strasberg's Actors Studio in New York wins the applause of a select audience.

February 9, 1956 Marilyn holds a press conference with Sir Laurence Olivier at the New York Plaza Hotel to announce her next project: the filming of Terrence Rattigan's play *The Sleeping Prince.*

February 25, 1956 After a year of self-imposed exile, Marilyn returns to Hollywood.

May 3, 1956 The shooting for *Bus Stop* begins. This is the first project largely chosen by Marilyn herself, including the director, Joshua Logan, and the material, based on a successful Broadway comedy. Marilyn's friend and partner Milton Greene is responsible for stills and makeup, and she selects her own costumes. In spite of these concessions and her successes, her New York psychiatrist has to be flown in to stabilize her emotionally.

May 14, 1956 The cover story for *Time* is about Marilyn.

June 2, 1956 After the filming of *Bus Stop* is concluded, M.M. returns to New York.

June 29, 1956 Marilyn weds Arthur Miller in a civil ceremony.

July 1, 1956 A marriage to Arthur Miller according to Jewish rites is held; Marilyn had converted to Judaism shortly before. At a press conference she reports: "We're so congenial. This is the first time I've been really in love. Arthur is a serious man, but he has a wonderful sense of humor. We laugh and joke a lot. I'm mad about him."

July 14, 1956 The newlyweds arrive in London and hold a press conference with Sir Laurence Olivier to announce the newest project, the first of the Marilyn Monroe Productions, Inc.: *The Prince and the Showgirl.*
A Marilyn craze has been sweeping England for weeks. But now the newspapers and magazines outdo each other with headlines and exaggerated inanities: "She walks. She talks. She really is as luscious as strawberries and cream." (*London Evening News*) The reports on her arrival push the speech of Prime Minister Anthony Eden – a warning about the serious economic crisis – onto page 2. Marilyn's dependency on medication becomes more acute during the difficult and emotionally trying filming, and her New York psychiatrist has to be flown in over the Atlantic after Paula Strasberg, Marilyn's constant companion, returns to New York earlier than planned.

October 29, 1956 Marilyn is presented to Queen Elizabeth II at a Royal Command Film Performance.

November 20, 1956 Marilyn and Arthur Miller leave England after finishing shooting for *The Prince and the Showgirl* and finally set off to Jamaica on their belated honeymoon.

December 18, 1956 Marilyn is on a radio show in the Waldorf-Astoria.

Spring 1957 Her business partnership, Marilyn Monroe Productions, Inc., as well as her friendship with Milton H. Greene, falls apart. Greene's comment on the failure:
"I thought I'd seen them all; being in the business I'd seen so many models and actresses. But I'd never seen anyone with that tone of voice, that kindness, that real softness. If she saw a dead dog in the road, she'd cry. She was so supersensitive you had to watch your tone all the time. Later I was to find out that she was schizoid – that she could be absolutely brilliant or absolutely kind, then, the total opposite."
Marilyn's detached reply: "My company was not set up merely to parcel out 49.4 % of all my earnings to Mr. Greene for seven years!" *(Time,* April 29, 1957, p. 58)

June 13, 1957 The premiere of *The Prince and the Showgirl* is held at Radio City Music Hall, New York.

August 1, 1957 Marilyn suffers a miscarriage after a two-month pregnancy. The loss of the child evokes a new emotional crisis, and she makes her first suicide attempt.

August 4, 1958 Shooting begins for *Some Like It Hot.* Marilyn's contradictory behavior, exaggerated and uncooperative, surpasses her previous misconduct on sets. Scheduled to shoot at midday, she often doesn't appear until 6.00 p.m., if at all. She objects to the movie being filmed in black and white, instead of in color. She blames the studio for having replaced Frank Sinatra with Jack Lemmon. She doesn't like working with Tony Curtis. She has problems with the director, Billy Wilder, who managed to survive *The Seven Year Itch* four years earlier, goes through hell for the next four months – for a film that becomes the most successful comedy ever on screen.

September 19, 1958 Marilyn is admitted to Cedars of Lebanon Hospital for "nervous exhaustion."

November 6, 1958 Filming of *Some Like It Hot* is completed.

December 17, 1958 Marilyn has a second miscarriage.

March 29, 1959 *Some Like It Hot* premieres.

Early 1960 Filming of *Let's Make Love,* a comedy directed by George Cukor, begins. The leading male role is played by Yves Montand, after refusals by Gregory Peck, Cary Grant, Charlton Heston, and Rock Hudson. A love affair with Yves Montand ends in November.

March 8, 1960 Marilyn Monroe receives the Golden Globe Award as "Best Actress in a Comedy" for her role in *Some Like It Hot.*

July 18, 1960 Filming of *The Misfits* begins in Nevada. Arthur Miller wrote the script for Marilyn; John Huston is the director. With Marilyn in the leading roles are her idol, Clark Gable, and

Montgomery Clift. During the shooting of the film Marilyn makes a pact with her friend and press agent Rupert Allan: if one of them is thinking of suicide, that person agrees to call the other to talk him or her out of it. In case the other person is not in and a message has to be left, they decide on the password "Truckee River." Marilyn makes a similar suicide pact with Lee Strasberg.

August 26, 1960 Marilyn Monroe suffers a nervous breakdown during the shooting for *The Misfits* and is flown to Westside Hospital, Los Angeles.

September 5, 1960 She returns to location.

November 4, 1960 *The Misfits* is completed.

November 11, 1960 A press bulletin announces that the marriage to Arthur Miller is to be dissolved.

November 16, 1960 Death of Clark Gable. During the Christmas holidays, the thirty-four-year-old Marilyn alarms her lawyer by asking him to draw up a new will.

January 20, 1961 The divorce from Arthur Miller is granted in Ciudad Juarez, Mexico.

January 31, 1961 Premiere of *The Misfits.* Many critics are less than generous in their reaction to Marilyn's performance as Roslyn Tabor, an unhappy divorcée. Details of her mental problems, her dependence on medication and alcohol reach the public.

February 7, 1961 Admitted to Payne Whitney Psychiatric Clinic of New York Hospital. She calls Joe DiMaggio in Florida who immediately comes to New York to get her out. On the evening of the fourth day she is smuggled out of the clinic through the cellar.

February 11, 1961 She spends the next three weeks in the psychiatric division of Columbia Presbyterian Medical Center.

March 7, 1961 As Marilyn leaves the clinic, she is beseiged by a horde of reporters and camera teams to an extent unparalleled in all the years of reporting on her private life. Marilyn has to be escorted through a cordon formed by sixteen policemen and hospital security personnel to her waiting limousine. Joe DiMaggio is Marilyn's chief support at this time. She flies to Florida where Joe is coaching his former team, the New York Yankees. This year Marilyn is not able to work; two more hospital stays follow.

November 19, 1961 At Peter Lawford's beach house in Santa Monica she meets President Kennedy. Rumors spread that she has sexual relationships with him and his brother Robert.

Early February 1962 Marilyn finds a house in the exclusive section of Brentwood (California). The secluded house on a dead-end street is not far from doctors and friends, like Dr. Greenson and Peter Lawford. Marilyn continues to see the Kennedy brothers in Lawford's villa.

February 1, 1962 Dinner in honor of Robert F. Kennedy.

Bancroft, Donna Corcoran. Marilyn plays Nell, a psychotic woman working as a baby-sitter.

17 MONKEY BUSINESS
20th Century-Fox, 1952. Produced by Sol C. Siegel; directed by Howard Hawks. Cast: Cary Grant, Ginger Rogers, Charles Coburn. Marilyn repeats her role as a dumb blonde secretary, Lois Laurel.

18 O. HENRY'S FULL HOUSE
20th Century-Fox, 1952. Produced by Andre Hakim; directed by Henry Koster. Cast: Charles Laughton, David Wayne, and many more. Marilyn plays a streetwalker.

19 NIAGARA
20th Century-Fox, 1953. Produced by Charles Brackett; directed by Henry Hathaway. Cast: Joseph Cotten, Jean Peters, Casey Adams. Marilyn as an adulterous, murderous wife named Rose Loomis.

20 GENTLEMEN PREFER BLONDES
20th Century-Fox, 1953. Produced by Sol C. Siegel; directed by Howard Hawks. Cast: Jane Russell, Charles Coburn, Elliott Reid, Tommy Noonan. Marilyn is Lorelei Lee in this musical comedy.

21 HOW TO MARRY A MILLIONAIRE
20th Century-Fox, 1953. Produced by Nunnally Johnson; directed by Jean Negulesco. Cast: Betty Grable, Lauren Bacall, William Powell, David Wayne, Rory Calhoun, Cameron Mitchell. Marilyn is a nearsighted gold digger named Pola Debevoise.

22 RIVER OF NO RETURN
20th Century-Fox, 1954. Produced by Stanley Rubin; directed by Otto Preminger. Cast: Robert Mitchum, Rory Calhoun, Tommy Rettig. Marilyn plays a hardened saloon singer.

23 THERE'S NO BUSINESS LIKE SHOW BUSINESS
20th Century-Fox, 1954. Produced by Sol C. Siegel; directed by Walter Lang. Cast: Ethel Merman, Donald O'Connor, Dan Dailey, Johnnie Ray, Mitzi Gaynor. Marilyn Monroe plays Vicky, a nightclub singer.

24 THE SEVEN YEAR ITCH
20th Century-Fox, 1955. Produced by Charles K. Feldman and Billy Wilder; directed by Billy Wilder. Cast: Tom Ewell, Evelyn Keyes, Sonny Tufts. Marilyn Monroe is a gorgeous blonde in the upstairs apartment.

25 BUS STOP
20th Century-Fox, 1956. Produced by Buddy Adler; directed by Joshua Logan. Cast: Don Murray, Arthur O'Connell, Betty Field, Eileen Heckart. Marilyn is Cherie, an abducted, would-be chanteuse.

26 THE PRINCE AND THE SHOWGIRL
A Warner Brothers Presentation of a Film by Marilyn Monroe Productions, Inc. and L. O. P. Ltd., 1957. Produced and directed by Laurence Olivier. Cast: Laurence Olivier, Sybil Thorndike. Marilyn is Elsie Marina, the showgirl.

27 SOME LIKE IT HOT
United Artists Release. A Mirisch Company Presentation of an Ashton Picture, 1959. Produced and directed by Billy Wilder. Cast: Tony Curtis, Jack Lemmon, George Raft, Pat O'Brien, Joe E. Brown. Marilyn plays Sugar Kane, an alcoholic singer in an all-girl band.

28 LET'S MAKE LOVE
20th Century-Fox, 1960. Produced by Jerry Wald; directed by George Cukor. Cast: Yves Montand, Tony Randall, Frankie Vaughan, Wilfrid Hyde-White. Marilyn is the Broadway actress Amanda Dell.

29 THE MISFITS
United Artists Release. A Seven Arts Productions Presentation of a John Huston Production, 1961. Produced by Frank E. Taylor; directed by John Huston. Cast: Clark Gable, Montgomery Clift, Eli Wallach, Thelma Ritter. Marilyn plays Roslyn Tabor, an ex-nightclub singer.

30 SOMETHING'S GOT TO GIVE
20th Century-Fox, 1962. Produced by Henry Weinstein; directed by George Cukor. Cast: Dean Martin, Cyd Charisse, Phil Silvers, Wally Cox. Unfinished.

Selected Bibliography

Arnold, Eve. *Marilyn Monroe: An Appreciation.* New York: Alfred A. Knopf, 1987.

Bernard of Hollywood. *Requiem for Marilyn.* Buckinghamshire: Kensal Press, 1986.

Conway, Michael, and Mark Ricci. *The Films of Marilyn Monroe. With a Tribute by Lee Strasberg and an Introductory Essay by Mark Harris.* New York: Citadel Press, 1964.

Crown, Lawrence. *Marilyn at Twentieth Century-Fox.* London: Planet Books, 1987.

de Dienes, André. *Marilyn Mon Amour.* München: Schirmer/ Mosel, 1986.

Fahey, David, and Linda Rich. *Masters of Starlight. Photographers in Hollywood.* Los Angeles: Los Angeles County Museum of Art, 1987.

Halsmann: Portraits (Selected and edited by Yvonne Halsman). New York: McGraw-Hill Company, 1983.

Mailer, Norman. *Marilyn.* New York: Grosset & Dunlap, 1973.

Miller, Arthur. *Timebends.* New York: Grove Press, Inc., 1987.

Monroe, Marilyn. *My Story.* London: W. A. Allen, 1975.

Riese, Randall, and Neal Hitchens. *The Unabridged Marilyn: Her Life from A to Z.* New York/Chicago: Congdon & Weed, 1987.

Shevey, Sandra. *The Marilyn Scandal. Her True Life Revealed by Those Who Knew Her.* New York: William Morrow, 1987.

Spada, James, and George Zeno. *Monroe.* New York: Doubleday, 1982.

Stern, Bert. *Marilyn Monroe: The Complete Last Sitting.* München: Schirmer/Mosel, 1982.

Summers, Anthony. *Goddess: The Secret Lives of Marilyn Monroe.* London: Victor Gollancz Ltd., 1985.

Photography Credits